I0813215

FEASTING AND FASTING IN OPERA

Feasting and Fasting IN OPERA

From Renaissance Banquets to the Callas Diet

PIERPAOLO POLZONETTI

The University of Chicago Press Chicago & London

The University of Chicago Press, Chicago 60637
The University of Chicago Press, Ltd., London

Published 2021
Printed in the United States of America

30 29 28 27 26 25 24 23 22 21 1 2 3 4 5

ISBN-13: 978-0-226-80495-8 (cloth)
ISBN-13: 978-0-226-80500-9 (e-book)
DOI: https://doi.org/10.7208/chicago/9780226805009.001.0001

This book has been supported by the Margarita M. Hanson Fund of the American Musicological Society, funded in part by the National Endowment for the Humanities and the Andrew W. Mellon Foundation.

Library of Congress Cataloging-in-Publication Data

Names: Polzonetti, Pierpaolo, author.
Title: Feasting and fasting in opera : from Renaissance banquets to the Callas diet / Pierpaolo Polzonetti.
Description: Chicago : University of Chicago Press, 2021. | Includes bibliographical references and index.
Identifiers: LCCN 2021005729 | ISBN 9780226804958 (cloth) | ISBN 9780226805009 (ebook)
Subjects: LCSH: Food in opera. | Opera.
Classification: LCC ML1700 .P66 2021 | DDC 782.1—dc23
LC record available at https://lccn.loc.gov/2021005729

♾ This paper meets the requirements of ANSI/NISO Z39.48-1992 (Permanence of Paper).

Contents

PART III

The Effects of Feasting and Fasting

*

Prologue

What Is Food Doing in Opera?

I will never forget that night in the 1990s, though it was twenty-five years back. A fellow musicologist was skidding down an icy street in Ithaca, New York, in his rusty Subaru Legacy. The car moved like a sled with no brakes. I guessed where he was going and decided to follow him. He headed to a run-down diner to celebrate New Year's Eve alone. Perhaps he deserved to celebrate: he'd spent weeks in seclusion studying feasting and fasting scenes in Verdi's operas, grazing on peanuts, fortune cookies, granola bars, and s'mores made by toasting marshmallows under his desk lamp. He was obsessing about a recurrent pattern he saw in every Verdi drinking song or piece of banquet music. All our conversations in the corridors of Cornell University's music department revolved around this: that no matter the prevailing mood of the scene—whether a bride is being forced to marry a man she loathes, or terrorists are plotting to stab the governor at the masked ball, or lovers are sadly watching their mates flirt with others—when food is involved, the accompanying music is always uplifting.

Sitting in front of his plate at the diner, the musicologist jotted down the first law of operatic gastromusicology: "No meal can be sad." He picked up his napkin and whispered, "Bakhtin!" This glorious phrase by the great Russian literary theorist would make a terrific first footnote: Mikhail Bakhtin, *Rabelais and His World*, trans. Hélène Iswolsky (Bloomington: Indiana University Press, 1984), 8: "No meal can be sad."[1] He bent and kissed his pen: Time for a toast! The musicologist took a sip from a can of Dr. Pepper towering over a meager hamburger bloodied with tomato ketchup, the condiment camouflaging the meat's unpleasant flavor. His eyes lit up as a sneer of retribution illumined his face. He drew a chart on a napkin with arrows and keywords representing the way a meal conjures up positive things and often keeps catastrophe at bay. Consistent patterns within the large theoretical framework that guided his analysis of conviviality in Verdi's operas revealed seven fundamental laws of operatic gastromusicology: (1) No meal can be sad; (2) No starvation can be happy; (3) Sharing a meal or drink is a socially cohesive event; (4) The presence of food or drink excludes immediate catastrophe (unless the food or drink is poisoned); (5) The act of feasting itself is morally neutral, but a feasting group (or individual) is morally negative when contrasted with a fasting group or individual; (6) A fasting individual is a hero, and a hero is always sober; (7) Music and text may lie, but gastronomic signs never do.

The fourth law made the musicologist as happy as the first: it reassured him that the unappetizing hamburger he had been forcing down, unless deliberately poisoned, was now going to save his life and usher him into a happy new millennium. He burst out laughing and cried, "No meal can be sad!" A skinny waitress with a white ponytail smiled at him, put out her cigarette, and brought him a red, white, and blue popsicle: "On the house!"

"Thank you! Thank you!" he said, awkwardly shaking her hand. "The popsicle is the lifesaving *sorbetto*, as in Verdi's *Masked Ball*!" Not understanding or caring what he was talking about, the woman replied, "Everything is gonna be fine."

"Yes! Exactly!" said he, with an expression of pure joy grounded in the faith engendered by the gastronomic sign he was sucking on.

Ten minutes later a sharp pain was devouring his stomach. Before dying in the diner's filthy restroom, he ruled out his being the object of a plot. Who would have deliberately poisoned him? And why? Impossible: everybody he knew ignored him and couldn't care less whether he was dead or alive. A chasm opened between the musicologist's theory and his real-life situation, like the mouth of hell in *Don Giovanni*. He had stumbled over a chunk of ice without suspecting there was an iceberg under it: in opera, eating and drinking are parts of a consistent code embedded in operatic conventions, but they do not always correspond to real life.

About midnight, I stepped into the diner's restroom and found the musicologist propping himself up on the toilet, nearly dead. His left hand was grasping a bundle of annotated, greasy napkins and the right held a pink plastic lighter that he was too weak to click. With his last breath, he begged me to burn his wretched notes or flush them down the toilet. I took the napkins with me and left him there. I gave a generous tip to the waitress, who was asking her coworker if she'd seen the pink lighter she'd left by the cash register.

If you're reading this story, it's because I finally managed to turn his notes into a publication. I dedicate this book to that poor fellow scholar. I am deeply indebted for the findings I practically stole from him. May his soul rest in peace.

I cooked up this story with a pinch of truth, but you should take it with a large grain of salt, as a cautionary tale about the alluring risk of conflating the opera stage with real life. One challenge of writing this book was the need to deal with parallel universes, the stage and the world, with characters and audience as guests seated at the same table but severed by an invisible divide, with half indulging in operatic food and the other half in mortal food. Time and time again, I experienced how that divide could be porous or disappear altogether. This book starts by exploring a world before this divide existed. In Renaissance banquets, the actions of the guests during the meal were as relevant as the performance of the artists entertaining them with music and theater. In the early stages of opera, eating during performances shaped operatic dramaturgy. As audiences were indulging in solid and liquid refreshment, opera often represented conviviality according to a consistent and highly meaningful code.[2] In opera, sharing and consuming food define characters' identity and relationships.

A memorable meal in opera is Don Giovanni's final supper, served by his starving servant Leporello. His dinner is interrupted by the statue of the Commendatore, the man he murdered at the beginning of the opera. The ghost rejects Don Giovanni's invitation to dine with him, explaining that "those who eat heavenly food do not eat mortal food." At the same time, he invites the libertine to dine with him in heaven. Don Giovanni accepts, but he refuses to repent (the necessary *laissez-passer*) and is plunged into hell, where he roasts in the fire in front of horrified spectators both onstage and offstage. The impossible attempt to share a meal by characters separated by the operatic divide between characters onstage and the audience demonstrates the chasm between the physical and metaphysical worlds. In Prague or Vienna in the late 1780s, audience members who were partaking of chocolate, coffee, and other refreshments during the performance were connecting to the banquet scene more viscerally, allowing the illusion that the fourth wall could melt in their mouths.

The operatic dining table is a diaphanous membrane that occasionally meshes with reality. In opera banquets we might recognize familiar social rituals of gathering to share foods, yet opera is a distorting mirror of reality. It converts a meal into an essential component of a complex symbolic iconography, embedded in a system of dramatic conventions that bear little relation to the reality of its time, let alone the reality of today. Like food in painting, food in opera becomes a signifier revealing aspects of drama and general culture. To access the significance of food in operatic culture, we need to start by paying attention to it.

Most operas include moments when food or drink are consumed, shared, or rejected, affecting our perception of the drama, often in subliminal ways. As soon as we start noticing them, we realize they are pervasive and always meaningful, though it is often hard to differentiate the decorative use of food from the meaningful and symbolic, a challenge aggravated by stage directors' free addition or subtraction of convivial elements in modern productions. In Verdi's *Traviata*, as in Puccini's *Bohème*, friendship and love are sealed and celebrated by sharing food and wine, whereas food disappears in the tragic endings as the heroines die of consumption. At the beginning of Meyerbeer's *Les Huguenots*, the Protestant Raoul refuses to participate in a banquet and toast with Catholic companions, foreshadowing the massacre at the end of the opera. Similarly, in Verdi's *Les vêpres siciliennes*, Sicilian freedom fighters and French occupying troops seal a truce with a toast. Some refuse to drink together, anticipating the final slaughter. The score of Verdi's *Otello* is drenched with wine as Cassio becomes hopelessly intoxicated, whereas Sir John Falstaff can hold his sherry and imbibes mulled wine to prevent catching cold after being thrown into the chilly waters of the Thames.

In the last act of Bizet's *Carmen*, the flavor of Spain is re-created through the onstage presence of oranges, boisterously advertised by a chorus of fruit sellers. This effect can also be found in Gershwin's *Porgy and Bess*, reproducing the street cries of the strawberry woman and the crab man, and representing both the use and abuse of alcohol. And speaking of strawberries, as I write during the COVID-19 pandemic, I think of Britten's *Death in Venice*, where strawberries sold by street vendors are linked to the spread of a contagious disease. Food is so pervasive in opera that over the past two decades, when going to the opera and talking to operagoers and scholars, I have had innumerable epiphanies. As a game, if we allow one grocery item per opera, we can build an operatic grocery list: chocolate (Pergolesi's *La serva padrona*); coffee (Rossini's *Il turco in Italia*); water (Wagner's *Die Walküre*); wine (Mascagni's *Cavalleria rusticana*); beer (Puccini's *La rondine*); beans (Berg's *Wozzeck*); milk (Humperdinck's *Hansel und Gretel*);

galushki (Mussorgsky's *Boris Godunov*); mushrooms (Shostakovich's *Lady Macbeth of the Mtsensk District*); fish (Prokofiev's *Betrothal in a Monastery*); whiskey (Brecht and Weill's *Rise and Fall of the City of Mahagonny*); schnitzel (Brecht and Weill's *Die sieben Todsünden*); asparagus (Brecht and Weill's *Die Dreigroschenoper*); and strawberries (Britten's *Death in Venice*). The list could continue. Each of these food items carries symbolic meaning that is often context-bound: for instance, in *Hansel und Gretel*, milk stands for childhood, and smashing the milk pitcher initiates a journey of coming of age; in *La rondine*, beer is presented in opposition to champagne as a way of contrasting simplicity with luxury, while in *Les Huguenots*, beer identifies the Protestants as opposed to the wine-drinking Catholics. The interpretation of the meaning of each specific food item needs to be contextualized, and generalizing about the meanings of ingredients is risky: for example, strawberries have a different meaning in *Porgy and Bess* than they do in *Death in Venice*. Yet, like the imaginary musicologist in the opening story, in this book I strive to conceptualize gastronomic laws and functions in opera and to sketch a theory of gastronomic gestures, rituals, and signifiers while looking on both sides of the fourth wall separating the stage from the audience.

Food in opera has five primary functions: social, intimate, denotative, medicinal, and dietary. The first and most common function is public, which is to say social, and often political. We see this function in convivial situations, as conviviality literally means to live together—*cum vivere*—and companions means those who share bread. This is also evident in toasts made to seal pacts and alliances. "Sharing food," as anthropologist Gillian Crowther points out, "is instrumental in creating social groups, and it forms loyalties and obligations."[3]

The second function of food in opera is intimate. In this case, sharing food may express a union between two friends, family members, or lovers. It can be used for seduction or—when not shared—denotes a selfish appetite for both food and sex (as in *Don Giovanni*).

Whereas the first two functions define relationships, the third denotes identity. Certain kinds of food or drink may strongly characterize groups or individuals by defining their social class, ethnicity, nationality, or gender (American male gold miners in Puccini's *La fanciulla del West* drink whiskey, and some smoke cigars, as do the Americans Pinkerton and Sharpless in *Madama Butterfly*).

The fourth function of food in opera is medicinal. This is the power of food or drink to directly affect a character's health or behavior. Examples include the representation of the effects of caffeine (as in the coffeehouse opening of Mozart's *Così fan tutte*), magic potions (as in Wagner's *Tristan und Isolde*, as well as in *Götterdämmerung*), medical remedies, chocolate, alcoholic beverages that intoxicate characters visibly and audibly, or poison (a popular snack in opera seria).

The fifth function of food is dietary, referring to the real-life practice of eating in the theater (whether, when, and what audience members ate in past centuries while attending opera performances), or real-life dieting by singers to shape their bodies for expressive purposes, which has only recently become significant in our cinematic and television culture. Soon after starting this project, I abandoned the idea of organizing the book as a systematic investigation of these five functions, mainly because they often overlap, and considering them separately was not only tedious but also artificial. It is nevertheless important to keep these functions in mind in order to navigate the polyvalence of feasting and fasting in opera.

What most interested me as a line of inquiry throughout this book is that in opera, as in real-life society, food not only is fuel or nurture but has meanings and purposes that make it a defining component of human identities and cultures. As food scholar Massimo Montanari shows, food is a manifestation of human culture, above and beyond food culture itself.[4] To fully grasp this concept, one needs to revert to some pioneering studies in the field of anthropology. Claude Lévi-Strauss maintained that in human culture five basic codes correspond to our five senses. Eating represents a privileged code because "not only does cooking [*cuisine*] mark the transition from nature to culture, but through it and by means of it, the human state can be defined with all its attributes."[5] In another seminal anthropological study, Mary Douglas stresses the significance of food as a code allowing us to unpack meaningful patterns in human society: "If food is treated as a code, the message it encodes will be found in the pattern of social relations being expressed. The message is about different degrees of hierarchy, inclusion and exclusion, boundaries and transactions across the boundaries. Like sex, the taking of food has a social component, as well as a biological one."[6]

Anthropological and social studies of food consumption are useful but are insufficient when approaching opera, which engages only two of our five senses: taste, smell, and touch can be stimulated only indirectly through hearing and sight. Food in opera is meaningful but flavorless, often odorless, and obviously textureless. Because singers cannot sing with their mouths full,[7] to represent eating and drinking opera relies on music and language, and even more rarely on action. Through music, composers convey the sensation of a full or empty stomach, the flavor of meat or vegetables, the longing for food, or the effects of coffee or alcohol. Moreover, eating and drinking scenes in opera convert food and drinks into what Gian-Paolo Biasin, in a book about food in the novel, calls "gastronomic signs."[8] They retain meanings they have in real life within a theatrical culture regulated by operatic conventions. Priscilla Ferguson, another anthropologist, considers the difference between "food" and "cuisine" a defining distinction between biology and culture. She alerts her readers that "food refers to the material substances we humans consume to meet the physiological requirements for sustenance; food is what we eat to live."[9] However, considering that in opera food is never consumed for sustenance, I use the terms "gastronomic sign" and "food" virtually interchangeably.

Notwithstanding its limited ability to directly engage the five senses, opera combines and manipulates a broad variety of audible and visual resources to stimulate or evoke all sensory perceptions. Music-theatrical genres have always had an omnivorous appetite for different codified classes of signs and expressive domains: music, sung poetry, acting and body movement (choreographed or not), stage sets, props, costumes, lights, and so on. Opera borrows codes besides and beyond the verbal and musical domains, such as fashion (costume and furniture design), weaponry and armed fighting, the body and its shape and gestures, and, last but not least, eating and drinking. I try to confront this protean monster without cutting off any of its tentacles, using gastronomic signs as an entrée for accessing opera as a whole.

In their approaches to opera as a multimedia art form, musicologists have slowly abandoned past hierarchical attitudes rooted in eighteenth-century debates on the priority of music over text or vice versa. Still, in the 1980s Carl Dahlhaus wrote that "when we speak of 'musical dramaturgy'—dramaturgy that makes use of musical means—we should refer *only* to the function of music in the creation of drama." This stems from his proposition that "music alone creates the drama," which in turn justifies Joseph Kerman's conception of opera as "drama in which music is the essential constituent."[10] The corollary is that "in opera, the dramatist is the composer."[11] In more recent musicological practice, Dahlhaus and Kerman are sitting ducks ready to be shot and roasted. After Pierluigi Petrobelli reflected on the three-system theory of opera (text, music, and drama), Fabrizio Della Seta expanded it into a theory of operatic dramaturgy as a network of systems or domains of expression. Here exoticism, for example, results from intersections of verbal and musical systems with staging.[12] Harold Powers and James Webster explored semiotic fluidity through an analysis of multivalence, and Carolyn Abbate and Roger Parker theorized the incongruence among opera's expressive domains.[13] Scholars began to understand opera as an art form resulting from a dialogue or clash among competing creative agents, in which staging, lighting design, props, and so on are not merely ornamental aspects but an integral part of a rich bundle of resources and expressive domains. Sergio Durante has observed that the analyst is often tempted to establish a hierarchy among the operatic expressive domains because of the nature of the traditional analytical toolbox,[14] which is a habit of the analyst that does not necessarily reflect the nature of the object of analysis. Alessandra Campana proposes inspiring examples of nonhierarchically affected analysis of stage manuals, lighting design, and special effects as equal parts of the operatic text.[15] Exemplary to this extent are Mary Ann Smart's study of gestures in nineteenth-century opera, calling attention to the signifying power of body movements and actions,[16] and David Levin's analysis of *mise-en-scène* as an essential component of the creative process. Levin's approach allows for an appreciation of how modern productions can affect the meaning of original works, but it also shows the resilience of opera under radical staging, such as Peter Sellars's postmodern productions of Mozart's operas, which Levin sees as examples of cultural translation.[17]

Sellars re-presents Don Giovanni as a Harlem gangster: in the banquet scene he appears eating takeout from McDonald's that includes chicken nuggets in lieu of pheasant, and soda in lieu of Marzemino wine. Words sung by the characters are so recognizable to opera fans that the English subtitles can depart only in insignificant details. Thus *versa il vino* remains faithfully "pour the wine," while *Eccellente Marzimino* is translated as "A good year" when Don Giovanni raises his paper cup of soda; *fagiano*, however, is faithfully translated as "pheasant," even while he munches his chicken nuggets—this line works as comic sarcasm, as does referring to soda as "champagne."[18] Some details can be adjusted, but eating itself in this scene cannot be eliminated or replaced by some different action. Only table manners and menu can change without entirely deleting previous textual strata, for the table music accompanying Don Giovanni's meal is more congruent with pheasant and wine than with fast food and soda. For this reason I take into account the original sources (the libretto and the music score) as I attempt to understand gastronomic signs in opera. They allow us to become fully aware of the consequences of cultural translations when looking at creative modern stage productions that depart significantly from original sources. The original sources are important not because they are more authoritative, or because they reflect the intention of the authors. In fact, librettists and composers are often passive agents when it comes to the representation of food, following norms and archetypes imprinted in the collective unconscious of their own time and culture, which change with changing tastes and manners of production and consumption.[19] Yet, when it comes to gastronomic signs, the original sources are the closest representation of the eating and drinking culture that shaped them, with or without the authors' full awareness.

This book participates in this ongoing exploration of the different expressive means used in opera, attempting the double focus on both food in human society (what audiences eat and how) in the first part, and food culture on the opera stage (what characters eat and how) in the second part, with an emphasis on early opera, and in the last part, with an emphasis on Romantic and post-Romantic operas. Most of the repertory explored here is Italianate opera from Monteverdi to Puccini, even though I make reference to operas outside that chronological frame and tradition. This choice is informed not only by my expertise but also by the special and intimate link between food and opera culture that formed in Italy during the Renaissance and still continues in different and often innovative forms. I chose examples and repertories based on questions and approaches that I find stimulating, and not simply to cover ground. I hope, though, to provide food for thought and tools for thinking about many other cases and repertories. Rather than giving anybody indigestion, I wish to stimulate my readers' appetites.

PART I

Convivial Beginnings

Opera was born and nourished at a time when conviviality was a vital aspect of social life. There are many traces of the convivial spirit that shaped the beginning of operatic culture, but we do not find them in the vast literature of music history. In the first three chapters of this book, I will attempt an archaeology of opera, which is to say, of operatic theory and practice before the early written descriptions of opera performances that date from around 1600. Long before then, elaborate Renaissance banquets included music and theater as essential parts of the kind of multisensory experience that would eventually become a defining characteristic of opera. The reason modern narratives about the birth of opera neglect the links between music, drama, and food has in part to do with the modern experience of opera, which became akin to a religious ritual, where eating and drinking were highly inappropriate. As I show in chapter 4, however, roughly until Wagner, going to opera still was a convivial experience, at least insofar as eating and drinking during a performance was admissible and even encouraged.

The history of opera before 1600 that I want to tell starts in chapter 1 with an examination of the convivial gatherings of the humanist academies that produced the body of theories from which opera was born. My narrative then proceeds backward in time, as in an archaeological excavation, where the upper strata are more recent than the lower ones. Classical Greek culture is by no means the beginning of the prehistory of opera. One need only pick up the shovel and keep digging to extend it back to the epic singing of

Demodocus at Alcinous's banquets in Homer's *Odyssey* or to the highly dramatic Paleolithic paintings at Cro-Magnon, revealing in their dynamism, color, and rhythm a formidable musical sensibility.

In chapter 2, I gather traces of how banquet culture and banquet art developed production strategies and aesthetic orientations that led to opera. In chapter 3, I focus on a fifteenth-century convivial event that included the performance of a seminal operatic prototype: Politian's *Orfeo*, which ends with a wild drinking chorus of bacchants. Chapter 4 explains why the practice of eating during opera performances stopped in the course of the nineteenth century and why it should be reinstated as a means to energize opera culture.

CHAPTER ONE

The *Symposium* and the Birth of Opera

The story goes that opera was invented in Florence about 1600. The earliest surviving scores and libretto for *Euridice*, based on the myth of Orpheus, were produced there and then. Beyond this familiar narrative, a look at the symposia of the Florentine academies that came up with the theories of music drama leading to early opera productions offers evidence that opera was first theorized at the banquet table. Indeed, opera was a humanist attempt to re-create processes, modes, and rituals of creative production typical of Greek classical culture, which included conversations at table accompanied by music and drama. This tradition can be traced back to Plato's *Symposium*, retrieved by Italian Platonist humanists such as Marsilio Ficino, who had a tremendous influence on late Renaissance musical philosophy, which shaped early opera.[1]

A well-known anecdote about the creation of opera is the one Giulio Caccini offered in the dedication of his printed score of *L'Euridice*, with a libretto by Ottaviano Rinuccini. Here the Roman singer and composer thanks his patron Giovanni Bardi and acknowledges his "camerata" as an academic team whose studies led to the retrieval of ancient music drama.[2] Caccini's account has contributed substantially to the legend that the Bardi Camerata was the think tank that single-handedly conceived opera, despite much evidence to the contrary. The myth has been in part debunked,[3] but like every myth it contains a kernel of truth: the leading role of academies and their members in developing music-dramatic theories that led to the invention of opera.

Other academies, as well as artists without academic affiliations, contributed important music-dramatic ideas and practices to early opera. Two such academies were named Umidi (humid) and Alterati (altered), suggesting that a generous amount of alcohol was served during meetings. I will focus on the minutes of the meetings of the Alterati, which, together with the published speeches and essays of their members, provide a gold mine of information on the relation between conviviality and early theories of opera. While their convivial rituals have been studied far less than their theories, they are equally relevant to an understanding of their discourse on operatic theories and modalities of sharing aesthetic and intellectual experiences.

In Praise of Alteration

The Alterati, to which both Rinuccini and Bardi belonged, was, according to Claude Palisca, "the [academy] that contained the greatest number of musical amateurs."[4] An eighteenth-century study by Domenico Manni shows that their debates and theories were still influential during the Enlightenment. Manni records that the Alterati first met in 1569, choosing as their logo a bucket of grapes with a motto traceable to Horace's "Quid non ebrietas designat?" (What does alteration not unlock?)—a rhetorical question suggesting that alteration can unlock everything.[5] Horace writes to his friend, the lawyer Torquatus, inviting him to a vegetarian lunch, to be accompanied by a carefully chosen wine produced in the year 26 BC in Minturno, close to where Falanghina wine is still produced. The Roman poet and master orator framed his praise of wine within two rhetorical questions, presenting it as a desirable stimulant to a beneficially altered state of mind: "What is it that inebriation cannot make possible? It unlocks secrets, turns hopes into reality, thrusts the unmoving into the battlefield. Wine frees hearts from the load of anxiety, teaches new art. Have not plentiful cups always made every man eloquent, and given comfort to the poor?"[6]

Members of the Alterati were admitted with nicknames and emblems, usually containing references to wine or other alcoholic beverages.[7] In December 1574 Giovanni Bardi entered the Academy as "Il Puro" and used as his insignia a flask for distilling pure brandy with the motto "I am altered and I distill" (Alterato io raffino). Distilling was a trendy profession and magical activity at the time, subject of a number of treatises on natural magic and often used as a philosophical metaphor for separating purity from impurity, incorruptible from corruptible matter, and ultimately as a way to manipulate the forces of nature and abstract its essences.[8] Ottaviano Rinuccini, who probably could not hold his liquor during the endless speeches, was "Sleepy Head" (Sonnacchioso). Other members had even more colorful names. Vincenzo Martelli was simply "The Drunk" (L'Ebbro). Senator Popoleschi was "Dizzy" (Lo Svanito) and used as his insignia a wine cask and grapes with the motto "In those I hope" (In quelle spero). Giovanni de' Medici, who presumably had a better head for liquor than Rinuccini, was called "Steady" (Il Saldo); a wine cask was his emblem. Federico Strozzi's emblem was just a cap filled with wine. Pietro Ruccellai was called "The Humid" (L'Umido), while Eleonora de' Medici's nickname was "Burning" (L'Ardente), suggesting that after a few glasses she became a hothead, as did Cavalier Ricasoli, called "The Flamer" (L'Infiammato). Bishop Alamanni chose the motto "Sweet in autumn" (Dulcius in autumno), the time of grape harvest. Archbishop Bonciani, called "Sour" (Aspro), had an emblem of a wine cask exploding. The most notable prelate in the academy was Cardinal Maffeo Barberini, who was elected in 1623 as Pope Urban VIII, continuing in Rome his mission as a passionate supporter of opera. His emblem was a grapevine adorned by laurel branches with the motto "And fruits not its own" (Et non sua poma), a reference to grafting techniques described in the second book of Virgil's *Georgics* (Agricultural things) (2.82), a part of the poem that begins by praising Bacchus and wine.

Reenacting Plato's *Symposium*

The Alterati's convivial gatherings and philosophical conversations were explicitly modeled after Plato's *Symposium*. In the opening speech, delivered at the academy's banquet on the night of February 16, 1575, the academy regent, Giulio del Bene, addressed the other guests by confessing that "while ruminating about what we could reason about tonight, I picked up Plato's book . . . and looking into his *Symposium* I saw that neither Plato nor the erudite Ficino—who walking in Plato's footsteps brought him back from memory to the present—were much concerned with banquets, types of food, cooks, nor by sobriety, but were concerned with speculative reasoning and knowledge."[9]

Although the primary reason for Plato's gathering was not to consume food and wine, such sustenance was needed if participants were to engage in philosophical discourse. In fact, "as man has two natures, body and soul, so he needs to feed both." But in a typical conflation of Aristotelianism and Platonism, del Bene explains that "the soul without food to keep her alive cannot engage in discussions or in contemplation," and reasons that "like us, [the ancient Greek philosophers] used to eat a light meal to nourish the body so that then they could nourish the soul with great study."[10]

How light the meal was is hard to say. Del Bene seems to imply that they had antipasti before the opening speech and afterward a serious banquet that supported conversation about the paper that had been read. Their diet for philosophizing was based on fruit and white meat. For a different supper, held during the summer, they bought an impressive amount of fruit (strawberries, grapes, prunes, pears) and white meat (six legs of veal, six turkeys, three capons, twenty-four doves or pigeons), along with other ingredients for cooking. In addition to the food listed, which probably served more than thirty people, the Alterati consumed a generous but not excessive amount of wine (twenty-one bottles of generic red, plus three nicer bottles of "Greco di Chianti").[11] The wine was a social lubricant that altered the state of mind enough to allow the free flow of ideas without provoking a bacchanal.

Alteration and Music Theater

Del Bene's speech discusses alteration in relation not only to the effects of wine, but also to those of music and drama.[12] The premise of the speech was Ficino's translation of and commentary on Plato's *Symposium*, which had created a long-lasting trend of convivial philosophy informing Italian Renaissance academies. Ficino begins the proem of his commentary with an anecdote about Plato's final supper: "Plato, father of philosophers, the day of his eighty-first birthday, on November 8, washed his hands, sat at the dining table, and died."[13] With this Ficino relates the death of Plato to the death of Plato's teacher Socrates, who also died shortly after his lethal last meal.

Ficino's major contribution to bodily, mental, and spiritual health is his *Three Books on Life*, a work that abounds in recipes and reflections on food. It starts with a proem addressed to Lorenzo de' Medici in which he evokes "Bacchus, the supreme prelate of priests," rather than Apollo, "for [Bacchus] perhaps heals more salubriously with his nourishing wine and his carefree jollity than [Apollo] with his herbs and songs."[14] Notwithstanding this playful dismissal of Apollo, Ficino, as a practitioner and promoter of Orphic music therapy, believed deeply in the medical and spiritual healing power of music.

Del Bene's definition of the concept of "alteration," based on Ficino's earlier idea of music as psychologically therapeutic, captures an essential function that opera will have as a form of collective healing and education.

We see here in embryo the idea of music drama as a "school of feelings," to borrow Lorenzo Bianconi's definition of opera's pedagogical value.[15] Del Bene, in fact, envisions music drama as a powerful way to alter how and how much spectators feel without altering what they think or what they are. His theory of alteration stems from the dialogue of Eryximachus in Plato's *Symposium*, where the legendary physician admits that, although drinking is an unhealthy habit, Socrates can drink a lot of wine without affecting his mind (176c–176e). The phenomenon is so revelatory of the mind's ability to remain lucid that Alcibiades, who tried in vain to seduce Socrates, proves that no matter how much Socrates drinks, the wine would not affect his rationality (214a).

Starting with the *Symposium* and borrowing also from Aristotle's *Physics*, del Bene provides a definition of alteration that explains why drinking does not affect the personality and ethical values of the true philosopher: "Alteration is a mutation of accidents while the subject remains the same."[16] What he means is that identity and personality (the subject) do not change when the brain is affected by accidental altering agents. Alteration is also "a motion in quality" (moto nella qualità), causing an increase or decrease of the intensity of a passion without altering true identity. The causes of alteration are stimulants that entice the subject. Unappealing sensations do not alter us, since they are blocked out. For example, bad odors stop affecting people when they become used to them, and after a while soldiers stop paying attention to the noise of artillery. Conversely, we are deeply altered by pleasant stimulations such as sweet scents and harmonious sounds.[17] At the end of his speech, del Bene announces a "sumptuous banquet," "precious wines," "dances and songs," and "superb music and masks and other things that invite to Venus's and Bacchus's delight." He invites his fellows "to feed the soul rather than the body" and insists that they must all "get drunk and altered with the desire to learn."[18]

The noble purpose of alteration is to turn from vice to virtue. In this context, del Bene recapitulates the pedagogical purpose of the liberal arts in Plato's *Republic*, pointing out that music teaches us to be ordered and well balanced (composti bene) in our souls. Among the liberal arts, music moves the sentiments (affetti) no less than rhetoric. By delighting us and lifting us up (delettarci et sollevarci) music is a powerful means of alteration.[19] Music, in fact, alters body and soul in a different way than rhetoric does, because it is made of numbers rather than words. Music is rational (based on ratios), while rhetoric is logical (based on Logos). By applying numbers to sensible things, del Bene explains, harmony (concento) alters the mind in ways that are both beautiful and delightful, "as you have just experienced," he adds: an indication that both music and food were present during the Alterati banquet.[20]

Music's power, as mastered by the mythical figure of Orpheus, affects animal and human behavior in a medicinal way, because it mechanically triggers psychophysical reactions like a drug, like alcohol. For this reason the myth of Orpheus occupies a prominent role in early opera as well as during banquets, as we shall see. The medicinal power of music was of great importance to humanist philosophers, first and foremost Ficino, and to the music theorists of the Florentine academies, such as Girolamo Mei and Giovanni Battista Doni, who tried to re-create it, like alchemists, by experimenting with mathematical theories and by translating and studying Greek music-theory books. The idea that well-regulated music acts as a healing drug or as a healthy food can be found even in Baldassare Castiglione's *Book of the Courtier* (1528), one of the most widely read books on good manners (including table manners), where music is praised as "medicine for souls" (medicina di animi) and "the most gratifying food for the soul" (gratissimo cibo di animo).[21]

Music Drama Therapy

The link between food's medicinal properties and early theories of music drama is even clearer in a speech on purgation in drama (or catharsis) that Lorenzo Giacomini delivered at an Alterati meeting in 1586. Giacomini extends del Bene's argument by pointing out that music alone, without a staged dramatic text, cannot trigger the highest form of alteration. Giacomini combines Platonic mysticism with scientific and medical discourse in his observations on the alterations produced by food and wine: "Food and wine, warming up and wakening spirits and strengthening the body, lead to cheerfulness. On the other hand, making the senses heavy through murky and impure vapors and the loss of internal heat leads to sadness and fear and makes us appear lazy, sluggish, and useless."[22]

Giacomini continues by saying that the effects of theater are not unlike the effects of ingested substances, especially the central and most beneficial effects, which are "purgative." Giacomini's concept of purgation conflates Aristotle's theory of *catharsis* with medical theories:

> Purgation appears to belong to the body and its humors. Healing is produced by contrary means or by purgation with purging medicaments,

> which move the bodily humors that are not capable of moving by themselves. This kind of medicament is called in Greek *catharsis*, which means purgation, and the medication that has this virtue is called purgative. It works not as a contrary or enemy of the humor, but as its friend. So the rhubarb, the aloe, and the black hellebore juice, once received in the stomach, transmit their temperature to the limbs by natural similarity that they have with the humors of the hot-tempered, the phlegmatic, and the melancholic. [The medicament] has the power of the magnet on iron or amber on straw, to attract the humor not only from nearby veins but from the most remote parts of the body . . . and to lead it to the place where it spreads its quality, which is the stomach, from where, having made it heavier and having stimulated its motion, the stomach expels it. What I say is confirmed by the medical authorities Hippocrates and Galen.[23]

Giacomini's medical reinterpretation of Aristotelian poetical catharsis leads him to the groundbreaking idea that representing pathological emotional states (affetti) would purge their dangerous effects through a controlled homeopathic cure. In his medical culture, tears are still conceived, as they were in medieval medical culture, as condensed melancholy humor. This is why Giacomini is convinced that expelling them by crying is therapeutic, especially when the crying is induced by delightful art that counterbalances suffering with beauty.[24]

The new purgative therapy consists of causing the secretion of tears through music and drama. Giacomini follows the classical theory that endows music with the power to trigger emotions mechanically. Unlike the Neoplatonists, however, he points out that music without dramatic poetry is beneficial only to the body and does not lead to the highest form of purgation. He uses the example of mercy (misericordia), consisting of "abhorring somebody else's suffering." Compassion leads to justice, which in its highest manifestation is the desire for the common good and the well-being of others. But it cannot be attained by music alone, writes Giacomini, because there must be a poetic representation of the actions of characters before we can empathize.[25] Here the idea of medical purgation conflates not only with Aristotle's dramatic idea of catharsis, but also with a Catholic idea of purgation (from which comes the concept of Purgatory) as spiritual healing and purification from sin, in which, during the fasting of Lent, a restricted diet goes hand in hand with redemptive spiritual exercises such as meditation and charity.

Giacomini's intent is pedagogical and medical rather than primarily ethical. Like Lucretius, whom Giacomini quotes at the beginning of his essay, he believes that bitter medicine needs to be sweetened, a prescription formulated much later in a Mary Poppins's song: "A spoonful of sugar helps the medicine go down."[26] We are more inclined to take a purgative, such as an emotionally taxing situation in a tragedy, if it is offered in a way that delights us "with beautiful metaphors, sweet poetry, mellifluous music, festive dance, magnificent stage sets, splendid costumes, [and] poetical artifice."[27] The list of powerful purgatives for the mind includes all the essential ingredients of opera.

The new form of tragedy with music must not block dangerous emotions and desires but must stimulate them so as to purge them. Repressing these emotions turns them into pathologies: "Pain, exuberance, libido, [and] anger: when, without offense to virtue, they are let out, they assuage more easily. They calm down when released within a certain measure and for a limited amount of time, instead of being violently restrained and repressed."[28]

The medical redefinition of *catharsis* as psychophysical and spiritual purgation leads Giacomini to the idea that staged musical drama can cure what in Freudian terms may be called psychopathologies, caused or aggravated by repression.[29] This remarkably modern idea informs opera from its beginnings all the way to Wagner and beyond. One of opera's therapeutic qualities, throughout its history, has been its ability to awaken and channel undesirable emotional states and purge them with "a spoonful of sugar."

CHAPTER TWO

The Renaissance Banquet as Multimedia Art

The Renaissance dining hall was a precursor to opera. Large-scale, complex banquets proved essential to the formation of operatic culture, which developed where courtly banquets were the norm. Cooking, serving, and performing had to be perfectly coordinated to offer a fully engaging experience, to provide guests (audience) with a feast for all the senses: an orchestrated succession of elaborate dishes served promptly and accompanied by a well-planned program of artistic events, including music and drama. Moreover, theatrical behavior was expected from both hosts and guests, as it would later be in the opera house. As Eugene Johnson shows in his study of early operatic theatrical spaces, in the seventeenth century the space of the banquet and the space of the theater often coincided. For the 1565 Medici-Habsburg wedding celebration in Florence, Antonio Vasari adapted the Salone del Cinquecento in Palazzo Vecchio, previously used as a government meeting space, to function at the same time as a banquet hall and a theater (something similar happened in Siena, Bologna, and elsewhere). He raised the ceiling and created a seating arrangement allowing gentlemen and gentlewomen to enjoy the spectacle of the theater performance (the *intermedi*), as well as the spectacle of the magnificent guests looking at one another (something Vasari himself recognized as essential to the success of the evening)—not to mention the spectacle offered by the virtuoso architects of special effects for the *intermedi*, and their resourcefully snappy conversion of a humdrum public space into a theater/banquet/dance hall.[1] Opera, created shortly afterward in Florence, would preserve for centuries the interactive theatrical culture of the banquet hall, in which people shared a space where politics, entertainment, and conviviality converged.

Healthy Pleasures

Ancient banquets in Greece and Rome, as described by Homer and Virgil and in Plato's *Symposium*, were complex rituals designed to stimulate the senses as well as the intellect. Renaissance banquets, as Anthony Cummings shows, were inspired by classical models, but they also departed from them as integration of gastronomy, medical knowledge, and the performing arts increased. Moreover, the new scientific approach to music as medicine encouraged the use of music to promote digestion.[2] Renaissance banquets were part of a larger cultural project of retrieving and modernizing classical heritage through a creative synthesis of Christian and pre-Christian models in search of the cultivation of a wholesome soul (or mind) in a wholesome body.[3] Bridging art and science, courtly gastronomy was deeply involved in this cultural project.

One of the earliest widely circulated Renaissance gastronomy books is an erudite essay on "honest pleasure and health" (*De honesta voluptate et valetudine*, 1475) by the humanist Platina, prefect of the Vatican Library and the author of a controversial history of the popes. In his dedicatory letter to Cardinal Bartolomeo Roverella, Platina assures the prelate that after studying Cicero, Aristotle, Plato, Pythagoras, Zeno, Democritus, Chrysippus, Parmenides, Heraclitus, Epicurus, Seneca, and Lucretius, he concluded that "the way to happiness is the voluptuous desire stemming from the honest pursuit of cures for the improvement of human health."[4] The book presents food ingredients and recipes with their medical properties, including several dishes made with cannabis that can be considered early instances of medical marijuana.[5]

For Platina, eating is part of a holistic approach to life. To this end he offers recommendations on where to live, where and when to eat, and how to set the table. He also advises against unhealthy habits such as sexual intercourse during hot weather and engaging in activities, like chess or cards, that may cause unsettling emotions immediately before or after a meal. Platina addresses the importance of healthy living, including exercising in the morning and choosing physical activities appropriate for one's age and lifestyle. Eating is an essential aspect of the healthy and wise regime. *De honesta voluptate* was extremely influential abroad: as Barbara Wheaton documents in her study of early French cuisine, the first edition in French translation,

Platine en françois (Lyons, 1505), followed by a German translation, was tremendously important for its unprecedented concern with diet and also because "Platina served as a model of the educated gentleman who took food seriously."[6]

With the emergence of formal treatises on how to prepare large banquets, beauty became as relevant a concern as health. Together with science and philosophy, the visual and performing arts began to play an important role in convivial rituals that sought balance and health in individuals and in their social interactions.

Carefully prepared and beautifully presented food was part of a quest for cosmic harmony, a pursuit that conflated Platonic multisensory and synesthetic mysticism (as in the myth of Er recounted at the end of Plato's *Republic*) and the spiritual value of food and wine in Catholic liturgy.[7] It is no coincidence that many books on banquet art and cooking, as well as records of banquets combining cuisine and performing arts, were produced for or under the patronage of church leaders. Nor should it surprise us that the most spectacular Renaissance pictorial representations of banquet scenes centered on key moments in the life of Jesus: his first miracle, the transformation of water into wine at the wedding at Cana (as in Veronese's famous painting), the Last Supper (represented by Leonardo, Pietro Perugino, and Tintoretto among others), and Jesus's feasts in the houses of Levi (Paolo Veronese) and Martha (Joachim Beuckelaer, Diego Velásquez, Vasco Fernandes). Biblical banquets in Renaissance iconography can also have negative connotations, however, when there is no sharing or when greed triumphs over generosity as in the parable of the rich man and Lazarus (Leandro Bassano) or the feast of Herod (Domenico Ghirlandaio, Donatello, Francesco Botticini, Gregório Lopes, and many others). The often dramatic, even theatrical, representation of these scenes sheds light on both sacred and secular meanings and functions of food and conviviality.[8] "In drawing on the wider phenomenon of court banqueting," as art historian Christina Normore points out in her discussion of a fifteenth-century Flemish painting representing the wedding at Cana, the picture "further hints at the porous nature of the boundary between the high art of painting and the low arts of the table with their messy mixture of the visual, the theatrical, and the culinary."[9]

Banquets as Performance

Banquets with music and drama were well-planned and carefully staged rituals offering performing opportunities both for guests and for a team of competent artists. These sculptors, artisans, landscape artists, choreographers, dancers, musicians, actors, and chefs collaborated to produce elaborate sugar creations, paintings, and sculptures in and around the dining room, dances for both professional dancers and guests, handsome clothes and jewelry, painted or embroidered linens, often folded like complex origami fabrications, splendid silverware and china, flowers, scented water, music, and drama.

One of the most interesting treatises "on stewardship," or how to organize and direct banquets, is *Dello scalco* (Ferrara, 1584) by Giovanni Battista Rossetti, steward of Lucrezia d'Este, the Duchess of Urbino, granddaughter of Lucrezia Borgia. In organizing banquets, he explains, the steward's job is "to satisfy all the senses: the eye with cleanliness, beautiful things, and inventions; the ear with music and refined entertainments; the sense of smell with well-prepared dishes; the taste and touch with perfect condiments that will be as varied as people's tastes."[10] Normore observes a similar approach to sixteenth-century banquets (a century before Rossetti) by Valois Burgundian rulers in southern France and today's Lowlands, showing how the mixed-media nature of these feasts required a highly coordinated effort by artists and artisans working with different materials and media (culinary art, music, theater, sculpture, architecture, poetry). The result was a form of interactive and "multiauthored" creative process that challenged the emerging idea of the isolated genius. Such a process eroded boundaries between materials and media, the static and the animate—as in the case of events presented between the courses (the so-called *entremets*) by musicians, actors or automata, machines, and fountains—and reconfigured boundaries between guests and performers, elaborate food dishes, and decorative objects, hence erasing the separation of spectator and spectacle.[11]

The Renaissance banquet was an event. Like opera, it used prescriptive texts (manuals and recipe books) and was often recorded in descriptive accounts. This differs little from the records of such early opera as the original editions of the score of Monteverdi's *Orfeo*, which mixes prescriptive notation and descriptive explanations of how certain pieces were performed at the time of the premiere.[12]

Banquet-art manuals are the best sources for studying banquets as a performing art. The proliferation of this genre of literature parallels the unprecedented rise of manners manuals such as the two international bestsellers of the time, Baldassare Castiglione's *Book of the Courtier* (1528) and Giovanni della Casa's *Galateo, or Rules of Good Manners* (1558). Together with Erasmus's *Manners for Children* (1530), these were the first books in European history devoted to good manners. As Norbert Elias remarks, they were seminal in the development of the modern "civilizing process." They expressed the needs of a "society in transition" and "the increased tendency of people to observe themselves and others."[13] Edward Muir, in his cultural history of the Renaissance, sees manners manuals as a new school of acting devoted to rituals for controlling unpleasant emotions and dangerous appetites and impulses.[14] The development of opera as a place where audiences go to observe and be observed is closely related to the codification of table manners practiced and tested in banquets that functioned as rituals of collective performance.

A canonical text on banquet art is *On Banquets, Food Compositions and General Table Setting* (Ferrara, 1549), written by Cristoforo di Messisbugo, steward of Cardinal Ippolito d'Este of Ferrara.[15] Messisbugo's work appeared in seventeen editions from 1552 to 1626, which is to say during the most fertile time of experimentation leading to the creation of opera.[16] The book takes into account every aspect of a convivial event affecting sensorial perception and its intellectual elaboration. The structure of the banquet allows guests to express their competence as virtuoso performers of ritualized social behavior; the dining table becomes a self-reflecting stage where guests are both audience and actors.

In Messisbugo's banquet, music does more than create an elegant but generic sonic background, as in today's restaurants, where there is no direct link between specific dishes and specific pieces of live or recorded music. For Messisbugo, there is an intimate correlation between the variety of musical pieces and timbres—of sound qualities prescribed for each course and the recipes for specific dishes. At a general level, the creativity of combining ingredients corresponds to the variety of genres of music (dance, madrigals, theater), as well as to the variety of instruments and their combinations: shawms, recorders, dolzaines and other kinds of bagpipes, citterns, viols, lyres, trombones, cornetti, portative organs, harpsichords, and other newly invented instruments.

A Dinner of 150 Dishes

A fish feast in Ferrara on Saturday, May 20, 1529, was offered by the twenty-year-old archbishop Ippolito II d'Este—destined from birth to be a high-ranking prelate—before he was appointed Cardinal of Ferrara. Named after his uncle, Cardinal Ippolito I, Ippolito II became a bishop before he turned ten. His ecclesiastical career path was smoothed by his mother, Lucrezia

Borgia, the illegitimate daughter of Pope Alexander VI.[17] As a generous sponsor of the arts, Ippolito dedicated his life to the pursuit of beauty, culminating in the building of Villa d'Este in Tivoli, which was decorated with ancient sculptures and spectacular high-tech fountains.[18] The banquet on May 20 took place in the Este palace of Belfiore, which was destroyed by fire one hundred years later. Among the art treasures that survived the fire is a pictorial cycle of the Muses, now housed in museums around the world. Two of them, Thalia and Polyhymnia, are holding and surrounded by edible fruits and grains (grapes, oranges, and wheat), giving us a glimpse of the union of food and the arts.[19]

Ippolito offered his feast to fifty-four noble ladies and gentlemen, including Ippolito's brother Ercole II, Duke of Ferrara, and his wife Renée, daughter of King Louis XII of France.[20] For this reason the dishes and music celebrated the union of French and Italian cultures. The banquet started at 9:00 p.m. and ended at 5:00 a.m. It began with an hourlong comedy with "divine music of various voices and instruments," recited in the hall adjacent to the garden of the palace. One can imagine the aroma of food coming from the kitchen, stimulating the guests' appetites. As the comedy reached its happy ending, the guests proceeded to tables out on the veranda. Later the musicians would be stationed under a canopy on the left of the garden where they could not be seen from the tables, although they were present "onstage" while the guests processed to their seats. At this time and during the appetizers, four musicians dressed in livery followed the guests, one playing the cittern, another a lute, the third a harp, and the fourth a flute. The quartet performed a galliard that was danced by four young couples. This piece functioned like an operatic overture: a prelude to the unveiling of the stage set.

The table was adorned with flowers and the coats of arms of the host and guests; napkins and tablecloths were folded artfully. The music of the quartet continued as the guests washed their hands with scented water and tackled the antipasti already arranged on the tables: sweet bread soaked in milk, marzipan biscotti, starch and almond-milk pastries called *pignoccati*, cake of egg whited and cream with rose-scented water called *cavi di latte*, and colorful salads of herbs and citrus fruits arranged to form coats of arms and letters. There were sweet wines and pine-nut pastries, caviar, cold fish dishes, asparagus, and anchovy salad. These were topped off by painted sugar sculptures representing Venus, Bacchus, and Cupid.

Sugar sculptures were a staple at Renaissance banquets. The earliest on record were made for a banquet for Isabella d'Este given in 1490 in Mantua, about the time and in the place of first performance of Politian's *Orfeo*. That occasion featured "artful sugar inventions representing cities, castles, animals and more."[21] Creations of this kind sometimes had input from great artists such as Giambologna or experts in Spanish-Arab pharmacology, who firmly believed in the curative properties of confectionary.[22] As Barbara Wheaton shows, in sixteenth-century France the art of confectionary was strongly linked to magic, as in the case of recipes by the magician Nostradamus. The discipline was also indebted to Italian confectioners and pharmacologists, as shown by the circulation of such printed books as *The Secrets of the Reverend Seigneur Alexis of Piedmont* (Venice, 1555).[23] Medicine, cuisine, and art converged in the construction and deconstruction of these ephemeral creations; a literal form of art consumption, they were destined to be both enjoyed and destroyed.

The guests participated as listeners, viewers, and diners, and also as actors. Their first performance task was self-control.[24] The table overflowed with colorful, beautifully arranged food, but they knew this was only the beginning of an eating marathon. What they did not know was how long the marathon would last. The chief steward had been instructed by the young archbishop to plan a total of almost 150 dishes, each delivered on either fifteen or fifty-four plates, depending on whether it was meant to be shared or was in individual servings. Here is a complete list of dishes and events in the order of presentation. With one clear exception (marked as entremets/intermezzi), music was performed during the meal and not only between courses.[25]

Description of the banquet at Belfiore (Ferrara) offered by Archbishop Hippolito d'Este on Saturday May 20, 1529.

9:00 p.m. predinner show: *farsa* (comic play) with music for various instruments and voices

10:00 p.m. procession to the table
ANTIPASTI (already on the table)
Dance accompanied by cittern, lute, harp, and flute

1. sweet bread and milk
2. marzipan biscotti
3. almond-milk pastries
4. egg white and cream cake with rose-scented water
5. herbs and citrus salad

6. asparagus salad
7. anchovy salad
8. wine and pine-nut pastry flans
9. pastries with caviar meatballs
10. cold boiled tuna with parsley
11. cold barbels in sweet sauce
12. sugar sculptures of Venus, Bacchus, and Cupid

[ACT 1]

1st Course
"Sublime harmony" of three trombones and three cornetti

13. trout pastiche
14. hard-boiled eggs with French sauce
15. sturgeon "milk." Fried pickerel and other fish spleens with oranges, cinnamon, and sugar
16. boiled sturgeon garnished with *agliata* (black garlic sauce) representing the coat of arms of the Este family
17. sixty fried bream
18. white starchy soup called *diamante*
19. flaky pastry pizzas
20. small fried fish from the river Po

2nd Course
Dolzaina, trombone, and German flute

21. pine-nut shell pastries with fatty cheese
22. boiled pickerel with white sauce covered with borage flowers
23. golden soup
24. cold turbot with lemon
25. large eels called *miglioramenti* with sugar and cinnamon
26. fried lamprey
27. tench with French-style dressing and covered with *sabba* (grape syrup)

3rd Course
Harp, flute, harpsichord

28. *biancomangiare* (white cream) with fried pickerel
29. French big lilies (*fiordiligi alla francese*)
30. "Cibibo" soup of Malvasia with sugar and cinnamon
31. potage of small tuna

32. large pickerel on the spit with vinegar
33. fried sardines with oranges
34. large shrimp
35. minced sturgeon on the pan, English style

4th Course

Dolzaina, violone, two bagpipes, cittern

36. pickerel cooked in wine, Flemish style, with minced citrons
37. Sicilian rice
38. grilled twaite shad
39. Neapolitan *nizzole*, also called *villanata* (hazelnuts cooked with butter, cinnamon, and sugar)
40. spiny spider crab
41. boiled sturgeon with salsa
42. German fried round dough

5th Course

43. little pies from Lombardy
44. *narvoli* [?] German style with onions
45. large fried pickerel covered with *brognata* glaze (prune, onion, pomegranate juice, honey) and confetti
46. lentils
47. dark sops (toast soaked in hot orange juice and wine with ground almonds, raisins, and cinnamon, sugar and orange juice) with pickerel
48. eel pies
49. grilled sturgeon fillets
50. fried freshwater minnows

Entremets/Intermezzi: Comic masks from Bergamo and Venice, jesting around the table

[ACT 2]

6th Course

Vocal music sung by the duke's singers, including Giovanni Michele, Mr. Gravio, and Mr. Giannes del Falcone

51. fried carp with "bastard sauce"
52. grilled pickerel stomachs with pepper, vinegar, and spices

53. *fiadoncelli* (dough flans) filled with raisins, egg yolks, sugar, and cinnamon
54. pickerel *tomaselle* (spiced fish cakes covered with orange juice and sugar)
55. green frittatas with pine nuts and raisins
56. fried mushrooms
57. tomato and cheese soup (*marzolini*)
58. Milanese *offelle* (filled pastries)

7th Course

A tambourine player comes out of the bower and accompanies four young couples and an illustrious lady dancing around the table "la bassa Spagna," "la Rogarsa," and "il brando."

59. black broth of *reine* (large carp) and almonds
60. braised pickerel stew
61. fried allis shad with sugar and cinnamon
62. soup with raisins
63. marinated barbs [*Barbus barbus* is a river fish]
64. caviar frittatas
65. German pies filled with marzipan
66. carp pies

8th Course

Three recorders, three bagpipes, and violone play music while jesters perform comic sketches

67. pastries with French cream
68. butter treated with sugar and rose water
69. artichokes
70. olives
71. fried stuffed pasta called "gloves"
72. cooked apples
73. almond dough (*pasta reale*)
74. oyster pies

9th Course

No live entertainment

75. 1,000 oysters
76. oranges and pears

At this point the *piffari* (probably shawms) play while the table is cleared. People think the banquet is over, but waiters come back with fresh silverware and napkins and bring more courses, introduced by dough sculptures representing naked moors, male and female, with golden laurel crowns, and flowers and greens covering the genitals.

[ACT 3]

10th Course

No music until the salads are brought in, then Mr. Ascanio plays his newly invented instrument, a *fagotto* (prototype of a bassoon).

77. rosewater sweets
78. salad of herbs and flowers
79. fresh caviar
80. pan fried carp on a bed of salad
81. *bottarghe* (botargo, or fish roe)
82. Spanish butter and bread
83. shrimp tails and citron salad
84. salted sea bass

11th Course

A splendidly dressed young lady comes out of the bower and sings a madrigal, accompanying herself on the lute

85. fried trout tails
86. sweet creamy yellow soup made with cinnamon, saffron, and butter
87. German style chopped sturgeon in orange sauce
88. Florentine *tortelli* (sweet pasta stuffed with raisins, pine nuts, sugar, and cinnamon)
89. Venetian mussel potage
90. French eggs
91. fried flounder with oranges
92. *stellette* or star-shaped dough

12th Course

Five singers perform "canzone alla Pavana in villanesco"

93. sweet pine-nut rolls
94. large stuffed shrimp
95. fried sardines
96. French potage of dab (*passera di mare*)
97. French bread cooked with cherries
98. pies *alla lombarda*

99. twaite shad in yellow broth
100. clam soup

13th Course
Consort of five viols

101. French carp pies
102. small flans with cheese, eggs, and *pasta reale* (almond dough)
103. fried *guoi* in yellow sauce
104. fried shrimp and other small river fish (*pescaria di fontane*)
105. spinach sauce on bread slices
106. potage of eels (*miglioramenti*)
107. cassata
108. fried dough

14th Course
Piffari (shawms) play a moresca dance in the light of torches, danced by "farmers" pretending to cut the grass in the garden

109. Milanese *tortelli*
110. fried calamari
111. Hungarian soup
112. fried young pike
113. fried spinach tortellini
114. grilled sea bass
115. shrimp with French dressing
116. Neapolitan *maccheroni* with sugar and cinnamon, covered with cheese

15th Course
No music until the last dish of the course

117. tall rice pies with cinnamon
118. fried soft-shell crab covered with orange slices, sugar, and cinnamon
119. tall fried dough with raisins, pine nuts, orange juice, sugar, and cinnamon
120. brown crab
121. fried fish of various kinds
122. grilled mackerel with onions and sauce
123. farro with sugar and milk
124. heads of pickerel with gold-colored mouths on white gelatin

As the fish heads are brought in, a singer comes out of the bower singing in the style of Orpheus and playing the lyre.

16th Course
Four French boys sing ornamented songs (*canzoni di gorga*)

125. cherry pies
126. Italian tartlets
127. large date pastries
128. sweet French gelatin spiced with cinnamon, cloves, nutmeg, saffron, and cardamom (*gelatina chiara alla francese*)
129. fried oysters with lemon slices
130. fresh fava bean pies with yolks and cheese
131. small Italian doughnuts
132. prunes in sweet sauce

17th Course
No music

133. fresh fava beans
134. cheese from Piacenza and *marciolini* (tomatoes)
135. cherries
136. raw baby artichokes
137. chestnuts in rose petals
138. giuncata cheese with herbs and anise
139. milk and honey
140. *zaldoni* (large wafers)

End of the courses proper. The table is cleared and guests wash hands in scented water.
[Desserts and fruit]
Mr. Alfonso della Viola presents his music for six voices, six viols, one lyre, one lute, one cittern, a trombone, a large recorder, a medium-size recorder, a German flute, a *sordina* [treble violin or kit], two instruments played with plectra [*strumenti con penna*, probably psalteries, lutes, or harpsichords]. "This music was so well concerted that each one thought to have been lifted to the heavens."

141. dressed orange, citron, and lemon peels
142. sugared lettuce, melons, almonds, and other fruit
143. apple quince
144. gelati

145. pieces of marzipan sweets
146. torroni
147. pine-nut, pistachio, and melon seed confetti with cinnamon

A this point waiters serve flavored toothpicks and clean napkins.

AFTER DINNER: Gifts and final moresca dance.
The Monsignor Hippolito d'Este orders brought in a silver model ship filled with precious presents for the guests. At 5:00 a.m. shawms play and twenty-four dancers dressed in livery come out of the bower holding torches lit on both ends. After they dance a moresca, everyone goes home.

Source: Cristoforo di Messisbugo, *Banchetti, compositioni di vivande et apparecchio generale di Christoforo* [*sic*] *di Messisbugo allo Illustrissimo et Reverendissimo Signor il Signor Don Hippolito da Este, Cardinale di Ferrara* (Ferrara: Giovanni de Buglhat and Antonio Hucher & C., 1549). In Messisburgo, Libro nuovo nel quale s'insegna il modo d'ordinar banchetti . . . (Venice: Spineda, 1600), 9r–14v.

Translating Renaissance menus is difficult, for many of the names of the dishes, and most of the recipes, have disappeared, and some animal species then used for food are now extinct (getting served in large quantity at banquets did not help preserve endangered species). Notwithstanding the patriotic efforts of modern chefs and gastronomists who argue the continuity in gastronomic tradition, today's taste is far removed from Renaissance courtly cuisine. Likewise, most of the music played during the banquet was remote in style and performance practice from what we know today. It was semi-improvised, often on instruments no longer in use, and we have only a general idea of what it sounded like. In addition to the strangeness of sounds and flavors, the amount of food served would be absurd today. Guests used to meals of this kind knew how to pace themselves, as they also knew the unspoken rules of when to talk and when to chew and listen. The syntax of the meal—the succession of courses—required a knowledge of the form, which was different from normal meals or even from our high-table multicourse meals. For example, in a modern dinner it would be unconventional to begin with sweets. When Barbara Wheaton describes a medieval French banquet's menu as "disorganized," she does so as a modern observer of a distant culture who does not relate to it in accordance with its own logic.[26]

It would be more productive to approach the study of food and the music of Renaissance banquets with an anthropological awareness that we are observing a distant and very different world, and with the historical imagination of archaeologists trying to reconstruct a lost civilization from fragments of material culture. I agree with Gary Tomlinson, who emphasizes the need to understand the Renaissance in the economy of otherness and difference, siding in this respect with postmodern historiographical approaches such as those of Michel Foucault and Peter Brown.[27] As the protagonist of L. P. Hartley's novel *The Go-Between* wrote about his own past, "The past is a foreign country; they do things differently there."[28]

The large scale of Messisbugo's banquet at Belfiore would not make sense in a modern restaurant, but it presents similarities to the syntax of classical theater, which would soon inform the dramaturgy of opera. The structure of the banquet, and its division into courses composed of different dishes, resembles the division of a classical dramatic work into acts and scenes, with the latter defined by entrances and exits of the characters (or dishes). The sweet dish, the boiled fish, the fried fish, the pastries, the soup: each will come back, dressed differently, in later courses, like characters in a play. This is unlike a modern meal, where items like soup never return in a later course.

The division into what I refer to as acts is based on an articulation provided by performing arts events of different kinds. The end of the first "act" of the Este banquet was marked with performances of comic intermezzi featuring commedia dell'arte masks, an unmistakable point of articulation—a substantial entr'acte—between two large time units. The second act of the banquet featured vocal and instrumental music and ended with a fake finale: the table was cleared in the middle of the ninth course. Guests were fooled into thinking they had survived the meal, but then a fresh tablecloth, silverware, and napkins were brought, and the third and longest eating act—the merciless addition of over seventy more dishes—began. The cardinal had played a mean trick on those guests who believed they could finally stop pretending to be moderate with the oysters and oranges and start indulging a little more freely. The very last "dish" brought in, mercifully, had no food in it, but only toothpicks and clean napkins to signal the long-awaited fall of the curtain.

There was another structural difference separating the antipasti from the rest of the meal. After the antipasti, musicians could no longer be seen. Yet music's role and thematic link to the meal remained meaningful, and starting with act 2, musicians, dancers, and actors began to make occasional entrances into the dining space, so that they could once again be both heard and seen. This differentiation between two modes of music production was to become an essential music-dramatic technique used in opera. One mode stages actors as dramatis personae producing music in their world, while the other presents music and sounds with no visible source: hidden commentary belonging to a different reality.[29]

Links between music and food were as carefully planned at the localized or small-scale level as at the large. In the first course, for example, the warm "sublime harmony" produced by three trombones and three cornetti introduced warm food after cold appetizers: hard-boiled eggs, fried fish, boiled fish organs, soup, and puff-pastry pizza called *pizza sfogliata*. The solemn sound of the brass consort alerted the guests to allegorical meaning in the dishes served, mostly celebrating the Este family, such as French sauce on eggs for the French-Italian connection and—most important—a boiled sturgeon garnished with a black garlic sauce ("agliata, sapore incarnato") to represent the host's coat of arms ("che rappresentava la impresa di sua Reverendissima Signoria"). Recipes for garlic sauces were given elsewhere in the book: crushed whole nuts were mixed with garlic, salt, fish or meat broth, and different spices to make sauces of different colors (saffron for yellow, for example). The "salsa incarnata" was dark, the result of a lengthy process of refining the foam from boiling carobs, layering it on top of the garlic sauce, and leaving it to cool, with the option of adding blackberries to darken the color. It was most likely used to decorate fish with the image of a black eagle that, together with lilies, was part of the Este coat of arms. Interestingly, the flavor of garlic was associated with lower-class status, contrasting with the noble image of the eagle. This was not the only element of the feast to cross social boundaries.

In the fourth course, most remarkably, earthy food—a Sicilian rice dish, a German fried doughnut, and a Neapolitan popular dish called *nizzole* or *villanata* (literally, country dish)—was accompanied by music with a distinctly folk flavor: an ensemble of bagpipes, bass, and cittern. And in the fourteenth course, dancers dressed as farmers performed a dance in which they pretended to mow the grass in the garden, then danced Moorish dance while guests ate dishes from various countries: Milanese *tortelli*, shrimp in French sauce, Hungarian soup, and sweet Neapolitan macaroni. Exotic music and country food entered the table of the princes but were recast in a higher style.[30]

In the second course, fish with French sauce (tench, "rivestite alla francese," no. 27) was accompanied by music that included the dolzaina, a sweet-sounding double-reed instrument, and possibly by French songs. At the start of the third course, a dish called "Fiordiligi alla Francese" (dish no. 29) represented the union of the Este family with the French royal family, whose symbol was the fleur-de-lis or lily flower (*fiordiligi*), which also appeared in the coat of arms of the Este family. The music, produced by harp, recorder, and harpsichord, expressed international coalition rather than local color. Conversely, toward the end of the meal another refined French dish ("gelatina chiara alla francese," no. 128) was served while four French boys sang their own repertory of highly ornamented songs.

The climax of the banquet was the musical and culinary representation of the myth of Orpheus. Right before this "number," the music-dramatic part of the banquet reached its climax. A strange-looking and likely weird-tasting dish was brought in: fish heads with open mouths colored in gold and laid on white jelly (no. 124). One of the musicians entered the dining hall playing a lyre and singing in the style of Orpheus ("venne fuori uno dalla frascata con una lira cantando al modo d'Orpheo divinamente"). Such singing was a healing and spiritual practice developed by Marsilio Ficino. Because it was improvised it is now lost, but traces of it and its magical power were integrated into the operatic productions in 1600 of *L'Euridice* by Caccini and Peri.[31] Drama, music, healing, and food came together. The open golden mouth of the fish was perhaps a reference to the mythic power of Orpheus to enchant and heal through music. But the severed head recalls the tragic ending of the story, when the bacchants cut off Orpheus's head and threw it into the sea, where it floated while still singing (Ovid, *Metamorphoses* 11.1–55).[32]

At the very end of the banquet, there was a second Moorish dance. As we have seen, the first one was performed by dancers dressed as working farmers. The second moresca was performed by twenty-four dancers holding torches lit on both ends. Likely this was another reference to the drunken bacchants butchering Orpheus with sticks and stones while nearby, as Ovid narrates, "strong, sweating farmers were attending the fields" (*Metamorphoses* 11, 32–33). The moresca was used for that very purpose in Monteverdi's *Orfeo*, first performed at the court of Mantua in 1607; it appears as the very last page of the printed edition.[33] With its wild and tipsy rhythm, this dance is ideal to represent the end of a banquet in which an enormous amount of food was accompanied by an equally generous amount of wine. At dawn, the archbishop's guests left the palace eight hours after their arrival—altered by wine, dance, theater, music, and food.

Banquet Production and Casting

Renaissance banquets were collaborative art productions realized through a carefully planned communal effort. As such, together with allegorical parades and church rituals, they paved the way for the formation of strategies that would become essential in opera productions. Complex convivial events were multisensorial in nature but, more important, they helped develop a system of organized teamwork in which a large number of people with different professional roles coordinated their work under strict time constraints. Considering the perishable nature of the food, the fish dinner described above could not have been produced otherwise. Courses of dishes on individual plates had to come out of the kitchen together. Each course had to be timed with the accompanying music or drama. What happened in the kitchen of a prince was comparable to the busy, tightly timed teamwork that would soon happen, and still happens, behind the scenes of an opera house. Normore observes that "major feasts required substantial input from multiple creators at all stages of their development," and this "multiauthored approach" adapted "patterns of collaboration employed from small manuscripts to massive altarpieces," with the difference that banquets and their entremets "complicate the separation between media and makers."[34] In other words, while we observe an altarpiece we forget the process that took place to make it. When we enjoy perishable food and live music, the moment of creation nearly overlaps the moment of consumption, reminding us that the work itself can exist only as something happening, as a performance, which is nonetheless the result of a prolonged and coordinated effort of a large number of organized people.

Rossetti's *Dello scalco* builds upon Messisbugo by perfecting the organizational aspect of banquet art. In its opening pages, as in the front matter of an opera libretto detailing the cast, we find a list of staff members involved in the production. The most important role was that of the chief steward, followed by his assistants, and then the accountant, the butler or pantry manager (*dispensiero*) a baker and pastry chef (*panattiero*) and flour assistant to the baker (*ufficial delle farine*), the cellarer, the wood and fire team, the chief cook (*maestro del tinello*) supervising the kitchen staff and tools, the sommelier (*bottigliero*), and a hierarchically organized army of menial undercooks, waiters, and servants.[35]

Each role is described in terms not only of skills and responsibilities, but of personality and appearance. Rossetti writes that the *bottigliero* needs to know everything about "most perfect water" and the qualities and effects of all kinds of wines, and how to mix them; he also needs to dress neatly, have a happy, red face, and be extremely polite.[36] The executive chef (*sopra cuoco*) must be amiable (*amorevole*), very neat in dress and personal hygiene, faithful, and careful, while the chef de cuisine (*cuoco*) must be strong, quick, precise, and sober and must have a sharp sense of measure; his team of cooks must be endowed with similar qualities.[37] The description of the personality and behavior of the steward himself goes on for several pages: he should be tall, able to lead and command by quiet gestures, and he must dress in a humble but respectable fashion. He needs to be perfectly clean, more cheerful than melancholy, and have a pleasant complexion. Yet he cannot be a smiling mask: he must be sensitive, ready to understand the mood of his subordinates and superiors, likable but firm, giving his subordinates the impression that he pays attention to what they are doing even when distracted by some other business. He needs to know how to be respected and loved, but also feared and obeyed.[38] The amount of detail and subtle behavioral analysis in this description bears comparison to Machiavelli's portrait of the prince, or to Castiglione's description of the courtier.

Rossetti shows great care for all that affects not only taste but also sight: in other words, how to set the stage. He invites the steward to pay attention to the choice of linen and silverware as well as the disposition of cold food, especially fruit and salads, and, as in a theater production, the lighting of the dining room. The steward should also keep odors under control, blocking the unpleasant ones and enhancing the good ones through fragrant, refreshing scents produced by baskets and garlands of lemons, oranges, and soaps and containers of scented water and flowers.[39] As for the sense of hearing, Rossetti reminds his readers that not every occasion requires music. He classifies convivial gatherings hierarchically, ranging from formal banquets (*banchetti*), to large suppers (*cene grosse*), to more intimate or domestic suppers (*cene desinari domestici*). Every kind of banquet requires different stage sets, props, and even styles of acting, as in the theater. Inviting guests for dinner means setting the stage using gastronomic and visual signifiers to cue them to the appropriate behavior, or to acting their role in pitching the right rhetorical level.

Banquet as Theater

A comparison of the banquet descriptions by Messisbugo and Rossetti, written thirty-five years apart, reveals a gradual blurring of the dividing line between real life and theater (intended as performance space). Rossetti documents a banquet offered by Isabella d'Este in Urbino that featured plenty of music and drama as well as dramatic music: "Every course was served with various kinds of music performed on various instruments and voices, which continued after the meal for the dance."[40] In addition, each course was announced by a fanfare of trumpets and drums, occasionally supplemented by firecrackers. This particular use of instruments can also be observed in several other banquets Rossetti described.[41]

By the time of Rossetti (1584), the large-scale form of three courses and *frutta* had emerged. At another banquet offered during the February carnival season for a reunion of the Este family with princes of Tuscany and ambassadors for Venice, the structure of the event was remarkably elaborate.[42] Rossetti describes the "stage sets" of tablecloths, napkins, lights, and sugar sculptures: the curtain rises, so to speak, with a presentation of the table itself—the tablecloth folded to create twelve arches dividing dishes filled with sugar figures of cupids "playing tricks in a thousand different postures" around a sugar sculpture of Venus armed with sugar weapons. A second table had its tablecloth folded to create fortified castle walls with battlements; on the towers were positioned a great number of sugar figures of soldiers brandishing various weapons. At the center of the table, the battle continued with red sugar soldiers armed with pikes and arquebuses attacking the castle perimeter. The table for the princes, similarly adorned, was disposed to allow a plain view of all the other tables. As in a theater, the highest-ranking audience members had the best seats. The dinner hall was illuminated by putti that appeared to be flying without support while bearing golden sticks holding white torches. The dishes entered on painted tables, each carried by two men, and were announced by a fanfare of drums, trumpets, and firecrackers. The steward's assistants were dressed in black velvet livery embroidered in silver, and the princes were served by twenty-four young men dressed in white satin and black velvet coats and wearing silver swords.

As was customary, the three courses comprised up to twenty dishes each. Given the season, they were predominantly pasta and meat dishes. The first course, for example, consisted of the following dishes, each presented to the guests on sixteen identical plates: meat pies (*pasticci*) decorated with mythological stories of the labors of Hercules (referring to Ercole I, Duke of Ferrara); cold peacocks in white sauce with golden feet laid on dishes covered with golden citrus leaves; capons in white dough with silver-colored heads and feet on plates covered with silver-colored laurel leaves; partridges breaded in French style on dishes with gold-colored bread; sliced skinless salami; ox tongue salted and sliced in the shape of olive leaves; sliced *sumata* (salted fat from pork belly, similar to bacon); *offelle sfogliate* (puff pastry); marzipan sculptures of dragons colored in gold and silver; *biancomangiare* (blancmange or white pudding, a staple since the Middle Ages); peacock meat covered with jelly and laurel leaves; decorated pheasant pies; plates of cheese from Lodi; *marzolino* goat cheese from Florence; salads of endive, lettuce, and sprouts, and also citrons.

The main show was offered after dinner. The tablecloths were removed, the ceiling opened onto a solarium with a fake sky, and fireworks gave the illusion of thunder and lightning. The goddess Flora appeared, floating on a cloud while throwing flowers and singing an aria announcing the end of the winter. Rossetti recorded all the texts, sung to instrumental accompaniments. After the vocal music ended, the *pifferi* played dance music. Special effects continued during the all-night dance, including a parade of allegorical carts. Early in the morning a breakfast was served with more desserts, sweet soft drinks (*acque zuccherate*), and dessert wines. The music carried on as cupids brought bouquets of flowers, flasks of scented waters, and precious soaps.

During yet another banquet, offered by Cornelio Bentivoglio, the intermezzo between the first and second courses was a staging of the Orpheus myth, complete with special effects giving the illusion that Orpheus could sing polyphonically by himself: "Orpheus entered the hall playing and singing with three voices that did not appear to be in his company."[43] The fifteen hollow animal forms covered by fake furs that followed him contained the dishes of the second course. To the guests' astonishment, the steward took the plates of food out of the animals and sent them to the tables while Orpheus continued his magical polyphonic song.

From Banquet to Opera

By the time court opera began, the size and complexity of banquet art were unparalleled: a printed account of the 1608 Florentine wedding banquet of Cosimo de' Medici to Maria Maddalena of Austria comes complete with engraved illustration and notes that two hundred musicians played at the gargantuan wedding banquet.[44] The grammar of the banquet followed the by-then conventional partition into two or three courses composed of up to twenty dishes each, with "codas" of fruit and desserts. What was in Messisbugo an implied formal organization had become, from Rossetti on, a codified convention.

The link between opera and food had grown intimate. One of the earliest opera composers and producers, Emilio de' Cavalieri, was employed in Florence as steward—director of banquet shows—at the end of the sixteenth century, right before the earliest intense operatic experiments began.[45] Meanwhile Catherine de' Medici was organizing spectacular festivals in France that deployed food, music, drama, and dance as part of aesthetically unified events called masquerades.[46] That the tradition of multisensory banquets had been perfected and was being explicitly presented as theatrical is evinced by the title of another book on banquets, the *Very Noble Theater of Banquet Art*, dedicated to Cardinal Giacomo Rospigliosi, the nephew of Pope Clemens IX, who was also a prolific opera librettist.[47] Banquet art was no longer part of opera's prehistory, but part of the same culture. Early courtly operas were in fact often represented during festivities that also featured elaborate banquets.

The direct link between staging opera and staging banquets, however, was far from new in the seventeenth century. To track down its origin we need to keep digging into the past and look, as we will do in the next chapter, at Politian's *Orfeo*, first represented at a Mardi Gras meal in Mantua in 1480.

CHAPTER THREE

Orpheus at the Cardinal's Table

The first attempt to set the Greek tale of Orpheus as musical theater, Politian's *Orfeo*, was made in fifteenth-century Mantua, a propulsive center of the humanist movement promoting the creative rediscovery of antiquity. The music for this early opera was improvised, in line with what humanists believed was the performance practice in classical Greek theater. Modern music historiography has relied heavily on written music texts, confining this opera to the prehistory of the genre, even though it was transmitted through a literary text that implied unwritten performance of music, dance, and action, inserted in a broader performative context that the extant text alludes to but does not capture in full. A propos of Monteverdi's *Orfeo*, written over one hundred years later, Mauro Calcagno conceptualizes "performance" in a broad sense: it "encompass[es] four different realms of culture within societies: entertainment, education, ritual, and healing."[1] These four realms can be ascribed to banquet art but also, as we shall see, to proto-operas conceived as part of a banquet, such as Politian's *Orfeo*.

It is obvious why the myth of Orpheus—a singer who used the power of music to affect animate and inanimate things—was the earliest secular play with music in the vernacular and the earliest attempt at re-creating a form of musical theater that, energized by the spirit of emulation of classical theater, departed from medieval norms. Less obvious is that the first presentation of *Orfeo* took place during a banquet and included scenes of conviviality that related both directly and symbolically to the conviviality offstage, thus blurring the division between fictional and nonfictional realities, between audience and stage.

In a letter published at the head of the libretto, Politian mentions that the work was part of the "carousing" hosted by the Cardinal of Mantua. This and other contextual evidence suggests that *Orfeo* was first performed during a banquet on Mardi Gras 1480, as a convivial ritual of transition from carnival's final day of feasting to Lent's fasting and purgation of body and soul.[2] There was, in other words, an intimate link between the reality the audience experienced and the fictional world of this piece of early musical theater. The host of the banquet was Francesco Gonzaga (1444–83), Cardinal of Mantua. During his pastoral mission, he organized many sumptuous gatherings that included music and theater.[3] The convivial practices of Cardinal Gonzaga and other church leaders worried Cardinal Pietro Riario, the nephew of Pope Sixtus IV, who, while himself indulging in lavish meals, expressed his pious concern for his fellow cardinals' diet and spiritual health.[4] In 1476 Riario denounced the "scandal of banquets organized by cardinals" and encouraged more sober and moderate communal meals consisting of only two modest courses: one of roast meat or fish, and one of boiled or stewed meat, introduced by a pasta dish and followed by cake or fruit. Compared with a regular banquet, the menu Riario prescribed was indeed modest. Riario also opposed performing music and theater during the meals, believing the participants should follow the monastic tradition of listening to readings from Scripture. No restrictions on drinking wine were recommended.[5] It seems obvious, then, that Cardinal Gonzaga offered his carnival banquet and the performance of *Orfeo* in defiance of the Roman Curia.

Politian's *Orfeo* as Operatic Prototype

The literary text of Politian's *Orfeo* occupies a minor position in the literary canon as the earliest complete text of a secular play extant in the Italian language. For this reason it has received considerable attention from scholars of Italian literature, who paid no attention to the genre of this play as musical theater. In so doing, they continued the approach of the most illustrious of the earliest commentators, the poet and literary scholar Giosuè Carducci, who defined Politian's *Orfeo* as "azione teatrale" and gave credit to it as "the very first attempt at a non-sacred dramatic text in Italian" but did not mention music at all.[6] On the other hand, music historians—most notably Nino Pirrotta—recognized its importance as an early example of staged music drama in which song was conceived not as incidental, but rather as an essential component of the dramatic fabric, recognizing its value as an operatic prototype more than a hundred years before Caccini's and Peri's settings of *L'Euridice* and Monteverdi's *Orfeo*, which are all based on the same classical myth. These early seventeenth-century operas were influenced by Politian's work, which was widely disseminated in printed editions.[7] If it took so long to convert Politian's prototype into a steady practice of operatic composition, it is because musicians were relatively slow at developing the efficient system of semi-improvised, rhythmically fluid music that would become essential for setting dialogic sections and monologues between arias and ensembles. This was the recitative, accompanied by basso continuo, first introduced about 1600.

No modern scholar, to the best of my knowledge, has noticed that Politian's *Orfeo* was rediscovered in the eighteenth century and perceived then—during one of the most fertile moments in opera history—as an operatic archetype. A copy of Politian's text was owned by one of the most distinguished and innovative eighteenth-century librettists, Apostolo Zeno.[8] In 1776 Father Ireneo Affò, who prepared the first critical edition of Politian's poetic text, presented it as an exemplary case of music-dramatic art in which "the musician served the poet and singing followed the harmonic notes of the poetical language." He also portrayed Politian as a skillful librettist: "Politian, composer of the *Orfeo*, had the task to write in a variety of poetical meters, so that the music would be inventive and pleasant, and he did so, I believe, in the most commendable way."[9] Before Affò's edition, the text had been printed in 1749, 1751, and 1765, two hundred years after the last Renaissance printed edition. It was published again in 1782, then disappeared from the book market for more than a hundred years.

Affò's edition was reprinted again in 1924,[10] inspiring Alfredo Casella to write a half-hour-long chamber opera based on Politian's libretto. Casella's work was adapted by the fascist writer Corrado Pavolini, who attempted to tame it by cutting, among other things, the lines celebrating homosexual love that Orpheus sings after failing to rescue Eurydice from Hades. Casella's work was first performed in Venice's Teatro Goldoni in 1932 during the new fascist celebration of Italy's artistic and cultural heritage as Greek-Roman classical. Casella himself, indeed, defined Politian's text as "pure classicism."[11] Politian's *Orfeo*, its origin as a semi-improvised live and lively banquet event discounted, was transformed into a monumental relict, like the ruins of the Roman Forum.

Improvisation and Trance: Baccio Ugolini as Orpheus

The date of February 15, 1480, for the banquet and first performance of *Orfeo* is also corroborated by the short sojourn in Mantua of the first interpreter of the title role, the singer and lyre player Bartolomeo Ugolini, called Baccio,[12] a disciple of Ficino and a member of his Platonic Academy. The casting of a follower of Ficino as the first Orfeo sheds further light on the philosophy of this operatic prototype. As Karol Berger points out, "From the start Ficino associated Orpheus with the idea of recovering ancient music"; Politian was well aware of that when he compared Ficino's lyre to that of Orpheus.[13] As a skilled diplomat, Baccio was often on the road, and he usually traveled with his lyre. He was greatly admired as a singer-improviser and lyre player by many other intellectuals and aristocrats of the time, and most of all, by Ficino and Cardinal Gonzaga, who appointed him bishop of Gaeta in 1494. Lorenzo de' Medici sent him to Naples on a diplomatic and cultural mission to retrieve ancient relics and coins, and he tasked him with commissioning a splendid new Orphic lyre from a Neapolitan instrument maker.[14]

Baccio was not a professional musician. Like Ficino he was a Catholic priest, but as a typical humanist of his time he was open to non-Christian spirituality. Like Ficino, the philosopher and magician Pico della Mirandola, and other members of the Florentine Platonic Academy, Baccio was initiated into Orphic singing as a spiritual and healing practice. As Pico maintained, "Nothing is more effective in natural magic than the hymns of Orpheus, if the correct music, intent of the soul, and other circumstances known to the wise were to be applied."[15]

Although the music of the first *Orfeo* was improvised and does not survive in any written source, the text was transmitted in a myriad of copies. These present remarkable variants, however, suggesting that *Orfeo* went through continual rewriting. It is also possible that some of the variants were actually records of semi-improvised performances that included the invention or variation of poetic lines.[16] Taking into consideration the convivial rituals for which the Mantuan *Orfeo* was designed, we realize that Politian's concept of classicism was not something to be preserved forever and admired at a distance, but was meant to be consumed fresh. Like food, it was part of the ephemeral art of the banquet. In his dedicatory letter, Politian writes that he expected this tale to be destroyed like his hero Orpheus, slaughtered by bacchants.[17] He implies not so much that its literary quality was substandard as that its nature was short-lived like the splendid sugar sculptures served at the banquet.

The semi-improvised nature of the event was a response to Plato's critique of writing in *Phaedrus*, a text Ficino quotes in a letter to Baccio:

> Plato adds that some very unskilled men are thus possessed by the Muses, because divine providence wants to show mankind that the great poems are not the invention of men but gifts from heaven. He indicates that in *Phaedrus* when he says that no one, however diligent and learned in all the arts, has ever excelled in poetry unless to these other qualities has been added a fiery quickening of the soul. We experience this when we are inflamed by God's presence working in us. Such force carries the seed of the divine mind.[18]

Ficino, who taught at the Platonist Academy in Florence, knew that in *Phaedrus* Plato presents a comprehensive exposition of sacred frenzy: "The greatest of blessings come to us through madness, when it is sent as a gift of the gods." To Ficino, Baccio seemed more likely to experience the sacred mania Plato writes about in *Phaedrus* precisely because he was not a virtuoso singer in total control of his art.[19]

Phaedrus is relevant as well for its discussion of the modes of performing a text in a way that alters both body and soul. In *Phaedrus* Socrates presents a critique of written language (274a–275e), preferring instead the "living and breathing word, of which the written word may justly be called the image" (276a). In his commentaries, Ficino explains that the reason Socrates does not read Lysias's speech on love himself, but prefers to hear it recited by young Phaedrus, is that sound is the means by which daemons allow the spiritual body to vibrate in sympathy with the physical body.[20] Ficino emphasizes the point that the most divine frenzy comes from the Muses "through song and poetry," and that poetry without song is empty, for "the person who approaches the threshold of poetry without the frenzy of the Muses, trusting that by a certain art he will emerge as a good poet, is empty himself."[21] Poetry needs sound—and even better, musical sound—to affect the spirit and body. A listener is more deeply affected than a reader. Sound is essential to trance. Ficino writes about trance:

> Whoever experiences any kind of spiritual possession is indeed overflowing on account of the vehemence of the divine impulse and the fullness of its power: he raves, exults, and exceeds the bounds of human behavior. Not unjustly, therefore, this possession or rapture is called frenzy and alienation ["furor quidam et alienatio"]. But no man pos-

sessed is content with simple speech: he bursts forth into clamoring and songs and poems. And frenzy, therefore—whether the poetic, hieratic, or amatory—when it proceeds to songs and poems, seems to be released, and properly so, as poetic frenzy. And since poetic song and verse demand concord and harmony and every harmony is entirely included in the scale of nine (as I show in the *Timaeus* with music), the number nine seems rightly to have been consecrated to the Muses.[22]

Dangerous Lessons from Orpheus

Renaissance banquets were occasions to celebrate and to learn. The music and theater represented during the feasts, as well as the food served and the table sculptures and objects accompanying the meal, were all carefully chosen to allow guests to reflect on ideas and values related to living together, from the intimate level of the loving couple (Orpheus and Eurydice) to the bonds within society at large. Yet as a carnival banquet it also offered a reversal of gender and societal norms. Normore shows how gender reversals were often implied in fifteenth-century entremets (a term designating both live shows and inanimate objects). She cites the case of a Netherlandish aquamanile used for washing hands during banquets, representing Phyllis, the beautiful mistress of Alexander the Great, and his tutor, the great philosopher Aristotle, who had advised Alexander to stay away from her. After seducing the old man, Phyllis rode him like a horse. The aquamanile portrays her dominating and humiliating the wise man, riding him while grabbing his hair with one hand and his buttocks with the other.[23] The reversal of gender and ethical norms has multiple, seemingly contradictory functions: as a cautionary tale, a stimulant for convivial conversations, or to distract and entertain by providing aesthetic and erotic stimulation.

The banquet of Cardinal Gonzaga was offered to honor a double betrothal: that of Clara Gonzaga (daughter of Federico I, lord of Mantua) to Gilbert Montpensier of the house of Bourbon, and the introduction and de facto betrothal at age six of Isabella d'Este to the fifteen-year-old Prince Francesco Gonzaga II (1466–1519).[24] Isabella would eventually become a leading figure in the Italian Renaissance. She was a typical "prince" of the age of Machiavelli, exerting power indirectly through manipulation and dissimulation in a political world where assassination, seduction, and intrigue were the norm. As a patron of the arts, an organizer of splendid banquets, a singer and lute player, and a skilled diplomat, Isabella rivaled her younger sister-in-law, the notorious Lucrezia Borgia.[25] The latter, and the excitement of splendid but dangerous Renaissance feasts, would inspire Gaetano Donizetti, over three centuries later, to end *Lucrezia Borgia* (Milan, 1833) with a lavish banquet and drinking song, during which the guests unknowingly toast each other with wine Lucrezia has poisoned, killing them all—including, accidentally, her own son.

Andrea Mantegna's frescoes for the "wedding chamber" (*Camera degli sposi*) in the Gonzaga castle of San Giorgio in Mantua, completed by 1474, testify to the strategic importance of weddings in courtly life and politics. The room was commissioned by the cardinal's father, the Marquis Ludovico, to welcome his wife, Barbara of Brandenburg; it long retained a double function as both private and public space. The married rulers, and the marquis's formal meeting with his son, recently elected cardinal, are the most important scenes in the complex cycle of frescoes.[26] Today these frescoes still illuminate the cultural milieu of the earliest operatic experiments, presenting a vivid sense of "theatrical immediacy" and carefully staged postures.[27] The scenes are framed by motifs of fruits and vegetables, and a spectacular oculus in the ceiling shows putti holding fruits and looking down on the scene. The cells in the vaulted ceiling present mythological themes, including three episodes from the story of Orpheus: Orpheus playing the lyre, enchanting Cerberus and a Fury in the underworld, and being killed by the bacchants.

Karol Berger has shown the similarities between Mantegna's representation of the bacchants killing Orpheus and similar representations of this episode in contemporary art, including a drawing by Albrecht Dürer created twenty years after Mantegna's frescoes, with the inscription "Orpheus the first homosexual." Berger points out that in this cultural context, "the bereaved Orpheus" was seen "as a threat to heterosexuality."[28] Further along these lines, Mauro Calcagno observes, "The Dionysian *sparagmos* [bacchant] is included twice among the mythological narratives" in the private wedding rooms of the Gonzaga castle but excluded from the iconography of the Orpheus myth in the more public space of the Palazzo del Te, the magnificent Gonzaga residence, also in Mantua, in which the painter Giulio Romano was asked to single out the Apollonian aspects of the myth.[29] The drama of Orpheus is thus a counterpoint to the domestic and political themes dear to the Gonzaga family and adds depth to the polyphony of signifying voices echoing in these private rooms. Following both Calcagno's and Berger's suggested paths of inquiry, let us now look at Politian's representation of female Dionysian frenzy.

If the story of Orpheus functioned as a parable of marital faithfulness, the inclusion of gender struggles complicated matters. In the staged version of the tale, Politian provided a comprehensive narrative on the nature and risks of love. As Rinuccini, Striggio, and other librettists later did, he combined two versions of the myth: Ovid's *Metamorphoses* (10.1–85, 154–218, and 11.1–83,) and Virgil's *Georgics* (4.453–527). A humanist philologist and scholar of classical literature, Politian painstakingly annotated these Latin texts while preparing his poetic text in Italian.[30] His intent, set forth in the dedicatory letter, was to revive Latin poetry and Greek mythology and disseminate them to his audience in the vernacular.

At the very beginning, Mercury demands attention from the cardinal's guests and gives a short plot summary, such as might be found in a modern opera libretto.[31] After Mercury's plot summary, the beginning of *Orfeo* focuses not on the protagonist but on the erotic frenzy (*amor humanus*) of the young shepherd Aristaeus, who tells the older shepherd Mopsus how he fell in love with the singer's bride at first sight and lost his mind: "E mia mente d'amor divenne insana" (and my mind became insane with love) and also lost his appetite: "Ma sempre piango, e' l cibo non mi piace" (But I always cry, and food does not please me).[32] In the following aria (called *canzona*), Aristaeus, like Orpheus, sings to the woods. In the refrain he repeats, "Listen, woods, to my sweet words / since my nymph does not want to hear them" (Udite, selve, mie dolci parole / Poi che la ninfa mia udir non vuole). In the first stanza he imagines that his sheep, sympathizing with him, also refuse to drink and eat.[33] The aria has a comic flavor, charged with sexual innuendo, as, for example, in the remark that the nymph, who loves another, does not care for his *fistula* (a term referring to a folk pipe but also used to describe injuries caused by anal sex), or the evocation of the sympathy that the "horny" herd feels for him ("cornuto armento," where horns are a symbol of cuckoldry).[34] Aristaeus is affected by an eating disorder resulting from an imbalance of appetite, or a disharmonious desire. That Aristaeus is a comic and generally negative character helps the audience view him as a moral warning against the excesses that will eventually affect the protagonist of the drama.

Edifying Lessons

Orpheus's entrance is far more somber: we first hear him after the announcement of Eurydice's death, singing "Let us cry together then, unhappy lyre" (Dunque piangiamo, o sconsolata lira).[35] We are then transported to the underworld, where he sings to Pluto, the king of hell, reminding him of his abduction of his own wife Proserpina, and asking her to give Eurydice back "for the sake of the apple that you, queen, once liked" (pel pomo ch'a te già, regina, piacque).[36] As Orpheus mentions a pomegranate, Proserpina begs her husband to accept his plea.

This reference to the myth of Proserpina comes from Ovid's *Fasti*, or *Book of Days*, which Politian translated and used to advise the painter Botticelli.[37] Book 4 is on the month of April, claimed by Venus as her own. It celebrates the abundance of flowers and food, culminating in the festivities and banquet of Proserpina's mother, the blonde Ceres, goddess of crops and agriculture.[38] Seeing Proserpina among some young girls picking flowers, Pluto abducts her and takes her to the kingdom of death. Her mother, after much searching and crying, strikes a deal with Jove, who grants that Proserpine can break the wedding bonds "if only she has kept her fast," for it is not granted to those in the world of the dead to eat the food of the living (as the ghost of the Commendatore will one day declare in Mozart's *Don Giovanni*).[39] Jove sends Mercury to the underworld to check on the girl's diet and, alas, finds that she has not kept her appetite in check: "The ravished maid did break her fast on three grains enclosed in the tough rind of a pomegranate." After Ceres threatens to stop the crops and fruits from growing, Jupiter allows Proserpina to leave the kingdom of Pluto, but only for six months of each year.[40]

On the last day of carnival, when *Orfeo* was performed, the myth of Proserpina, and the reference to the pomegranate, would have been a powerful reference to Lent, with the obligation to fast starting only hours after the end of the banquet. Proserpina's pomegranate was thus a reminder of the difficulty of controlling human appetite, and of God's clemency and compassion in forgiving human frailty. Less than a year later, Botticelli painted the *Madonna della Melagrana*, a Madonna sharing a pomegranate with her son Jesus. In this painting, as in other Christian iconography, the fruit is an allegory prefiguring Christ's descent into the underworld, his victory over death on Easter Sunday, his victory over sin, and his compassion for the sinner.[41]

Orpheus fails in his mission, as Mercury anticipated, by "looking back while singing gay lines" that are not recorded, since they were probably improvised on the spot by Baccio.[42] Then, for the first time in Politian's libretto, the pattern of eleven-syllable lines (*endecasillabi*) is broken by Eurydice. The indication "parla" (speaks) indicates that the music is disrupted.

In two seven-syllable lines (*settenari*) and a single *endecasillabo*, Eurydice tells her husband that "too much love has destroyed both: I am taken from you because of your folly" (Oimè, che' l troppo amore / N'ha disfatti ambedue. / Ecco ch'io ti son tolta a gran furore).[43] In later operatic librettos the mixture of *settenari* and *endecasillabi* with free rhyme or no rhyme (called *versi sciolti*) would typically be set as recitative but understood as spoken language even when sung, since the erratic patterns of note length and accent imitate spoken language. Orpheus likewise responds in *versi sciolti* ("Oimè, se' mi tu tolta, / Euridice mia bella? O mio furore"), ending with the fateful word "furore" that, uttered by Eurydice, summoned the Furies.[44] It is likely that Baccio stopped singing at this point, breaking the music's spell. The plot then hurtles to its catastrophic end: Orpheus resolves to emulate Jove, who loved the boy Ganymede, or Apollo, who loved Hyacinthus. Politian follows Ovid's version in alluding to Orpheus's songs of homoerotic love stories (*Metamorphoses* 10, 154–218), enraging the bacchants.

A Wild Drinking Song

Politian's *Orfeo* is the only operatic version of the Orpheus myth before Jacques Offenbach's *Orphée aux Infers* (1858) to end with a wild drinking song representing female frenzy and the drunkenness of the bacchants. For the final hours of carnival, the last scene of *Orfeo* is a tragicomic bacchanalian orgy, conceived within Politian's understanding of sacred Dionysian rituals. As is typical of carnival role reversals, the musical tale ends with women performing a ritual: Orphic songs (medicinal or magic ritual use of music) were sung, as far as we know, only by men. Those in the Platonic circle led by Ficino, including Baccio, occasionally celebrated and practiced homoeroticism in line with the idealized love preached in Plato's *Symposium*.[45] Women were excluded from these circles, which generated a lot of controversy.[46] The female chorus of the bacchants in *Orfeo* indeed can be seen as a reaction of victims of cultural exclusion from the part of the homosocial group of which Orpheus becomes the emblem and hero after he comes out from the underworld (and out of the closet).

The final scene begins with the leader of the bacchants inciting her companions to kill Orpheus and cut him in pieces. That the butchering happens offstage did not prevent Politian from giving the audience a taste of blood. After the slaughter a woman comes back, holding the head of Orpheus:

Torna la baccante con la testa di Orfeo e dice:

O o! O o! mort'è lo scelerato!
Euoè! Bacco, Bacco, i' ti ringrazio!
Per tutto 'l bosco l'abbiamo stracciato,
Tal ch'ogni sterpo è del suo sangue sazio.
L'abbiamo a membro a membro lacerato
In molti pezzi con crudele strazio.
Or vadi e biasimi la teda legittima.
Euoè Bacco! accetta questa vittima![47]

[The bacchant returns with the head of Orpheus and says:

Euoè Bacchus! Accept this victim!
Euoè! Bacchus, Bacchus, I thank you!
All over the woods we thrashed him,
Until every twig was soaked with his blood.
We ripped him apart limb by limb
In many pieces with cruel torment.
Now he can go and blame his wife.
Euoè Bacchus! Accept this victim!]

The image of a bacchant holding a man's severed head would have recalled a well-known piece of local statuary: Judith beheading the Assyrian general Holofernes. About twenty years earlier, Donatello had represented the biblical heroine who freed the Jewish city of Bethulia from Assyrian occupation (this same story would, in the eighteenth century, be dramatized in Pietro Metastasio's *La Betulia liberata*, also set by Mozart). Donatello represented Judith beheading the king while pressing her right foot on his groin. Art historian Adrian Randolph defines this sculpture as "the most important political statue in fifteenth-century Florence," showing how Judith represented both justice and the "sexual triumph" of the chaste over a licentious general.[48] In the Medici garden, where the sculpture was originally placed, Judith was staged in a sort of dramatic dialogue with other figures, including two sculptures representing Marsyas, the faun who challenged Apollo in a musical contest, and a sculpture of Priapus with his phallus erect but covered and an inscription addressing a "thievish girl" whom he threatens with his "concealed weapon," likely addressed to the nearby statue of Judith. This garden complex, then, could have been a representation of the reversal of gender norms that points to the reestablishment of male power without implying that one is order and the other disorder.[49]

After the sculpture was moved to the Piazza della Signoria, the religious reformer Savonarola was burned following a Catholic auto-da-fé "under the stern gaze and admonitory gesture of Donatello's *Judith*."[50] As Randolph also documents, thirty years earlier, in 1469, for a wedding banquet in the Medici house the statue of Donatello's *David* was placed in the main courtyard where the dining tables for the men were arranged, while the bride and unmarried women were seated in another part of the courtyard near the statue of Judith. "In this festive context," Randolph writes, "the image of a powerful woman, who adorned herself, attracted a man, plied him with wine, and then killed him, would seem to fall squarely within the trope of the woman-on-top."[51] The bacchant holding the head of Orpheus presents clear similarities with the way Judith was perceived in the culture of the time.

In her influential gender study of music, *Feminine Endings*, Susan McClary writes that Monteverdi's *Orfeo*, "even without the expurgated ending featuring the Bacchantes . . . delivers a host of mixed messages: is Orfeo a hero or a transgressor? Virile or effeminate? Rational or mad?"[52] In Politian's version, these questions seem to multiply: Who would win the final battle? Who is the chastised and who is the avenger? Who represents tyranny and who brings justice? Is beheading a punishment or a liberation? After all, in his letter on divine frenzy (*De divino furore*), Ficino interprets Plato's sacred madness as a state in which, as he describes it, "the mind, detached from the body, is moved by divine inspiration."[53] The representation of the severed head of Orpheus is the signal initiating Dionysian ritual.

After the recitative-like utterance of the solo bacchant, the meter of the lines shifts to a less dialogical and more songlike rhythm of eight-syllable lines (*ottonari*). The chorus sings a two-line refrain alternating with stanzas sung by the bacchant. This poetical form is typical of drinking songs. The text has a structured organization of lines, and the accents marking the rhythm occur periodically.

El coro delle baccante	[*Chorus of bacchants*
Ognun segua, Bacco, te!	Everybody follow you Bacchus!
Bacco, Bacco, euoè!	Bacchus, Bacchus, euoe!
Chi vuol bevere, chi vuol bevere,	Whoever wants to drink, whoever wants to drink,
Venga a bever, venga qui.	come drink, come here.
Voi 'mbottate come pevere	You are all chugging like funnels,
I' vo' bever ancor mi!	but I want to drink too!
Gli è del vino ancor per ti.	There is wine for you too.

Lascia bevere imprima a me.
Ognun segua, Bacco, te!
Bacco, Bacco, euoè!

Io ho voto già il mio corno:
Damm'un po' 'l bottazzo qua!
Questo monte gira intorno,
E 'l cervello a spasso va.
Ognun corra 'n za e in là
Come vede fare a me.
Ognun segua, Bacco, te!
Bacco, Bacco, euoè!
I' mi moro già di sonno:
Son'io ebria, o si o no?
Star più ritte i piè non ponno:
Voi siate ebrie, ch'io lo so!
Ognun facci com'io fo:
Ognun succi come me.
Ognun segua, Bacco, te!
Bacco, Bacco, euoè!
Ognun cridi: Bacco, Bacco!
E pur cacci del vin giù.
Po' co' suoni faren fiacco:
Bevi tu, e tu, e tu!
I' non posso ballar più.
Ognun gridi euoè!
Ognun segua, Bacco, te.
Bacco, Bacco, euoè.[54]

Let me drink first.
Everybody follow Bacchus!
Bacchus, Bacchus, euoe!

My cup is already empty:
get that damn cask over here!
This mountain is spinning around
and my brain is turning to mush.
Everyone now run here and there
as you see I am doing.
Everybody follow Bacchus!
Bacchus, Bacchus, euoe!
I'm dead tired now:
Am I drunk, yes or no?
I can't stand on my feet:
now you must get as drunk as I am!
Everybody now do what I do:
Everybody swig like I do.
Everybody follow Bacchus!
Bacchus, Bacchus, euoe!
Everybody shout: Bacchus Bacchus!
and then gulp down more wine.
Then we'll be tired of music.
You drink, and you, and you!
I can't dance anymore.
Everybody cry euoe!
Everybody follow Bacchus!
Bacchus, Bacchus, euoe!]

Politian was well versed in highbrow classical and classicist poetry, but here he resorts to dialect such as *mi* and *ti* for *me* and *te*, and *'n za* for *in qua*, and lowbrow colloquialisms such as "'mbottate come pevere," giving the impression of the woman's belly becoming a wine barrel (botte) with its mouth a large wooden funnel (*pevera*), a term also used to allude to the vagina.[55] Politian also inserts rhythmic and formal inconsistencies. Many of the *ottonari* lines, in fact, are defective by being a syllable or two too long (as in "Chi vuol be-ve-re, chi vuol be-ve-re" or "La-scia be-ve-re imprima a me"). These irregularities draw the rhythm of the song off balance, giving the impression of tipsy stumbling, most likely enhanced by action during the song. The text itself thus reveals that the song was staged, sung, and danced. It prescribes actions (drinking, emptying cups, and passing the wine around), sound (*suoni* referring to both vocal and instrumental music), and body movements (wild, unstructured running and dancing).

To imagine the sound of this chorus, one may look at Renaissance drinking songs. They were written and performed in a variety of styles ranging from relatively complex polyphony to rollicking bacchanals, with music incorporating popular styles, as in Guillaume Dufay's elegant but captivating *chanson*, "Adieu ces bons vins de Lannoys."[56] Considering the style of poetry in this last chorus in Politian's *Orfeo*, it is likely that it had some kinship with folk or popular music idioms. During banquets, as we have seen, it was common to present dishes and music that evoked regional and popular culture. To imagine the musical style of *Orfeo*, Pirrotta evokes Politian's spring celebration song, "Ben venga maggio" (Let's welcome May), for which we do have music notated by an anonymous musician. This song, like carnival songs (*canti carnascialeschi*), popular religious songs (*laudi*), and motets of the time of Savonarola, belongs to a style in between lowbrow and highbrow, and to both the written and the oral traditions.[57] The text of "Ben venga maggio," however, is free from dialect. The music has a gripping rhythm, repeating short phrases enough to captivate the ear and then varying, almost unexpectedly, accent placement, meter, and phrase length. The three-voice polyphony adds a consonant but thick texture by having the voices proceed homorhythmically: they all sing the same words and syllables together while melodic lines move in different directions. The sophisticated and erudite aspects of the music remain half-hidden to give an impression of immediacy, but they are there to guarantee courtly finesse, like peasant dishes revamped for a court banquet.

The final bacchanal of *Orfeo* probably shared some of these features, but the dialect, movements, and gestures suggest a less sophisticated and more hypnotic and rhythmically driven musical setting. With its carefully planned alternation of solo verses and choral refrains, seemingly careless rhythmic irregularities, and frantic dance and athletic movements, this piece could have produced an effect of structured frenzy.

In a bacchanal ritual, music, dance, and alteration would be the essential ingredients of a trance, a Dionysian "telestic mania," as Plato defined sacred frenzy inspired by Dionysus. Rouget, who analyzed the description of telestic frenzy in *Phaedrus* and in the broader context of ancient Greek culture, classifies four kinds of sacred frenzy discussed in *Phaedrus*: the prophetic from Apollo, the music-poetic and artistic from the Muses, the erotic from

Aphrodite (Venus), and the "telestic" or ritual trance by possession from Dionysus (Bacchus). This trance originates from pathologies triggered by ancient offenses to a divinity, and the trance provides divine power, while rites of purification grant recovery and release from troubles. In the final analysis, the purpose of the trance is therapeutic.[58]

In *De vita coelitus comparanda*, Ficino addresses the "natural power of speech, song, and words." It is in this context that he observes, "There is indeed in certain sounds a Phoeban and medical power, as shown by the fact that in Apulia whoever is stung by the tarantula is stunned and lies half-dead until he hears a certain sound proper to him. Then he dances along with the sound, works up sweat, and gets well."[59] The reference to Phoeban Apollo is consistent with Ficino's puzzling insistence, in his *Commentaries on Phaedrus*, on the affinity of Bacchus to the Apollonian (meaning medical) furor. Ficino comments on Socrates's erotic furor that "since he has become ecstatic [excessus] through Bacchus, the Apollonian daemon immediately enraptures him perchance (for Apollo is closest to Bacchus)."[60]

Politian's bacchanal may have been inspired by tarantism, a phenomenon recognized in his own time as a living relic of telestic mania. This would explain the shift to low style adopted by the chorus, in contrast to the elevated style of Orpheus and Eurydice. But there is more: the pattern of accents in Politian's chorus fits the tarantella rhythm, which is based on a combination of iambic cells (a long, accented note plus a short, unaccented note), interspersed with intensifying groups of three short notes and ending on a long, accented note. One can sing the syllables of Politian's lyrics under the notes of a tarantella, such as the one the composer Luigi Ricci used in the comic opera *La festa di Piedigrotta*. Here the tarantella is sung in front of a tavern where people eat and drink copiously.[61] This tarantella was likely adapted from a dance piece present in the Neapolitan oral-tradition repertory, where it remained until today, as documented—among other sources—by a 1954 Folkways recording of the piece for ocarina, castanets, and tambourine.[62]

Another characteristic of tarantella music is a sudden shift of modes (in

Figure 3.1. Hypothetical setting of the bacchants' drinking chorus from Politian's *Orfeo* on the traditional tarantella motive, appearing in Luigi Ricci, "Piedigrotta: Commedia in 4 atti di Marco D'Arienzo, musica di Luigi Ricci, rappresentata al Teatro nuovo l'anno 1852," MS. copy I-Nc 3.3.18-19, 2 vols., vol. 2 (3.3.19), 4r–20v.

modern terms, alternating major and minor sections). In Platonic music theory, the ethical power of music to trigger emotions is exerted by harmonic and melodic configurations proper to each musical mode. The properties of the tarantella are therefore both rhythmic and harmonic, making it a powerful musical remedy. The cry of the *tarantate*—the possessed women—is based on "ah-eee," not too dissimilar to the "euoe" (pronounced "e-u-ŏ-é") of the bacchants. Anthropologist Ernesto De Martino, in his study of tarantism, relates *tarantate* to Dionysian rituals.[63] He does not claim a direct similarity between the bacchants' "euoe" and the *tarantate*'s "ah-eee," but he relates the latter to ancient Greek female rituals associated with the myth of Io (the maiden transformed into a cow and then back into a woman), whose name reproduces a ritual cry onomatopoeically. The sound also relates to various female orgiastic rituals in ancient Greek culture, which permeated Greek colonies in southern Italy, including those of the bacchants.

As in southern Italian culture, Greek women were particularly inclined to Dionysian orgiastic rituals because, as De Martino points out, "the harsh social pressure exercised on the female world in an androcratic type of society leads to the return of the repressed in the form of ciphered neurotic symptoms incompatible with any cultural order whatsoever."[64] In his chapter on "musical catharsis," he also relates Apulian tarantism to ancient Greek rituals for curing real or symbolic bites of poisonous animals in which the music exerts magical or medical power. This is the case for musical formulas (*epodai*) recorded by Plato to cure bites of snakes and scorpions. The same cultural explanation may apply to the tale of Orpheus. As De Martino writes, "The famous legend of Orpheus and Eurydice, which originally narrated the success of Orpheus's attempt to use music to steal the young Eurydice, bitten by a snake, away from Hades, might be taken in support of the use of musical enchantment to treat and bring back to life maidens 'bitten' by poisonous animals."[65]

Can we hypothesize for this opera a connection between Eurydice and the bacchants? And what would be the implications of a more extended female alliance than has been so far recognized? In her study of early operatic settings of the myth, Alexandra Amati-Camperi, along with Susan McClary, denounces the relegation of female characters to secondary importance both in the opera repertory and in critical literature on opera and focuses on music-dramatic similarities between the female characters Eurydice, the messenger, and especially Proserpina, but understandably not the bacchants, whose voices will no longer be heard after Politian, at least not until Offenbach.[66]

Rather than providing a moral ending in which meaning is disclosed, this early opera practices what the Alterati theorized a hundred years later. The opera stages catharsis that lets out "pain, exuberance, libido, anger" in an unrestrained and unrepressed, but controlled, frenzy, caused by and resulting in alteration.[67] It appears, therefore, that the theories of the Florentine academies, and especially those of the Alterati, did not anticipate or engineer opera but only continued the humanist tradition of music and drama as part of banquet culture.

CHAPTER FOUR

Eating at the Opera House

During the first act of a Met production of Gaetano Donizetti's *Anna Bolena*, I drank a few cups of rooibos tea and ate a couple of slices of freshly baked banana bread with nuts and chocolate chips. The refreshments helped me get past my lack of sympathy during the opera's beginning when Anne Boleyn, having left her true love out of naked ambition, feels forlorn and neglected by Henry VIII. During my third cup of rooibos, Anne's new crown turned out to be a crown of thorns, as she herself admits (1, 12: "un serto io volli, e un serto ebb'io di spine"). The queen was starting to grow on me. The second act was a whole new ball game: Anne ends up in prison, condemned to the block after a page boy incriminates her under torture. The king's new mistress, Anne's cousin and former friend, is racked with guilt but still driven by ambition and by infatuation for a ruler who is a pathological narcissist. As in *Lucia di Lammermoor*, Donizetti dramatizes the protagonist's madness to lucidly denounce injustice. By this point I had transitioned from rooibos to gin.

This episode happened on the evening of April 27, 2020. I was not in an opera theater. I was enjoying opera, food, and drink sitting comfortably on my own couch. Much of the country was in the midst of a lockdown on account of the COVID-19 pandemic, and New York's Metropolitan Opera had been offering "Nightly Met Opera Streams." Other opera companies had been doing the same: San Francisco, Vienna, Berlin, Paris, London, Milan, Turin, Parma, Venice, Palermo, and many other theaters in countries including Spain, Portugal, Poland, Bulgaria, Greece, and Israel.[1] Opera had never been so accessible. The tragic irony was that while opera fans enjoyed unprecedented access to their favorite form of entertainment, opera artists were facing unprecedented hardship. Equally extraordinary, we could experience opera while having a drink or even a meal—highly unusual in the modern age.

In today's opera culture, eating or drinking during a performance is unacceptable. Yet this prohibition is relatively recent in the long history of the genre. For the two centuries after public, commercial opera was first created in Venice during the carnival season of 1637, asceticism like that practiced in the theater today would have seemed very odd. Public opera in Venice was marketed as a pleasurable and entertaining experience. Eating at the opera was the norm rather than the exception.[2]

Street Food at the Opera

The earliest experiments in opera were conceived and performed in palaces, often for courtly or academic gatherings with an exclusive audience. As we have seen, music theater was part of festivities at banquets that were presented with elaborate menus. In the palace, courtiers observed a long-established etiquette of good manners that regulated behavior, whether at the dining table or while attending performing arts events. As Roland Barthes writes in *Elements of Semiology*, "The menu is concocted with reference to a structure," and as such it illustrates an "alimentary language" with its "rules of exclusion," "rules of association," and "rituals of use" allowing for "alimentary *rhetoric*."[3] In the absence of a menu—or even a shared meal—eating prepared food functioned in a very different way than at a banquet or in a restaurant.

At seventeenth- or eighteenth-century opera performances, snacking was the preferred mode of eating. Even when full meals were eaten, they were casual and without menu or table settings. Eating at the opera followed what Pierre Bourdieu in his sociological study of taste defines as the "free-and-easy" meal of the people (franc-manger populaire), void of "the habitus of order," the strict sequences of dishes, and the grammar of the structured meal.[4] These customary practices in public opera houses were a sign of democratization, and they often came in opposition to attempts to regulate and impose order.

Not all public theaters, admittedly, observed and enjoyed the same level of freedom and democratic inclusion. During a public performance in Siena in 1677, the local lord and patron of the arts, Cardinal Flavio Chigi, provided "liquid refreshments for the noblewomen in the audience and the singers backstage": being served a drink at the right moment signaled social distinction.[5] But in most public opera theaters there was no need to wait for refreshments to be served. Food and drink concessions became an important part of the theater's economy, and as such they needed to sell as often as possible to as many people as possible. As early as 1681, Cristoforo Ivanovich writes of four financial instruments used to enhance the profits of Venetian opera productions: the entrance tickets (bollettini che servono di passaporta), the rental of seats (scagni che s'affittano pure ogni sera), the rental of boxes (affitti de' palchetti), and the price food stands paid for permission to sell refreshments (la contribuzione convenuta per botteghini, che servuono di rinfreschi).[6] Selling food and drinks was a source of income for both the impresario and the seller, who was called the *scaleter*: "Other income was to be had from the selling of refreshments (the *scaleter* who sold a sort of doughnuts, and the *caneva* for the sale of wine)."[7] While the rental of seats and entrance fees went to the opera company, the impresario (at least in the documented case of impresario Marco Faustini) received whatever money came from box rentals and food concessions. City laws issued by the *magistrato delle pompe* prohibited bringing full meals to the theater in order to ensure that audience members would buy food and drinks from the official concessions.[8] All this evidence shows that selling food and drinks was a substantial aspect of the opera business.

In the early twentieth century, the historian Giulio Bistort published *Il magistrato alle pompe*, a book on past Venetian regulations of public behavior, from banquets to gondolas, carnivals, excessive cleavage in women's clothes, and so on. Bistort spends a full chapter on eating at the theater. In it he records a city law, issued on December 21, 1711, that banned dinners (*cena*) in the opera theater by prohibiting picnic baskets (*ceste*) and items used to set the table (*apparecchi*). On August 2, 1749, another law had to be issued, probably because of transgressions of the first, stating that "dinners, parties and refreshments are strictly prohibited in the theater boxes."[9] Further evidence for the consumption of substantial food at the opera can be found in a memoir, presumably written at the beginning of the nineteenth century, by Giovanni Rossi, another historian of Venetian laws. This narrative of the decadent final years of the Republic of Venice is reminiscent of the twilight of the Roman Empire. During this Napoleonic era, opera audiences started to eat more substantial meals than snacks: "In the last years of the Republic the San Cassiano theater became a place for bacchanals, where people used to have little suppers between the acts, amazingly eating even meat pies (*carni pasticciate*), roasted coots (*folaghe arrostite*), in total freedom, without setting the table, both in the boxes and in the pit."[10] Rossi was shocked by the "total freedom" with which the opera audience indulged their appetites in places where there were no tables, no first or second courses, and of course no table manners. At the end of the nineteenth century, the musicologist Taddeo Wiel looked at Venetian legislation against public disturbances issued in the middle decades of the eighteenth century. Although the regulations he cites make no mention of food or drinks, Wiel interprets them as an implicit ban on eating at the opera.[11] According to Wiel's narrative, the early Florentine court opera paved a road to Wagner that was interrupted (for almost three centuries) by degenerate public opera.[12] Wiel sees the eighteenth-century lax practices on food inside the theater as corrupt and faulty, since they encouraged the audience to be disengaged and distracted, and he claims that "lengthy recitatives encouraged the audience to chat, drink coffee, and eat sorbetti."[13] Wiel's problem is not with the use of recitative or with feasting, but rather with the audience's uncivilized and rowdy behavior, "screaming, whistling, . . . throwing flowers, papers with celebratory poems," and even tomatoes.[14] Bistort's and Wiel's testimonies provide useful information to be taken with a grain of salt, as they were generated during the formation of a modernist attitude toward highbrow art, when intellectuals were fiercely opposing distraction on the part of past audiences, who in their opinion did not take opera as seriously as modern audiences did.

Disorganized eating and drinking at the opera have been and still are perceived as symptoms of a lack of order and good taste, notwithstanding the high-class status of the audience, who paraded in their fashionable clothes, coiffures, and jewels, using coded body language, courting and deploying other modes of regulated social interaction. First in Venice's public opera and soon elsewhere we witness a centrifugal trend pushing even aristocrats away from the structured code of courtly manners. In her study of eighteenth-century Italian opera, Martha Feldman describes opera seria in these terms: "With food, drinks, gambling, visiting, reading, cards, lotteries, games—sometimes even brawls—on top of listening, watching, and people watching, Italy's commercial theaters were not just the most splendid but the maddest in Europe." This prompts Feldman to reflect on the "pervasive tension in opera seria between fixity and license, both on stage and in the listening practices in the house."[15] In other words, like other scholars, Feldman perceives a contradiction in the contrast between the unrestrained behavior of the opera audience and their formal, codified dress, not to mention the highly codified and sophisticated idiom of opera characters: the formal conventions regulating their actions, gestures, and music. Another scholar of early opera, Margaret Murata, remarked a propos of the violent disturbances and disorders at the Teatro Capranica in late seventeenth-century Rome, "Not tradition, written constitution, or rules of hospitality could completely control behavior in a venue like the public theater."[16] The great majority of the operagoers Murata described belonged to the upper and middle classes and brought along their butlers and waiters, who were well trained in table manners and practiced them regularly during meals. However, in the opera house the dominant culture was not the aristocratic culture of court and palace, but the all-inclusive culture of the marketplace and piazza, of festive times that bring people together in a common space where they can behave in a less controlled way. In the piazza, as in the opera theater, great art (as in the architecture of churches, palaces, and fountains) was in fact the stage for a kind of public behavior that was much more relaxed than inside the palaces or churches.

In the baroque, rococo, and neoclassical eras, the piazza and the opera house mirrored each other in form and function. Architectural historian Rudolf Wittkower has clarified the aesthetic of urban planning and the function of the public space from the high baroque to the middle of the eighteenth century in the context of Pietro da Cortona's 1657 modernization of Santa Maria della Pace and its piazza in Rome. The new baroque piazza represents a step away from the Renaissance in that it embraces theatricality: a specular relationship is established in both the piazza and the new horseshoe-shaped floor plans and vertical rows of boxes typical of the new public opera house. As Wittkower writes, "Although the regularly laid-out piazzas had a long tradition in Italy, Cortona's design inaugurates a new departure, for he applied the experience of the theatre to town-planning: the church appears like the stage, the piazza like the auditorium, and the flanking houses like the boxes."[17] Both spaces were conceived theatrically, to allow the architecture itself and the people inhabiting it to be part of a reality that appeared constantly staged. Both spaces were designed to display power, but at the same time they allowed the public to challenge or criticize power by voicing reactions through body language and words. Absorption, enthusiasm, disruption, and indifference were all meaningful ways people could assert their presence as active listeners and viewers. The theater boxes allowed privacy analogous to the balconies of private houses on the piazza, but they also, like small stages surrounding the main stage, provided the opportunity to be seen, and therefore to turn domestic privacy into public display. In some cases, as during the carnival of Venice, the piazza functioned as an actual theatrical space as well as a space for selling and eating food, and especially for butchering and eating meat before the mostly vegetarian meals of Lent.[18]

The eighteenth-century art and architecture critic Francesco Milizia complained bitterly about the presence of boxes (*palchetti*) in public theaters, and not only for aesthetic reasons (they do not allow architects to erect majestic pillars and other imposing architectural ornaments that recall ancient theaters), but also because they impair the public function of the classical theater by reproducing a domestic space within and in conflict with a public place: "That so-much praised commodity that boxes allow privacy and invisibility is not conducive to decency. One great advantage of public theater is to be in a public space. In one's own house . . . people may unleash their passions, but they would restrain them in public, when seen by a greater number of onlookers, so that they will show in public an appearance of decency and civility that they may lack in private and strive to appear as they should be." Milizia loathed the behavior typically seen in the boxes, which he describes as incessantly strolling from box to box to visit other people, chatting, flirting, and slicing and eating cold cuts (trinciando freddure).[19] Imagining the theater of the future, he envisions a space that would replace boxes with balconies (as modern opera theaters would do). In an illustration of the ideal theater, he still includes two "gran caffè" accessible from the main floor and balconies and two additional cafés for parties (caffetterie in tempo di festini), as an attempt to regulate and confine, rather than eliminate, eating in the theater.[20]

A much discussed and reproduced oil painting attributed to Giovanni Michele Graneri portrays an opera in the Teatro Regio of Turin about 1740 (fig. 4.1). Here we see a waiter serving refreshments during what appears to be an intensely dramatic moment: a chained, kneeling character begs mercy from another, who seems to be singing an aria. Strikingly, people appear to be eating and drinking during a very tense moment in an opera, possibly its climax, when a figure in charge of or above the law (typically a sovereign) exercises the power either to grant or to deny mercy, with all the resulting consequences.[21] In our opera theaters today, eating during such a scene would likely be interpreted by other audience members as a callous public display of lack of interest or empathy. The same behavior at a baseball game or movie theater or even a Met live opera broadcast at home or in a public theater signifies no lack of interest (consider munching popcorn during an especially tense twist in the action).[22]

Margaret Butler, in her studies on opera in eighteenth-century Turin,

Figure 4.1. Giovanni Michele Graneri (previously attributed to Pietro Domenico Olivero), *Teatro Regio di Torino*. Oil on canvas, c. 1752. Turin, Palazzo Madama, Museo Civico d'Arte Antica, inv. 534/D. Courtesy of the Fondazione Torino Musei.

reminds us that Graneri's painting opens a window on a typical opera seria night in Turin, about which she writes, "Performances at the Teatro Regio lasted approximately five hours; in the intervals and, indeed, while the opera was being performed, theater-goers bought things (jewelry and other fineries) from vendors who sold them along the theater's main staircase, and refreshments at the shop; they also gambled at its casino."[23] We also know, from Milizia's late eighteenth-century treatise on ancient and modern theater that among the many amenities of the Turin opera house were stoves for cooking (*fornelli*).[24]

Graneri's Turin opera house presents many similarities in style and composition to his works portraying marketplace piazzas.[25] His painting of a vegetable and fruit market represents people in the square watching and being watched by others from tiers of windows in the buildings surrounding the marketplace, like spectators in opera boxes. As in his image of the Teatro Regio, it is a high-tension moment: the winning numbers of the lottery are about to be announced. It could be a moment of mercy granted or denied by chance, a life-changing moment for somebody who might have gambled a fortune and who will experience, under the eyes of everybody else, either bliss or damnation. Such a moment produces in the spectators a wide range of emotions: joy, pity, horror, regret, envy, admiration, contempt, or indifference. Graneri was not only a painter and a man of the piazza (as can be inferred from his predilection for this subject) but, as a professional violinist in the orchestra of the Turin opera house, somebody who knew the culture of opera intimately.[26] As he suggests through his analogy of opera house and marketplace, the theater was perceived as a meeting place where people could perform a range of behaviors, all equally tolerated. Public opera developed as one of the most socially interactive and dynamic forces of the Age of Reason, no matter how conservative the ideas expressed in the drama.

The theater and the piazza reinforced and staged social differences, but they also allowed mingling, and voicing reactions in the lingua franca that Mikhail Bakhtin calls the "language of the marketplace," deploying the "nonofficial freedom" of language and gestures, especially during carnivals.[27] The unofficial speech of the marketplace, such as curses, cries, and abuse are "liberated from norms, hierarchies, and prohibitions of established idiom." As such, they "create a special collectivity, a group of people initiated in familiar intercourse, who are frank and free in expressing themselves verbally. The crowd was such a collectivity, especially the festive, carnivalesque crowd at the fair." The marketplace was spatially and culturally separated from official places of power: "palaces, churches, institutions, private homes [that] were dominated by hierarchy and etiquette."[28] But the demarcations were porous, allowing social permeability, the crossing of borders, and the mingling of the classes and their languages. The opera theater was a center of power, typically situated in the heart of an urban capital and frequented by the most powerful and influential citizens, often wealthy patrons of the theaters or sponsors of specific productions, to whom operas were often dedicated.[29] Yet it functioned very differently from the palace and its court, mirroring, in a theatrical way, the openness of the public square. The barrier was economic—the price of the ticket—but in the more fluid economy of the time, opera was accessible to a broad portion of urban society. In Venice, which was the main international opera center, all classes had access to the theater, and it was often the lower classes who determined an opera's success or failure. The status of the opera house as an official theater allowing for a controlled mingling of classes in a piazza-shaped space permitted public opera to become a haven for a controlled public exercise of freedom. Eating at the opera is symptomatic, then, of a parallel increase in the consumption of music, language, and ideas during the Age of Reason.

Sorbet Absorption

Among all the items sold at the food stands at the opera theater, the most iconic is perhaps the "sorbet." This cold concoction even informed the nomenclature of opera, as attested by the term "sorbet aria," or *aria dei sorbetti*, denoting an aria of scant dramatic or musical interest. However, as we have seen, the Graneri painting of Turin's opera house shows refreshments that look like *sorbetti* being served during a climactic moment, providing strong evidence that eating sorbets during an opera was not a sign of lack of attention to or importance of any moment of the opera. Absorption, in other words, could and did happen while sorbets were eaten in the auditorium of the opera, though when people felt it was a good time to stretch their legs they would also go out to get a sorbet at the ice cream concession.

In eighteenth-century Italy, the term *sorbetto* was used for a broad variety of cold drinks and sweet iced treats, including ice cream or gelato and actual sorbets. The practice of enjoying cold beverages and snacks was widespread, especially in Italy. The Comte d'Espinchal, in his *Journal d'émigration* (1789), writes that in every opera theater in Italy, large or small, people would eat gelato, served in the corridors and boxes. Stendhal was far from disturbed by this: in fact, he appears to have been positively impressed by the *sorbetti*, writing in 1817 that Milan's La Scala was famous for its "divine" sorbets. At the Teatro Valle in Rome, too, archival material repeatedly refers to the sorbet and gelato concession (Cabarè di gelati).[30] Gaetano Savonarola, in his *Galateo dei teatri* (1836), writes that everybody, even people on the main floor, indulged in "hot and cold drinks, oranges, sweets, sorbetti, and beer," and they occasionally threw fruit (mostly apples) at the singers on the stage.[31] In Naples, the *sorbetta* (gelato concession) and the taverna that served drinks and food at the Teatro dei Fiorentini were very lucrative, the reason rent negotiations between contractors and managers were complex and carefully outlined in contracts.[32]

In eighteenth-century Naples, sorbets and ice creams were no longer exclusively associated with luxury and aristocratic tables, as they had been in the Renaissance, but became street food, available to people from all classes.[33] As Melissa Calaresu observes in her study of eighteenth-century ice cream culture in Naples, the easy access to gelato allowed a "permeability . . . between plebeian and elite culture reflected in the movement between interior and exterior spaces."[34] Joseph Addison, who visited Naples from 1701 to 1703, feared mutinies if snow was sparse, claiming that for Neapolitans snow is as dear as nutritious foods in other countries. Later in the century, Henry Swinburne commented on the passion for "iced water" and other snow-based refreshments in Naples, shared by the entire population, including beggars.[35] Giuseppe Baretti, in his *Account of the Manners and Customs in Italy* (1768), reported that iced beverages and snacks were widespread in all of Italy and consumed at any time by people of different classes.[36] The physician John Moore, who visited Naples in 1777 and 1778, calls iced drinks "luxuries of the lowest vulgar."[37] Like drinking coffee, eating ice cream was perceived as a moment of sociability not attached to social status, an invitation to conversation and the exchange of news and ideas, a small luxury accessible to almost everyone.[38] Sorbets were the most typical snack in the opera theater, reinforcing the analogy between opera theater and piazza.

Period recipe books, often accessible in inexpensive editions, include an impressive variety of flavors for both sorbet and ice cream. Snow is always the main ingredient. To it one could add lemon, either juice or chunks, mandarin oranges, strawberries, chocolate, cream or butter, pistachios, barley or regular coffee, pears, jasmine, raisins, eggs, vanilla, chestnuts, or liquors.[39] Filippo Badini, in his medical treatise and recipe book *Sorbetti* (1775), claims that iced drinks, and especially sorbets, are the product of "refined human reason and society." In his Enlightenment-era approach to the matter, he lists the kinds of ice cream or sorbet that are good for treating various medical conditions, from gastrointestinal problems to psychological conditions and lack of sexual appetite: when invigorated by cinnamon and coffee, this refreshing snack could turn people "steaming hot."[40] Like coffee and chocolate, cold treats not only were good, they were also considered good for you, an essential recommendation in an increasingly medicalized culture.

If sorbet was considered a healthy snack, something good for body and mind, why did the *aria del sorbetto* have a reputation as an undesirable piece usually interpreted by low-ranking singers in the cast? Marco Beghelli proposes an interesting hypothesis about the sorbet aria, claiming it was typically the first aria of the second act, sung after a meal had been eaten between acts, either in the boxes or outside the auditorium. When the curtain went up again, spectators may still have been enjoying the last course of the meal, a *sorbetto*. He supports this hypothesis based on evidence from metaoperatic moments in opera librettos about opera, from Cimarosa's one-act farce *L'impresario in angustie* (Naples, 1786) to Filippo Celli's comic opera

Il corsaro, o sia un maestro di cappella in Marocco (Rome, 1822). Beghelli concludes that by 1826 people probably had stopped eating *sorbetto* at the opera theater. In this year, in fact, Peter von Lichtensthal writes, in the past tense, about "arias for secondary roles, called also *arie del sorbetto*, because during their performance audience members *used* to have sorbets served to them in their boxes."[41] The implication is that some arias were so lacking in musical and dramatic interest as to signal that it was time for a snack. In the revised version of his essay, Beghelli specifies that the sorbet aria was not an aria during which the *sorbetti* were served, but an aria of so little interest that the audience would linger in the foyer and by sorbet concessions outside the auditorium, waiting for better musical numbers before going back in. These insignificant numbers might include the first two arias of the second act. Beghelli admits that a systematic study of librettos by Metastasio does not support this hypothesis; however, some revisions of the original librettos present evidence that productions that had escaped the author's control occasionally slotted in sorbet arias for the beginning of the second act.[42]

Intermissions between acts of a heroic opera may seem a logical moment to step out of the auditorium today, yet in former times they were often filled with what, for many, was the best entertainment: ballets and comic intermezzi. Experienced operagoers knew that during the opera itself, not everything was worth attention. Public opera developed as a chain of recitatives and closed numbers, orchestrated and with a clearly demarcated beginning and end. This formal architecture, often referred to as "number opera," satisfied several types of conventions and requirements called *convenienze* in Italian operatic lingo: a term suggesting that their purpose was functional or convenient for both artists and audiences, since they provided for alternating action, reactions, dialogues, reflections, pronouncements, and such.[43] It would be a mistake to assume that opera audiences were engaged only by factual action. An important convention was to vary the type and intensity of numbers, assigning different aria types to the same singers, and alternating singers of different rank. It is true that the most beautiful and difficult arias were assigned to the stars—the primo uomo (usually a castrato) and the prima donna in heroic opera, and the primo buffo and prima buffa in comic opera—but it is also true that climactic moments needed to be built through recitatives and less intense numbers.[44]

In period sources, simple recitatives (without the orchestra) are occasionally described as tedious, especially by non-Italian audience members. Charles de Brosses, who visited Italy from May 1739 to April 1740, thought the recitatives were so unbearable that diversion was necessary: "Chess is perfect for filling the emptiness of these long recitatives, and music [meaning arias, duets, and other numbers] for breaking one's excessive concentration on chess."[45] Yet only those who knew the plot well or cared only for the music could afford to get distracted during recitative sections, since recitative is where dramatic action, narration of past events, and unfolding of the plot takes place. Recitatives could even be powerful music-dramatic moments. Giuseppe Tartini, who played violin in opera houses at the beginning of his career, reports that the only time in his life when he witnessed an episode of collective trance was during a recitative that at every performance chilled the entire audience, changing the color of their faces and causing complete absorption.[46]

Arias by marginal characters also appear to have been ideal moments to take the long-awaited sorbet break. However, composers would also occasionally write these numbers to help launch the career of a young artist. A case in point is Barbarina's "L'ho perduta" at the beginning of the last act of Mozart's *The Marriage of Figaro*. It comes after three long acts, when the audience might have been tired and likely to linger in the sugar-baker's café at Vienna's Burgtheater, where the opera was first produced in 1786. Barbarina's aria parallels the arias of the Countess at the beginning of the second act, "Porgi amor," and "Dove sono" in the middle of the third, which are laments for the loss of a husband's affection. For beauty and emotional content, they can hardly be compared to Barbarina's aria, but both women, in these lyrical utterances, appear alone onstage, without other characters listening or distracting our attention. Barbarina was first interpreted by a twelve-year-old Austrian singer at the beginning of her career, Anna Josepha Francisca Gottlieb, a singer-actress who had started acting in spoken theater as a child prodigy at age five. Mozart invites us not to miss Barbarina's piece, but rather to pay closer attention to it. To start with, this is the only piece in the whole opera set in a minor key, adhering to the sentimental style. Stefano Castelvecchi demonstrates how the combination of *sensibilité* and eroticism in this aria was indeed explosive, inviting an irresistible voyeuristic absorption by the audience.[47] It is through this simple aria that Mozart succeeded in launching the career of his first Barbarina: in 1791, Gottlieb created the role of Pamina, the princess in *The Magic Flute*.[48]

All things considered, times for snacks and drinks outside the auditorium were probably not planned by composers or librettists. People who had attended multiple performances, as was customary at the time, would have stepped outside at different moments during the same opera. Count Zinzendorf attended eighteen performances of *Le nozze di Figaro*, as we know from his diaries, and in this he was a typical eighteenth-century operagoer who, as Dexter Edge commented, "treated the Burgtheater as a kind of outsize salon."[49] If the Burgtheater or any opera house functioned as a salon for many audience members, that does not mean the art was of lesser value. There is no doubt that salon culture, in Vienna and elsewhere, was the ideal venue for the production and circulation of great art, notwithstanding, or probably because of, its relaxed atmosphere. As Waltraud Heindl writes in her account of Viennese salon culture, "Foreign visitors in Vienna . . . were stupefied by the Viennese capacity for food and drink," from the variety of soups and meat dishes to the renowned cakes of Bohemian origin, to coffee and other drinks. Heindl also points out that the "Biedermeier period is known for its eating and drinking habits," a culture in which Franz Schubert was fully immersed.[50] If one of his friends had a sorbet during the performance of one of his Lieder, that would not have made the piece a "sorbet Lied." In Mozart's or Schubert's time and culture, eating during a performance did not signal lack of interest, but rather showed the opposite. During interesting moments, as in Graneri's painting of the Turin opera, people did not dare to leave their places, so they consumed food and drinks in the auditorium of the theater, like baseball fans who are glued to the action taking place during the game while holding a hot dog and a can of beer. In short, people might have been eating sorbets during any kind of recitative, duet, ensemble, or aria, but during the "sorbet arias" the sorbet, rather than the aria, would have been the main attraction.

Food Disorders

Regular opera seasons typically coincided with the time of carnival. It was during carnival that Venice, where public opera was first introduced, was flooded with the most visitors.[51] Like the marketplace, carnival represented unofficial truth, as Bakhtin insists, different "from the serious official, ecclesiastical, feudal, and political cult forms and ceremonials."[52] As we have seen, Politian's *Orfeo*, the earliest experiment with opera, was produced during a carnival banquet. In that case, however, carnival happened in a context where the ordered syntax of the menu and the code of table manners prevailed. A very different context is carnival in the marketplace, where inclusiveness made it appear to be a utopian "banquet for all the world,"[53] a feast in which the consumption of food and drinks was utterly disordered.

A seventeenth-century English tourist, John Evelyn, found himself in Naples during carnival 1645, and he recalls a mob of "courtesans (who swarm in this city to the number, as we are told, of 30,000, registered and paying a tax to the State) flinging eggs of sweet water [candies] into our coach, as we passed by the houses and windows."[54] The next year, notwithstanding snow and cold weather, Evelyn went to Venice for Mardi Gras "to see the folly and madness of the Carnival," where he again noticed the habit of throwing "eggs of sweet water."[55]

Eighteenth-century travelers to Italy were taken aback not only by the wild behavior of people in the street during carnival festivities, but by the consumption of food and unkind disposal of leftovers by opera audiences. Most of these witnesses were musicians and intellectuals who found distraction detrimental to their work, and they do not necessarily represent the perception of the general public. Benedetto Marcello is a typical aristocratic musician who despised the opera show business then current, for example, describing with caustic irony the central role of the café in the economy of the opera house. Marcello calls it a *botteghino*, a term still in use but nowadays referring to the ticket office. The *conduttore del botteghino* would typically offer free drinks to the musicians, the impresario, and other professionals. Neapolitan prima donnas were also accustomed to being invited to lunch and dinner by rich merchants. The impresario, however, sold poor-quality drinks and junk food to the general public: "coffee with barley," toasted bread, odd mixed drinks with fanciful names made of cheap liquor and sweetened with honey, sorbets made with sulfuric acid as artificial lemon flavoring, treated with potassium nitrate and containing ash instead of salt; chocolate made with a concoction of sugar, wild cinnamon, almonds, acorns, and wild cocoa; table wines and plain cheap food at four times their normal price.[56]

Jean-Jacques Rousseau is a typical intellectual who was eager to show off his superior sensibility. Having fallen in love with Italian opera in Venice from September 1743 to August 1744, he was annoyed by the scant attention people around him paid to the opera itself. As he recounts it:

> I soon contracted that passion for Italian music with which it inspires all those who are capable of feeling its excellence. In listening to barcaroles, I found I had not yet known what singing was, and I soon became so fond of the opera that, tired of babbling, eating, and playing in the boxes when I wished to listen, I frequently withdrew from the company to another part of the theater. There, quite alone, shut up in my box, I abandoned myself, notwithstanding the length of the representation, to the pleasure of enjoying it at ease unto the conclusion. One evening at the theatre of

> Saint Chrysostom, I fell into a more profound sleep than I should have done in my bed. The loud and brilliant airs did not disturb my repose. But who can explain the delicious sensations given me by the soft harmony of the angelic music, by which I was charmed from sleep; what an awaking! What ravishment! What ecstasy, when at the same instant I opened my ears and eyes! My first idea was to believe I was in paradise.[57]

Charles Burney's travelogue documenting his trips to the Continent to collect material for his *General History of Music* is a precious source for understanding eighteenth-century rituals of attending music and opera events. As a protoanthropologist of music, he maintains a relatively neutral position. In July 1770, Burney attended a couple of comic operas in Milan, the first being a "science-fiction" opera with a revolutionary message, Piccinni's *Il regno della luna*.[58] The second was *L'amore artigiano*, a libretto by Carlo Goldoni set by Florian Gassmann, a performance that featured plenty of food and drink on both sides of the footlights. Although the opera was relatively short, the event lasted from eight to midnight, in part because of the extensive dances. Burney's description offers a vivid picture of how the economy of attention worked during a long opera event:

> The theater here is very large and splendid; it has five rows of boxes on each side, one hundred in each row; and parallel to these runs a broad gallery, round the house, as an avenue to every row of boxes: each box will contain six persons, who sit at the sides, facing each other. Across the gallery of communication is a complete room to every box, with a fireplace in it, and all conveniences for *refreshments and cards*. In the fourth row is a *pharo* table, on each side the house, which is used during the performance of the opera. There is in front a very large box, as big as a common London dining room, set apart for the Duke of Modena, governor of Milan, and the *Principessina* his daughter, who were both there. The noise here during the performance was abominable, except while two or three airs and a duet were singing, with which everyone was in raptures: at the end of the duet, the applause continued with unremitting violence till the performers returned to sing it again, which is here the way of encoring a favourite air.[59]

Unlike Rousseau, Burney does not complain about people's playing cards or eating, but only about the noise they make, especially when applauding, which would happen after moments that captured the audience's attention.

Managing the economy of attention by offering plenty of moments for distraction was also common practice in Burney's native England. From 1750 to 1790, the King's Theater of London offered refreshments in its coffee rooms, as well as the opportunity to play cards during performances of Italian opera.[60] A bit of doggerel written in the 1780s complains about the resulting chaos:

Here, some o'er streams of coffee pouring,
There Johnny Brute in vulgar snoring
Proclaims his taste for singing
Whilst vast applause is ringing![61]

In London people could buy printed librettos together with refreshments from "fruit women," the former to ensure the enjoyment of long operas in a foreign language, and the latter to have something to throw if the performers failed to please.[62] The *Universal Register* reported incidents of people's throwing apples and oranges, and other witnesses noted that the cheap upper gallery was occupied by sailors, prostitutes, and servants who occasionally threw fruit and water into the pit.[63] The behavior of the audience at Covent Garden and Drury Lane during English opera events was no better: the *Times* reported "beaux talking extremely loud [of their] racing, drinking, wenching, sparring" and "orange girls presenting their wares out of all time and season."[64] The elegant Pantheon Opera House had a built-in coffee room, card rooms, smoking and lounging rooms, and restrooms. Opera patrons could visit these facilities at any time, and people did in fact drink coffee, play cards, and so on during performances.[65] At both the Pantheon and Little Haymarket, "box-keepers" were on hand who would run errands for those members of the audience who preferred not to leave their seats, including such tasks as bringing refreshments from the coffee room. Meanwhile, behind the scenes beer, bread, and cheese was served for the crew.[66]

About Naples, Burney writes that "the acts are necessarily so long, that it is wholly impossible to keep up the attention, so that those who are not talking, or playing at cards, usually fall asleep."[67] Opera also offered the opportunity to divert one's attention from physical discomfort. On a Saturday night, still in Naples, Burney had a bad headache, but he tells us: "I determined to try the medicinal power of music at Piccini's [*sic*] opera, and found that, though it did not cure, it alleviated the pain, and diverted my attention from it."[68] Earlier in September, while in Florence, he attended two performances of *Le donne vendicate*, another Goldoni libretto set by Piccinni in which food played a prominent role. The opera starts in a dining room with a table set for supper (sala con tavola apparecchiata e lumi), and the characters singing in chorus "Long life to whoever eats and drinks happily!" (Viva chi mangia e chi beve giocondo). Goldoni requires that they actually eat and drink onstage ("*Casimiro, Roccaforte, Volpino e Flaminio con quattro donne mangiando e bevendo*"), inviting each other to renew toasts: "Beviamo un'altra volta," "Dunque beviamo").[69] One can imagine some in the audience joining in the toast by lifting their own glasses. Burney notices that in this case the audience is far from distracted and in fact shows a remarkable appreciation and an "extraordinary good humour," reporting that "the crowd and applause were prodigious . . . and at the close of all, it was rather acclamation than applause."[70]

Beyond food's presence in and at the opera, operatic music was often used as an appetizer, as when Lord Hamilton invited Burney for a meal in Naples. Before dinner, guests were entertained by "a fat friar, of the order of St. Dominic, who came there to sing *buffo* songs; he accompanied himself on the harpsichord in a great number of humorous scenes from the burletta operas of Piccinni and Paisiello."[71] Dinner itself lasted until two in the morning. The following night, Burney had dinner with Lord Fortrose, and after dinner they had the honor of hearing a musical *digestif* sung by the legendary castrato Caffarelli, accompanied by a "complete band" until 11:00 p.m.[72] Opera and food went hand in hand, both in the theater and in the salon, where favorite opera pieces were often performed as chamber music.

Even court opera imitated public opera habits. Food and drink were served in the private theater at Eszterháza, where Joseph Haydn was active as an opera composer, stage director, impresario, and conductor in the service of Prince Esterházy. János Malina, in his study of the Italian opera repertory at Eszterháza, estimated that over a thousand opera performances took place there from 1776 to 1790, and he determined that there was a café in a one-level building adjacent to the opera house where coffee, tea, hot chocolate, almond milk, and lemonade were served. The café had billiard tables, and the hostess, wife of the set designer Pietro Travaglia, was an expert billiard player.[73] Esterházy documents related to theater production from a slightly earlier period include bills for drinks. On December 17, 1764, for example, the musicians drank twenty-six carafes of *officier Wein* (house wine for high-ranking court functionaries) and beer. The *Operisten* (the cast) were served more precious wine: three bottles of Tokay, half a bottle of Frontiriak (muscatel), six bottles of Weisser (a Riesling), burgundy, champagne, and vermouth.[74]

In the venues where Mozart's operas were first produced, opera audiences also had access to refreshments whenever they wanted them. In Prague during the first performance of Mozart's *Don Giovanni*, theater servants reportedly brought beer and sausages to the spectators, who also demanded lemonade and almond milk.[75] As for Vienna, it is not surprising that the diaries of Count Karl von Zinzendorf, a passionate operagoer who often documented his meals and opera experiences, never wrote about a meal he ate at the opera. At least in Vienna, real meals always happened before or after an opera performance.[76] With a very few exceptions, eating at the opera was more grazing and snacking than eating full meals, which is probably why Zinzendorf did not bother to comment on such a common and unremarkable habit. In the Vienna Court Theater (or Burgtheater), where Mozart's *Le nozze di Figaro* and *Così fan tutte* were produced, food was present in abundance, even though music histories do not mention it. Daniel Heartz, in his thorough study of this theater, focuses exclusively on architectonic aspects that he believes were strictly relevant to the artworks represented on stage. The plans of the parterre reproduced in his essay nevertheless suggest that there were plenty of spaces outside the auditorium where coffee and food concessions could have been located.[77] More relevant are the theater's account books, which show space for a food concession managed by "Zuckerbacker," a confectioner who served as a manager of the opera house café.[78] Under "Income/Receipts," an entry headed "Receipts from sugar-baker stock/goods at German plays" specifies that "Friederich Schreckleb, theater sugar-baker, is freed from having to pay anything for the theater year 1776."[79] Instead of paying rent, the sugar-baker had to provide refreshments for free, presumably to the theater administration and affiliates: "A deal was made with sugar-baker F. Schrekleb, that he has to deliver free of charge all the refreshments required for the plays and singspiels—liquors, coffee, tea, chocolate, punch and other warm drinks as well as all pastries."[80] It is safe to assume that refreshments continued to be sold when Lorenzo Da Ponte managed the opera (1789–91), although the account books for those years are lost. We do not know of any policy regarding the areas of the theater where refreshments could be consumed. At the present stage of research, it is difficult to estimate conclusively how widespread eating at the opera was, in part because opera historians tend to disregard this aspect when summarizing their findings. Nevertheless, it is undeniable that drinking and eating at the opera house, often during the performance, were common not only in Italy but also in many other countries. In certain venues in France, however, audiences did start to abstain from food and drinks during performances earlier than elsewhere.

French Taste and Distaste

The case of France is particularly interesting, largely because during the Age of Reason France became the model for taste in fashion, food, and culture in general, imposing on Western culture ideas of what was tasteful and distasteful. This happened slowly, since at first France was more a follower than a leader. In 1754 Jean le Rond d'Alembert wrote in an article on "cuisine" of the *Encyclopédie* that fine cooking ("la bonne chère") was introduced into France by an army of Italian cooks brought to the royal court by Catherine de Medici.[81] This anecdote links the beginning of courtly haute cuisine to the introduction of Italian music, at first in the form of the elaborate multimedia banquet art including proto-operatic allegorical music-dramatic representations. Many of Catherine's spectacular court festivals or "magnificences" were strategically planned to pave the way for reconciliation of Protestants and Catholics during the extremely tense time of religious wars. As the historian Roy Strong maintains, the attempt by the court-sponsored Académie de poésie et de musique to retrieve the ancient power of music, united with theater and dance, was part of the reconciliatory cultural politics informing the court *fêtes*, as was the case for the large banquets planned during these *fêtes*.[82] The St. Bartholomew's Day massacre of Huguenots marked the failure of Catherine's attempt at reconciliation, a theme explored in Giacomo Meyerbeer's opera *Les Huguenots*.

If it might be a myth that Italian cooks introduced haute cuisine to France, it is a fact that Italian musicians introduced opera, but public opera struggled for a long time in a nation where the central government maintained strong control over the genre. As a result, "food disorders" were less common in France. Evidence shows that refreshments were available—but not to everybody and not everywhere in the theater. For example, a report on the visit of Russian diplomats in August 1668 records that during a performance of a comedy with ballet at the Théâtre du Marais in Paris, the Russians "requested some wine, which was brought to them." Two days later, during another performance, the Russian ambassador and his son were presented with "two great basins, one with dried fruits and the other with fresh fruit. . . . They did not eat of this, but drank and thanked the actors."[83] It is rare to find similar accounts, and one suspects these instances were exceptions rather than the rule.

In the following century the Paris Opéra, the Comédie-Française, and the Comédie-Italienne operated under the management and supervision of entrepreneurs appointed by the king. Public access was granted to paying patrons. Norms, regulations, censorship, and fines created a highly controlled climate substantially different from the Italianate model of public opera. Opera continued to be a hub for sociability, but in a less relaxed environment than in other countries. As David Charlton writes, "Courtly ambience was a main point of definition at the Paris Opéra," where people went to socialize and network, including at the opera café, in the basement of the building.[84] A painting representing a performance of Jean-Baptiste Lully's *Armide* in the Palais Royal, made in 1747, about the same time as the painting of the Turin opera performance, shows a different opera ritual from Italy. While people in the pit—mostly intellectuals—pay close attention to the opera, the aristocrats in the boxes are too busy looking at each other and chatting. As Neal Zaslaw notes in his commentary on this painting, "The nobility and bourgeoisie in the three tiers of boxes go to the opera frequently, because it is the favorite gathering-place of high society."[85] Unlike the Turin audience, nobody here is eating, and there is no seating in the pit.[86] In his influential cultural history of French music, *Listening in Paris*, James Johnson writes about audience behavior at the Palais Royal, "In 1750 it was unfashionable to arrive at the opera on time," and people "lingered over their weak ale or chocolate in the opera's dark café," confirming the custom of consuming refreshments in designated areas outside the auditorium.[87]

During the nineteenth century, the gap widened between provincial theaters, where refreshments could be enjoyed during the opera, and more serious institutions in Paris, where the audience's behavior was controlled. In Gustave Flaubert's *Madame Bovary*, the protagonist Emma attends a production of Donizetti's *Lucia di Lammermoor* in Rouen. When she felt faint during the intermission from "the smell of gas mingled with that of human breathing," her husband Charles "ran to the bar to get her a glass of barley water," spilling most of it on the shoulders of a lady "who, feeling the cold liquid tricking down her back, screamed like a peacock, as if she were being assassinated."[88] In provincial cities like Bordeaux, opera was often performed in establishments called café-concerts, where patrons paid nothing to attend the performance but, as in many jazz clubs, needed to order drinks and food. It was in these Bordeaux café-concerts that the first African American opera composer, the New Orleans native Edmond

Dédé, worked as musician and in-house composer starting in 1865, writing songs, operettas, and ballets.[89] The illustration shown here represents one of the theaters where Dédé worked, with people moving around and having drinks during a performance of an opera. Children are included in the illustration to advertise the establishment's respectability and family-friendly atmosphere (fig. 4.2). Racial discrimination probably blocked Dédé's dream of composing opera for the more sophisticated Parisian venues where people did not consume drinks and snacks during the show.

An exception to this rule can be found in the novel that inspired Verdi's *Traviata*, Alexandre Dumas fils's *La dame aux camélias*. Here the first encounter of Armand (Alfredo) and Marguerite (Violetta) takes place at the opera, where she indulges in sugared raisins and other sweets during the performance.[90] It is possible, however, that Dumas resorts to this narrative stratagem to emphasize the heroine's defiant personality: a femme fatale

Figure 4.2. Café-concert Grand Alcazar de la Bastide in Bordeaux. Courtesy of the Archives municipales de Bordeaux.

unable to restrain her appetites and desires who breaks with the norms, even at the opera.

The propriety of Parisian audience behavior—which has become today's normative mode of listening in concerts and operas—emerged only at the end of the eighteenth century, at first sporadically and in isolated cases and spreading gradually over the course of the nineteenth century. This phenomenon has attracted the attention of scholars in the past two decades, inspiring pathbreaking studies such as Christopher Small's *Musicking* and Johnson's *Listening in Paris*.[91] Anselm Gerhard also shows the development in post-Revolutionary French bourgeois audiences of more and more restrained behavior, displayed to claim class status and gentility by distancing middle-class manners from those of the working class.[92] In the 1830s and 1840s, with the formation of a broader opera audience, people started to behave better by today's standards. As Daniel Snowman writes, "With *embourgeoisement* came a new *politesse*," and people started to question whether it was more polite "to eat beforehand or afterwards" or to imbibe "an interval drink" with the people sharing their box.[93]

In 1806 Napoleon inaugurated a new Théâtre de la Cour at the Tuileries Palace with Ferdinando Paër's *Grisélidis* (*Griselda*). General Charles-Alexandre Durand recollected that all the new political establishment was present, and that everybody was required to dress in the best formal attire. Footmen in the emperor's livery handed out ice creams (*glaces*) and other refreshments to everyone in the hall (outside the auditorium) during the intermission between the acts.[94] In an 1808 theatrical almanac, Pierre-Joseph Charrin observed that in Paris, unlike Italy, "people do not gamble or eat at the opera, but listen in total silence."[95] Parisians preferred dining before or after the show. This became part of a long-lasting operatic ritual that inspired Wagner's theatrical reforms. The theaters were situated near the most fashionable cafés and restaurants.[96] Balzac recounts in his essay on drugs (*Traité des excitants modernes*) that in 1822 he ran an experiment on the effects of alcohol. After allegedly drinking many bottles of wine and smoking cigars with a friend, he arrived at the Théâtre Italien completely drunk. This is probably why, during the overture to Rossini's *La gazza ladra*, he experienced a sort of ecstasy and perceived the whole orchestra as one vast instrument. A lady commented that he was feeling the wine (Ce monsieur sent le vin), to which he replied, "Non, Madame, je sens la musique."[97] Not being able to sip wine during the opera, people sometimes binged before the opera started. After 1830, the opera district near the boulevard des Italiens was frequented by singers, composers, and opera fans and became known for wonderful food at the Café de Paris, Italian gelato at Tortoni (where Rossini hung out) and, closer to the Opéra, the Café Riche, immortalized in Guy de Maupassant's 1885 novel *Bel-Ami*, offering expensive French cuisine, champagne, and refreshments served in splendid tableware. Meanwhile the Opéra café served refreshments to the theater's patrons, but—again—not in the auditorium.[98]

The new habit of eating and drinking before or after the opera benefited and fueled the nascent restaurant business in Paris. The formation of the silent audience in France coincided with the invention of the restaurant that offered food as a high-taste aesthetic experience of culinary art to whomever could afford it—unlike previous taverns, cabarets, catering, and hotel dining services that provided a public place to gather, socialize, and be nourished with only secondary concern for good taste.[99] As Rebecca Spang shows in her history of the restaurant in France, the word "restaurant" transitioned in the early decades of the nineteenth century from the name for a restorative bouillon offered in some locations at specific times of day into a new model of offering various foods at flexible mealtimes. The new printed menu looked like a concert program. The à la carte restaurant impressed and often puzzled clients with long and complicated four-column menus listing many wines and dishes with unusual names, requiring that patrons have high competence in making decisions about the order and the pairing of courses and wines. Connoisseurs relied on published gastronomic guides, inaugurating a genre of gastronomic criticism comparable to music criticism, such as the *Almanach des gourmands* by theater critic Alexandre Grimod de la Reynière. For the first time kitchens were hidden from public view (not unlike the orchestra hidden in the pit in Wagner's new opera theater), while diners—now on public display and conscious of being observed while eating a meal—found themselves pressured to control their posture and bodily noises.[100]

Etiquette at the concert hall and the opera house became consistent, regardless of the repertory performed, and audience members were compelled to suppress their bodies to avoid making noise or calling attention to their physical presence by moving or assuming unusual postures. Richard Leppert links the formation of the still and silent public to the emergence of visuality and visibility as the main mode of perception and representation. This resulted in a contradiction between the physicality of what we see (the embodied presence of musicians and performers) and the abstract nature of the art produced (music). As Leppert explains, physicality is not completely suppressed for paying listeners, who consume music as a source of embodied and experiential pleasure.[101] The corollary to this theory is that the listening public is reduced to a projection of physicality (an image), as the desires and sounds of the body are suppressed. At the concert hall, we are expected to appear as disembodied images, a painted backdrop representing a generic attentive public. Yet, as Cormac Newark points out in an article provocatively titled "Not Listening in Paris," audiences at the opera were often listening without hearing.[102] Performing attention did not result in paying attention, as so often happens in a lecture hall where the required etiquette encourages the audience (whether students or professional scholars) to pretend absorption even while lost in other thoughts and dreams.

Wagner's Fast

Wagner's mission as a music dramatist was to sustain genuine absorption. To do so he needed to go further than French opera and change the entire operatic culture, from composition to performance, from the architecture of the theater to the rituals of attending opera. In his view the Parisian model failed because, designed to distract and entertain, it created fake absorption, generating a "fleeting glance," as David Levin writes in his interpretation of Wagner's critique of French opera. Wagner's goal of commanding and retaining the audience's unconditional attention required "an entirely different regime of operatic spectatorship" where audiences could no longer "pick and choose" but were "expected to pay attention."[103] Wagner's reformist zeal, reminiscent of Lutherans' zeal to retrieve the spirit of Christianity's origins, started as a reaction against corrupt (popish) Italian and French models of production, which he regarded as shabby, consumeristic, commercial, and ultimately detrimental to the theater's purpose as an educational and spiritual force. Wagner abhorred as marketing strategies the concept of "the show" as a source for utilitarian gain, materialistic pleasure, and sheer entertainment. In *The Art-Work of the Future* (*Das Kunstwerk der Zukunft*, 1849), he envisioned opera as the revolutionary rejection of a public theater corrupted by the capitalistic, commercial Italianate model, which he linked to Roman decadence, with its "repugnant spectacle of . . . utilitarianism," where public life, having replaced beauty with the "absolutely useful" and thus "having sunk to a mere general expression of universal egoism, had no longer any care for the beautiful." "Public utilitarianism" was no virtue for Wagner, who defined it as "the satisfaction of the belly." To denote public utilitarianism as decadent, Wagner makes consistent use of food metaphors, as when he writes about "useless prescripts of utility, where the public care was concentrated on the catering of food and drink."[104] This is why in opera Wagner bans catering as a useless utility, detrimental to the nourishment of the spirit.

Wagner's early experience of Italian opera was in a provincial German theater, now known as the Goethe Theater in Bad Lauchstädt, where he conducted Mozart's *Don Giovanni* in 1837. In his *Autobiographische Skizze*, published as early as 1843 in the *Zeitung für die elegante Welt*, he recollects that Mozart's "*Don Juan* was distasteful to me, on account of the Italian text beneath it: it seemed to me such rubbish."[105] He found the production itself equally distasteful: in the theater boxes one could see "younger and older ladies equipped with their knitting and the necessary refreshments" (jüngere und ältere Damen, mit ihrem Strickstrumpf und den nötigen Erfrischungen). To Wagner, this opera house was a *Scheune* (barn),[106] and the Bad Lauchstädt ladies were rural and uncivilized, modern orgiastic bacchants, mortal enemies of Orpheus, armed with knitting needles, drinks, and smelly sandwiches.

Wagner's ideal theater became a reality when he built the first "opera theater of the future" in Bayreuth, in which, as Evan Barker aptly puts it, "the entire attention of the audience is to be focused on nothing other than what is being performed on the stage. Social events have no place in the theater."[107] His creation of Bayreuth for his epic opera cycle coincided with a deep reform of audience behavior: no more knitting and refreshments. Once the Wagnerian model became the standard, opera became a ritual in which self-abnegation and abstinence were practiced in search of an experience comparable to ascetic religious services. In *Art and Revolution*, indeed, Wagner laments that after the classical Greek era, theater lost its original religious value: "To the Greeks the production of a tragedy was a religious festival," while "*our* evil conscience has so lowered the theater in public estimation, that it is the duty of the police to prevent the stage from meddling in the slightest with religion."[108]

In respect for Wagner's ideals and the purpose of his art, it is right to fast during a performance of the *Ring*. That does not mean it is equally right to abstain during operas differently conceived. The women of Bad Lauchstädt understood something Wagner was not willing to acknowledge: that refreshments and knitting enhanced their experience of *Don Giovanni*. Mozart, like many previous and contemporary opera composers, allowed for an alternation of absorption and distraction, the latter being necessary to recharge and maximize the former. Opera from Monteverdi to bel canto (and in some cases to verismo) offered a distinctive form of absorption as part of a ritualized but loosely structured social event. We will never be able to fully understand this repertory until we realize that refreshments, games, and freedom of movement were not detrimental; they were part of this past operatic culture, just as they are in many jazz and blues live-music events.

Feeding Attention in Blues, Jazz, and Opera

Today music enthusiasts can enjoy a gumbo and a beer at Buddy Guy's Legends in Chicago while listening to refined and thought-provoking blues, or have cocktails or dinner at a world-famous jazz club like the Blue Note in New York while listening to some of the best musicians of the moment. At the Chicago Lyric Opera or at the Met, on the other hand, they can eat or drink only in designated areas outside the auditorium. The reason behind this divide is ideological. The blind adaptation of Wagnerian ideals to pre-Wagnerian opera has not been beneficial to the enjoyment and understanding of the rituals of performance and consumption of a genre of musical art that can be compared to live jazz and blues events.

Recent experiments in opera production show promising signs of change. In 2012 the Haymarket Opera Company of Chicago began allowing drinks at tables on the main floor during performances of baroque operas by Charpentier, Handel, Purcell, Alessandro Scarlatti, and Telemann. Their venue, the Mayne Stage Theater, had originally opened as the Morse Theater in 1912, when it functioned as a vaudeville and movie theater. A hundred years later it operated as a "multipurpose entertainment venue" with an attached gastro-pub called Act One that offered a full service of food and drinks at the tables and in its restaurant area. The venue hosted jazz, world music, rock concerts, stand-up comedy, dance shows and parties, as well as Halloween shows like the rock musical *Zombie Prom*, which served "spooky drinks" at all times. Occasionally there was also baroque opera.

This postmodern attitude toward the performing arts serendipitously reproduced an authentic experience of baroque opera.[109] The Haymarket Opera Company played period instruments, adhering to other historically informed performance techniques and staging the operas with authentic costumes and stage sets. The Mayne Stage production sets were designed and painted by a classicist architect and artist, David Mayernik. In his book *The Challenge of Emulation*, Mayernik proposes a postmodern neoclassicist idea based on a dialectical reconciliation of invention and imitation through emulation, which, although it implies an idea of competition between the imitated and the imitating, in the best cases results in a new invention adapting imitated art to new circumstances. Changing the model is not simply to assert originality, but rather to adapt emulated art to new contexts without depriving it of the meaning accumulated through tradition.[110] Emulating opera rituals, rather than selectively reproducing past performance practices, should be the best path to the artwork of the future and a strategy to make opera culture not only survive, but thrive again in different times.

To tackle the challenge of producing meaningful cultural translation of past works for new times and contexts, we can benefit from ethnomusicological wisdom that shows how the making of art and the rituals of art consumption are intimately interconnected.[111] When we try to separate art from its natural cultural habitat, we may miss the point not only about art's reception, but also about art's form and meaning. John Blacking, criticizing the Gestalt psychological foundation of the Berlin school of ethnomusicology, emphasizes "the importance of cultural experience in the selection and development of sensory capacities."[112] Considering the intimate relation between operatic structures and styles and operatic cultures helps us understand opera better. As Blacking envisioned in the early 1970s, "musicology is really an ethnic musicology": ethnomusicology should indeed be musicology tout court, at least if we are interested in the study of music as human experience.[113] Another influential ethnomusicologist, Mantle Hood, alerts us to the risk of approaching musical cultures by focusing exclusively on the parameters of sound organization we are trained to analyze and talk about in musicological discourse. What escapes our perception are all those aspects and parameters that he defines as "the untalkable of music," including sensory stimulations that are too often dismissed as extramusical:

> Imagine a performance of Indian music in Madras, perhaps in September, the house smells of curry still wafting in from the kitchen, pungent incense ameliorating the effects of oppressive heat and humidity, the clinging weight of light cotton clothing. Now think of the same music in a gigantic concert hall in New York City in November, when the air is dry, the night cold, warm clothing a heavy encumbrance. How shall we label that kind of untalkable, "positive/negative energies generated by the total atmosphere"? . . . Might this untalkable be "the relative energies of inspiration"?[114]

What happens to Indian music when exported from Madras to New York also happened to opera when exported from Mozart's Vienna to today's Vienna.

The history of the American variety show is an enlightening case, because opera went through the process of eliminating food and drink from the auditorium slightly earlier than American vaudeville. In both we observe similar patterns in the imposition of social norms that sanitized and sterilized the artwork, taking it away from its natural habitat. While drinking and snacking were allowed in early concert/saloon shows, they gradually disappeared with the formation of more refined vaudeville at the end of the nineteenth century. Robert Sneider, in his study of New York vaudeville, shows that the demise of drinking and eating at the Bowery Theater in New York and in concert saloons of the city was gradual and informed by the pursuit of respectability modeled after the classical concert hall and opera hall: in 1873, Tony Pastor's self-defined "opera house" still offered "best quality of ales, wines, liquors and cigars to be had at the saloon inside the theater." Pastor eventually "banned drinking in the auditorium and confined it to an adjoining saloon." In the 1890s, after he moved to premises in the Tammany Building, he sought a more inclusive audience, welcoming children, women, and middle-to-upper-class families. According to police reports, "Pastor's theater had no connection with any place where liquors were sold," and he "labored industriously to make the variety show business a successful one by dissociating it from the cigar-smoking and beer-drinking accompaniment."[115] The New York vaudeville scene slowly parted from the culture of saloons, leaving audience members with a dry mouth and an empty stomach. That was the price this art form had to pay in order to be taken more seriously.

Blues and jazz music proved slightly more resilient to the pervasive practice of shutting the audience's mouth, in part because a more recent, memorable tradition proved that this music has no less value or expressive power when performed in clubs and restaurants than when performed in concert venues. In *Thinking in Jazz*, ethnomusicologist Paul Berliner examines the interaction of improvised music making and audience behavior, showing how the latter influences the former. No matter the form, "Every music performance is a dramatic presentation for listeners and improvisers alike. In a sense, both groups play interactive roles as actors from their respective platforms," Berliner writes, emphasizing that "performers and listeners form a communication loop in which the actions of each continuously affect the other."[116]

Playing in jazz clubs where drinks and food are served can be distracting, frustrating, relaxing, or exciting, depending on the level of engagement of both artists and audience. Attention in such an environment is not imposed but has to be earned by engaging listeners. Audiences and musicians share an intimate space where, as in a dining room, absorption and indifference are immediately obvious through body language and sound. Even Wynton Marsalis, one of the main proponents of the concept of jazz as American classical music, to be performed in highbrow institutions like Lincoln Center and Carnegie Hall, declared, "I would rather play in a great room with atmosphere than in Carnegie Hall. The shabbiest little room can be great if the people, the vibes, the feeling, the love is there."[117] Coleman Hawkins once refused to play in an all-you-can-eat smorgasbord restaurant whose manager told the musicians to "keep the volume down so table conversation may be carried on."[118] Hawkins, who had never turned down a gig because of the presence of food or drinks, felt he had no chance to reach out to his listeners. This episode, however, seems the exception rather than the rule. As Ira Sullivan told Berliner in an interview, playing in clubs can be a rewarding challenge:

> The dinner jazz clubs are what make the challenge of playing and trying to reach people even greater. . . . People come here to meet old relatives and to talk and eat and have a few drinks. That can't be changed. But every once in a while you play so strong beautiful that suddenly you hush up an audience like that, and it's a great feeling of accomplishment you feel. Like you've given them something special even if they don't really recognize what it is you've done for them. You've reached them where they didn't know they can be reached.[119]

To some musicians, the food and drinks typical of the jazz club are such a natural part of their habitat that "some artists have even sought to reproduce the spirited atmosphere of the nightclub within the more acoustically controlled setting of the recording studio. Cannonball Adderley brought friends, food, and libations along when he made the *Inside Straight* LP at Fantasy Studios."[120] These examples and others show that even for "serious" jazz (i.e. after the end of the jazz era), a semiconvivial, relaxed environment can promote a frank relationship with the audience.[121] While one cannot lay down a principle that feasting is more or less conducive than fasting to the appreciation of music and theater, it is clear that audience behavior, including conviviality, changes the way music is conceived, structured, performed, and perceived.

It is hard to get over the bias that a highbrow art can take place only where the body is suppressed in order to free the mind. Yet it is difficult to imagine that the food and drinks served during Renaissance performances caused a highly refined art form such as the madrigal to be perceived as less serious or distracted listeners. The problem is that, since then, table manners have changed as well. The Renaissance good manners handbook, Castiglione's *Book of the Courtier*, instructs people how to negotiate relaxation and attention, explaining when it is proper to talk and when it is time to be quiet.[122] Perhaps this is a book worth rereading. I remember one night in Chicago when Buddy Guy stopped playing and told some people who were chattering at the top of their lungs that if they wanted to talk loudly among themselves they should go somewhere else, but that they were welcome to stay if they had any interest in his songs. Having a pint during a blues concert should not authorize us to take music less seriously than in a concert hall.

When considering whether it is appropriate to eat at the opera or in a blues or jazz club, etiquette is the most important issue. What is really at stake is to find the best conditions for an art form that, like transplanted trees or animals, may not thrive outside its natural habitat. As in the last century of the history of jazz, the period reports and later historical narratives from the first two centuries of public opera—the golden age for opera attendance, number of productions, and active opera theaters—provide two contradictory narratives: one of audiences that appear to have suffered from attention deficit disorder, and the other of live events that unleashed more passionate and enthusiastic reactions than ever. The contradiction is easily reconciled when we realize that operagoers of the past had developed a better economy of attention than present audiences, which is to say they had at their disposal more effective ways to manage their energy. The behavioral repertory of yesterday's audience, unlike today's, did not include pretending to be engaged when they were not. Wagnerian discipline is not effective when applied to opera conceived for an alternation of distraction and absorption. What matters, then, is not so much to let audiences quench their thirst or calm their appetite during live performances, but to adopt different modes of listening for different repertories. A responsible general ecology of opera and music can offer different environments, each congenial for the performance and experience of different repertories, and thus create the ideal conditions for audience members to be more honestly engaged. It may be impossible to re-create the original ecosystem of a lost musical culture, but we can try by experimenting with historically informed creative solutions and resorting to cultural translations that, in the spirit of emulation, produce analogies rather than replicas.

After many months of pandemic lockdown, I realized that being able to drink rooibos tea while watching opera sitting on my couch is far from re-creating the ideal ecosystem for this art form. The reality is, I would rather go hungry in an opera theater than enjoy food and drinks on my couch. Sharing the experience of music brings people together and enhances its flavor. I hope that one day we will be able to go back to the opera house and that future opera producers will better understand the importance of letting the audience drink a cup of rooibos while sitting in a theater.

PART II

"Tastes Funny"

Tragic and Comic Meals from Monteverdi to Mozart

The second part of this book reverts to representations of food and drink in early opera. Chapter 5 asks why some characters, like Iro in Monteverdi's *Il ritorno di Ulisse in patria* or Papageno in Mozart's *Die Zauberflöte*, are aware of their bodily needs while more serious characters are not. These and other operas demonstrate that appetite and thirst are symptoms of bodily realism, which, as Bakhtin shows, is a defining aspect of comedy. Chapter 6 explores representations of tyrants as libertines and libertines as tyrants in relation to their conflation of food and sex. Its main focus is Mozart's *Don Giovanni* as an opera that offers a much broader use of gastronomic signs than has been acknowledged. As shown in chapter 7, eighteenth-century comic opera also develops a system of categorizing characters based not only on their body awareness, but also on their taste (what they eat often reveals their class), a notion I borrow from Bourdieu's theory of links between taste and identity to show how gastronomic signs define identity in terms of gender, social class, and ethnicity.

CHAPTER FIVE

Comedy as Embodiment in Monteverdi and Mozart

Even if from the time of Monteverdi to Mozart opera audiences could eat and drink whenever they felt like it, the characters onstage could not. As soon as they ate—or even expressed appetite—they lost status; nourishing or desiring to nourish the body was perceived as a comic gesture. It is in this sense that food "tastes funny" in early opera: it works as a sign telling us we are entering Comedyland. A long-standing archetype linked comedy to the appetites of the lower body.

The marriage of comedy and food was introduced in classical Greek and Roman theater, where gastronomic signifiers were sometimes used to denote class identity and define relationships. In Aristophanes's *The Clouds* (1.1, 50–55) Strepsiades, while speaking about his interclass marriage, tells his son that he was a rustic who smelled of "wine dregs and cheese," while his wife, aristocratic and classy, smelled of "saffron, kisses, luxury, and delights." Plautus's *Casina* also abounds in references to wine and food, often used as metaphors, as when Lysidamus describes love as the most flavorful of ingredients and wishes cooks would use it as a spice, since nothing tastes good without it (*Casina*, 2.3, 217–22).

Food is as universal as love, and both are necessary to embodied souls. According to Aristotle, in fact, all *animalia* (besouled bodies) seek nourishment and reproduction to partake of the eternal and the divine (*De anima* 415a, 23–30). The etymological root of "comedy" is the Greek word κῶμος, a term that describes such different, related concepts as a "wine-soaked" Dionysian feast, "sleep" (which comes with much drinking), and "country village" (κώμη), where such feasts usually took place. Words related to comedy often denote freedom from urban norms and laws imposed by the centers of political power and, in the subjective sphere, from norms imposed by consciousness.[1] As Erich Segal comments on Aristotle's definition of comedy, "The universal comic concern with drink, sex, food, and invective is . . . what Aristotle would have categorized as 'trivial': the essential subject of comedy."[2] Attention to the appetites of the lower body makes the language of comedy politically destabilizing. Where there is appetite, there is the will to bring change. Analogously, as Plato anticipated in *The Republic*, comedy was perceived as more politically dangerous than tragedy, and to preserve the stability of the regime, Socrates advises against cultivating comedy in the ideal city (*Republic* 388e). This long-standing perception of comedy as challenging the established order informs the perception of comic opera: David Kimbell, a modern historian of Italian opera, presents the separation of heroic drama and comedy as "the most momentous aspect of the eighteenth-century determination to create order out of the inherited chaos."[3]

Opera buffa—the Italian term for comic opera—is related to *abbuffata*, a large popular feast kindred to today's buffet, denoting a meal with few or no restrictions on the sequence of courses or the quantity of food that can be eaten. Compared with formal high-table multicourse meals, the buffet is a freedom feast. By the same token, opera buffa disseminates democratic ideas to a greater extent than opera seria and presents more fluid music and dramatic conventions. Only in comic opera are characters aware of their appetites and able to be classified based on what they eat or desire, which denotes their class and ethnicity. Comic characters *are* what they eat. Whereas opera seria represents ancient noble heroes and deities, comic operas are usually set in the present and represent everyday reality. In comic opera, gastronomic signifiers are immediately understood as corresponding to contemporary food culture. Representations of social identity often implied a critique of the social and political system.

There is an overabundance of food and drink in comic opera, and librettos often specify what the characters eat or drink. Characters in opera seria are rarely found at the dining table. And even when they are, the librettos do not specify what they ingest, except for poison.

Serious Meals: Poison

The gastronomic gap between comic and serious opera increased after the Arcadian reforms in the early eighteenth century, especially at the hands of librettists Apostolo Zeno and Pietro Metastasio, who pursued an Aristotelian separation of genres. Present historiography accepts that the separation of comedy from serious drama took place gradually from the 1690s as a result of Aristotle's influence.[4] In his *Poetics*, Aristotle gives a historical account of how tragedy acquired dignity and magnitude by eliminating comic elements, stressing that sobriety and seriousness are distinctive aspects of tragedy (1449b20–29), identifying the tragic plot as the story of the tragic hero whose fortunes change from happiness to misery (1453a5–15) and the tragic dramaturgical principle that action is not essential to tragic drama, while music and spectacle can enhance its dramatic power (1462a10–15).

Stefano Arteaga, in the late eighteenth century, writes that the librettist Silvio Stampiglia (1664–1725), founding member of the Arcadian Academy of Rome, was "one of the first to purge [*purgar*] the melodrama [*opera seria*] of the mixture of seriousness and buffoonery" (*buffonesco*) and also purged opera seria "of too complex plots and of too satiating [*sazievole*] special effects."[5]

Opera seria was purged of references to food as well. The numbers speak for themselves (fig. 5.1). Out of Metastasio's twenty-one opera seria librettos, only two contain references to food or drink.[6] The output of the most prolific and influential eighteenth-century buffa librettist, Carlo Goldoni, is similar. Out of Goldoni's eighty-four librettos published from 1732 to 1794,

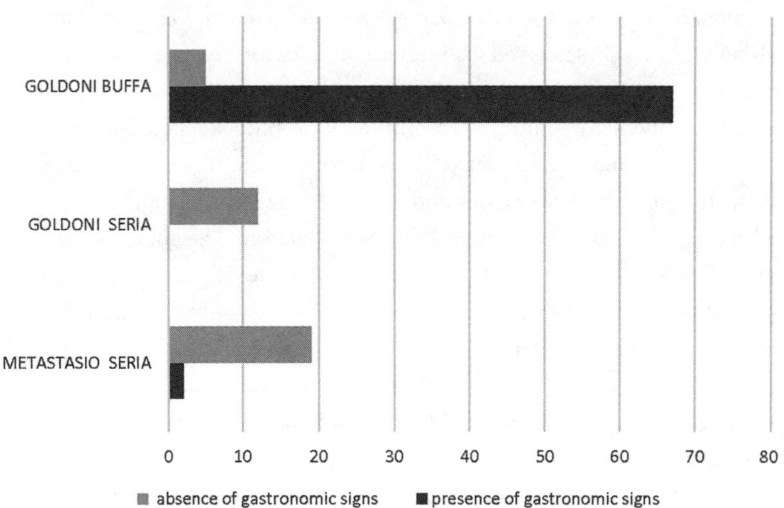

Figure 5.1. Distribution of gastronomic signs in *seria* and *buffa* librettos by Goldoni and Metastasio.

none of his twelve *opere serie* contain gastronomic signs, but of his seventy-four comic librettos, almost all contain references to them.[7]

Pietro Metastasio's librettos were set by every opera composer of the eighteenth century, and many other librettists took them as models for heroic music drama.[8] Metastasio himself considered the exclusion of *parti buffe* a fundamental achievement of his operatic reforms, though he did not shy away from "situations that, although not comic nor vulgar, could be at least festive and joyful."[9] With the disappearance of comic roles from serious dramas, eating and drinking scenes also disappeared, except for official banquets or incidents of poisoning. Also, food and drink in these official banquet scenes or toasts do not satisfy the appetite or quench thirst, but remain purely symbolic signifiers for celebration and interaction.

Of the two Metastasian operas with banquets, *Achille in Schiro* still presents traces of the mixture of comic and seria, as did its model, a late seventeenth-century libretto by Ippolito Bentivoglio that was so deeply contaminated by the mixture of genres that the publisher apologized because it "does not follow Aristotle's rules but rather the pleasant fashion of our time."[10] In remaking the libretto, Metastasio eliminated the comic roles of the old nurse and servant, as well as dances of monkeys and dwarfs. Yet, remarkably, he inserted a banquet scene (2, 6–7) that was not present in his source. During this scene, an emissary of Ulysses asks the king of Skyros to join the Greek army against Troy. Ulysses's secret mission is to find out whether the great hero Achilles is hiding in the island of Skyros. Achilles attends the banquet in plain view, disguised as a woman. While the men talk about war, Achilles is asked to entertain the warriors by singing and accompanying "herself" on the lyre. To make things worse, Princess Deidamia, whom Achilles loves, flirts with him, making onlookers suspect a "queer affection" (strano affetto) between the two women. Metastasio then carefully describes the offering of a cup of "smoking Cretan liquor" to Achilles, who offers it to Deidamia, revealing their affection. The chorus invites the guests to be carefree and festive. Although Achilles is fuming and about to stop his silly performance of languid love songs and reveal himself as a war hero among the other heroes, he holds his tongue until the banquet is interrupted by sounds of battle from outside. The opportunities for choral and light celebratory music in this libretto contrast sharply with the dramatic tensions, a strategy Metastasio reused in *Semiramide*.

The banquet scene in *Semiramide* involves the quintessential ingredient of the serious opera meal: poison. The banquet is held to announce and celebrate the spouse the royal princess Tamiri has chosen, who is expected to become the future king of Babylonia. The action opens with the rejected men plotting to poison the chosen one, Scitalce, by poisoning the cup Tamiri will offer him to seal their union. One of them, Sibari, will disclose the plot by showing the poison in a little vase to the other suitor, Ircano. Poison is the only visibly recognizable ingredient in the banquet; Sibari announces, "Here is the poison," while stage directions prescribe, *he shows him a little jar* (2, 1). Metastasio describes the set with great precision: *Royal house lit at night. Several glass cabinets all around displaying transparent jars. Lavishly prepared dining table ready for the meal with four armchairs around and one chair center front.*[11]

Cabinets full of glass jars glimmer under artificial lights, suggesting diaphanous, dematerialized bodies, like a chemistry lab for brewing toxic substances that cast a shadow over the entire meal.

In the banquet scene (2, 2), there are four armchairs for Princess Tamiri and her suitors, Scitalce sitting on her right, the allied conjurers Mirteo and Ircano on the left, while Sibari stands. Before the meal, as predicted Tamiri offers the cup to Scitalce to seal the engagement, but Scitalce unexpectedly declines, not being able or willing to commit to Tamiri, who then offers the cup to Ircano. Ircano, however, knowing its lethal contents, throws it to the ground, thus saving his life but rejecting Tamiri as well. The dinner party is completely spoiled at this point, even before the guests have a chance touch any food on the table or to sip their wine. They all leave their chairs, as Metastasio carefully prescribes, before the rejected princess sings a rage aria, "Tu mi disprezzi ingrato" in which she threatens Ircano for despising and offending her. Though there has been nothing convivial about this meal, Metastasio prescribes a festive, joyful celebratory chorus for the banquet. The contrast between the serene choral music and the nerve-racking tension in the drama anticipates Verdi's tragic irony. Among the many settings of this libretto, one original solution is in Nicola Porpora's version from the 1720s, which replaces the chorus in the libretto with serene *Tafelmusik*, a gallant and dignified minuet for wind band (oboes, flutes, trumpets, and horns) and strings.[12] The effect does not change: banquet music is disconnected from the drama, like happy music played in a restaurant regardless of how unhappy the customers might be.

When fifty years later Antonio Salieri parodied this poisoned-cup scene in his "heroicomic drama" *La secchia rapita*, he replaced the reference to generic poison in a transparent jar with poisoned chicken broth. When the Countess, who has been warned of the risk of poison during the banquet, asks about the broth, she gets a description of the recipe and its medicinal properties: a refined process of abstracting sweet juices from the breast of an unspecified animal, resulting in a rarefied brew of high quality that it is good to eat before a meal to promote digestion.[13] This comic revamping of Metastasio's famous *Semiramide* scene offers two examples of the representation of food in eighteenth-century comic opera that reflect a culinary culture increasingly aware of the medicinal and social powers of food, and of its ability to affect and shape the human body as well as the social body.

Opera and Embodiment

Sam Abel, a theater scholar and passionate opera fan, declares that "opera is about the human body, that opera is *embodied*," because its experience is "far more physical than discursive," more similar to a sexual experience than an intellectual one. For this reason Abel rejects "most musicology" as "fatally formal, entirely abstracted from the physicality of opera," instead embracing opera critics like Susan McClary, Catherine Clément, Michel Poizat, and Wayne Koestenbaum for breaking with the "stultifying orthodoxy" of traditional musicology and for being honest about subjective physical reactions to opera, inspiring a form of criticism that can "articulate this visceral response to operatic *performance*." Embodiment in this case happens at the level of interaction between artists and audience, when we see "opera as theater," which is to say, as "performed physical exchange between singer and audience."[14] When we change perspective and focus on the characters and how they feel, rather than on how they make us feel, we need to use the term "embodiment" in a different way.

I use "embodiment" to describe the characters' awareness of their bodies, that is, how much they let bodily appetites and needs influence their actions and reactions. Embodiment, in this case, informs how characters express themselves verbally, musically, and dramatically. Embodiment in this sense is the mode of comedy, whereas its opposite—disembodiment—is the mode of heroic or serious opera. The distinctive and defining mode of operatic comedy is the representation of embodied humanity. This is how Dante uses the term in the *Divine Comedy*. As Vittorio Montemaggi puts it, "Dante chooses to write the way he does, and to make his narrative as compelling as possible, because of his theological understanding of human embodiedness."[15] In opera, embodiment and disembodiment affect the music-dramatic fabric at many levels, such as the type of voices, the use of coloratura or other unrealistic styles of musical text delivery, the interaction or incommunicability among characters, the separation or identification of the bodies of the dramatis and singing personae—and the presence or absence of food.

Opera characters who express desire for or satisfaction with food assert their existence as living subjects in physical reality. Comic characters possess a special kind of subjectivity: bodily subjectivity, or letting their bodies influence their actions and reactions. Asserting subjectivity has been essential to the world of opera since the earliest stages, as Mauro Calcagno has shown. Opera uses "deictic" or pointing words: words that point to a subject and its existence in place and in time, anchoring the "I" to presence in the represented reality.[16] Eating and drinking, or expressing the desire to do so, have the deictic function of calling attention to the subject's existence in a tangible world, bonding subjects to their bodily needs and desires, grounding them to their earthly biological life.

In the rest of this chapter, I will look at two comic characters who are aware of their appetites: Iro, in Monteverdi's *Il ritorno di Ulisse in patria* (1640), and Papageno in Mozart's *Die Zauberflöte* (1791). Both operas mix serious and comic aspects, but they clearly distinguish between characters who do and do not display bodily subjectivity. Notwithstanding the chronological gap between the two operas, Iro and Papageno not only share appetite, as do many other comic characters, they are also rare examples of suicidal comic characters. Their tragicomic nature reveals that a definition of comic opera exclusively based on humor and laughter would be misleading. We need to look deeper, or lower, for an understanding of operatic comedy as embodied dramatic art.

Iro's Hunger

Monteverdi's *Il ritorno di Ulisse in patria* is the earliest known opera to use comic bodily realism. As announced in the title, the libretto is based on the story of Ulysses's return to his homeland, as recounted in the second half of Homer's *Odyssey* (books 13–24). The opera was first performed in Venice in 1640 in the public opera house of Santi Giovanni e Paolo. It soon became widely successful and influential, shaping the early developments of the genre.[17] Gastronomic signs in Homer's *Iliad* and *Odyssey* are pervasive and involve gods, heroes, and people of lower social class.[18] Embodiment is universal, but the modes and manners of expressing bodily desires and satisfying them reveal differences between heroes and fiends, gods and men, and civilized and barbaric characters.

During his peregrinations in search of his father Odysseus, Telemachus hears about his father's deeds in the Trojan War at two lavish banquets: the first at Nestor's palace in Pylos (book 3), and the second at Menelaus and Helen's palace in Sparta (book 4). Odysseus himself leaves the island of the beautiful nymph Calypso after a farewell feast (book 5), and sails to the kingdom of the Phaeacians, who welcome him with a spectacular banquet. One-third of the epic—the story of Odysseus's deeds and voyages—is recounted during that lavish meal, at the end of which, after drinking and eating overabundantly, the Phaeacians extend their remarkable hospitality by giving Odysseus a ride home to Ithaca, acting as "designated drivers." Their excessive hospitality enrages Poseidon, whose son Polyphemus had been blinded by Odysseus. Earlier in the tale, the Cyclops, eating and drinking by himself, had wolfed down the flesh of Odysseus's companions, and Odysseus blinded him after getting him drunk with the wine. The elegant convivial feast of the Phaeacians and Polyphemus's solitary cannibalism are opposite modes of eating: one represents civilization, the other, barbarity.[19] In opera, these two modes still inform the difference between tyrannical solitary eaters in opera, such as Don Giovanni and Scarpia in Puccini's *Tosca*, and characters who share food with generosity and civility.

Monteverdi stages the Phaeacians' love for the good things of life in their jovial chorus "In questo basso mondo" (1, 6), celebrating the materiality of our "low world, where men get whatever they want." The chorus echoes Lorenzo de' Medici's bacchic song (*canzona di Bacco*) "Quant'è bella giovinezza," a carnival song (*canto carnascialesco*) that identifies the ephemeral pleasures of youth as life's only pleasures: wine, food, and love.[20] Monteverdi's chorus is reminiscent of such *canti carnascialeschi*, but it presents no reference to conviviality.

Monteverdi's opera, in fact, eliminates all the positive convivial scenes in the *Odyssey*; only the simple food offering of the swineherd Eumaeus survives when Odysseus returns to Ithaca disguised as a beggar (book 14). Monteverdi's Odysseus, however, unlike Homer's, does not touch the food. The only banquet scene represented in the opera is that of the suitors (2, 12, set in the "palace courtyard where a banquet is being prepared"), which becomes a bloodbath when Odysseus returns before the food is consumed.

Iro is the ultimate comic character of the opera. He is a glutton, beggar, and buffoon, eating scraps at the suitors' table. Contrary to the opera's literary source, he is the only character in the tale who eats. For him food is man's only joy. Federico Malipiero's seventeenth-century translation of the

Odyssey describes Iro as a "buffone," and Malipiero fleshes out his character by explaining that "because of his insatiable appetite he had a stomach that could never be filled with enough food and was ostentatious of his appetite, acting as if he were always starving, as is customary for those who worship their belly as their God."[21]

Once the massacre of the suitors causes Iro to lose access to free food, he commits suicide. Ellen Rosand sees Iro's death as analogous and parallel to the death of the philosopher Seneca in Monteverdi's *L'incoronazione di Poppea*: "By choosing death Seneca asserts victory of the spirit over the senses, affirming the stoic value of suppression of instinct. Iro, who chooses death to save himself from hunger, asserts the opposite, the power of the body, of base appetite over mind."[22] Nonetheless, Iro's suicide scene remains a puzzling moment in the opera, first because it represents a significant departure from Homer's epic poem and second because, unlike Papageno's suicide attempt, Iro dies—which is at odds, to say the least, with the comic nature of his role. To make sense of Iro's suicide, we must understand seventeenth-century operatic comedy in terms of bodily realism rather than in terms of humor.

Iro's style of singing is as realistic as operatic singing could ever be at this time in history.[23] Comic-realistic singing is typically syllabic when representing speech utterances. It uses coloratura passages, but only to represent laughter or other emotional states that would cause the human voice to prolong the sound of syllables or to reiterate or modulate their pitch. For the same reason, Iro's singing is fragmented when the voice is broken by emotional reactions, and the delivery of text speeds up or slows down as a result of a physiological reaction to emotional responses. This style of text delivery is at the opposite end of the spectrum from that of Minerva, goddess of reason, who deploys overwhelming, florid coloratura to represent concepts rather than physical reactions. Minerva does not react to emotions, she causes them, and her mind controls her voice. But in Iro's case his lower body—his stomach—controls both his mind and his voice.

Iro's final lament and suicide scene is a case in point. It takes place after Ulysses kills the suitors. Starting with an alternation of seven- and eleven-syllable lines (*versi sciolti*, a poetic form privileged by the librettist Giacomo Badoaro),[24] Iro soon messes up the meter by a slip of the tongue, calling the suitors (proci) swine (porci).[25] When he realizes this he corrects himself, thus adding two syllables to the *settenario*, an effect Monteverdi amplifies by repeating "i porci":

O dolor, o martir che l'anima attrista.	[Oh pain, oh torment saddening the soul!
O questa rimembranza	Oh, what remembrance
Di dolorosa vista.	of a painful sight!
Io vidi i Proci estinti,	I saw the suitors extinguished.
I Proci, i porci furo uccisi.	The suitors, the swine were killed.
Ah, ch'io perdei	Ah, that I lost
Le delizie del ventre e della gola.	The delights of the belly and throat.
Chi soccorre il digiun, chi lo consola?	Who will relieve my starving, who will soothe it?]

Iro's lament begins with an overstretched D^1, harmonized as the fifth of the tonic G against a growling bass constructed of rapidly ascending scales alternating with dropping octaves, a "sonification" of Iro's hungry stomach.[26] The stomach music suddenly turns doleful as the G sonority shifts from major to minor to accompany Iro's sobs on "dolor" and "martir," then a melodic slow octave descent from E^1 to E, touching the lower D on the words "estinti Proci" to represent the fall and death of the suitors. Iro's voice then sinks to the bottom D—the lowest pitch in the piece—on the word "brame" (cravings) as he asks, in a rhetorically awkward descending melodic line spanning D^1 to D, "who will tolerate now the craving of your immense appetite?" (chi più della tua fame satollerà le brame?). Four measures later, as he sings the word "caverne" (caverns) in the context of a self-delivered verdict, "no longer will you find anyone who would like to fill the hungry caverns of your vast stomach" (Non troverai chi goda / empir del vasto ventre / l'affamate caverne). In the quick final section of the number, a 3/1 meter presto, the low D returns, always harmonized as the fifth of the tonic chord, expressing desire, appetite, and the emptiness of his stomach, which continue to drive him, to move him, even after he resolves to silence them by causing the death of his own body (the libretto does not specify how he dies). It happens again on the word "vinta" (conquered), dramatizing his resolution to defeat hunger, his mortal enemy. The last melodic drop to the low D happens at the very end, as Iro finally resolves, "Let my body feed the hungry tomb" (vada il mio corpo a disfamar la tomba). "Tomba" is his last word, at the end of a descending line musically painting his descent into the grave, completing a trajectory to the lowest yet harmonically suspended pitch that can be described: craving → caverns of the empty stomach → hunger → grave. When at last Monteverdi sets *tomba* on two long, repeated syllables reiterating the low D, harmonized again as the empty fifth of the tonic G, the tragic irony is revealed: at the end of the lament the grave is as hollow as his stomach was at the beginning. The grave becomes a stomach.

Iro sings his lament mostly syllabically, but Monteverdi breaks this plain and clear delivery of the text with excessive repetition of words and syllables, typical of someone in distress, at the borderline of stuttering. When Iro asks, "Who will relieve my starving, who will soothe it?" the word "chi" (who) is repeated six times in two measures—"chi chi chi chi chi chi"—reproducing onomatopoeically the cry of the rooster in Italian ("chichirichì"). Forty measures later, when he holds the note D^1 on "chi" for a considerable length, he establishes a tonal link between this chicken sound and the concept of the grave, reinforcing the idea that Iro is turning himself into meat for food. The addition of improvised simple figurations by flutes or recorders could enhance this effect.[27] The only coloratura in the piece is also used realistically, to reproduce hysterical laughter when he reminds himself "you will not find anyone who will laugh at the gluttonous triumphs of your throat" (Non troverai chi rida / Del ghiotto trionfar della tua gola).

Iro's death could also be related to, or even a commentary on, the radical Aristotelian materialism of the natural philosopher Cesare Cremonini. Rosand suggests that Cremonini "questioned, among many other things, the immortality of the soul."[28] Cremonini played a guiding role in the development of modern science during the time of his colleague at the University of Padua, Galileo Galilei. Both were investigated by the Inquisition, but unlike Galileo, Cremonini was acquitted. There has never been any evidence that Cremonini doubted Catholic dogmas; his alleged atheism and belief in the mortality of the soul cannot be substantiated based on his writings: it is a myth created much later by free-thinking French historians.[29] It is nevertheless undeniable that Cremonini was a careful reader of Aristotle. As such, he was well aware that in *De anima*, Aristotle claims "the soul is inseparable from its body" (413a), a claim that supports both the mortality of the soul and its opposite, the immortality of the body and its resurrection. For this reason Aristotle has been brandished both by Catholic orthodoxy and by those who depart from it.

Interestingly, Iro reappears in the opera alongside the shades of the killed suitors (ombre de' Proci), who are wandering in a desert in the underworld (3, 2). They are souls without bodies. The libretto warns us that "the scene is sad and can be left out": in opera of this time, there is nothing comic about disembodied souls. *De anima* claims that the primary function of the soul (anima) is to move (animate) the body. It is a form of dynamic energy triggered by desire: at the simplest level, a desire to nourish the body. "Hunger," as Aristotle explains, "should be defined as a certain mode of movement of a body" (403a).[30] To have appetite, one needs both a body and a soul: "since nothing except what is alive can be fed, what is fed is the besouled body and just because it has soul in it. Hence food is essentially related to what has soul in it" (416b). Aristotle's corollary is that eating and sex are essential to locomotion and internal movement of the body, its growth and decay (432b).

Eating and sex are related in Monteverdi's operas, though they manifest themselves in different comic characters. In *Il ritorno*, old Iro has in mind nothing other than nourishment, but there is nothing in the minds of the young maid Melanto or her suitor Eurimaco other than sex. Their singing expresses the desires of the lower body in a way that is distinctive of sexual attraction and related to appetite for food through the use of food similes in their language. In their erotically charged duet (1, 2), their initial lyrical effusions awaken their sexual appetites, which they express realistically in fragmented melodic lines, as if their hormonal reactions were arresting their voices. This happens around the evocation of a specific flavor: "sweetness." The sweet lies the man tells the woman are, for Melanto, "dolci bugie." She repeats these words, her voice unable and unwilling to complete the sentence: "le tue dolci. . . . Le tue dolci. . . . Le tue dolci bugie." She holds the word "dolci," which in Italian means either candy or desserts, in her mouth to enjoy it longer, like a gourmand. The sweet morsel ignites a second lyrical and melodic effusion. Then, after an excited, recitative-like exchange, the final section begins, once again, on the word "dolce." Now the two lovers call each other "my sweet, sweet, sweet life" (dolce, dolce dolce mia vita). At the climax of the duet, they intertwine in a final embrace, similar to that of Nero and Poppea in the final duet in *L'incoronazione di Poppea*. The lovers bless their "knots," hoping they "will never untie," while the orchestra binds them tighter in contrary-motion counterpoint. The tonal focus of this duet is D, the sonority associated with Iro's stomach and his hungry grave.

"Tonal focus" is a term Karol Berger uses in his analysis of Monteverdi's *L'Orfeo* for the moment when Eurydice's shade utters the word "dolce" as she sees her lover for the last time, saying that this last sight is at once "too sweet and too bitter" (vista troppo *dolce* e troppo *amara*). Berger observes that "as her body evaporates into a cold shade, the musical coherence of her diction too, threatens to dissolve, going in and out of tonal focus."[31] Although true for Eurydice, it is pointedly not so for Melanto or Iro, who remain tonally grounded, with only expressive minor inflections and no disorienting chromatic excursions. Melanto's death, unlike Eurydice's, turns her not into a shade, but into meat. After the massacre of the suitors, the punishment for "those women who were the suitors' harlots" (book 23) is to be turned into game, birds hunted for food. Telemachus hangs the young women by the necks from a single rope and sadistically enjoys the macabre spectacle, watching them "dying while convulsively jerking their feet." Homer compares Telemachus's victims to dying birds, inviting the reader to be complacent about watching their final agony: "as *we see* in the woods mockingbirds, doves, and similar birds caught in a net, agitating their little wings."[32] The simile turns the dying girls into an image of flesh destined for the dining table. In the opera, however, Monteverdi's librettist deflects: it is Iro who, before dying, symbolically metamorphosizes through his sounds into an edible bird, a chicken.

In literature from the time of Rabelais to Monteverdi's contemporaries Cervantes and Shakespeare, Mikhail Bakhtin identifies a fundamental turning point.[33] The human body and its appetite become the center of "grotesque realism" and its typical exaggeration of body size and desires, especially those related to eating and drinking.[34] In the case of Cervantes's *Don Quixote*, Bakhtin identifies in Sancho Panza an emblematic figure of grotesque comic realism. We can see how well it applies to Monteverdi's Iro: "In Cervantes' images of food and drink there is still the spirit of popular banquets. Sancho's materialism, his potbelly, appetite, his abundant defecation, are on the absolute lower level of grotesque realism of the gay bodily grave (belly, bowels, earth) which has been dug for Don Quixote's abstract and deadened idealism."[35]

The actual bodies represented in comic realism "did not cut off the umbilical cord which tied them to the fruitful womb of the earth,"[36] reason enough that Bakhtin emphasizes the importance and power of comic death, "devoid of all tragic or terrifying overtones," because "death is the necessary link in the process of the people's growth and renewal, it is the 'other side of birth.'"[37] It is in this sense that Bakhtin defines grotesque realism as "directed toward the underworld, but earthly and bodily," making of the tomb a "bodily, creative grave."[38] Death is part of the cycle of life, and "feeding the grave" with one's own body is feeding the earth. What regulates the life and death in this world is time, which, in Bakhtin's words, "kills and gives birth," and for this reason "time is simultaneously ironic and gay."[39]

Time, sung by a bass, makes its entrance in the prologue of *Il ritorno*, evoked by the personification of Human Frailty, sung by an alto voice, lamenting that Time is also her enemy, giving her life and death. Time replies, "Nothing is safe from my tooth: it chews, it savors" (salvo è niente dal mio dente / Ei rode, ei gode), warning that, like the cannibal Polyphemus, he eats mortals. Monteverdi emphasizes the point by stretching and repeating the words "tooth," "chews," and "savors," thus providing an opportunity for the singer to ornament the notes with a "trillo," which, according to Giovanni Conforti and Giulio Caccini, unlike our modern trill, is a quick repetition of the same note, making the words "dente" or "rode" into a sonic rendering of the act of chewing.[40]

Iro loves to eat, but he hates sharing food. His eating is profoundly antisocial. In the royal courtyard where they are getting ready for the banquet, Iro orders the disguised Ulysses to go somewhere else. Ulysses responds by mocking Iro: he is a "man of large size" (huomo di grosso taglio) and "broad perspective" (di larga prospettiva), "gray and old" (canuto ed invecchiato), a "pot-bellied knight" (cavaliero panciuto).[41] Musically, Ulysses wins: he is able to use madrigalisms and prolonged syllables, but Iro's threats and replies are reduced to incoherent fragments by his fears and rage. The short fight (breve contrasto) that follows is accompanied by harmonically static music based on fourths and fifths, using strings to imitate martial trumpets. Homer stages it as a boxing match: pure action without words (book 18), but in Malipiero's translation Ulysses threatens, "I will break your teeth and with a punch I will make your veins explode in your breast, making you vomit blood." This is indeed what happens: Ulysses breaks Iro's jaw, while the suitors almost laugh themselves to death (morivano dalle risa).[42]

The sickening violence of Homeric epics becomes typical of grotesque comic realism by Rabelais's time—not too long before Monteverdi—when it acquires a symbolic valence typical of the carnival rituals of destruction of the old order to make way for something new. Bakhtin points at the analogy between, and conflation of, "the dismembered body and its anatomization" and comic banquet scenes.[43] The example he analyzes in detail is the thrashing of the Catchpoles during the wedding banquet in the fourth book of *Gargantua and Pantagruel*, where the "anatomizing enumeration of injured organs" and the bloody thrashing is at once both realistic and symbolic. "The Catchpoles," as Bakhtin writes, "are the representatives of the old law, of the rights of a world that is dying and receding," and for this reason "the beating is a feast of death and regeneration." Feudal princes and kings are replaced with new ones, and it is for this joyful revolutionary force that "the thrashing itself has a special solemn and festive character; it is administered at a banquet."[44]

The banquet massacre at the end of the *Odyssey* is also a story of regenerating a political regime by butchering a corrupt aristocracy (the "proci/

suitors" are killed like "porci/pigs") and bringing back a reborn king. It can be seen as a critique of the degeneration of the market-driven economy in the Venetian republic, where commercial opera was invented, entangling the experience of opera in the unregulated, casual, convivial, and erotic exchanges that took place in public theaters. Odysseus is the reborn and regenerated king who, in order to regain power, must become a new man. This is clearer in Monteverdi's opera than in Homer, and it occurs where the opera radically departs from its literary source. In the second act, Odysseus/Ulysses is devoured by the earth, and his son Telemachus vents his horrified reactions in surprisingly serene major sonorities, crying out, "What do I see? This voracious earth swallows the living, opens mouths and caverns craving human blood," and "the rocks swallow human flesh." The key of G major continues as he sees Ulysses reborn from the earth in his youthful appearance, prompting a shift from recitative to an arioso moment: "Falling is not so bitter, if we learn that by dying we are rejuvenated." The words dying and rejuvenating (se col morir ringiovenir) are repeated in five ascending tetrachords over a descending bass line to represent musically the contrast between rising (rejuvenating) and falling (dying).

In Homer (16.180–220), however, the earth does not swallow Ulysses. Instead, Athena/Minerva, the goddess of reason, changes him into a youthful hero. This departure from Homer is as significant as Iro's added suicide scene. For Monteverdi and Badoaro, the old hero's regeneration by being swallowed and regurgitated by the earth was more important than faithfulness to their literary source. Bakhtin observes how the myth of Ceres, the earth goddess, is an emblematic story of death and regeneration, of what he calls "the creative grave."[45] Ceres is the goddess of crops and agriculture, of feasting and abundance, but through her daughter Proserpina she is also associated with the underworld, with spiritual and material rebirth. In Wagner's *Ring*, it will be the earth goddess Erda who will call for the regeneration of a system corrupted by gold and the vulgar thirst for economic and material power. But Wagner's gods, unlike the new Ulysses, do not listen to her, and they march into their twilight like the suitors in Odysseus's Ithaca.

Papageno's Appetite

In Mozart and Emanuel Schikaneder's *Die Zauberflöte*, Papageno is a comic character who, like Iro, is determined to feed his belly. Unlike Iro's, Papageno's suicide attempt fails. He is saved by the three boys just before his famous duet with Papagena celebrating love and reproduction. Whereas the heroic Odysseus and the comic Iro are incompatible characters who fight when their paths cross, in *Die Zauberflöte*, embodied comedy and disembodied heroic drama unfold side by side. The comic Papageno and the heroic prince Tamino are on the same team, and they are tested together with different results. For example, when the three boys prepare a nice dining table for them (2, 16, "*unter der Terzett setzen sie den Tisch*"), Tamino abstains from food and instead plays the flute, while Papageno enjoys the meal and comments on the skill of Sarastro's cook. Similarly, when Tamino's beloved Pamina sings her heartbreaking G-minor aria lamenting the loss of her lover, Papageno eats and praises the chef and the cellarer (2, 19, "Der Herr Koch und der Herr Kellermeister sollen leben"). Comparing Papageno's relationship with Prince Tamino and Iro's relationship with King Odysseus reveals an epochal change of attitude toward embodiment and its link to social class, which can be described as a shift from incompatibility to dialectical confrontation.

When they first meet, Prince Tamino asks Papageno, "Tell me, my funny friend, who you mayst be" (1, 2, Sag mir, du lustiger Freund, wer du seist?). The question is perfunctory, as he has already defined Papageno's status and role by calling him "funny." The lower-status comic character, surprisingly, laughs back at the Prince and his "dumb question," telling him, "I am a man, like you" (Wer ich bin? Ha! [aside] Dumme Frage! [aloud] Ein Mensch, wie du).[46] Papageno does not see differences among men. He is a Rousseauvian man in a state of nature, appearing, in the illustration for this scene inserted in the original libretto, in a costume with feathers on his head and body, similar to contemporary representations of Native Americans, who were at the time associated with the mythical *bon sauvage*.[47] When Tamino then introduces an economic distinction by informing us that he is a powerful and wealthy prince, the son of a ruler of lands and people, and then asks Papageno how he lives, he gets a simple and straightforward answer: "by eating and drinking like all men" (von Essen und Trinken, wie alle Menschen). This equality of the stomach's need threatens the social status of the prince, at least in the world of opera, where heroic characters do not eat.

The gastronomic signs of Papageno's diet that classify him need to be historically contextualized. He tells the prince that he works for the Queen of the Night in exchange for "Wein, Zuckerbrot, und süße Feigen," foods that open a window on a global market bridging Europe (wine), the Middle East (sweet figs), and America (sugar). Moreover, the expression "Zuckerbrot und Peitsche" (sugar bread and whip), corresponding to carrot and stick in English, evokes the condition of slavery in sugar plantations.[48] The punishment the three ladies inflict on Papageno—the "whip"—reinforces the reference to slavery: "Instead of wine have some water," is the verdict of the first lady, and "instead of sugar bread, this stone" (und diesen Stein statt Zuckerbrot), adds the second, while the third silences him by locking his mouth, where food goes in and words come out, "instead of sweet figs a padlock on your mouth," triggering the quintet "Hm hm hm hm hm hm hm hm." What Papageno eats defines his social status—a laborer in exchange for food, punished by being deprived of using his mouth for speech and nourishment.

In 1791 sugar drove the discourse of an abolitionist campaign in Europe and North America that asked people to boycott the system of human trafficking by abstaining altogether from sugar and rum. The pamphlet "On the Propriety of Abstaining from West-India Sugar and Rum" makes a strong argument against supporting the trade. The author, attributed to William Fox, asks his readers, "Can our pride suggest to us that the rights of men are limited to any nation, or to any colour?" and provides horrifying descriptions of flogging ("at every stroke of the whip flesh is cut out") and the testimony of Benjamin Franklin who claimed that the real color of sugar is red like the blood of plantation workers ("sugar is thoroughly dyed scarlet"). Most important, the author presents human trafficking as the failure of the entire Age of Enlightenment: "We, in an enlightened age, have greatly surpassed, in brutality and injustice, the most ignorant and barbarous ages: and while we are pretending to the finest feelings of humanity, we are exercising unprecedented cruelty."[49] If Papageno's "Zuckerbrot" links him to the contemporary debate about slavery, his Bildung trajectory also tells a story of liberation from the culture of slavery in which he and his unredeemed counterpart, Monostatos, participate as both victims and perpetrators.

Modern critics have not been kind to Papageno, seeing his attachment to the body as a symptom of baseness and shallowness. This is due to a long-standing dualistic conception opposing mind and body, which Mozart challenged and dismantled. Jacques Chailley writes that Papageno is "lacking courage and intelligence, and therefore he is unworthy of initiation."[50] Rose Subotnik stresses how Papageno is "enslaved by bodily needs—for food, drink, and sex."[51] Carolyn Abbate argues that Papageno is subject to automatic impulses, which justifies Mozart's choice of the mechanical, metallic sound of his magic bells.[52] Karol Berger draws a parallel between Papageno and Monostatos, calling them "two versions of *l'homme moyen sensual* . . . who care mainly about satisfying their bodily appetites." However, Berger also points out that they belong to opposite realms and that they complete opposite itineraries. To simplify his argument, Monostatos, privileging war and hate, hence rape and abuse, starts with Sarastro and ends with the Queen, while Papageno, privileging peace and love, starts his journey in the Queen's dark power but ends in Sarastro's enlightened realm.[53] From the first aria to the last duet, Papageno never renounces material desires; instead, he changes his attitude toward them.

At first Papageno sees women as objects that can be traded for sugar. In his first lied, "Der Vogelfänger bin ich ja," women and food appear to be interchangeable, like goods for trade and consumption. In the second stanza of this "catchy" strophic song, he wishes he could set his nets and traps to catch girls. In the early performance tradition, a third stanza was added, in which Papageno wishes he could trade the girls he traps for sugar, then give the sugar to the one who will be his wife and the mother of his child.[54] By the final duet, he no longer sees women as objects that can be traded for sugar, but sees them as companions to achieve the love that, as he explains in culinary terms, "spices up our life" (2, 7, würzet unser Lebenstage) and makes "woman and man reach for divinity" (Man und Weib, und Weib und Man / Reichen an die Gottheit an). Their joyful celebration of sex and procreation is material and transcendental, embodied and spiritual.

Papageno's Bildung story is encoded in Mozart's careful tonal plan. Papageno's opening lied is in G major, which Jacques Chailley labels as "the key of frivolity," setting Papageno apart from the more serious and philosophical prince.[55] But naming G major as "the key of frivolity" backfires when we follow the complete thread of Mozart's tonal narrative technique that bridges the different dramatic moments: G major is pivotal to the achievement of the happy, enlightened ending. In the second-act finale, Papageno once again plays his panpipe, calling Papagena. Out of desperation for not finding his "little maid of a wife" he attempts suicide in a G-major aria injected with extended G-minor passages and is saved in extremis by three boys who remind him of his magic bells. After a C-major section we hear the final love duet in G major that begins ("Pa Pa Pa Pa"). At the end of the piece, G major serves as dominant function to modulate to C minor, the key area dramatizing the last appearance of the dark forces: the Queen of the Night, now allied with the tyrannical Monostatos, accompanied by her faithful Three Ladies. As they are suddenly defeated by the appearance of the solar Sarastro, C minor opens up to its relative major, the symbolically charged key of E-flat. E-flat major is generally interpreted in this opera as the key of enlightenment and Masonic initiation, and it is also the key of the duet between Papageno and Pamina. Papageno's initial philosophy of life as pleasure, leading him to the corollary "love is pleasure" and to its tragic consequence that without love there is no pleasure, hence no life worth living. The final duet then reaches a new understanding of love as a divine force, not exclusively as consumption of pleasure, or in opposition to it, but as a higher synthesis of pleasure and love.

In *Il ritorno di Ulisse in patria* and *Die Zauberflöte*, Monteverdi and Mozart mingle comic and serious characters, genres, and situations. Iro and Papageno have in common their attachment to bodily appetites, leading them to believe a body that cannot satisfy its urges is not worth living in. Their suicide attempts, traditionally a seria prerogative, are tragicomic, with the comic element rooted in bodily realism and subjectivity. The presence of bodily subjectivity in both characters does not make them similar; in fact it stresses the differences between the two precisely in the different attitudes toward the body and its needs. If Iro's appetite is monomaniac—exclusively focused on nourishment—Papageno experiences a broader variety of appetites. Even in the case of food, Iro cares only for substance and quantity, but Papageno is able to appreciate food for its taste and quality. This leads to a diversification of the gastronomy represented by specific food signifiers, such as wine, sugar bread, and sweet figs, each carrying a specific reference that also points to a geographical origin, a system of production, and a mercantile exchange loaded with sociopolitical implications.

Ultimately, Papageno is saved from carrying out his suicide attempt because the appetites of his lower body are not exclusively focused on the belly but include sexual desire, manifesting itself as a desire to procreate. This sets him apart from other Mozartean characters experiencing sex drive without the intention to procreate, such as Cherubino and Don Giovanni. Whereas Iro chooses death, feeding the grave, Papageno embraces life, the divine force of love that generates new life. With the final duet between Papageno and Papagena, Mozart sends a powerful and often neglected message: that the lowest characters' awareness of their lower bodies presents an alternative to purely intellectual enlightenment, namely the positive power of the body's appetites to counterbalance the dark appetites of the mind.

CHAPTER SIX

The Insatiable

Tyrants and Libertines

In the world of opera, tyrants and libertines have prodigious appetites, but unlike comic characters, they are insatiable. Operatic tyrants rape women, cheat on their partners, and, like lower-class comic characters, eat and drink, compromising their status as seria protagonists. Their true desire, in fact, is for something out of reach for human beings: power unchecked and unbounded. Plato depicts tyranny as the most degenerate form of government: tyrants are unable to restrain their insatiable appetites, especially their erotic desires, and their thirst for power leads them to put themselves above the law (*Republic* 571a–576e). Tyranny is degenerate because it is grounded in injustice, a negative force that generates internal divisions (*Republic* 351d). In this chapter we will encounter operatic tyrants and libertines at the dining table, which divides rather than unites.

Our point of departure will be seventeenth-century Venetian opera, namely a collection of librettos belonging to the library of Apostolo Zeno, one of the most influential eighteenth-century opera seria librettists.[1] Like Monteverdi's public operas, the seventeenth-century Venetian operas from the Zeno collection present a fertile mixture of comedy, heroic drama, and tragedy. They planted the seeds of many long-lasting conventions regarding the representation of the body in opera. As in the previous chapter, our destination will be Mozart—specifically *Don Giovanni*, an opera centering on the quintessential tyrannical libertine.

The Tyrant's Table

In *La saggia pazzia di Giunio Bruto* (The wise madness of Junius Brutus, 1698), the title character, the legendary founder of the Roman Republic, is leading a conspiracy of freedom-loving citizens against the tyrant Tarquin. The opera, whose plot is derived from Cicero and Livy, is a celebration of Venetian republican ideals and government, which were under constant pressure from the absolutist regimes of the time.[2] Cicero portrays Tarquin as the quintessential tyrant who delights in lawless violence and, unable to control his lust, rapes the virtuous Lucretia. He depicts Junius Brutus as a hero who "lifted from his fellow-citizens the unjust yoke of oppressive servitude" and "led a revolution" to establish the Republic.[3]

Tarquin's banquet takes place not in a dining hall but in a garden, which is a darker, more dangerous place at night. The libertine's purpose in organizing the banquet is to seduce Volunia, Junius's beloved. To add tension to this already stressful convivial gathering, we are informed that Volunia's brother plans to poison the tyrant (1, 6). The banquet scene (1, 11) begins with the servant Gilbo, who, like Leporello in *Don Giovanni*, complains about his status by singing "il servir / è un morir" (serving is dying). The scene is filled with asides in which the guests express their hidden feelings about the tyrant. Tension rises as Tarquin's wife enters and sits at the dining table (1, 12). Tarquin starts the toast but is interrupted when Junius Brutus rushes in (1, 13) and snatches the cup from Tarquin's hand intending to drink it, unaware that the cup had been poisoned. Volunia's brother snatches the cup and smashes it on the ground, making Tarquin suspect it was poisoned. The party is spoiled, and the act ends with a dance of pages clearing the table (*segue il ballo di paggi che levano le mense*). Although a banquet is by definition a communal meal celebrating unity and companionship, the tyrant's table represents a divided family, and in this case the divided family represents a divided, unjust government. The opera ends with Tarquin's troops fighting the rebels and with his defeat and the victory of liberty, celebrated in the quartet, "Libertà, libertà" (3, [17]), representing the episode in 509 BC that put an end to the monarchy and inaugurated the Roman Republic.

Il Vespasiano, a libretto by Giulio Cesare Corradi set to music by Carlo Pallavicino, became one of the most successful and widely disseminated operas from 1678 to 1695 and was still performed in England as late as 1724.[4] The emperor Vespasiano, interpreted by a bass, is a good ruler, but his horrible sons are the real protagonists of the opera: Titus (often remembered for destroying Jerusalem in AD 70, causing the Jewish diaspora) and Domitian are both interpreted by castrato singers.[5] Domitian, determined to snatch the imperial scepter, tries to seduce his brother's wife Arricida during a banquet in the royal dining hall, bringing the first act to a climactic end (1, 6–20). The banquet scene opens while the dinner table is still being prepared ("sala dove si preparano le Regie Mense"), as if to awaken the appetite. The libretto prescribes table music onstage: a small band and castrato singers performing under pergolas ("pergolati in alto con musici e suonatori").[6] Domitian sings his first aria at the beginning of the banquet, celebrating violence as a ruler's infallible weapon: "massacres, mourning, fire, deaths" (Stragi, lutto, incendi, e morti). The aria features a trumpet obbligato anticipating Domitian's melody, based on a descending fifth and octave and rapid sixteenth-note coloratura passagework on "armi" (weapons). As we have seen, trumpets were often used during high-table events to announce courses. In this case the trumpet conflates two functions—a call to the table and a topos of war and royalty—as if to suggest the image of a tyrant ready to devour his subjects. After the aria, Domitian orders Arricida to his table. In this first phase of a long and painful aggression, asides are the typical mode of communication. In asides, Arricida declares her hatred for her tyrannical brother-in-law, and he shamelessly announces that he will satisfy his desires against her will (1, 7, "A tuo dispetto appagherò le mie voglie"). After telling her he plans to rape her, he forces the woman to sit at his table, and the banquet begins with a "bizzarra sinfonia."[7]

Arricida understandably has no appetite and does not touch food or drink, which Domitian takes as a rejection of his hospitality. In front of the other guests, he orders her to give him her "sweet mouth" ("porgi la dolce bocca") and to show him her naked breasts ("svelami il seno"). She fights him off, and the virtuous captain Licinio begs the tyrant to show some respect. Domitian kicks him to the ground ("gli dà un calcio rovesciandolo per terra"), pronounces his death sentence, and continues his sexual assault on Arricida, who attempts, unsuccessfully, to leave the table (1, 19).

After this violent episode, Domitian nonchalantly orders sparkling wine. At the sound of a capriccio sung by a castrato, he feels drowsy ("musico canta a capriccio, in questo mentre Domitiano vien preso dal sonno"). The music and text of the "musico" imitate the style and modal flavor of *ottave* improvised by Venetian gondoliers.[8] The song conjures up the great beauty of the breasts and lips of a woman who, by her rejection of the poet, turns the paradisiacal image into an inferno. Unlike Orpheus with Charon, however, the *musico* does not succeed in making the monster/tyrant fall asleep. Like Puccini's Tosca, the female victim defends herself by taking up a table knife and wishing that the tyrant king might sleep forever (dorma sonni di morte un re tiranno). Unlike Tosca's attempt, however, hers fails. Domitian orders soldiers, "Take her to my rooms, where I will vindicate myself with an assault of kisses" (Trahetela a mie stanze / Con assalti di baci / Vendicarò quest'alma). The scene ends with Arricida's rage aria, declaring she intends to defend her virtue to the death. This banquet too ends with a dance of pages clearing the table (*ballo de paggi che levano le mense*). The opera resolves with Vespasian's intervention as a sort of deus ex machina reconciling the two sons fighting against each other, forgiving Domitian, and inviting them to ban hatred from their hearts. The scene climaxes with the appearance of the real deus ex machina, Apollo, presiding over the final dance of the four elements, as if to say that a change in the nature of a tyrant like Domitian is a miracle.

A third tyrant from the Zeno collection of seventeenth-century Venetian operas is Sardanapalus, the title role in Carlo Maderni and Domenico Freschi's 1679 *drama per musica*, who at the end of his dissolute life faces his tragic destiny with courage. In the preface (*argomento*), the librettist Maderni describes Sardanapalus's debauchery vividly: "Sardanapalus, the last king of the Assyrians, was a monster, the most lustful and lascivious of the time." He recounts the peculiar tastes of the libertine king: he particularly liked to dress like a woman while having sex with two maidens at once.[9] This detail, like the overall portrait of this Oriental tyrant, is thanks to Greek historian Diodorus Siculus, who, as one can read in a Venetian edition available at the time of the opera's composition, presents the last Assyrian king as feminine (effemminato), an extravagant ruler who styles his hair and dresses like a concubine (vestito da concubina, vestito et acconcio da bagascia), gesticulates "like a whore" (con gesti di puttana), has forsaken his gender (del sesso suo scordato), and uses aphrodisiac food to stimulate libidinal appetite (con cibi di libidine incentivi).[10] Both the gender and sexuality of Sardanapalus break the established rules and norms of seventeenth-century audiences. He is able to indulge in this behavior thanks to his absolute power.

The first scene of the opera, the prologue (added after the premiere), introduces three deities—Bacchus, Ceres, and Venus—celebrating wine, food, and sex and inviting all the beautiful women in the audience to enjoy pleasure. Considering that the opera was performed during carnival and that the audience was eating and drinking during the opera, the prologue places the audience within the opera's frame. The moral standpoint of the drama is equally ambivalent, as the opera condemns the lascivious tyrant but also invites the audience to take pleasure in life and offers a voyeuristic display of sensuality in scenes of baths, dining halls, and seraglios. The correspondent of the French newspaper *Mercure galant* reported that all four opera theaters active that year in Venice attracted an extraordinary number of viewers, and they singled out *Sardanapalo* for the beauty of its machines, sets, and costumes, which corresponded to the quality of the instruments (la bonté des instruments) and the beauty of the music.[11]

The first scene of the first act conforms to the *argomento*: the king appears cross-dressed, embroidering in the company of young women, who embrace him and praise his youthful, feminine beauty.[12] Given the tessitura and the fact that women were not cast as male rulers, the role was probably interpreted by a castrato (the part of Sardanapalo is notated in the soprano clef). Roger Freitas convincingly demonstrates that at this time "castrati played amorous leading roles not in spite of their physical distinctiveness, but because of it." He explains that "a womanish demeanor in the seventeenth century was considered rather a sign of too great a taste for women" and shows that there was a general belief that excessive sexual activity with women would cause a man to forget his biological gender.[13] Because Sardanapalo is represented as a boy who has not yet turned into a man (the women call him "giovanetto amante," or very young lover, in the opening chorus, 1, 1), his soprano voice is appropriate to express and embody his youth. Like the cross-dressed role of Cherubino in Mozart's *Le nozze di Figaro*, Sardanapalo's soprano voice realistically represents his prepubescence.

A different case of cross-dressing is provided for the old nurse Dirce, who, like all operatic nurses of this time, is interpreted by a tenor to convey old age realistically. To advertise the beauty of her mistress Nicea to Sardanapalo, she tells the king in recitative that her lady is at present stark naked, taking her bath, and sings a G-minor aria comparing the young woman's breasts to cliffs lashed by waves of milk (1, 18, "Le sue poppe son due scogli / Flagellati da un mar di latte"). The images of milk and breasts are fleshed out by repeated, rapid, ascending sixteenth-note scales on "flagellate" (lashed), landing on slower, reiterated quarter notes on "latte" (milk). This aria employs the languid effects of the harmonic minor scale with an ascending G-sharp and descending G-natural; the E-flat produces mild exoticizing effects in proximity to G-sharp. The nurse knows how to choose and mix the ingredients of this metaphoric aphrodisiac, which does not fail to whet the appetite of the lascivious tyrant.

Later in the opera Dirce tells Nicea's lover Baleso, with sadistic pleasure, that Nicea is in her bath with Sardanapalo, who, "like a bee in love, flies onto the breasts of Nicea to harvest the sweet honey of Love from the flower of her beauty."[14] While the dramatis persona is a woman, the singer's persona remains a man, able to empathize with the male gaze. Gender ambiguity and reversals are pervasive in this opera; in addition to Sardanapalo and Dirce, Princess Armisia is represented as a courageous huntress who, after singing a formidable virtuosic hunting aria with trumpets ("Già sfida la tromba," 1.12), kills a wild boar onstage. She donates it to Tersiste, the Moorish slave of her lover, General Arbace. In the accent typical of Italian blackface slaves of the commedia dell'arte tradition, Tersiste rejoices at the idea of eating it half boiled and half roasted (1, 13, "Mi in Palagiu portar, e voler tostu / Mezo alessu mangiar, e mezo arrostu").[15] Later Tersiste claims to adore only Bacchus and the best Brazilian tobacco; only drinking and smoking bring him happiness (2, 17). Tersiste's pipe tobacco makes the fourth wall as blurry as smoke itself, since many in the audience would have known that Assyrians living in the seventh century BCE could not have known about Brazilian goods. The point of this historical inconsistency was to modernize the story, presenting it as something that could possibly happen to the audience.

The final banquet scene (3, 14) is yet another representation of a divisive communal meal. Before the scene begins, the audience has been informed that the king is planning to draw lots to determine which woman will be his wife. He can't choose between Nicea and Armisia, both engaged to other men—Beleso and Arbace—whom he also invites to the banquet just so he can poison them in front of their sweethearts. Armisia, however, has another plan: to instigate a mob rebellion against the tyrant (3, 12). The scene is again filled with asides in which characters plot against each other. As soon as the eunuch slaves serve the food (1, 15), the banquet is interrupted by trumpets announcing not a new course, but a rebellion against Sardanapalo, who abandons the dining table when he hears the warlike sound (1, 16) and orders his palace to be burned. He shows courage, however, by throwing himself into the fire ("qui si getta corraggiosamente tra le fiamme e s'abbruggia"). The last line is given to Armisia, introduced by the trumpets whose sound marked her hunting aria: "This is the way tyrants and libertines end." This banquet later inspired the famous decadent painting by Eugène Delacroix showing Sardanapalus enjoying the slaughter of women as a slave serves him a drink while his enemies are about to burn his palace. The final punishment of the libertine-tyrant at the end of Sardanapalo's supper also anticipates *Don Giovanni*, whose earliest literary sources date from the time of this bizarre seventeenth-century opera.

Don Giovanni the Cannibal

The modern Spanish aristocrat Don Giovanni may appear less exotic than the ancient Assyrian king Sardanapalus. During his final lavish meal, Don Giovanni comments on the savory food prepared by his personal chef: "Ah, what a flavorful dish!" (Ah che piatto saporito). His servant Leporello, however, watching his master eat, responds in an aside with a rhyme that points at his uncivilized, barbaric appetite ("Ah che barbaro appetito!").[16] This two-line exchange locates Don Giovanni's appetite in the liminal zone between civilized aesthetic appreciation (eating for the pleasures of the educated palate) and uncivilized ravenous gratification.

Don Giovanni's appetite for food and for women has been aptly described by Nicholas Chong in his essay on *Don Giovanni*'s "Last Supper" as a "conflation of sexual and gastronomic appetites."[17] I suggest that this conflation leads to a figurative representation of Don Giovanni as a hunter and devourer of women. Don Giovanni's poetic language equates women to food; his use of the refined allegories and metaphors that abound in opera seria represents him both as a civilized poet and as a cannibal.

Cannibals had been synonymous with exotic and barbaric culture since Homer's Polyphemus and Herodotus's anthropophagi. In the age of global exploration, cannibalism was often evoked to denigrate non-Western cultures,[18] but also as an example of alternative refinement.[19] Shirley Lindenbaum argues that in the eighteenth century cannibalism was both repulsive and seductive, sometimes mixed with eroticism.[20] Rogério Budasz illustrates how the encounter of Jesuit missionaries and Brazilian cannibals (the Tupinambà) produced an impressive quantity of early ethnographic discourse in which attraction and repulsion went hand in hand. The missionaries compared the cannibalistic rituals to a "witches' sabbath," but they were also seduced by the beauty of the songs accompanying those barbaric rituals.[21] As Budasz points out, "Jesuits in Brazil were especially worried by the natives' 'bad habits'—drinking fermented *cauim* and engaging in cannibalism, polygamy, and revenge wars—that could hamper the religious and political project of subjecting them to the Catholic Church."[22] Gluttony and lust are therefore deployed in describing the natives in order to suppress and terminate cannibalism, portrayed as a form of moral aberration, but not without acknowledging the seductive quality of the music accompanying cannibalistic rituals.[23]

The conflation of the appetites for food and for sex is not unique to Mozart's *Don Giovanni*, but only in this opera is the libertine represented, figuratively, as a cannibal. Antonio Salieri explored the conflation of food and sex in two operas. Salieri did not miss a single performance of Mozart's *Don Giovanni* in the late 1780s, and ten years later he wrote an opera on Shakespeare's insatiable Falstaff (1798), anticipating Verdi's rendition of the corpulent English libertine.[24] While it is possible that Salieri's inspiration was the success of Mozart's *Don Giovanni*, he had already explored this theme in 1773 when he set Carlo Goldoni's spoken comedy *La locandiera*, in which the astute innkeeper Mirandolina seduces a misogynist by preparing and serving him an exquisite meal.[25] Unlike Falstaff and Don Juan, Goldoni's female seducer is a typical product of the Enlightenment, conferring on both women and the lower classes the opportunity to advance in status through the power of intellect. Perhaps this is why the first Viennese performance of the opera was formally dedicated to women.[26] Mirandolina, like Serpina in Pergolesi's *La serva padrona*, manipulates the appetite of her higher-class male prey: she is a skilled huntress of men. But unlike Serpina, she is financially in control and able to make a living through her own manual and administrative work as a chef and innkeeper. As Maggie Günsberg observes in her study of gender in Goldoni, the comedy "portrays a subversive female character who is not recuperated by patriarchy through remarriage. In other words, her subversion is successful."[27]

As a character, Don Giovanni, unlike Mirandolina, belongs to the tradition of libertine aristocrats of the baroque era. Like the other libertine aristocrats we have encountered so far, he is a late product of the Counter-Reformation, a figure who usually provokes a religious condemnation of aristocratic sin rather than an ethical and secular denunciation of social injustice and ruling-class corruption. Da Ponte and Mozart's version, however, while adopting the religious discourse on sin, also adapts it to the Enlightenment political concerns.[28]

The representation of appetites for sex and food in *Don Giovanni* is deeply rooted in early baroque culture. A comedy by Tirso de Molina, staged in Seville and Naples in the 1620s, already featured an extensive final banquet scene and included as dramatis personae both high-ranking aristocrats and lower-class characters such as fishermen, shepherds, and servants.[29] This comprehensive social microcosm is typical of baroque comedy, akin to Shakespeare's theatrical world, where high and low classes and rhetorical levels coexist onstage while keeping their boundaries (interclass marriages are a taboo). These baroque origins explain why Don Juan presents himself in works of different or ambivalent genres: commedia dell'arte scenarios, Molière's spoken comedy *Don Juan, ou Le festin de Pierre*, and even a heroic opera, *L'empio punito* (the punished rake, Rome 1671), featuring, like *Sardanapalo*, a castrato singer in the role of the aristocratic libertine.[30] The baroque roots of the Don Juan myth remained vigorous well into the eighteenth century. Even after the separation of comic and serious opera genres, *Don Giovanni* librettos retain this ambiguity of genre, oscillating between the comic and the serious and spaces in between, including the pastiche *La pravità castigata* (The castigated depravity, Brno 1734), where Don Giovanni is listed as a *parte seria*); a tragicomedy by Goldoni (*Don Giovanni Tenorio*, Venice 1736); a ballet by Angiolini with music by Christoph Willibald Gluck, *Le festin de Pierre* (Vienna, 1761), featuring a final dance of Furies as in his more famous *Orfeo ed Euridice*; the one-act farce by Giovanni Battista Lorenzi, *Li due gemelli ed il convitato di pietra* (Naples 1783), and finally the metatheatrical version by Giovanni Bertati, *Don Giovanni, o sia Il convitato di pietra* (Venice 1787), which was one of the most direct sources of Da Ponte's libretto. The list of music-dramatic works featuring Don Giovanni is much longer; I selected a small set of examples to show the wide variety of genres and the oscillation and cross-fertilization of seria/buffa genres.[31] All these works condemn Don Giovanni as a sinner. As Anthony DelDonna shows, the 1783 Neapolitan production of Lorenzi's *Li due gemelli ed il convitato di pietra* was heavily based on a commedia dell'arte scenario (Casamarciano), featuring the Pulcinella mask in the role of the libertine's servant. At the end of Lorenzi's version, Don Giovanni confesses and names his carnal sins, though he does not repent. The purpose of this confession, then, is primarily to give the audience a lesson about the spiritual nature of the libertine's vices. He does this after taking part in a banquet by the funeral monument of the Commendatore, who serves him vipers, toads, and other venomous creatures for his final meal: through contrapasso (as in Dante's *Divine Comedy*) his appetite for delicious women is punished by an offering of revolting dishes.[32]

The nature of Don Giovanni's sin can be understood in the frame of the relation between the hunger for sex and the hunger for food in Thomistic theology. Da Ponte, who had been educated for the priesthood, was very familiar with this theological doctrine, as well as with Dante's *Divine Comedy* in his later career as a professor of Italian at Columbia College in New York (now Columbia University), where he also taught Dante.[33] Thomas Aquinas identifies avid desire (*cupiditas*) as the root (*radix*) of all capital sins, together with pride (*superbia*), which is also "inordinate appetite" (*inordinatum appetitum*).[34] While *cupiditas* is generated by "turning to exchangeable goods," *superbia* is "turning away from God."[35] Aquinas groups gluttony and lust together in his exposition of the seven capital sins stemming from *cupiditas* and *superbia* (*inanis gloria*, *invidia*, *ira*, *tristitia*, *avaritia*, *gula*, *luxuria*). Both lust and gluttony are driven by appetite for the good of the body (*bonum corporis*), whose satisfaction causes pleasure. "Without such a pleasure there cannot be any happiness," Aquinas explains, giving credit for this idea to Aristotle's *Nicomachean Ethics* ("Delectatio, sine qua felicitas esse non potest, ut dicitur in I et X *Ethics*, et hanc appetunt gula et luxuria").[36] Unlike such sins as envy or melancholia that are caused by a destructive aversion to good, the desire for food and sex are an attraction to something good and productive, preserving one's biological life as well as the continuity of the species. The fascination with the Don Juan myth has to do with the excitement and fear of crossing the line between good and evil, an archetypical human characteristic defined, since the biblical recounting of Adam and Eve's expulsion from Eden, through the link between food (the forbidden fruit) and sex.[37]

Religion and politics (Aquinas and Plato) converge in Mozart and Da Ponte's *Don Giovanni* in a potentially explosive intersection of Christian morality and revolutionary ethics. While sin fundamentally hurts the sinner by creating a distance from the supreme source of bliss, social injustice shifts attention to the predator's victims. When we take this into consideration, we understand why feminist musicologist Kristi Brown-Montesano in 2017 (at the peak of the Me Too movement) urged operagoers and musicologists to "hold Don Giovanni accountable" for his crimes against women (not for his sins), claiming that "the only way to make *Don Giovanni* worthy of our time, if indeed that is possible at all, is to listen more closely to the women."[38] Yet *Don Giovanni* provides one of the most powerful arguments against the abuse of power not only in interpersonal relations, but in society at large, and banning the opera from our theaters would be eliminating an important arena for reflection on the evil of sexual abuse.

We can also recognize how the character of the libertine is presented as a brute using heightened senses like a beast of prey. Shortly after raping Donna Anna and killing her father, his appetite is awakened by the approach of Donna Elvira: "Shush! I can smell a female" (Zitto: mi pare / Sentir odor di femmina). This puts an abrupt end to his conversation with Leporello, who comments on his master's "perfect sense of smell" (Che odorato perfetto!). The climax of this encounter is Leporello's aria "Madamina il catalogo è questo," where the women his master has conquered are grouped into different "courses" according to geographical origin, social class, body shape, and age. The catalog reads like the menu of a formal banquet. It resembles an earlier catalog aria that lists the courses of a banquet in Giuseppe

Gazzaniga's *La vendemmia* (first performed in 1778). That aria parades an enormous amount of food, mostly game—which is to say, hunted animals turned into food.[39]

In Leporello's aria, the slower pace of the second part breaks with the convention of the buffo bass patter aria, which normally accelerates toward the end. As John Platoff observes, "Instead of musical compression and excitement, there are expansiveness, relaxation and the individualized expression of particular text lines," presenting a "more subtle and truly human comedy."[40] Platoff's point is that Mozart's shift to the slower tempo, a triple-meter andante con moto, seems to invite his audience to pay closer attention to each woman he catalogs: the "gentle blond," "the faithful brunette," "the fat one," "the skinny one," "the tall majestic woman," "the petite one," and so forth. For Don Giovanni, who, figuratively, has just eaten a gargantuan meal, this section of the aria might convey a sense of fatigue. His stomach regains its appetite only at the vivacious setting of "the petite one" (la piccina), repeated nine times in sixteenth notes, contrasting with the longer note values used for the other body types: Don Giovanni can eat nine small ladies, while he can only take in two tall ones (la grande, repeated twice) and one fat lady (la grassotta, not repeated).

Don Giovanni's cannibalistic appetite surfaces again when he meets the farm girl Zerlina at her wedding. In his seduction scene (1, 9), he tells her that, as an aristocrat, he cannot tolerate the thought that her "sugar-sprinkled face" (viso inzuccherato) could be "mauled by a dirty peasant" like her husband. Taking her "fresh and good-smelling fingers" (quelle dituccia candide e odorose), Don Giovanni imagines that he is touching the soft, creamy cheese known as *giuncata* (parmi toccar giuncata). A refined and fashionable contemporary recipe book, *Il cuoco piemontese perfezionato a Parigi* (The Piemontese cook perfected in Paris) recommends pairing creamy cheese with sugar.[41] By pairing Zerlina's "sugar face" with her "creamy cheese fingers," Don Giovanni proves himself a refined eater. The gastronomic signifier becomes a social signifier, telling us he is a civilized gourmet who belongs to the higher class. And yet his figurative desire to eat a human being is a form of cannibalism. Don Giovanni is a cannibal with exquisite taste, like the character Hannibal Lecter in *The Silence of the Lambs*, who confesses, "I ate his liver with some fava beans and a nice Chianti."

Mozart's music for the ensuing duet literalizes the metaphor. Don Giovanni wins over Zerlina in the duettino no. 7, "Là ci darem la mano," in which he desires to take the hand he just touched and smelled, the hand of creamy cheese with sugar on top. In this duet, his advances and her responses are musically staged as a progressive closing of the sonic space between the two. Don Giovanni's first phrase lasts eight measures; Zerlina gains distance by replying with a ten-measure phrase, then loses it, until progressively shorter exchanges end up with overlapping entrances. This compression of space choreographs a hunt where the prey finally falls into the predator's mouth. This particular chase ends with a series of puns: Don Giovanni calls Zerlina "diletto," meaning delightful, with the double entendre "di letto" (good in bed). The sex-food correlation is expanded in the climactic *a due*, "Andiam, andiam mio bene / A ristorar le pene," meaning let's go to calm the pangs [of love]. But *ristorar* also means to feed (from which, "restaurant"), and "pene" is also the Italian word for penis.[42]

At the beginning of the second act, Leporello asks his master to renounce women. Don Giovanni replies, "They are more necessary than the bread I eat" (Lasciar le donne! Sai ch'elle per me / Son più necessarie del pan che mangio). Shortly after this other cannibalistic metaphor, in his canzonetta no. 16 ("Deh vieni alla finestra"), he attempts to seduce Donna Anna's maid with music by singing to her, "You, who have a sweeter mouth than honey, who have sugar in the middle of your heart" (Tu ch'hai la bocca dolce più che il mele / Tu che il zucchero porti in mezzo al core). These lines belong to the last stanza of the strophic song: it is the climatic expression of cannibalistic desire. Turning women into food is turning them from humans into commodities. Kenneth Bendiner interprets representations of food in art, especially when food is a metaphor for sex, precisely in terms of "fetishism," as "a replacement of a living subject by an inanimate object," reminding us that in Marx's socioeconomic theory of power relations and in Freud's psychoanalytic theory of sexual relations, "fetishism is a means of control."[43] The only women Don Giovanni compares to food are in fact lower-class women: a farm girl and a maid. They are women at the bottom of the social food chain. The opera therefore labels as uncivilized a social system where social predators can hunt down vulnerable people, turn them into things, and even consume them for their own pleasure.

The Bait

Don Giovanni uses food, wine, and music as bait to seduce, or rather to hunt. The two aspects are related: he uses food to hunt, and he hunts to consume his prey. Because of his unquenchable desire, though, he constantly risks falling into his own traps. The final and lethal bait is his dinner invitation to the Commendatore he murdered and his acceptance in return of the ghost's invitation to dine in the netherworld.

The first time Don Giovanni uses food as bait is at the wedding of Zerlina and Masetto (1, 8), when he offers them his protection as a feudal lord. On this occasion he orders Leporello to take the farmers to his palace and give them "chocolate, coffee, wines, hams" (cioccolatte, caffè, vini, prosciutti). He chooses the bait carefully, items that are high in quality and status, but not too refined for peasants' palates. Most of all, he wants them to be served plenty of wine. Leporello, in his report to Don Giovanni on how he executed the orders (1, 15), recounts, using the present tense to evoke the events most vividly, "I make sure they all have drinks, both men and women: they are already half drunk, some are singing, some are joking, others keep drinking." Excited by the report, Don Giovanni resolves to carry on with his baiting strategy, launching his first-act aria 11, the "champagne aria."

Edward Dent maintains that "Fin ch'han dal vino" is called the "champagne aria" because of an obsolete "wrong" performance tradition in German countries of staging Don Giovanni holding a glass of champagne while singing. Dent observes that "there is nothing whatever in the words to suggest that Don Giovanni himself is drinking at this moment."[44] In other words, representing Don Giovanni drinking would be as absurd as representing a fisherman eating the bait off his own hook. Indeed, Da Ponte's text makes it clear that Don Giovanni's intention is to make others drunk, not himself:

Fin ch'han dal vino
Calda la testa
Una gran festa
Fà preparar.
Se trovi in piazza
Qualche ragazza
Teco ancor quella
Cerca menar.
Senza alcun ordine
La dama sia
Chi 'l minuetto
Chi la follia,
Chi l'aleman[n]a
Farai ballar.

[As long as they have wine
heating their heads,
make ready for them
a big carouse.
If in the piazza
you run into any girl,
that one too
you must bring in.
Regardless of rank,
she shall be a dance partner.
You will let them dance:
some the minuet,
some the folia,
some the allemande.[45]

Ed io fra tanto	In the meantime,
Dall'altro canto	in some remote corner,
Con questa, e quella	with this one and that one,
Vo amoreggiar.	I want to make love.
Ah la mia lista	Ah to my catalog,
Doman mattina	tomorrow morning,
D'una decina	ten items at the least
Devi aumentar.	you must add.
(*Partono*).	(*Exeunt*).]

Although Dent is right to observe that the words do not suggest that Don Giovanni is drinking, the music tells a different story, which might actually justify the performance tradition of representing Don Giovanni holding a wineglass while singing this piece. I agree with Hermann Abert, who observes that in this aria "the whole sensual atmosphere intoxicates him in advance,"[46] but I would stress that the intoxication Mozart dramatizes musically is primarily the one caused by wine. It is worth noticing that while Da Ponte writes five-syllable lines, *quinari piani*, with a stable and steady rhythmic pattern combining dactylic (´_ _) and trochaic (´_) feet, Mozart upsets this pattern by setting the first two piano lines as dactyls and treating the ending of the verso piano (´_) as a limping *sdrucciolo* (´_ _). He does not do the same for the third line, giving the melody a sense of irregularity, increased by the different widths of the intervals between the two eighth notes, causing a hiccup effect on "vino" and "testa" and, in the woodwind and first violin parts, by the alternation of grace notes and trills. The musical hiccup or stumble represents Don Giovanni as already under the influence of alcohol.[47] That Mozart conceived "Fin ch'han dal vino" as a bacchic, orgiastic dance-song is clear from the tonal plan, which begins with a monotonous reiteration of the tonic in the bass, giving it an exotic flavor. Don Giovanni, who has already been culturally exoticized by representing him as a cannibal, is further exoticized in this song by representing him as a bacchant. The initial tonal stability is compromised by the chromatic descent in Don Giovanni's line as he tells Leporello to bring to the party every girl he meets in the public square ("ancor quella cerca menar"). *Menare* means to lead forcefully, or even to beat up or to manhandle, but it also had the "totally obscene meaning" (significato assolutamente osceno) of "to masturbate," according to a definition in the 1763 edition of the vocabulary of the Crusca Academy.[48] In the opera, the chromatic line on "menare" reveals that Don Giovanni is drunk with sexual desire, possibly fueled by onanistic fantasies. From this moment to the end of the opera, the plot unfolds as a tragic comedy: because of his unrestrained appetite for both the prey and the bait, a hunter falls into his own trap.

In the first-act finale, Don Giovanni continues to use food and drink to seduce, and to rape when seduction attempts fail, dangerously pushing his luck. The finale begins with a rhyme between "testa" (head) and "festa" (party), creating a subliminal link between loss of reason and the carnival-like festive celebration. Masetto, having forgiven Zerlina for flirting with the libertine aristocrat, admits that "we men are just weak-minded" (siamo pure deboli di testa). Immediately after, we hear Don Giovanni offstage, issuing orders to prepare everything for a grand party ("sia preparato tutto a una gran festa").

The entire stretched-out finale presents a continual movement away from the key of C major, associated with Don Giovanni's festive mode, the home key area where Don Giovanni weaves his web. Masetto is the first to bring the key to the dominant, while protesting that he does not want to hide from the libertine as his wife tells him to; he suspects that Zerlina wants to flirt with the Don. Don Giovanni's entrance is marked by an explosion of C-major sound with full wind fanfares, including trumpets and timpani, reestablishing the tonic. Don Giovanni wakes everyone from their wine-soaked slumber, only to invite them to have more and enjoy the wonderful refreshments (gran rinfreschi). He repeats the order in patter, a stereotypically comic text delivery, cementing the association of food and comedy, which makes him a fully embodied character regardless of his high social status.

Zerlina resists Don Giovanni in the next scene of the finale (1, 18), a seductive andante modulating to the pastoral F major with foregrounded lines in the woodwinds. We might expect a second capitulation, as happened in the similar duet "Là ci darem la mano," but this time the encounter is interrupted by the entrance of Masetto, moving away from the C-major trap. The Don's hunting does not stop here, though. He modulates back to C as he deploys music, along with food, as part of the bait. After a long section in which Donna Elvira, Don Ottavio, and Donna Anna steer far from Don Giovanni's tonal area, the refreshments are served to the accompaniment of music (1, 20). In the festive allegro, Don Giovanni and Leporello encourage the guests to drink and eat, anticipating that the girls will go crazy ("Tornerete a far presto le pazze"), ordering more coffee, hot chocolate, and sorbets as stimulants (Don Giovanni: "Ehi Caffè!" [*waiters bring in refreshments*] Leporello: "Cioccolatte!" Don Giovanni: "Sorbetti!"). As the refreshments are served, Masetto fears the worst: Don Giovanni fondles Zerlina while her husband "looks at them fuming."

The section leads back from E-flat to the bright C major in a passage that momentarily brings together friends and enemies, oppressors and oppressed in a boisterous hymn to freedom: "Viva la libertà!" Commentators have offered differing opinions about this passage. John Rosselli thinks "Libertà" hints at libertinism; Charles Rosen thinks it evoked political freedom in the revolutionary climate of the late 1780s. Robbins Landon sees it as Mozart's "tribute to Joseph II," Nicholas Till claims "libertà" refers to the "bourgeois individualist's quest for liberty," while Hermann Abert hears it as "bitter irony."[49] Perhaps "Viva la libertà" also refers to liberality with food, as the rhyme "libertà—generosità" suggests. After all, Don Giovanni provided generous refreshments at this party, as we have seen. I am not suggesting one reduce Mozart's majestic music to a thank-you card for being invited to the party; rather I think the musical hyperbole of the hymn is a conflagration of very different colliding desires and emotions.

The libertine tells two onstage bands to resume playing ("Ricominciate il suono"), instructing Leporello to form up the couples for the dance while he attempts even more forcefully to seduce Zerlina. In a passage that Abert understandably defines as a "contrapuntal masterpiece,"[50] Mozart superimposes different dances corresponding to styles appealing to guests of different social classes: a minuet for the aristocrats, a contradance and allemande for the lower classes, carrying out Don Giovanni's plan to vary the dances, as announced in the "champagne aria" ("chi 'l minuetto, / chi la follia / chi l'allemanna"). The scene ends with a rape attempt ("while dancing, he leads Zerlina near a door and tries to force her through"). She screams ("Scellerato!" Scoundrel!) in a tonally and rhythmically unstable section reaching keys distant from the tonic, along with tempestuous tremolos, crescendos, and all the orchestral forces unleashing chaos.[51] The rape of Zerlina, however, becomes yet another coitus interruptus as the other aristocratic characters catch the Don at it and comment that he is falling into his own trap ("L'iniquo da se stesso / nel laccio se ne va"). The only way out is to run away from his own party. The first-act finale closes on the tonic C major as the final chorus of his enemies declares that now "everything is clear" about the abuser's identity ("Tutto, tutto già si sa"), warning Don Giovanni that "the entire world will know of your horrendous crime" and "the lightning of vengeance will fall on your head."

In act 2, Don Giovanni plants his last bait by the tomb of the dead Commendatore (2, 11). After Leporello reads the inscription on the gravestone, promising a vendetta against the man who killed him, Don Giovanni jokingly asks Leporello to invite the Commendatore for dinner ("O vecchio buffonissimo! / digli che questa sera / l'attendo a cenar meco"). The ensuing dinner invitation duet dramatizes the mixture of comedy and horror, with the scared servant hearing the dead man's ghostly voice, the master threatening the servant with his sword, and the statue nodding to accept the invitation (a stage direction that Mozart was careful to indicate in the autograph score).[52] Alessandra Campana singles out this number, where the "visual register" is extremely relevant, to make a point about the importance of staging and acting in eighteenth-century opera, observing that "the Commendatore's nod is also the utmost performative utterance: an 'I do' that ends up being of a certain consequence." As Campana explains, this invitation to supper inaugurates a significant expansion of "the theatrical scope of the opera . . . to encompass supernatural events."[53]

The Libertine Supper

Both *Don Giovanni* and *Sardanapalo* end with a banquet where the libertine protagonist is seated at a lavish table eating a formal meal with an onstage band playing table music—as in a convivial ritual at the highest level. In both cases the banquet scene ends with the tyrant-libertine engulfed and roasted by flames. Unlike Sardanapalo, who sits at the table with his prospective lovers, Don Giovanni eats by himself. For this and other reasons, theologian Steffen Lösel sees Don Giovanni's last meal as a reversal of Christ's Last Supper.[54] Both suppers convey meanings that transcend the reality of the meal itself but could be expressed only at the dinner table, through a ritual of consumption and through gastronomic signs, such as wine or bread, charged with symbolic value.

As in the first-act finale, Don Giovanni's second-act banquet opens with triumphant music celebrating the joy of eating and the conviviality of the event. Woodwinds, trumpets, and horns open with a fanfare of dotted rhythms suggesting the nobility of the occasion. Nobility, however, is almost immediately marred by Don Giovanni's line about the money he spends for his own pleasure ("Già che spendo i miei danari / Io mi voglio divertir"), since no noble character, especially in opera, can mention money without compromising social status.[55]

The *Tafelmusik*, played by an onstage band of woodwinds and cello, has received considerable scholarly attention, primarily because of its meta-operatic quality. The band plays excerpts from popular operas of the time:

Vincente Martín y Soler's *Una cosa rara*, Giuseppe Sarti's *Fra i due litiganti il terzo gode*, and Mozart's own opera *Le nozze di Figaro*. Nicholas Chong has effectively rejected Dent's opinion that the three quoted excerpts have no meaning. Expanding on Daniel Heartz's intuition about the significance of these quotations and borrowing from Christopher Reynolds's theory of musical allusions, Chong explores a rich and intricate network of intertextual associations.[56] For example, the excerpt from *Cosa rara* alludes to a dramatic representation of a royal hunting party, and the specific quotation is from the aria "Come un agnello" (like a lamb), ending with the line "a dente asciutto / lei resterà" (she will remain with an empty mouth), which Chong relates to "Don Giovanni's indifference towards Leporello, whose mouth is literally empty while his master feasts." On a different level, the first line could have a religious meaning, related to Christ as sacrificial lamb (another possible reference to the Last Supper), which Heartz associates with Don Giovanni and Allanbrook associates with Donna Elvira.[57] The allusions would have been lost on people who did not recognize the operas or had no recollection of their texts or the dramatic situations. Yet they can still clarify paths of signification that are latent in the action represented onstage. As in a Renaissance iconography of the Last Supper, no detail is meaningless, including what appears to be purely ornamental.[58]

Like Christ's Last Supper, Don Giovanni's last meal is a homosocial event. This is understandable, considering that Jesus's last meal is eaten with his closest associates. In the case of the Spanish womanizer, it seems so out of place that modern directors often cast women as supernumeraries, going against the prescriptions of the libretto (as happened, for example, in the 2011 Met production directed by Michael Grandage). However, according to the libretto, no woman is present before Donna Elvira's unexpected, stormy entrance and after she leaves. All the characters and servants mentioned in the stage directions of act 2, scene 13, are male (Don Giovanni, Leporello, *suonatori* [male musicians], *servi* [male servants], and the Commendatore).

In modern psychology the Don Giovanni syndrome has been constructed as a compulsive search for sexual pleasure that cannot be fulfilled with women. In the 1950s, when homosexuality was considered a pathology, a study published in a journal of psychiatric illnesses presented Don Juan as a clinical case of repressed homosexuality whose womanizing results from a thwarted search for erotic pleasure in women.[59] The author of this clinical study, Lewis Robbins, defines Don Giovanni as an "incarnation of perverse sensuality," offering the case of a patient affected by a similar personality disorder. The patient recounted that he knew he disappointed his parents by not being born a girl; from age thirteen to twenty-three he drank and masturbated excessively, and in the next year he became an even heavier drinker and an incorrigible womanizer who enjoyed seducing his friends' wives. Finally he was hospitalized for "manic depressive psychosis," and in the mental institution he derived narcissistic pleasure from recounting his numerous affairs. After months of psychoanalysis and the "gradual breaking down of many characterological defenses," Dr. Robbins reports, "his dreams revealed strong latent homosexual tendencies and marked anal sadistic and particularly extreme narcissistic traits." He eventually confessed his "doubts about his masculinity" until "he finally realized that his sexual affairs were not unlike masturbation, in that he had little interest in the woman." Within the frame of Freudian psychoanalysis, the diagnosis is a textbook case of the Oedipus complex:

> It became clearer that the nucleus of this patient's conflict lay in his desire to possess his mother in an oral incorporative fashion. . . . Two solutions offered themselves to this dilemma: to displace the desire for the mother onto other married women, and, by the mechanism of incorporation, to ally himself with strong figures, and through a sort of psychological cannibalism obtain their potency. Thus was seen a man constantly in search of two things, the attainment of one of which resulted in the frustration of the other, and so the drama repeated itself endlessly, just as in Mozart's *Don Giovanni*.[60]

Thirty years after this clinical study of what we might call the Don Giovanni syndrome, Wendy Allanbrook thought that the last-act "finale reduces the dissolute life to a figurative onanism."[61] The diagnosis of Don Giovanni as homosexual or onanist (or both) is an attempt, typical of the twentieth century, to medicalize Don Giovanni's deviant sexual behavior as pathology. This type of discourse, Michel Foucault maintains, is a positivistic equivalent and replacement of the Catholic diagnosis of sin within the practice of confession. A Counter-Reformation opera can easily become a Freudian opera. According to Foucault, both Catholic examination of conscience leading to confession and Freudian psychoanalysis leading to psychotherapy deploy a technology of power aimed at marginalizing excess or deviation from what the system assumes, axiomatically, to be the "natural" norm (the heterosexual cisgender sexual attraction for the purpose of reproduction within the institution of marriage). The purpose is to constrain or repress "peripheral sexualities" ("perversions"), thus preventing them from undermining the normative purpose of sexuality. In this context Foucault writes specifically about "the prestige of Don Juan, which three centuries have not erased," revealing how "underneath the great violator of the rules of marriage—stealer of wives, seducer of virgins, the shame of families, and an insult to husbands and fathers—another personage can be glimpsed: the individual driven, in spite of himself, by the somber madness of sex. Underneath the libertine, the pervert."[62]

Contrasting with the critical tradition of interpreting Don Giovanni as a sinner or pervert is a critical tradition that we may call "beyond good and evil." This tradition promoted admiration for Don Giovanni as a Nietzschean *Übermensch*, a superior heroic and erotic man embracing the pleasures and joys of life and loathing egalitarianism, free to use and abuse women or any vulnerable class of people. In Frits Noske's words, the tyrant-libertine is a superman, "an existentialist hero *avant la lettre*," "a man who tries for total freedom," "freedom that can only be realized by obtaining total power."[63] The root of the tradition conferring heroic status on Don Giovanni is in the thought of the nineteenth-century philosopher Søren Kierkegaard, who explored a teleological suspension of the ethical in search of those truths that belong to the realm of aesthetics. In his reflection on Mozart's *Don Giovanni* in *Either-Or*, Kierkegaard eludes the theology of sin, presenting the libertine as the highest embodiment of what he calls the "spirit of sensuality." For Kierkegaard, Cherubino in *Le nozze di Figaro* represents the first stage of the spirit of sensuality: "the awakening of desire as dreaming." Papageno occupies the middle stage, which is "desire as seeking," a form of searching and growing, both physically and spiritually. Don Giovanni represents the third and final stage of the spirit of sensuality: "desire as pure desiring." This stage can be best expressed in music, which can overcome the limits of language to express yearning at a transcendental level.[64] In Mladen Dolar's opinion, Kierkegaard's "idea of music attains its completion in the idea of Don Juan" because "the inherently erotic quality of music is seductive and ephemeral."[65] Yet the erotic quality of the music expresses desire in itself, unbound and detached from the object of desire. In Carl Dahlhaus's opinion, Kierkegaard's idea of music in the case of Mozart's *Don Giovanni* is akin to Edward Hanslick's idea of "absolute music," of music expressed in an unmediated way.[66] This critical tradition presents Don Giovanni as a heroic aesthetician whose desire is no longer an appetite for material, consumable goods but a longing that transcends physicality, transfiguring sensuality into pure beauty, detached from the objects of desire. In this perspective Don Giovanni appears more idealistic than rapacious, more saint than sinner, more of a mystic than a cannibal, an idealist aesthetician rather than a predator on human flesh. No wonder Brown-Montesano denounces the idealizing of Don Giovanni's aesthetic experience, reminding us that nothing can redeem a rapist with an unquenchable thirst for power.[67]

When we direct our attention back to the representation of food, we see that Don Giovanni's aesthetic mission is not absolute or pure, but a deployment of power. Don Giovanni is hungry for real food, as Leporello observes when he sees him devouring his lonely meal. Giovanni's appetite is "barbaric." The food or wine he chooses may well appear to be informed by gastronomic taste—an aesthetic concern—but it is deployed as an assertion of hierarchical power. As we will see in the next chapter, taste and social class are strictly linked. For example, Don Giovanni expresses appreciation for the "eccellente Marzimino." In eighteenth-century Europe, only the upper classes had the privilege or the culture to appreciate, recognize, and compare wines and to buy a specific appellation. The boasting about luxury food widens the gap between the aristocratic libertine and his starving servant Leporello, who, like Zerlina, is at the bottom of the social food chain. During the dinner scene, the servant faints from hunger while watching his master eat ("mi par proprio di svenir")—at least until Leporello steals a piece of pheasant.

Pheasant is the second gastronomic signifier denoting class, since the aristocracy had the exclusive privilege of hunting wild animals on their lands. In iconography, the representation of game meat is always associated with luxury, the privilege of aristocracy, as well as with war and battlefield violence.[68] At banquets pheasant was often served with its colorful feathers on, making it beautiful and easily recognizable onstage. By eating this aristocratic food, Leporello ingests the signifier of aristocracy—a revolutionary act of proletarian expropriation. The gesture echoes Leporello's lines from the very beginning of the opera about his wretched status as a servant, "eating bad food and sleeping badly" (mangiar male e mal dormir). By eating pheasant he fulfills, at least fleetingly, his wish to lead the life of a gentleman and serve no more ("voglio fare il gentiluomo / E non voglio più servir"). Pressed by his master, he finally confesses, "your chef is so excellent that I wanted to try it." By putting an emphasis on the chef's art, Leporello confers nobility on his own appetite, redefining it as good taste and contrasting it to the barbaric appetite of his master.

The third gastronomic social classifier is the table music that represents opera itself, since only well-to-do people could afford to attend opera performances. In Michel-Barthélémy Ollivier's painting *The Supper of Prince de*

Conti at the Temple (1766), musicians providing live table music and hounds (representing hunting) signify the privileges of the aristocracy.[69] After the table music starts, it is Leporello who listens and recognizes the opera excerpts played by the onstage band. His lines are "bravi! *Cosa rara!*," "Evvivano *I litiganti*," and "questa poi la conosco purtroppo" (unfortunately I know this too well), referring to "Non più andrai" from *Le nozze di Figaro*. Remarkably, these lines appear in Mozart's autograph score but not in the original libretto. In other words, Leporello seizes and enjoys the type of music and food meant for the upper classes. By adding Leporello's line to his autograph score, Mozart acknowledges that the lower classes can be competent consumers of opera. Mozart is telling us that opera should be not a luxury item, but an essential nutrient. I experienced the truth of Mozart's insight myself when I had a chance to teach classes on *Don Giovanni* to students in prison. Some of the negative reactions I received in person and online, especially those against the idea of 'imposing' Mozart's opera on people who are typically excluded from this form of art, made me realize that even today many people find it harder to accept Leporello's taste for pheasant and opera than Don Giovanni's taste for human flesh.[70]

The table music excerpts are also meta-operatic references cracking the fourth wall, creating an intersection between the stage and real life. Mozart's addition of Leporello's reply—"unfortunately I know this one too well"—is self-referential, and for a moment it offers a glimpse of Mozart's empathy for and identification with Leporello and the lower classes. Similarly self-referential is Da Ponte's line for Don Giovanni, "eccellente Marzimino," which refers to wine from Da Ponte's native province, Trentino.[71] The latter associates Da Ponte with Don Giovanni and reveals how the conflation of food and sex was rooted in the librettist's own experience. In his *Memorie*, Da Ponte recounts that he wrote *Don Giovanni* at the same time as he was writing librettos for Martín y Soler and Salieri—and that he did so while drinking, eating, using tobacco (probably as snuff), and flirting with a young girl. He sets the stage first, as he would do in a libretto of an opera:

> A little bottle of "Tockai" on the right, the inkwell in the middle, and a box of Seville tobacco on the left. A beautiful sixteen-year-old girl (whom I would have preferred to love as a daughter, but . . .) was living in the house with her mother, who was taking care of the family, and she came to my room every time I rang a bell, which to tell you the truth, I rang very often, especially when I felt my poetic inspiration was cooling

> down. She was bringing me now a cookie, now a cup of coffee, or nothing but her beautiful face, always gay, always smiling and made precisely to inspire poetic inventions and witty ideas. . . . Sometimes she would sit by me without moving, without opening her mouth, without even blinking. She would stare at me intensely, lightly smiling, sometimes sighing, almost on the verge of crying. In short, this girl was my Calliope for those three operas and then for all the poetry I wrote during the following six years. At first I allowed her to visit me often. Finally I had to allow her visits less often, not to waste too much time in tender amorous fondling, at which she was an expert. The first day, between the "Tockai," the Seville tobacco, the coffee, the bell ringing, and the young muse, I wrote the first two scenes of *Don Giovanni*, two more of *L'arbore di Diana*, and more than half of the first act of *Tarar.*[72]

Don Giovanni's last meal not only bridges real life and theater, it also spans the world of the living and the world of the dead. To do so effectively, Don Giovanni is represented as fully embodied and immersed in his material existence, in contrast first to Donna Elvira and then to the Commendatore. When Donna Elvira interrupts his meal, she does so by singing in a less realistic style, using stretched-out notes and coloratura passages pleading for her lover's redemption by asking him to "change your life" (as in "che vita cangi"), intoning the word "vita" on an E-natural in the key of B-flat major, a tone that destabilizes the home key as it propels us instead toward the dominant through its applied leading tone. As in the act 1 finale, we hear Don Giovanni struggling to bring the music back to the tonic: down to earth where he fully belongs. In the episode with Donna Elvira in the last act, it happens on the phrase "let me eat" (lascia ch'io mangi). Even more forcefully, Mozart grounds Don Giovanni's praise of women and wine as men's nourishment ("Vivan le femmine, / Viva il buon vino, / sostegno [e] gloria / d'umanità") by writing a syllabic melody that emphasizes the accent distribution of the *sdrucciolo* line, and by setting the whole phrase as a clear drop from dominant to tonic. The tonic continues to exert its gravity in the final *a tre* with Donna Elvira pronouncing her final judgment that Don Giovanni has "a heart of stone if he has a heart at all." Lösel reads this line as a biblical allusion (Ezekiel 11:19, 36:26) to Pharaoh's hardened heart.[73] This line also provides a thematic allusion to the impending entrance of the man of stone. This episode, in fact, leads directly to it: Donna Elvira exits with a scream of horror as she runs into the walking statue. At this point Mozart dissolves the tonic through bold dissonances (G-sharp and B-natural leading to A and C against the B-flat in the bass) with her scream on A-flat against the bass raising chromatically from B-flat to B-natural.

As the Commendatore enters (2, 15), Mozart shifts to a different level of reality, crossing a bridge from the world of the living to the netherworld. Here we hear again the music of the overture. Hermann Habert warns us that it is misleading to hear the overture as program music introducing the final entrance of the stone guest; rather, Mozart uses this music twice "to symbolize the same otherworldly power" by means of "disembodied images" that "lack the tangible, three-dimensional reality."[74] The difference between the overture and the opening of 2, 14 is that in the latter the Commendatore starts not with the same grounded, funereal sonority of D minor, but rather with an unstable sonority: a shockingly dissonant and tonally ambivalent diminished chord (B-natural in the bass, F–G-sharp–D in the high-register strings and flute). Notwithstanding the dramatic slowing of the tempo from the molto allegro of the previous section to andante (evoking the slow pace of a funeral march), tonal grounding dissolves as the orchestra's full-throated diminished chord leads to a dominant seventh that resolves through a chromatic ascent of the bass (C-sharp–D). The latter is led to resolution in the doom-laden key of D minor by the unaccompanied vocal line of the Commendatore, which lands the name *Don Giovanni* on the minor tonic, hence burying him on his tonal ground. As the tonal resolution arrives, the continual syncopation in the accompaniment counteracts the gravitational force of the downbeats. The first violin line also undermines the D-minor tonic through uncanny insistence on "other" tones (E and G-sharp) using a dominant chord with a major seventh, unwilling to fall and resolve on the tonic, but rather lifting, rising to the otherworld. Don Giovanni then tells Leporello to bring another "supper" (cena) for his guest, who stops the order (ferma) on a diminished chord. Accompanied by shimmering tremolos in the upper strings, the Commendatore explains, hyperbolically and unrealistically stretching out syllables, that "those who eat heavenly food do not eat mortal food" (Non si pasce di cibo mortale / Chi si pasce di cibo celeste).[75] At this point the second-violin sixteenth-note scales start spiraling, chromatically rising toward the "cibo celeste" over the dematerializing tremolos. Scott Burnham convincingly describes this passage in terms of "uncanny" and "liminal experience," concluding that "Mozart's opera stages this juxtaposition of supernatural time and human time, stages the boundaries between Giovanni's now (his No to past and future), and the Commendatore's Always."[76] It is also possible that instead of a juxtaposition, Mozart is setting the table for an encounter.[77] The Commendatore, in a tense, chromatically ascending passage that switches from *decasillabi* to *settenari*, invites Don Giovanni to dine with him: "You invited me to dinner, now you know your duty, answer to me: will you now come to dine with me?") (tu m'invitasti a cena, / il tuo dover or sai, / rispondimi, verrai /tu a cenar meco?) Don Giovanni accepts, notwithstanding Leporello's pleas. He resolves ("ho già risolto") while tonally resolving on a C-major chord, the sonority of his first feast in the act 1 finale. The paradox is that Don Giovanni accepts on his own terms by refusing to repent. This refusal brings back a harmonic tension expressing disharmony at a cosmic, spiritual level, the missed chance of participating in the feast of celestial food for those who refuse to renounce mortal food.

Don Giovanni's perception of his damnation after he touches the cold hand of the statue is literally a gut reaction. He asks, "Who is twisting my guts?" (Chi m'agita le viscere?), a reminder that his attachment to the lower body and its appetite persists and weighs him down. In the libretto for Vienna in summer 1787, revised following the Prague premiere earlier the same year, stage directions describe Don Giovanni as being swallowed by the earth (*Don Giovanni resta inghiottito dalla terra*).[78] It is worth remembering that the embodied characters Bakhtin finds in comic realism never untie "the umbilical cord which tied them to the fruitful womb of the earth" and that their death is therefore "devoid of all tragic or terrifying overtones."[79] As we saw in chapter 5, Monteverdi represented the regeneration of Ulysses into a new hero by causing him to be swallowed by the earth: Ceres's "creative grave," in Bakhtin's words.[80]

In the happy ending of the Prague production, after Leporello announces that he is going back to the tavern to find a better master ("Ed io vado all'osteria / A trovar padron miglior"), he and the other lower-class comic characters, Masetto and Zerlina, wish for Don Giovanni's resting place to remain with Pluto and Proserpina, daughter of Ceres the earth goddess ("Resti dunque quel birbon / Con Proserpina e Pluton"). The divine comedy of this ending lies in the proclamation that justice is restored when the insatiable appetite of the earth, Ceres's grave, swallows and digests an insatiable tyrant and libertine.

CHAPTER SEVEN

Indulging in Comic Opera

Gastronomy as Identity

In comic opera, characters are, or wish to be, what they eat. Gastronomic signs define identity in terms of nationality, ethnicity, class, and gender. During the Enlightenment, when comic opera became an independent genre of great international appeal, representations of nourishment became embedded in discourses about wealth and health. I will begin by exploring the tenuous link between national opera traditions and national cuisines, then move to stronger and more meaningful uses of gastronomic signifiers to represent identity within the fictional worlds of operas. Oppositions between vegetables and meat or healthy and unhealthy foods started to shape a modern eating culture, a world where people were more willing and more able to choose what to eat and what to be. Eating habits began to position the subject in society in a complex transactional and fluid grid where gender, ethnicity, class, and education informed what ended up on one's plate.

National Traditions and Ethnic Gastronomies

Distinctive national culinary traditions did not emerge until the nineteenth century, when mass ethnic immigration, the rise of modern restaurants, and the production of national cookbooks contributed to codifying national and regional cuisines.[1] Food historian Massimo Montanari shows that (with the exception of macaroni, already identified with Italy in the Middle Ages), the formation of a comprehensive Italian gastronomic identity began in the late nineteenth century because of two main factors: first, Italian immigration to other countries (mostly the Americas), hence the perception of "Italian food" as ethnic cuisine outside Italy; and second, a cultural-political plan to manufacture a pan-national cuisine after the unification of Italy. The invention of Italian cuisine was engineered by Pellegrino Artusi, who produced the first Italian cuisine cookbook.[2] As we saw in chapter 2, Renaissance cuisine, in Italy and elsewhere, was in fact an eclectic mixture of national and supranational cuisine in which invention was more valued than tradition or authenticity.

Whereas European culinary practices were dominated by French international cuisine, national operatic traditions were superseded by a pervasive presence of Italian opera. Yet distinctive national opera traditions started to emerge or to consolidate.[3] The intersection between opera and cuisine is revealing. When we look at operas produced in various European nations, we observe a complex interplay between the nationalities represented onstage and local culinary cultures.

Mozart's Viennese singspiel, *Die Zauberflöte*, as we have seen, features gastronomic references to the Middle East and America. Papageno's diet—"wine, sugar loaves [*Zuckerbrot*], and sweet figs"—alludes not only to distant places (American sugar plantations, Middle Eastern dried fruit), but also to local foods (wine) and hybrids: *Zuckerbrot* was associated with American sugar plantations but was also recognizable as a local dessert. In another German *komische Operette*, *Der Bassa von Tunis*, familiar gastronomic signs are used to denote otherness: satire is produced by representing Muslims breaking their own dietary restrictions by drinking wine. This is not, however, a purely anti-Muslim stance;[4] smuggling wine from Christian countries to Muslim lands was a lucrative business, comparable to the black market in alcohol in the United States during Prohibition.[5]

In French *opéra-comique*, eating and drinking scenes or references are present in more than sixty librettos featuring Harlequin, the popular stock character from the commedia dell'arte. In his history of public theater in eighteenth-century Paris, Henry Lagrave writes that "no character is allowed to eat onstage, with the exception of Harlequin, for whom eating is one of his usual occupations."[6] The earliest opera we encounter in the ten-volume anthology *Le théâtre de la foire, ou L'opéra-comique* is *Arlequin roi de Sérandib* (1713). In it, Harlequin has been crowned king of the fantastic Oriental kingdom of Sérandib and makes his second-act entrance wearing a turban and carrying a wine bottle, accompanied by a cook. In his ensuing aria, Harlequin reassures the cook that he is very happy with his "ragout" and potatoes, and that he intends to double the number of the meals he eats daily; after the aria, the head eunuch brings him another bottle.[7] The French stew ("ragout") and wine Harlequin enjoys might seem to characterize this Italian play, popular in France, as French, but in fact French cuisine was the European standard at the time, and ragout was a staple in many countries. As sociologist Priscilla Ferguson puts it, French cuisine can be defined "as at once national and cosmopolitan."[8] Thus Harlequin is not "Oriental," notwithstanding his costume, and a comic effect is produced by the misfit of the character in the exotic world he is supposed to rule. Indeed, in the eighteenth century, foreign kings ruling occupied countries were no rarity: witness the many Italian states ruled by French, Austrian, and Spanish monarchs and the increasing number of colonies outside Europe. The subtle satire could be extended to the concept of alienation of the sovereign from his subjects. Harlequin is related to the commedia dell'arte role of Zanni, constantly eating and always hungry. Harlequin, however, is less of a stereotype: he is represented in hugely different situations, power positions, and places.[9] The fortunes of Harlequin in the Enlightenment are symptomatic of a trend to represent social identity in flux.

There were strong connections between French and English comic opera, as Daniel Heartz postulated in relation to John Gay's popular ballad opera *The Beggar's Opera*. Vanessa Rogers added considerable evidence of these bonds, including the French source of Gay's drinking song "Fill every glass, for wine inspires us." In the drinking and tavern scenes, satire about chocolate and coffeehouses reflects eighteenth-century convivial culture in England, which, like the rest of Europe, looked to France as an international model of good taste.[10] In this case too, representations of national practices merge with international taste and sensibility.

In Spanish tonadillas, local culinary culture is also recognizable alongside the ever-present French cuisine. Elisabeth Le Guin, in her study of the genre, shows that snacks were served during performances, and food was evoked or represented onstage. The associated critical discourse reveals Spanish "anxiety about foreign musical influences," evident in a late eighteenth-century article in the *Diario de Madrid* expressing concern that, by being too much exposed to Italian music, "our [Spanish] cooks would sing Italian arias, with the evident risk that they would put noodles, macaroni, etc. into our stews instead of mutton, ham, [and] chicken."[11] In Pablo Esteve's tonadilla *La avellanera y dos franceses*, a half-Moorish comic character called Granadina (from Granada) sings in dialect about the fine almonds she is selling (*aellanitas guelas*).[12] Later a Frenchman sings a dance-song (seguidilla) about a disemboweled pig, showing a magic lantern image of it to lower-class people gathered in a square. Comedy is produced by the opposition between the two numbers involving the Granadina and the French cooks. In the former, almonds denote the Andalusian Islam-influenced cuisine that uses almonds in abundance and thus defines Granadina's regional and ethnic identity. On the other hand the latter seguidilla represents Frenchmen, the ambassadors of refined taste, preparing tripe, a lower-class dish typical of popular feasts, which is less as a signifier of French cuisine than as a comic gesture. Mikhail Bakhtin singled out tripe as a lower-class food typical of grotesque realism, representing "the swallowing, devouring belly" or the stomach eating itself. As Bakhtin points out, "Tripe could not be preserved long; [it was] therefore consumed in great quantities on slaughtering days and cost nothing. Moreover, it was believed that after cleaning, tripe still contained ten per cent excrement."[13]

The tripe scene in the *La avellanera y dos franceses* is also a grotesque representation of an Easter meal that breaks a religious taboo, similar to the scene with Muslims drinking wine in *Der Bassa von Tunis*. In the "seguidilla de la lanterna," a Frenchman sings about butchering, with references to liver, guts, and blood: "Now you'll see how they cut the liver out of a pig and stitch together the guts into blood sausages, what a miracle!" (Ahora veran como sacan / los higados a un marrano / y de las tripas ilvanan / morzillas q.es un milagro). The entire chorus wraps up the scene with the lines, "and for Easter it'll be a lovely stew" (y sera de la Pasqua / lindo potaje).[14] The reference to meat reminds us of the end of Lenten fasting and the Paschal season, but satire is produced by the contrast between the nature of the feast and the grotesque disemboweling of a pig: the filthiest animal in Judeo-Christian tradition replacing the pure and innocent lamb traditionally served at the Easter meal.[15]

Boozing in Distant Lands

The representation of non-European nationalities and ethnic groups through the gastronomic cultures of the East and West can be exemplified by two operas based on librettos by Giovanni Bertati, the first representing China and the second, North America. *L'inimico delle donne* (The enemy of women, premiered in Venice in 1771) is a comic opera set in China, with music by Baldassare Galuppi.[16] It includes a banquet scene with no specific reference to Chinese cuisine, which seems a missed opportunity to use local food as a gastronomic signifier of a nation with distinctive culture and traditions that had begun to generate renewed interest from Europeans in the eighteenth century.[17] At the beginning of the opera, Italian visitors are afraid the Chinese are cannibals who will eat them on skewers, but they are soon disabused of this notion. Ralph Locke, in his study of exoticism in opera, points out that *L'inimico delle donne* represents China as a "highly developed society with a court culture that had parallels with the nations and empires of Europe," as does Gluck's *Le cinesi* (The Chinese women, Schloss Hof, 1754); both are devoid of musical markers of Asianness.[18] The Chinese society represented in *L'inimico* can, however, be both "utopic and dystopic": a trap for the traveling middle-class woman Agnesina that is eventually revealed to be, according to Adrienne Ward, a "site of sexual and moral deviation."[19]

The European visitors are invited to a banquet with the Chinese prince Zon-Zon, who is labeled *mezzo carattere* (between comic and serious) in the Venetian libretto. He is affected by melancholia that makes him indifferent to female charm. In act 1, this anti–Don Giovanni is presented with a list of over thirty female suitors. As in Leporello's list of conquered women, they are classified according to body type (the fat one, the skinny one, etc.), except that, unlike Don Giovanni, Zon-Zon despises them all. Eating with this prince proves to be a painful experience, as he lacks appetite for both food and sex and therefore delays and ultimately declines the serving of food. Like high-table European banquets, the banquet scene of the act 1 finale is accompanied by table music, a "sinfonia" played by an onstage band. The stage directions indicate that "at the sound of a symphony, Zon-Zon enters with the others and they are led by Sin-Sin to their established places around the table."[20]

The finale starts with two two-bar phrases, reminiscent of an aristocratic European minuet; it presents none of the Orientalizing stylistic markers classified by Ralph Locke (minor keys, harmonic simplicity with sudden tonal shifts, duple-meter marches, repetitive rhythmic patterns, loud dynamics).[21] The only exotic element is the Chinese court's lack of awareness of the effects of the wine the Italians present as homage to the prince, who decides to taste it before food is served. Zon-Zon orders the wine brought in during a passage whose majestic tone is undermined by an orchestral introduction with loud rapid descending sixteenth-note flights in the oboes and violins, to which the violins alone respond, after a pause, with a low, quiet, single note. The tipsy quality of the introduction anticipates the inevitable. The Italian travelers warn the Chinese that wine is stronger than tea, and repeatedly invite them to drink in moderation. But the prince and his courtiers cannot resist the novel drink and end up seriously intoxicated. It is true that, as Jürgen Maehder observes apropos of this scene, Bertati's knowledge of East

Asian genetic alcohol intolerance syndrome is superficial at best.[22] It seems to me that the Chinese people's reaction to alcohol is caused by drinking on an empty stomach, therefore a difference in dietary culture rather than in genetic predisposition. Yet the effects of wine are described with medical precision, in the context of Galen's theory of temperaments, as a feeling of a heat that spoils the prince's appetite. Galuppi sets the lines of the prince, "I feel a heat that spoils my appetite" (Sento un caldo che mi toglie l'appetito) as a fragmented, chromatic, descending melody over the dominant pedal, accompanied by a vertiginous legato accompaniment in the strings.[23]

The Italians' gastronomic gift of wine ruins the communal meal. The physiological reactions may suggest the difficult relationship of two cultures that are both refined but are separated by habits and rituals that make sharing the table challenging. The prince orders the food removed, and while the Italians protest that they have had nothing to eat, the closing tutti expresses dizziness, confusion, lack of balance, and nausea.

The representation of Native Americans is similar in Bertati's other libretto, *L'orfanella americana* (The American orphan girl; Venice, autumn 1787).[24] In this opera an aristocratic, corrupt English libertine mortally wounds a Native American chief, father of the girl he has attempted to seduce (a parallel to Don Giovanni). The Englishman attempts in vain to relieve the chief's suffering by offering to seal a truce by smoking a pipe, eating roast beef, and drinking rum with him. The substances denote the two cultures: tobacco for the Native Americans, rum and roast beef for the Anglo-Saxons. American colonists are characterized both as British through roast beef (a typical English dish) and "American" through rum, associated with New World sugar plantations. More civilized, urban Americans drank tea, as happened in the house of a wealthy Boston merchant at the beginning of Giovanni Paisiello's *Le gare generose*, another opera written at the time of the American Revolution. In this case, tea was a reference to the Boston Tea Party—a much celebrated event of the time.[25]

In *L'orfanella americana*, the English aristocrat corrupts the whole Native American tribe with rum, making them hopelessly drunk.[26] The Native Americans, like the Chinese at the banquet in *L'inimico delle donne*, are confused and fear their loss of control. The musical representation of the effects of alcohol does not imply a biological difference between ethnicities but reflects a lack of knowledge of the effects of European alcoholic beverages. One could contrast this with Rossini's representation of the pretended drunkenness of Count Almaviva in the act 1 finale of *Il barbiere di Siviglia i* or, in *La Cenerentola*, with the tolerance for wine of Don Magnifico, baron of Montefiascone and minister of wine, in his act I aria in which he legislates against mixing wine and water. These two European aristocrats know the effects of alcohol and stay in control, whereas the Chinese and Native Americans lack this knowledge and are disempowered. One can see how an increasingly medicalized culture is linked to a discourse on power and colonialism by representing the different psychophysical effects of substances on the brains and bodies of entire social or national groups.

Defining Social Identity after Goldoni

As we move from ethnic to social identity, gastronomic signifiers become more precise: they reflect a code that was well recognized by audience members. Eighteenth-century comic opera, especially Italian opera buffa modeled after Goldoni and including its offspring, such as Da Ponte's librettos, plays with existing conventions by using stock characters to represent stereotypes, redefine identity, and question the incongruities and tensions between subjective identity and social class, or between inherited identity and aspiration. This is the kind of comic opera that was most widely present in international opera circuits of the time. Goldoni was also responsible for a reform of comic opera that translated the conventions of the commedia dell'arte model into modern bourgeois reality, even when his utopian or dystopian comedies were set in fantastic lands.[27] In this operatic subgenre, gastronomic signs define social identity as they would have done in real life.

In his study of eighteenth-century food culture, Piero Camporesi shows that the age of heavy, gargantuan banquets ended with the Enlightenment, replaced by a taste for small, refined dishes and often by dietary restrictions motivated not by religious observances, but by an emerging ideology of health and ethical eating. Fashion itself required slim, agile bodies that celebrated a "growing demand for 'elegant simplicity,'" replacing the baroque taste for the bulky, curvy, fleshy body.[28] Fashionable ladies led the way by practicing "contrived anorexia" and, as Piero Camporesi puts it, "listlessness, faddishness, languid indifference to food, calculated lack of appetite, ornate affectation and ostentatious craving for physical lightness and intellectual agility became such widely fashionable mannerisms that even the ladies' table companions were infected."[29] To show off classiness, people had two options: either consume fashionable drinks or food or (pretend to) choose abstinence.

Goldoni, who wrote both heroic and comic librettos, was well aware that a heroic character could not feel or express appetite for food. In his comic operas, he often represents social aspiration as a struggle to hide appetite. The absence of food works as a gastronomic signifier, denoting not so much disembodiment (as in opera seria), but rather, ill-concealed embodiment.[30]

La contessina (The young countess) centers on the middle class's attempt to obtain aristocratic status by imitating high-class manners as a path to marrying up. Acting like aristocrats means showing little appetite, or justifying eating and drinking as a form of taste (aesthetic appreciation) or current vogue (for wholesome dietary choices). In *La scuola moderna*, subtitled *La maestra di buon gusto* (The modern school, or The teacher of good taste), "Maestra" Drusilla explains that "there are people who at dinner eat next to nothing, satisfying themselves with the title of 'Illustrious.'" In her aria "Per le strade" (On our streets), she expands on the concept expressed in the preceding recitative by singing about people who enjoy being addressed by their aristocratic titles in the streets while tormented by hunger and striving to conceal their appetites (2, 4). Another "fasting" opera, *Le virtuose ridicole* (The ridiculous women of virtue) represents affected intellectuals, both men and women, pretending to be interested in academic, scientific, and artistic matters. The opera shows that the pretentious intellectual elites are affected by the same eating disorder as pretentious social elites. Both groups repress their appetites to distance themselves from the overpowering bodily desires of the common people.

Il povero superbo (The proud poor man) represents a man who inherited a fortune and spent it all pretending to be an aristocrat. Completely broke, he hopes to get free food from a waitress who, in the first scene of the opera, had fed a humble beggar. Her very first words were "Eat, drink and be happy." The pretentious Cavaliere kicks the beggar out and tells her he needs to take chocolate for breakfast as medicine; without it, his stomach cannot digest anything else (1, 66–73). After she leaves the room, the smell of salami almost makes him faint, so he eats a couple of slices and drinks some wine. Caught in the act, he explains that he did it to cure a cough, and he complains about the poor quality of the wine and chocolate. This bad performance of taste and dietary choice to assert high-class identity was obvious irony, but it also reveals two new functions of eating and drinking in the Enlightenment: the hunger of lower-class people was not as comic as the hunger of aristocrats or intellectuals because it lacked the ironic clash between pretense and actual need. In the baroque era, laughing at poor people's hunger was a cliché, as in the representation of the Zanni type, but now opera showed a greater social concern. Laughing at poor people's hunger was no longer funny or acceptable.[31]

The Land of Plenty

Goldoni's *Il paese della cuccagna* (The land of plenty), first staged in Venice for the Ascension fair of 1750 with music by Galuppi, may seem, with its feasting rituals, to reproduce pre-Enlightenment carnival rituals, which Bakhtin describes as regulated events in which ethical values and morality are momentarily turned upside down.[32] In fact, the opera combines the new sensibility of the Enlightenment with much older comedy traditions. Goldoni shows off his classical erudition by revisiting the model of Greek Old Comedy, which, as Erich Segal points out, was "a wishful return to a time when everything was easier, food grew spontaneously, and there were no laws."[33] The opera also recaps the Renaissance tradition of the legendary paradise for gluttons, represented, for example, in Pieter Bruegel the Elder's painting *The Land of Cockaigne*, which, in art historian Kenneth Bendiner's perspicacious analysis, parades "both criticism and delight in the same imagery" through "the linkage of food and physical pleasure, whether condemned or praised."[34]

Il paese della cuccagna is one of Goldoni's midcentury satirical fantasies, set in a distant land governed by Lardone (literally, "Big Lard"), and supervised by Salciccione ("Big Sausage"). In this utopia, eating, drinking, and making love are not only encouraged but enforced by law. Shipwrecked sailors are welcomed to the Land of Plenty with a meal of "chickens, lamb, and roast goat, chunks of cheese, prosciutto and other foods, and wine flasks" and are invited to eat and drink in an aria (1, 4) "Mangiate, bevete!" (Eat, drink!) sung by Compagnone ("Big Companion"), whose role is to initiate the sharing of food. Keep in mind that the etymological root of "companion" is one [to share] bread with.

The gods of the Land of Plenty are Ceres, Bacchus, and Venus, patron deities of food, wine, and sex. In this blessed land, a libertine lady called Madama Libera preaches drinking, eating, and free love, presenting infidelity as a virtue in a world where morality is figuratively turned upside down by having the lower body (the belly and sexual organs) overtake the upper body (the heart and mind). However, the lower body no longer has the same meaning and value as in the premodern grotesque realism of Rabelais's world, instead becoming the focus of an emerging scientific culture that medicalizes eating and sexual habits. Madama Libera prays to Bacchus to make everybody's stomach into a distilling apparatus called an alembic (*alambicco*) so they can digest while eating (1, 7).

Turning the attention to the stomach as no longer the lower, less controlled part of the body but a chemical laboratory was a new development in Goldoni's time. As cultural historian E. C. Spary documents in *Eating the Enlightenment*, iatrochemical accounts of digestion deeply affected the perception of the body. "French physicians and their clients," Spary writes, "regarded the stomach as a somatic locus where digestive, moral, and even political upsets manifested themselves and through which appetite was expressed."[35] The stomach became the center of the body, processing substances that affect self, mind, and personality. The digestive system even affected the soul, at least in enlightened Catholic circles, where the encounter with God through the Eucharist was discussed in terms of digestion.[36] This unprecedented focus on the stomach and lower body was part of what Foucault and Foucaultian scholars describe as the French Enlightenment's progressive use of medicalization as social control.[37] The situation in France applied to every nation in Europe that followed French fashion and also internationally disseminated opera buffa.[38]

Il paese della cuccagna abounds with arias and scenes about food, with details about ingredients and recipes such as roasted and boiled meat (beef, pork, veal, poultry, pigeons); "pasticcios" (baked dishes made with pasta dough and usually cheese and meat, such as lasagna); "ragù" sauce with ground meat; pies and cakes, chocolate, and, of course, plenty of wine. The Land of Plenty thus stands for the time of plenty: carnival. But as in all reversal comedies, the conclusion is a reestablishment of law and order: in this case the arrival of Lent, the time of fasting. In the last act, the seria character General Oronte and his soldiers invade the Land of Plenty, capture the happy locals, enslave the men, and set the women to work as nurses in hospitals. The sad final chorus "Let's go, poor us, to work" (Andiamo, andiamo misere, / Andiamo a faticar) bookends the act 1 chorus "Sweet thing dear to humankind is eating without working" (Dolce cosa all'uomo amica / è il mangiar senza fatica). Peace, the precondition for abundance, relaxation, and love, is contrasted with war, which brings hardship and work. Liberty and libertinism are replaced by tyranny and forced labor. The golden age ends and increasingly corrupt ages follow, ending with the iron age, the time when "work conquered all."[39]

Goldoni scholar Ted Emery comments on the ending of this opera that "the radical Otherness of carnivalesque vice is identified and expelled in an act of ritual purification."[40] This is a widespread interpretation of carnival in Goldoni, following Umberto Eco's idea that carnival is a subversion both of order and of its final restoration.[41] I find this interpretation as unconvincing as Bakhtin's theory that carnivals are always revolutionary. Goldoni represents the complementary but opposite values that people experienced at different times of life or in different contexts: the alternation of Lent and carnival, work and holiday, church and theater, war and peace, sickness and health. The drama of human life unfolds in the alternation and cycling of these experiences. If Lent ends the season of carnival, it is only with the understanding that another carnival will come. After all, a world where every day of the year is either only fasting or only feasting would be neither sustainable nor desirable.

Performing Good Taste

Bakhtin describes the eighteenth century as a moment of decadence, claiming that rococo culture ended the era of popular laughter, of the unifying and free universal feast, and destroyed the "traditional link of wise and free speech with food and wine."[42] However, opera buffa, which Bakhtin does not acknowledge, was part of a new culture leading to a greater awareness of class identity, boundaries, crossings, and clashes. Foods denoted taste, culture, and social status as embedded in a mercantile, consumerist system. Food no longer united, it created distinctions. Excellent food and wine cost more than average comestibles, and characters onstage were often reminded of that price. Paintings of the marketplace from the Renaissance to the eighteenth century joyously celebrate abundance and accessibility, a well-ordered chaos regulated by the modern mercantile logic of monetary transactions.[43] As we saw during Don Giovanni's final banquet, the wealthy libertine mentions his spending ("già che spendo i miei denari") before consuming imported wine, aristocratic food, and operatic music. Luxury was a mark of distinction between the struggling majority and the privileged elites; it was, as Fernand Braudel writes, "an elusive, complex, and contradictory concept, by definition constantly changing,"[44] identifiable only contextually, in a specific market. A luxury item required an elevated price tag to be taken as a symbol of social success because in order to signal distinction it needed to be out of reach of the masses.

Gypsies did not belong to the same class system and had a different set of values, as can be observed in Giovanni Paisiello's *I zingari in fiera* (The gypsies at the fair), first staged in Naples in 1789, and afterward an enormous international success. In the first act, we see ordinary people sitting in a coffeehouse on the town square, buying and enjoying drinks. In the second act, gypsies in a camp in the remote countryside are happily drinking wine, smoking, and eating their preferred diet: roasted pheasant and smoked goat prepared by the gypsy woman Lucrezia. In her cavatina with chorus, she leads the dining group with such comments as "What are pheasants worth? Only Lucrezia can prepare such beautiful morsels."[45] In Paisiello's score she repeats *fagiani* (pheasants), the second time inserting a cadenza so she can ornament and embellish the word, figuratively dressing the birds to her own taste.[46] Pheasants here are a sign not of distinction but of gypsy culture, which is outside the logic of the social, economic, and even legal system that maintains distinction. Gypsies do not buy pheasants, they hunt them and roast them, reclaiming their natural and inalienable rights on the land.

Goldoni's comic opera about the Senigaglia fair (*La fiera di Sinigaglia* [*sic*], 1760) represents a completely different world regulated by market logic, showing the impact of a global economy even in a relatively small seacoast town in central Italy. The libretto abounds with lengthy discussions of pricing, percentages, gains, and losses. It names typical food items that the middle classes were seeking in order to show their good taste and, in doing so, to perform socially at a higher status level. The new "modern exoticism" of food made global foods more widely available, infiltrating even peripheral locations.[47] The barista Lesbina (labeled *caffettiera* in the list of roles) opens the opera by advertising coffee, rosolio (sweet aromatic liqueur), and chocolate. Later in the first act she laments that she is not getting paid for her merchandise (1, 14, "Chi mi paga il cioccolato? / Chi mi paga il mio caffè?").

Privileged classes have the time and resources to acquire and cultivate refined taste. In his sociological study *Distinction*, Pierre Bourdieu shows how music and food denote class, that what produces distinction is upper-class distaste for the facile ("le dégoût du 'facile'") and their preference for the complex, the sophisticated, the artful. Good taste is taste acquired through acculturation and economic transaction: the two are linked, since acculturation costs money and time.[48] Bourdieu, taking as his point of departure Claude Lévi-Strauss's cultural dichotomy between *le cru et le cuit* (the raw and the cooked),[49] shows how privileged people wish to distance themselves from necessity.[50] Indeed, appearing to be hungry—needing food for nutrition—makes one lose social status, while practicing self-control amid abundance appears virtuous. Indulging in food is justifiable only as an aesthetic experience.

Popular taste values the "simple and good": in the case of food, what is both fairly nutritious and not too elaborate. Popular food must also be familiar rather than exotic.[51] The upper classes may be free from the shackles of necessity, but they are bound by the requirements of etiquette, forced to perform their status if they wish to keep it. Conversely, the lower classes may be limited in taste to what is available, but they enjoy freedom from form. In their behavior they are less constrained, freer to express and satisfy appetite. Refined aesthetics in food or music may appear hypocritical, artificial, or pretentious from the perspective of popular taste.[52] In this regime the middle classes find themselves in the difficult position of struggling to perform refined taste while hiding unrefined taste, and most of all hiding the struggle.[53]

Bourdieu's theory, developed in the 1970s, may seem quaint now that the relation between taste and class has become less obvious and less consistent, but it still helps us understand how food defined class in eighteenth-century comic opera. It is important to keep in mind, however, that comic opera does not merely reproduce the logic of class distinction but challenges it through the power of laughter. Goldoni's reform of the commedia dell'arte tradition deviated from stock typology in order to represent and even cause or at least accelerate social mobility and intersectionality.[54] Identity in opera buffa is often relational, performative, and contextual. Goldonian comic opera uses the traditional division of characters into class types derived from the comedy of masks, but it challenges its conventions by unveiling incongruities between class identity and social status. Thus we must avoid the temptation to automatically link stereotypical characters in comic opera to a type or a social class. Associating comic types with low classes or seria types with aristocracy are common missteps in opera studies. In line with Bourdieu, we must break with linear thinking that ties specific properties (economic power, gender, age, social and ethnic origin, education, etc.) to social class. Bourdieu hypothesizes that social identity is a product of complex "networks of interrelated relationships . . . [and] the effect they exert on practices," first and foremost on the performance of taste.[55]

Actor-network theory (ANT), systematized by another French sociologist, Bruno Latour, is a fruitful model for studying the network of associations between different domains in opera. It dismantles the artificial idea that social classes and opera types are like containers; rather, it sees them as the products of associations. The forces establishing associations among heterogeneous elements are "actors," described by ANT as whatever or whoever establishes the connection.[56] In this theoretical framework, "social aggregates are not the object of an *ostensive* definition—like mugs and cats and chairs that can be pointed at by the index finger—but only of a *performative* definition," which is to say they can be established only by performing an action—by doing or saying something.[57]

Take the following example: In the comic intermezzo *La birba* (1735),

Goldoni represents an aristocrat, Cavalier Orazio, who gambles away his fortune. He laments in an aria how hard it is to work all day to to eat only bread and onion, whose taste reminds him of his personal financial ruin (2, 244: "Tutto il giorno affaticare / e la sera pan e cipola"). In this case, as in many other librettos by Goldoni, aristocrats are cast in buffo roles, subverting the conventional identity of noble characters as serious. Associations of class and taste are often dismantled and re-created by contingent choices and situations. Later in the same opera, Orazio's wife Lindora sings of aristocrats who are obsessed with French taste and fashion, but when they run out of money (as they often do) they end up eating polenta (3, 540–44, aria "Quanti quanti pareggini"), the cornmeal dish that was a staple for the masses south of the Alps.[58] The other filler-upper was dry pasta or macaroni, a food first mass-produced only in the eighteenth century and carrying, as today, a fluid association with class. In this case the gastronomic signifier for class is not simply the food item (pasta), but how it is prepared and served. The distinction between aristocratic macaroni and lowbrow macaroni can be clearly construed as Bourdieu's opposition of the simple or *facile* versus the elaborate or *difficile*: the servant's mac-and-cheese versus the aristocrat's elaborate pasta dish, as the baked pasticcio di maccaroni.[59]

In Goldoni's straight comedy *Gl'innamorati* (1759), baked macaroni is presented as a sophisticated plate, a *pasticcio di maccheroni*, in a menu that includes a French dish (*fricandò alla francese*), meatballs, roast liver medallions (*fegatelli arrostiti*), and herb soup (1, 7).[60] A macaroni pasticcio, at the time of Goldoni, was an elaborate dish: first, a ragù of ground meat and minced onion, carrots, and celery was prepared and sautéed in wine and olive oil, then tomato sauce was mixed with the pasta; the mixture was first boiled, then baked with a topping of béchamel sauce (butter, milk, and flour), and finally, the whole dish was sprinkled with grated parmesan cheese.[61] This intricate and refined manner of preparation is the source of the metonym *macaroni* as used in the American colonial tune "Yankee Doodle" to describe the hairdo of English dandies who affected continental manners after returning from the grand tour of Italy ("stuck a feather in his hat, / And called it macaroni"). This fashion even inspired the publication of a trendy "macaroni-spotting gazette," the *Macaroni and Theatrical Magazine*, first issued in 1772.[62]

The simpler macaroni appears in Goldoni's comic opera *La notte critica*, where the waitress Marinetta brings her lover Fabrizio a simple hot pasta dish wrapped in a handkerchief, hence without any elaborate condiments (2, 17). The smell attracts Marinetta's other lover, the servant Carlotto, who accuses her of infidelity (3, 6). The handkerchief of macaroni may have been a comic reference to Desdemona's handkerchief in Shakespeare's *Othello*.[63] Carlotto understands the macaroni as a sign of the woman's infidelity since, among people of his social class, macaroni appeals to the appetites of the lower body. In these two librettos, the same category of food is used not as a performance of taste, but to reveal true feelings and appetites.

The (Ig)nobility of Carnivore Aristocracy

In the eighteenth century, meat was more accessible to the wealthy classes than to the poor, and not just because of its higher cost. Game, which in theory could have been available to everybody at no cost, became the food associated with aristocracy owing to the exclusive hunting privileges granted to landowners (usually aristocrats) and their guests.[64] Game meat was not available in the marketplace; class status, rather than money, determined access to it. As Camporesi writes, game and "black and bloody meats" were clearly perceived as "patriarchal" (a term used in period sources) and "potent symbols of feudal conviviality and of barbaric aggression."[65] In paintings, as Bendiner shows, meat is often associated with feudal values like war and hunting, but also with luxury and materialism.[66] A perfect example is Mozart and Da Ponte's tyrannical, libertine aristocrat Don Giovanni, who, as we have seen, eats game (pheasant), an inescapable symbol of aristocracy and power, but devalues it by mentioning the costliness of the dinner. In doing so he replaces a preconceived association between aristocracy and the premonetary feudal economy with a new marketplace association, while preserving the association of game with hunting, essential to portraying the predatory libertine as a hunter of women.

For Goldoni the link between aristocracy and meat had strong but ambivalent connotations, and not only in his opera librettos. In his *Mémoires* he remembers accompanying his father, a medical doctor, to a feast in the palace of the illustrious Count Lantieri of Gorizia, an aristocrat from Friuli and his father's patient. Goldoni describes the event as elaborate and extravagant to the point of being exotic. It impressed him as not delicate, but abundant ("sa table n'étoit pas délicate, mais très-abondante"), consisting of an overwhelming amount of meat, including hares, pheasants, partridges, woodcocks, snipes, thrushes, larks, and other large and small game birds, presented on a large dish of meat formed by a leg of mutton or breast of veal. There were three soup courses, only one of them meatless; even the barley soup was full of meat gravy, which was believed to promote digestion. Wine was dispensed through a peculiar apparatus called a "glo glo," made of glass balls of various sizes connected by tubes that produced harmonious sounds when guests drank from it, transforming drinking into a pleasant concert.[67] The *Mémoires*, published in Paris in 1787, reflects contemporary reactions against the artificiality of courtly cuisine. The aristocrats' kitchen and dining table were presented as chemistry labs, opposed by a new culture of natural, heathier eating practiced by the emerging revolutionary bourgeoisie.[68]

L'Arcadia in Brenta is one of the many operas to present meat, together with other refined food items, such as rosolio liqueur and chocolate, as class signifiers. Daniel Heartz singled out this 1749 opera as an exemplary buffa and the one that inaugurated the long collaboration between Goldoni and Galuppi.[69] The opera portrays the life of leisure and the pleasures of expensive country villas along the Brenta River where, as Goldoni wrote, there were "grand amusements, dinners, balls, and shows; and there the Italian cicisbeism, without embarrassment or restraint, has gone further than anywhere else."[70] "Cicisbei" were courtly lovers of well-to-do married women; the word became synonymous with decadent aristocratic manners.[71] The protagonist, first interpreted in 1749 by the star buffo bass Francesco Baglioni, is Messer Fabrizio, a name that Count Bellezza announces with pomp, stating that the echo of his name resounds high and majestic ("L'eco intorno rimbomba / Il nome alto sovrano / Di Fabrizio Fabroni da Fabriano," 1, 9). The pomp of the line is delivered in rather unpretentious, unaccompanied recitative, anticipating the protagonist's unsuccessful attempt to assimilate with the aristocracy.[72] Like Goldoni's own father, Fabrizio struggles to entertain aristocrats and fashionable people, ruining himself financially to satisfy the whims and expensive tastes of his illustrious guests. He is already out of cash when the opera starts, as his servant Foresto warns him in the opening scene. By act 3 the guests are starving, and Fabrizio has nothing to offer them. Madama Laura thinks she *needs* chocolate as a medical treatment for her stomach condition (3, 1–4), while Lindora asks for just a small breakfast ("colazioncina") consisting of game meat appropriate to the aristocracy: "a pigeon, two quails, a partridge and a black francolin," accompanied by half a bottle of good wine (un piccione, / due qualglie, una pernice, un francolino / e una mezza botteglia di buon vino), to which Fabrizio replies that he can only serve polenta. Lindora is so hungry that she grudgingly accepts lower-class food. It is then the Count's turn to ask for a noble breakfast food: "a spherical pasticcio [meat casserole], two boiled birds, a roasted four-legged animal, a pie, milk, salad, and not too many pieces of fruit" (un sferico pasticcio / due volatile alessi, /un quadrupede arrosto, / torta, latte, insalata e pochi frutti).

Fabrizio's reply is a multitempo aria (3, 4, aria "A Lauretta la sua cioccolata"), commenting on the aristocratic diet and its inaccessibility to middle-class people. In the first section of the aria, marked andante, Fabrizio reassures his guests that they will be served the food and drink they desire. Galuppi sets this section in a slow, dignified pace, the rhetoric of body movements decreed for aristocrats. He writes simple imitation between the bass and the viola and contrary motion between the voice and the strings. This elementary contrapuntal texture gives a hint of highbrow style, but the lines are fragmented, with pauses inserted for lowbrow comic effects: "A Lauretta" [pause] "la sua cioccolata, a madama" [pause] "un tazzin di ristoro, e il rosolio a quegl'altri e il caffè" (a restoring cup, and rosolio to the others and coffee). The comestibles are set as stretched-out high Cs (the tonic), to let the hungry guests stop on the reassuring thought that they will be served. Yet the tonic sonority in the voice (C) is set against a bass that is always somewhere else. After the coffee, the bass hits the distant C-sharp on the more substantial "torta sfogliata," which in an eighteenth-century recipe book meant meat pies made of batter and flour dough.[73] The pie lands on an awkward modulation to D through a chromatic rise in the voice (F to F-sharp), after which Fabrizio tells his servant to be quiet and get the pasticcio ready. "Pasticcio," in addition to being a complex meat dish with dough, had also come to mean something messy, including an operatic concoction of pieces from different works or by different composers. He sings "pasticcio" on another high C, now a dissonance against the D sonority in the orchestra. In the next tempo section, an allegro, the tonality moves from D to G and the text is set in a faster, less dignified way: a 3/8 dance meter. Here the character acts without pretending, telling Foresto in an aside that there is no food and no money.

Let us revert to one more representation of meat as a signifier of the logic of feudal power. This is a catalog aria about meat dishes from Bertati's *La vendemmia* (The grape harvest) set to music by Giuseppe Gazzaniga.[74] The opera exists in many versions: in addition to the numerous productions in Italian cities, it was staged in Graz (1781), Prague (1782), and Dresden (1783) with a German translation in the libretto beside the Italian original, then in London (1789) with English translation, and Paris (1791) with French translation, while in places where Italian was more commonly understood it appeared without translation (Vienna, Eszterháza, and Lisbon).[75]

Count Zeffiro, the character who sings the food aria, although an aristocrat, is labeled in the 1780 Naples cast list as "buffo caricato" (the opera's buffoon) and characterized as a "flatterer and freeloader" (adulatore e scroccone)—as insubstantial as his name (the breeze Zephyr).[76] In the opening ensemble, Count Zeffiro is the only character to express appetite. Later in the same act, he sings his catalog aria to a middle-class protégé, Cardone, who is planning to marry a pretty shepherdess. The Count offers to be the shepherdess's cicisbeo, her gallant, and to provide food for the couple's wedding banquet; the menu parades before his disciple the Count's power and wealth. In the larger dramatic context, the aria has multiple functions: arousing and expressing appetite, using food to seduce a bride, and denoting class in an ambiguous way: high social status but lack of true nobility.

Different versions of the aria vary the food items listed. Comparing, for example, the Venice (1778) and Naples (1780) versions, the latter eliminates regional Venetian names of birds like *mazzorini* (mallards) and *Folleghette* (coots), praised in a dictionary of the time for their excellent meat.[77] The Neapolitan version inserts more greens and more sweets and, most important, eliminates the too-explicit references to aristocratic game dishes; unsurprisingly, such satire against the aristocracy was more tolerated in the Republic of Venice than in the Kingdom of Naples where, as Anthony DelDonna shows, the monarchy, aware of opera's power to influence public opinion, carefully monitored operatic texts and music.[78] The 1789 London production, featuring Nancy Storace and Francesco Benucci (who had been Mozart's first Susanna and Figaro two years earlier), adopts the text of the 1778 version, heavy on meat, except for the Venetian birds, which were replaced by peas and asparagus, the greens in the Neapolitan edition. The English version is a compromise between a literal and a cultural translation; it inserts typical English dishes like roast beef and puddings and exotic dishes from Britain's far-flung empire like turtle and pineapples, yet it keeps the foods that signify aristocracy everywhere: venison and other game, and elaborate meat dishes.[79]

The Count's catalog aria begins with a pretentious descending arpeggio on the notes of the tonic triad, in royal dotted figurations and a tempo maestoso. It is a horn fanfare, recalling aristocratic hunting sports and possibly making the double entendre of horns (*cornea*) as a symbol of cuckoldry, inserted as a prophetic reminder that the Count is planning to seduce his protégé's bride. At first the Count uses this haughty rhythmic and harmonic vocabulary to alert his interlocutor, "When you see who I am you will be surprised and dumbstruck" (Quando vedrai chi sono, / sopreso restarai);

then, in a chromatic ascent coinciding with a dramatic crescendo he warns Cardone that he will be awestruck (e stupirai di me). But the Count cannot sustain this high rhetorical level; soon his speech degenerates into patter, the style usually adopted by buffo roles, as he sings about "serving all the numerous guests at the wedding banquet" (per render ben servito / il numeroso invito).

After a cadenza on the dominant, the tempo shifts from maestoso to allegro, and food courses are paraded like a charging army. The fast pace is counterbalanced at first by a heavy repetition of the three notes of the tonic chord played in quarter notes by the whole orchestra. Instead of a slow crescendo, as we would expect in a catalog aria, the orchestra plays forte from the beginning, relentlessly pounding the tonic chord. On this heavy orchestral concoction, and using the same triad as the melody, the Count begins listing greasy appetizers, starting with "zuppe alla santé," a cream made by mincing celery and lettuce in butter and adding meat broth and béchamel sauce, served over toast.[80] On the same melodic material, the Count continues with boiled veal and fried brains (un gran lesso di vitella / un buon fritto di cervella), leaving quarter-rest pauses as if to allow his guest time to breathe between the courses.

The Count intensifies the pace by shifting to eighth notes as he introduces more courses; he mercilessly reduces the rests between the dishes, all the while remaining solidly grounded on the tonic. Now in rapidly alternating forte and piano dynamics, he lists a pie of chicken giblets (un pasticcio di regaglia), game casserole with pigeons and woodcocks (una gran carapotina, / con piccione e beccaccina). He finally slows down and modulates to C for an even heavier fricassee of sweetbreads (fricassè poi d'animelle), beef, pigeons with pappardelle pasta, and woodcock in salmì sauce, another meaty French-inspired dish (piccion grossi in pappardelle / un salmì con la beccaccia). Finally, the Count incorporates the pun "una nobil torta in faccia," meaning both a cake served together with the previous course and a cake thrown in the face (a classic in slapstick comedy). Gazzaniga sets the conclusion of Bertati's text, where the Count asks his interlocutor, "What do you say, what do you think? Isn't this making your mouth water?" (Che ne dici? Che ti par? / Non ti senti liquefar?) by reverting to the pompous dotted rhythm and, after a fermata, adding in simpler square quarter notes, "I can almost feel it in my mouth / How delightful, how tasty!" (Ah mi par d'averli in bocca / che dolcezza, che sapor!), as a final slip, unveiling his gluttony and lack of nobility because of his full awareness of his own body's uncontrollable reaction at the thought of mouthwatering delicacies.

The next section of the aria reverts to legato figuration in the strings and piano and long notes, dolce, in the oboes. Here the Count starts to present desserts—English pudding and French pudding (un bodino all'uso inglese / ed un altro alla francese)—but then subverts the syntax of the meal and goes back to meat in a low-class patter ill suited to noble dishes like roast pheasants garnished with small songbirds like warblers, ortolans, skylarks, thrushes, wild ducks, and coots (poi l'arrosto di faggiani / tordi grossi ed ortolani, / beccafichi, lodolette, / mazzorini, falanghette). He finally reviews the entire list of dishes, hammering it on a single tone in quarter notes, doubled by the bass to give it more substance, and in a continuous crescendo, climaxes again on the lines, "What do you say, what you think?"

The Count in *La vendemmia* is in some ways similar to the Count in *Le nozze di Figaro* or to Don Giovanni in Bertati-Gazzaniga's and Da Ponte-Mozart's versions. All revel in their power over others: Count Zeffiro through the carnivorous tastes of the nobility, Count Almaviva through the droit du seigneur, and Don Giovanni through the conflation of food and sex. Whereas Don Giovanni is omnivorous, Zeffiro is primarily characterized through his predilection for meat dishes used to denote social class, in a medical climate that has already started to question the healthfulness of meat-heavy diets, and in a social climate that was starting to link diet to ethical standards.

Vegetarians

Vegetables and fruit often denoted gender (women) and class (farmers). But in the second half of the eighteenth century, vegetarianism became the dietary choice performed of enlightened intellectual elites such as the economist Ferdinando Galiani and the radical revolutionary Maximilien Robespierre. The latter presented vegetarianism and abstinence from alcohol as signs of bourgeois virtue, opposed to the aristocratic decadence of the ancien régime.[81] Rousseau, in his *Discourse on Inequality* (1754), claims that before the development of inequality, humans were vegetarians. In a footnote added to the 1782 edition, Rousseau bolsters his hypothesis with ethnographic evidence that the inhabitants of the Lucayan archipelago, after being transplanted by the Spaniards to Cuba and Santo Domingo, died from eating flesh. He observes that carnivorous animals always fight, while those that feed on fruit are more peaceful, which is a distinction that might also apply, at least in theory, to human beings: "since frugivorous animals live among themselves in continual peace, if the human species were this latter genus, it is clear that it would have had a much easier time subsisting in the state of nature."[82] Tristram Stuart, in his book about the ideology of vegetarianism, points out that "Rousseau's social philosophy had a fundamental grounding in the vegetarian debate," beginning a trend of linking human and animal rights that culminated in John Oswald's revolutionary treatise *The Cry of Nature, or An Appeal to Mercy and to Justice, on Behalf of the Persecuted Animals* (1791). Stuart relates his treatise to contemporary essays by Thomas Paine (*The Rights of Man*, 1790), Mary Wollstonecraft (*A Vindication of the Rights of Woman*, 1792), and Herman Daggett (*The Rights of Animals*, 1792).[83]

In the comic intermezzo *Lisetta e Caican turco*, a decadent Turk meets a Western vegetable seller, a girl who advertises her wholesome produce: "Fresh herbs, new herbs / Here comes the greengrocer girl / Arugula, lettuce, fennel, salad!"[84] The score is not extant, but in Goldoni and Galuppi's *Il filosofo di campagna*, widely performed in the second half of the century, we have a good example of music describing vegetables: the simple Lesbina, servant of the rich farmer Don Tritemio, sings about the salad she is going to eat for dinner, praising fresh radishes and chicory as a way to tease her wealthy old suitor.[85] Her aria "Quando son giovine" offers a sonic rendition of a fresh salad. It is low in musical calories: the simple, pastoral F-major aria in 3/8, andante, evokes a natural setting, best suited to growing vegetables, while the texture is supremely light, scored for strings only, giving it lots of leafy melodic arpeggios and crisp octave leaps in the ritornello while keeping the melody as songlike as possible, as is appropriate to a popular canzonetta.[86]

In the second, faster section of the aria, Lesbina sings of a spicier food: beautiful chicory, ready to be harvested and eaten fresh. Personifying the chicory, she invites her suitor to take her and eat her now ("Mangiatemi presto / Coglietemi sù"). The purpose of the aria is to seduce the old master and begin an interclass relationship. It does so by conferring value on the food aesthetic of the raw, the fresh, the simple as better than the sophisticated, the prepared, the cooked.

The association of vegetables and fruit with the ambiguous pastoral setting allows interclass alliances among women. At the beginning of the act, Lesbina sings a duet ("Candidetto gelsomino") with her mistress Eugenia, daughter of Don Tritemio. Eugenia is a wealthy young woman and a seria character, in love with a young cavalier but destined by her father to marry against her will the wealthy old philosopher and landlord Nardo. Because Eugenia is a seria role, she does not sing about food in her duettino with

Lesbina (doing so would declass her to a comic role) but sings about flowers, comparing their freshness to the freshness and beauty of young women. The music of this duet, though, undermines the distinction: like Lesbina's canzonetta, it is a pastoral 3/8 andantino. The wealthy lady presents the first line, which is repeated by her servant and ally in a minor key, and, after reverting to major, it climaxes *a due*, as the women merge their voices and suspend their class differences.[87]

The ensuing aria by Eugenia reestablishes distinction in typical seria style with extended coloratura, musically illustrating the feeling of being in the middle of the stormy sea, far from the shore.[88] It reinforces the impression that in the duettino with Lesbina, Eugenia departed from her distinctive rhetorical level and met her servant on common ground. As such, this duet is similar to the act 4 duettino between the Countess and her servant in Mozart's *Figaro*, which also seals an alliance between women of different rank.[89]

At the end of the opera, Lesbina marries Nardo, freeing her mistress from the unwanted marriage obligation and at the same time raising her own social status. Notwithstanding their class differences, Lesbina and Nardo are compatible in aesthetics and ideology. Nardo's bucolic worldview is based on cultivating simple pleasures: eating with gusto and drinking good wine after working hard in the fields—a wholesome way of life he celebrates in his first aria, which he sings while holding a spade (1, 5). Nardo also values peace in his own house (2, 13) and cares nothing for the social status of his wife, but only for the nobility of her heart. In his aria "Se non è nata nobile / Che cosa importa a me?" (2, 14), he asks, "What do I care if she was not born into nobility?" Nardo's country philosophy and Lesbina's praise of fresh vegetables are both part of what we now identify as the ideology of the locally and organically grown and a rejection of artificial and processed food, a rejection that was part of the dietary philosophy of the Enlightenment, challenging the values of the refined, meat-eating aristocracy of the ancien régime.[90]

After 1750, natural and simple food became fashionable for health reasons as well, especially among a sector of society obsessed with popular science, trending medical theories, and dietary debates, all disseminated through pamphlets and literary journals. Antonio Cocchi, professor of medicine in Pisa, advocated a vegetarian diet in his widely translated and disseminated essays.[91] Jean-François Marmontel, a prominent French intellectual of this time and a member of the Encyclopédistes, wrote extensively about his diet, using a narrative that depicted wholesome primordial fruits and vegetables degenerating into artificial and unhealthy sophisticated cuisine but reaching a phase of redemption with the adoption of a new simplicity and sobriety in his own time. "Dietary enlightenment" assumed a double meaning: both the lightening of caloric content and the enlightenment of eaters who had acquired the knowledge necessary to make informed dietary choices. The political implications of the new dietary movement and the rejection of aristocratic taste were inescapable in the final years of ancien régime France.[92]

Marmontel was also a passionate supporter of Niccolò Piccinni's operas. His 1777 *Essai sur les révolutions de la musique en France* reads as a manifesto of Piccinnist aesthetics.[93] In earlier writings Marmontel had preferred the sentimental genre, or even the comic, to tragedy because such *petits sujets* appeared to him more "natural," allowing "sympathy and identification" and hence exerting a positive moral influence on society.[94] Piccinni became the major representative of *petits sujets* and sentimental opera with *La buona figliuola*. Its libretto by Goldoni, after Samuel Richardson's best-selling epistolary novel *Pamela*, examines class relationships in the context of an interclass marriage. Both the novel and the opera are exemplary works of the age of sensibility, aiming at naturalness and immediate expression of sentiments.[95] Northrop Frye, in his essay "Theory of Modes" sees *Pamela* as a "domestic comedy" based on the Cinderella archetype with its consequent rewarding of virtue by change of fortune and status. As such, *Pamela* differs slightly from other types of comedy, especially from what he labels "new comedy" (referring to Greek comedy after Aristophanes, especially by Menander) based on the attraction between two young people despite a patriarchal figure who is eventually defeated.[96] The new comedy as revitalized during the Renaissance does not necessarily have the "serious" moral content of the former type. Conversely, domestic comedy is sentimental and more serious in tone and content. Stefano Castelvecchi, addressing the ambiguity of genre of *La buona figliuola*, points out that Goldoni conceived it as a "third genre," close to the French *drame* but more serious and dignified.[97]

The character Cecchina is the emblematic *mezzo carattere*, a role between seria and buffa. The difference between Cecchina and the opera's most seria role, Marquise Lucinda, is clear in the music: Lucinda distances herself from the rest by singing extended coloratura passages and using distinctive seria rhetoric and style. More difficult to grasp is the difference between the *mezzo carattere* role Cecchina and the buffa role Sandrina. Their first arias (cavatinas) are both written in a simple, natural, gallant style. Cecchina appears in gardening clothes, singing her triple-meter cavatina in the pastoral key of F major. It presents a mixture of seria and buffa apparent in the elegant symmetry of phrases, with an arch-shaped melody of "affecting sweetness" and "touching" expressivity.[98] Sandrina's G-minor cavatina—the only minor-key piece of the whole opera—is more sentimental, similar to Barbarina's aria in the last act of *Figaro*, which is also ambiguous in the buffa-seria spectrum.

Sandrina complains about having to carry heavy fruit baskets.[99] Her style and utterances are certainly less elegant than Cecchina's, but they are equally moving and sincere. The libretto does not explicitly label these roles as buffa or *mezzo carattere* but instead calls Cecchina a gardener (*giardiniera*) and Sandrina a farmer (*contadina*). Mary Hunter notes that the transformation of Cecchina's occupation from maid in Richardson to gardener in Goldoni distances her from the shrew-maid type of *La serva padrona* and also creates a symbolic association with the flower garden: the cultivated, fresh, and natural landscape.[100] Franco Piperno observes that this is a crucial difference, since gardening was (and still is) considered an occupation more suitable to upper classes than farming. This is one of the symptomatic aspects of Cecchina's nobility, which will be revealed in the recognition scene.[101] In this case the gastronomic sign allows us to focus on the similarities between the two women rather than the differences. It is true that the farmer Sandrina mentions edible produce whereas Cecchina sings of flowers and ornamental plants (roses, jasmine, herbs, flowers). However, after her first cavatina, Cecchina tells us in recitative that she loves pruning and knows technical details about grafting wild trees to grow juicy plums and pears.[102] What the two young women have in common, notwithstanding the difference in their "blood," is their use of vegetarian gastronomic signs. They grow and harvest fruits and vegetables. Cecchina's true nobility, then, is different from that of the carnivore aristocracy. It might still be "blue blood," but it is certainly lower in cholesterol. Her nobility lies not only in how she feels about herself and others, but also in how she feeds herself and others. The heart and the stomach, from this time of history until our own, are no longer artificially separated but are naturally interconnected.

If it is true that gastronomic signs define identity in terms of nationality, ethnicity, class, and gender, it is also true that they make and remake connections and associations, often in unpredictable ways. The case of vegetarian food choices shows that during the Enlightenment, as soon as intellectual capital starts to be seen as an important asset, "smart" choices of affordable and sustainable food (the produce of the earth) have the power to act as signifiers of refinement, understanding, and virtue, regardless of wealth or birthright.

PART III

The Effects of Feasting and Fasting

In part 1 of this book, we looked at rituals and habits of consumption involving the audience, and in part 2 at gastronomic signs defining characters' identity along the serious-comic spectrum as well as in terms of ethnicity, class, and gender. In this last part, we will see the effects of feasting and fasting on characters, audience, and singers, starting in chapter 8 with two popular soft drugs: chocolate and coffee. Chapter 9 focuses on Verdi's operas, which let us explore how sharing food or wine, or refusing to do so, affects relationships. Chapter 10 is about the effects of fasting on the singer's body in the case of the prodigious diet Maria Callas undertook before her interpretation of Violetta in Verdi's *La traviata* in 1955. I identify this episode as a turning point in opera history, determining a collision between, and fusion of, the singer and the dramatis persona, until then perceived as separate entities.

CHAPTER EIGHT

Coffee and Chocolate from Bach to Puccini

Coffee and chocolate are the two most distinctive "soft" drugs of the Enlightenment. Both drinks were readily available in the seventeenth century but became popular only in the eighteenth, when they began to denote and shape lifestyle. Their effect on the brain and on general health was amply discussed in pamphlets and popular-medicine publications, and of course in coffeehouses, which generated new types of social interaction. Both public and domestic consumption created new rituals, often involving the display of china and tableware then in vogue. Representing consumption of coffee and chocolate onstage therefore meant pairing decorative props with the beverages being drunk by the audience in the theater.[1]

Americans and Turks

Coffee was at first associated with fashionable "Turkish" garb at the time of Soliman's visit to Louis XIV, and even though it quickly became assimilated into Western culture, erudite treatises by Johann Krüger and Giovanni dalla Bona presented coffee as the preferred drink of the prophet Mohammed, showing that its origin in Arab or Turkish cultures was not completely forgotten.[2] The title page of an early treatise on coffee, chocolate, and tea shows three men in their native attire seated around a table: a Turk with a cup of coffee, a Chinese man with a pot of tea and a teacup, and a Native American with a cup of steaming chocolate.[3]

The traditional association of coffee with Turkey is still present in Rossini's *Il turco in Italia* (1814). This comic opera is based on an original eighteenth-century libretto by Caterino Mazzolà, and it includes a scene involving an unfaithful married woman, Fiorilla, serving coffee to a guest, the Turkish Prince Selim (1, 9).[4] The mixture of illicit erotic energy and caffeine is explosive, especially in Rossini's hands. The scene, as described in the first edition of the libretto, is set in the opulent house of Don Geronio, Fiorilla's husband, with "elegant furniture" (appartamenti elegantemente mobigliati), including a dangerously inviting sofa. Fiorilla enters with Selim, ordering her servant to immediately prepare coffee for her guest. As she and Selim start to flirt, the coffee is brought in (è recato il caffè), which Fiorilla herself serves with great care for the ceremony, impressing the Turk with her elegant manners. The recitative leads to what first appears to be a love duet (no. 5 of the score). In a comfortable andante, interjected with nervous figurations in the violins and winds, Fiorilla warns her visitor that she does not trust Turks, who are known to have a thousand women at their service (Siete turchi: non vi credo). Selim's flirtatious defense modulates to the dominant key. The "duet" is interrupted by the entrance of the pusillanimous husband Geronio (1, 10), who comments in an aside, "Here we go, the two alone, tête-à-tête," (ecco qui . . . da soli a soli). He then timidly asks the couple, "Is it allowed? May I come in?" accompanied by sheepish trills and an alternation of piano and forte dynamics expressing his fear and rage. The duet evolves into a trio and shortly afterward into a quartet with the entrance of Narciso (1, 11), Fiorilla's cicisbeo, her "formal" lover. The music increases in complexity and dramatic tension, especially as Selim aggressively confronts Geronio and Fiorilla forces her cuckolded husband to honor the Turk by humbly kissing his robe. The temporary relaxation of pace in the slow tempo (largo) where Selim expresses his surprise at the behavior of Italian husbands picks up again as Fiorilla's cicisbeo displays his own jealousy for her unfaithfulness in an increasing tension that includes momentarily darkening minor harmonies: the storm is brewing, ready to break during the ensuing faster allegro vivace. The typically implacable Rossini crescendo leads to a final stretto during which the four characters express contrasting overexcited feelings of love, rage, jealousy, and scorn. Rossini's take on coffee shows how, in the early nineteenth century, the favorite drink of enlightened minds was an eroticizing drug stirring irrational passions.

Enlightening Drugs

Coffee was the trademark of the eighteenth-century Enlightenment, making it the preferred drink of fashionable intellectuals.[5] It did not denote social class, because it was broadly accessible and thus bypassed the logic of class distinction. By the late eighteenth century, coffee was drunk by virtually everybody, from aristocrats to servants and even the general populace, as disdainfully noted by Le Grand d'Aussy in 1782.[6] It denoted a caffeinated mental state rather than any particular social status, and its effect of making people more alert and clear-minded was associated with the new mentality of the Enlightenment.

One of the most enlightened journals of the 1760s was *Il caffè*. This periodical, run by Pietro Verri, was a pivotal venue for the formation of public opinion in Italy, publishing articles on a broad variety of political and cultural topics, including an endorsement of cuisine reform based on a dietary regimen that was lighter and more energizing than the heavy, complex foods of the previous age.[7] Popular periodicals like *Il caffè* were often read and discussed in public coffeehouses. The coffeehouses became the bourgeois equivalent of Renaissance humanistic academies, with the difference that they contributed enormously to the formation of the public sphere in the Western world. The public coffeehouse defined a particular strand of enlightened culture based on democratic debate.

Coffee was also drunk privately, often in large quantities. John Rice maintains that the manic hyperproductivity of most eighteenth-century composers was achieved under the influence of caffeine, as coffee consumption increased enormously between the times of Bach and Mozart—an avid coffee drinker whose operas *Don Giovanni* and *Così fan tutte* both mention coffee.[8]

Chocolate, unlike coffee, remained relatively expensive throughout the century and thus denoted a higher social status than coffee.[9] Like coffee, chocolate became a staple in urban Western culture, although its Native American roots were often remembered in historical accounts.[10] Although chocolate could be drunk in public places, it was perceived primarily as a cozy domestic drink.

Giovanni Pergolesi's *La serva padrona* is a case in point. The comic intermezzo in two parts is set entirely in a domestic space. It begins with the wealthy, aging bourgeois Uberto complaining about waiting for his servant Serpina to serve him chocolate, "aspettare e non venire" (waiting and not coming).[11] The aria's initial ritornello represents irritation through octave leaps in the bass and violins and reflects the growling of the stomach through sixteenth-note spasms beginning in the fourth measure, widening and contracting (F–E-natural vs. F–E-flat). Uberto's own melody expresses the wait with a stretched-out monotonic line that ends with a frustrated octave drop. The master's displeasure leads to an argument with Serpina, who refuses to prepare the chocolate and escalates the tension toward their first duet, "sempre in contrasti" (always arguing). This delay is the initial move taken by the cunning young maid to stimulate the old man's appetite and eventually trap him into an interclass marriage, thus raising her status from servant (*serva*) to mistress (*padrona*).

In Goldoni's comic librettos, chocolate, even when drunk by a group, is served and in a domestic space; the characters often emphasize the drink's health benefits. *Il viaggiatore ridicolo* opens with the following stage directions: *private room [camera] with chairs and table in Don Fabrizio's house, with Don Fabrizio, Donna Emilia, the Count sitting and drinking chocolate, while Livietta [the servant] stands and Giacinto [the waiter] serves the guests.* They all sing "How good is chocolate, when drunk in good company! It brings health and happiness for the whole day."[12] The "good company" is clearly restricted to the aristocracy, and the chorus emphasizes the link between wealth and health. Similarly, in Goldoni's *La conversazione*, wealthy characters praise chocolate's "taste and healthiness" (gusto e sanità).[13]

Like coffee, chocolate was the subject of lively discussions disseminated in popular scientific publications.[14] The medical literature on chocolate has combative and passionate overtones. For example, the medical doctor Giovanni Battista Felici maintains that chocolate causes melancholy if boiled with sugar until it forms a greasy butter (grasso butiroso). It is much preferable to serve it cold, even though it is not as tasty.[15] Felici's agenda is to promote healthy food to the detriment of taste. He assesses the medicinal properties of chocolate by estimating heat within Galen's classical medical system, based on the theory of the humors. Another doctor, Giovanni Battista Anfossi (not the composer), defends chocolate, mocking old-fashioned Galenic doctors who explain everything with the "mysterious words of dry, humid, hot, and cold."[16] He praises modern chocolate, free of the excessive spices used in the baroque era, and unlike his colleague he wholeheartedly defends its benefits in a great variety of recipes that make the drink appealing to different palates. Quoting modern medical literature, Anfossi claims that chocolate is especially good for women's and children's delicate stomachs, and he provides a long catalog of its benefits: "It comforts the stomach, facilitates digestion of all foods, allows [one] to breathe more freely, quenches the thirst, nourishes the body; it is diaphoretic, sudorific, gives pleasant vapors to the head, [and] induces quiet and tranquil sleep." The list reads like a catalog aria, increasing in rhythm and pace toward the end with a "stretto" section: "It cures languor, weakness, indigestion, vomit, cardialgia, gas, colic, swoons, tuberculosis, podagra, aphonia, hemiplegia, anorexia, nausea," and on and on.[17] This hyperbolic defense of chocolate illustrates the widespread medical discourse around this drink.

J. S. Bach at the Coffeehouse

"Schweigt stille, plaudert nicht / und höret!" Bach's Coffee Cantata begins by telling the audience to "be quiet, stop chatting and listen," where "höret" is sung on an F-sharp, clashing with the G in the bass to make the point that it's time to stop the noise.[18] The opening reminds me of that night in Chicago at Buddy Guy's Legends when Buddy Guy stopped playing and told a disruptive group of friends who were chattering and laughing at the top of their lungs to shut up and listen. Like Bach's cantata, Guy's songs often addressed serious topics in a playful tone "A Man and the Blues," for example, is introduced by a guitar solo with slow, arching lyrical phrases, until Buddy Guy hammers repeatedly on the blue note E-flat against the C-major chord, after which the melodic phrases become more euphoric and confident, describing, with almost clinical precision, blues as a state of mind.[19] The song, when performed in a club with bar service, can swallow the audience.

Bach's cantata was first presented at Zimmermann's café in Leipzig about 1735.[20] In this coffee shop, Bach directed the collegium musicum until Gottfried Zimmermann, the coffeehouse's owner, died in 1741. The first line of Bach's coffee cantata ("Sweigt stille, plaudert nicht") acknowledges the audience as part of the physical space and soundscape of the cantata itself.

Addressing the audience's noise produces a "presence effect," to borrow a term used by Hans Ulrich Gumbrecht in *Production of Presence*, as it fully belongs to the culture of presence where the body of the actor coexists with the bodies of the audience.[21] By telling people to be quiet, the first line of the cantata projects onto the music score the shadow of a sound the audience casts on the venue: a coffeehouse. That sound shadow also evokes the interaction between the musicians and their rowdy, hypercaffeinated audience, amplifying the presence effect.

In his influential book *The Structural Transformation of the Public Sphere*, the philosopher Jürgen Habermas writes that coffee culture was distinctive of the Enlightenment because it allowed democratic and intellectual exchange and interaction.[22] It was not always an inclusive culture, however. For Bach's first thirty years, Leipzig's lively coffee culture excluded women: a 1716 public ordinance banned "the presence and service of all female persons in coffee-houses."[23] But the ban soon gave way. In 1725 a tourist guide to the city advertised "the eight licensed public coffee houses have provided entertainment for people of all rank, ladies and gentlemen," one of them being Zimmermann's, which, as stated in an announcement of musical concerts in the city for the year 1736, offered weekly musical events performed and attended primarily by university students, a rowdy crowd who were also attentive to trendy music and topics.[24]

If women could attend Bach's coffeehouse concerts less than ten years after they were banned from the city cafés, this was due to their fierce resistance. Katherine Goodman reconstructs gender tensions at the time, writing that "Bach's *Coffee Cantata* was written and first performed in an intellectual atmosphere charged with antagonism about the role of women in cultural life. It amounted to a gender war."[25]

Doctors were also unsuccessfully preaching the dangers of women's drinking coffee both in private and in public. A treatise on the subject was published by the physician Daniel Duncan in Leipzig in 1707. The frontispiece shows women playing cards and chatting while drinking coffee, with a caption reading, "And if we drink ourselves to death at least we do it according to the current fashion."[26] As David Yearsley demonstrates in his latest book on Bach, women's response was immediate: in 1715 Madame Eleonora Charlotte Leucorande published a pamphlet claiming that "coffee is an excellent means to prevent excess of wetness [in women]," and that is why in Leipzig women who drink coffee look and are healthier, since coffee "keeps their blood healthy, relaxing circulation when necessary, so that in marriage they can become blessed mothers." Both defenders and detractors of the health consequences of caffeine consumption seem to agree that, as Yearsley puts it, "the beverage makes women more masculine, and therefore more difficult to control."[27]

Gender troubles are the focus of Bach's cantata, which begins with a father, Schlendrian, ranting about his inability to control his daughter Ließgen. In the ensuing recitative, he tells her to give up coffee. Ließgen replies that she needs coffee for medical reasons without it she could "become like a shriveled-up roast goat" (ein verdorrtes Ziegenbrätchen). She then sings her aria, "Ei, wie schmeckt der Coffee süße" (Oh, how sweet the coffee tastes). The flute introduction is a sweet but jittery line rapidly alternating eighth notes, sixteenth notes, sixteenth-note triplets, and thirty-second notes, in a restless juxtaposition of legato and staccato articulations. In the equally jittery vocal line, Ließgen obsessively repeats the word "coffee" nineteen times. Unfortunately, many performances of this piece seem to have been recorded under the influence of chamomile tea rather than coffee. Two convincing, well-caffeinated performances are the version by Emma Kirby and the Academy of Ancient Music, conducted by Christopher Hogwood, with Lisa Beznosiuk on the flute, and a version sung by Sumi Jo, which speeds it up even further, aided because the Concertgebouw ensemble uses a modern flute.[28] It seems that to perform this piece well the interpreters need to have been drinking coffee, or at least to be willing and able to simulate its effects.

Those in the audience who were drinking coffee not only were listening to the aria, they were part of its subject. On February 7, 2020, I attended a live performance of the Coffee Cantata at the Herbst Theater in San Francisco; coffee was served in the foyer, but giant signs were posted at the entrance instructing, "Water Only in Theater." The tenor's opening words—"Be quiet, do not chat"—were rendered preposterous by the announcement that had already instructed the audience to turn off cell phones. Rather than a presence effect, the relocation of the piece from the coffeehouse to a still, formal concert hall produced a distance or absence effect.[29]

Coffee and Chocolate in *Così fan tutte*

Like the first audience for Bach's Coffee Cantata, the original audience for Mozart's *Così fan tutte* could smell and taste coffee. In the Viennese Burgtheater where *Così* was premiered on January 26, 1790, people were drinking hot and cold beverages before and during the performance, producing a presence effect that would make the arguments and drama in the opera more real and relevant.

The representation of coffee, chocolate, and other gastronomic signs in *Così fan tutte* provides a fresh perspective on the debate over whether the opera contradicts or confirms the statement in its title that "all women behave the same way." More precisely, it encourages us to ask whether men, as well as women, act and react predictably as a result of chemical stimulation. The opera's subtitle, *La scuola degli amanti* (the school of lovers), emphasizes how both sexes are tested (*delle amanti* would have restricted the gender to women).[30] Debates on gender roles and identity were a hot topic in coffeehouses from the time of Bach's Coffee Cantata to the premiere of Mozart's *Così fan tutte*.

The opening scene of Mozart's opera is set in a public coffee shop (*bottega di caffè*) in Naples, a city still renowned for the high quality of its coffee. The importance of the setting is obvious when we consider that Mozart copied it down in the autograph score.[31] Two men, Ferrando and Guglielmo, are persuaded by an old libertine philosopher, Don Alfonso, to test the fidelity of their respective fiancées, Dorabella and Fiordiligi.

In the coffee scene, Mozart represents men as acting, or reacting, under the influence of a chemical substance. As an avid coffee drinker, Mozart was familiar with the effects of caffeine and reproduced them in his music, represented in the instrumental opening of the scene by rapid arpeggios over a bass filled with pulsing octave leaps, fast alternation of piano and forte dynamics, and quarter notes and eighth notes fragmented by pauses to musically cardiograph the effects of caffeine: shortness of breath, rapid pulse, tachycardia, palpitations, and arrhythmia. The violins introduce the caffeinated melody later sung by the two young men, alternating falling anacruses and dotted figurations with trills launching speedy ascending notes, also fragmented, like the throbbing bass, by rests of three different lengths. After a scant four measures, Mozart shifts to triplets and longer ascending tirades, replicating the sensation of light-headedness. The rhythmic variety and intensity are not only energizing, but also exhausting, since they happen over a prolonged tonic chord: Mozart represents, with medical precision, chemically stimulated excitement.

The rest of the scene is a theatricalized representation of a coffeehouse debate that, consistently with Spary's description of similar debates, involves epigrammatic satire, philosophical disputes for the production of "playful, secular knowledge," and the "settlement of philosophical disputes," abounding with playful violence, so that "conversations often apparently ended in brawls as clients sought to defend their honor in the face of verbal insults or philosophical disputes."[32] Ferrando and Guglielmo indeed react violently to Don Alfonso's claim that there is nothing special about Dorabella and Fiordiligi, since "they eat like us" (mangian come noi). The implication is that all women, like all men, are subject to the appetites of the lower body.

As the young men invite Don Alfonso to unsheathe his sword, the old philosopher replies, "the only duels I engage in are at the [dining] table" (e duelli non fò se non a mensa). After they agree to wager a large sum on their women's fidelity, we learn, in the final number of the scene (terzetto no. 3) that Guglielmo plans to spend his winnings on a banquet (convito), to which he will invite Don Alfonso and other guests (convitati). This invitation leads to the moment where the three characters sing together about the toasts they are going to make (E che brindis' replicati) at the end of the adventure. It is at this climactic point that the trio moves from the dominant back to the closing tonic to project their imagined ending.

The continual references to food in the opera stimulate appetite at all levels. To increase the effect, the entire test of the women's fidelity is conducted on an empty stomach. Toward the end of the act (1, 12), Guglielmo asks whether they are going to eat, to which his companion responds that at "the end of the battle, dinner will taste better" (A battaglia finita / Fia la cena per noi più saporita). A meal does indeed come at the end of the opera, but it turns into a convivial battlefield or dueling ground, as anticipated in Don Alfonso's line. After the two men manage to seduce each other's girlfriends, they reluctantly take part in a wedding banquet served, most unusually, in the women's palace, with all the paraphernalia of an aristocratic meal (2, 15): Tafelmusik, played by a small orchestra upstage (orchestra in fondo), silver tableware (doppieri d'argento), four waiters in formal attire (quattro servi riccamente vestiti), and a chorus of servants and musicians playing instruments (coro di servi e suonatori). And yet, during the toast Guglielmo wishes, in an aside, that the unfaithful women would drink poison instead of wine (a bevessero del tossico), and the feast is interrupted by the return of the women's original partners. As the libretto instructs, "the servants take the dining table away and the musicians leave in a hurry," hence there is no communal meal sealing the reestablishment of the original couplings. The only thing in the men's stomachs is the coffee they drank at the beginning of the first act and the wine they drank during the toast.

The public and semipublic spaces of coffee and wine are contrasted to the domestic spaces of the women's elegant chamber and the attached garden. We know that the garden is also an orchard because of a casual comment Ferrando makes to his friend's lady that the trees have "more leaves than fruits" (2, 5). Fruit trees were typical of aristocratic gardens of the time and provided delicacies for sophisticated tables.[33] They also recall the biblical Garden of Eden, where forbidden fruit is ready to be eaten. Da Ponte's use of gastronomic signs spans the modern world of trendy culinary fashions and traditional biblical allegory.[34]

Da Ponte describes the role of chocolate carefully when Despina prepares it and her mistresses reject it (1, 8–9). The gastronomic sign acquires different meanings and functions, both realistic and symbolic. In the recitative, chocolate is first used to convey Despina's socially progressive stance. As the stage directions in the libretto prescribe, the scene is set in an "*elegant room with several chairs, a table, etc.*" where "*Despina is preparing the chocolate*," complaining about her status ("What a wretched life to be a maid!"). She reflects that she has been slaving away all day. The smell of the chocolate prompts her to denounce the injustice of inequality: "It's half an hour that I've been whipping, the chocolate is ready and I can only smell it while my mouth is dry? Isn't perhaps my mouth like yours, well-bred ladies? And why then do you get the substance and I get only the scent?" At this point she can no longer resist and resolves to try it, but the ecstatic gustatory moment is interrupted by the sudden entrance of the ladies: "By Bacchus, I want to taste it. Damn it . . . it's so good! Somebody is coming! (*she wipes her mouth*). Good heavens, it's my mistresses: Ladies your breakfast is ready."[35] The two well-bred sisters, however, are so upset by the departure of their lovers that they reject the inviting breakfast: *Dorabella, Fiordiligi coming in in a desperate state of mind etc., Despina serves the chocolate on an elegant tray. Dorabella flings it to the ground. In front of the unbelieving Despina, they both take off all their womanly ornaments* and ask for a dagger and poison to commit suicide. The hyperbolic tone, parodying opera seria, prompting Dorabella's rage aria "Smanie implacabili" (Implacable anxieties, making me restless).

As already discussed, access to chocolate was perceived as access to wealth and health. As in the case of Leporello's stealing pheasant from Don Giovanni's lavish table, Despina's theft of chocolate crosses social boundaries. As a comic character, though, she shows more appetite than the two sisters, whose stomachs have been closed by their tragic separation from their partners. The rejection of chocolate—not only food but also a healthy drink—is caused by anxiety, but it also amplifies anxiety: Dorabella's "Smanie implacabili," set in an allegro agitato tempo marking. Mozart provides with medical precision a musical dramatization of the anxiety provoked by the absence of or withdrawal from chocolate. Dorabella's descending melodic line encompasses the huge span of an octave plus a third in only four measures, but it is immediately fragmented by pauses breaking syllables in the middle: "sma[pause]nie im[pause]placabili." The melody is accompanied by a tachycardiac pulsing bass and nervously palpitating waves of triplets in the upper strings.

Notwithstanding this medical precision, *Così fan tutte* debunks excessive medicalization. The act I finale satirizes mesmerism, which in France was a radical belief in medically manipulating interpersonal bonds, from the most intimate level of single bodies to the body politic. The French Mesmeric Society preached a scientific approach to social bonds based on a mechanistic conception of human relationships understood as a system of magnetic attractions and repulsions. One of its founding members—Guillaume Kornman—tested his wife's fidelity, generating a sensational public scandal that inspired the plot of the opera.[36] A confrontation between the French playwright Pierre Beaumarchais (author of the Figaro saga) and Kornman started in 1781 and culminated in a public pamphlet war a few years later when Antonio Salieri, an acquaintance of Da Ponte and Mozart, was living and collaborating with Beaumarchais. Beaumarchais attacked the banker and defended his unfaithful wife, who had been locked in a prison for prostitutes, revealing that Kornman had encouraged his wife's lover and created opportunities for illicit encounters between them, probably as a test in "animal magnetism." It is likely that the early unusual spelling of the name of the character Guglielmo as "Guilelmo" in the original libretto and in Mozart's autograph alluded to Guillaume Kornman. Mozart may even have met the real-life Guillaume. In 1778 Mozart's father Leopold wrote from Salzburg to Wolfgang Amadeus in Paris asking him to bring music scores and his book on violin playing to "Messieur Kornman etc.: Banquiers."[37] It is possible that the intention was to obtain a loan, thanks to their mutual acquaintance, Dr. Anton Mesmer, for whom Mozart had played piano in the late 1760s and had produced his singspiel *Bastien und Bastienne* in the doctor's villa. After Mesmer moved to Paris in 1778, Kornman and his lawyer appropriated mesmerism and turned it into a weapon of political and social control. By alluding to this scandal and debunking mesmerism in the opera, Da Ponte and Mozart, in line with Beaumarchais, opposed the ideology of oppressive medicalization of sexuality being promoted by the French mesmerists.

The title of the opera, therefore, does not essentialize unfaithful women but focuses on behavior by describing what they do (*così fan tutte*) rather than what they are (*così son tutte*). It is Despina, in her aria no. 12 ("In uomini") who essentializes men, explaining to the two sisters that "all men *are* made of the same dough" (di pasta simile *son tutti* quanti). She emphasizes *son tutti* quanti by repeating it over a monotonic bass with the tonic on every dotted quarter note, doubled by the woodwinds that add a grace note to each one. The repetition and rhythm depict the act of kneading the dough. Despina is the rare case of a female character who refers to men using food metaphors; in the course of the opera she compares them not only to dough, but also to figs and apples.

Entr'acte: The Dead Composers' Café

I remember the coffee that the philosopher Vittorio Hösle used to brew for me in his house in South Bend, Indiana, as some of the best in my life, in part because the aroma of the exciting beverage went so well with our conversations. Among his numerous publications he wrote a best-selling book titled *The Dead Philosophers' Café* in which he imagines a coffeehouse where philosophers from different epochs gather and debate.[38] I wonder what a *Dead Composers' Café* would be like. I can imagine Bach running into Mozart, offering him a freshly brewed coffee and having a casual conversation prompted by the flavor and smell of their hot beverage:

Bach: People think you represent the New and I the Old. Yet in your opera you still represent coffee as a drink for men only, as it was in Leipzig back in 1715, even before my time at Zimmermann's! While your men drink coffee in a public house, your women stay home and drink chocolate. My Ließgen instead drinks coffee, like a man, even without her father's permission. Who's the arrow then, and who's the circle, Herr Mozart?

Mozart (*smiling and nodding*): Touché! (*he takes a sip of coffee, thinks for a few moments and continues*) . . . and yet, your cantata represents a girl with a problem of substance addiction and ends with a trio singing "Die Katze läßt das Mausen nicht / Die Jungfern bleiben Coffeeschwestern" [Cats do not give up mousing, girls remain coffee-sisters], as if to say women's behavior is predictable, like cats with mice. Ergo . . . at least you seem to agree with me that 'così fan tutte.'"

Bach: Ah. . . . sehr gut, you got me, young friend . . . sehr gut! Perhaps you and I are also addicted to coffee like my Ließgen: "Così fan tutti" or, shall we say "Così *facciamo tutti*"? Ah ah ah!

I imagined this absurd conversation while sitting still and silent at the Herbst Theater in San Francisco, missing the coffee I had to dump in the water fountain before entering the auditorium. Listening to the Coffee Cantata without being allowed to drink coffee seemed to me as surreal as imagining Bach and Mozart chatting away.

Puccini, American Coffee, and Other Treats

Fortunately, before the Coffee Cantata I had two shots of "Illicit Espresso" at a place called the Contraband Coffee Bar, which injected me with enough caffeine to keep me awake until the next morning. During that sleepless night, I tried to recollect whether American characters in opera drink coffee. They do, but not until *The Girl of the Golden West*, and not espresso, which seems to be illicit in opera too. In *Madama Butterfly* American characters drink "milk punch and whisky" while toasting their nation and singing "America Forever." Milk punch, originally from Scotland, became a typical American cocktail. Benjamin Franklin imported the recipe after his five-year sojourn in England. In his version, which he personally annotated in 1762, it involves brandy, lemon juice, nutmeg, sugar, and milk.[39] Both liquors betray the Anglo-Saxon identity of the two American characters, as was the case for eighteenth-century Bostonians drinking tea in Paisiello's *Le gare generose*.[40] In Puccini's opera, the clash between Japanese and American cultures is represented gastronomically as mistrust for food served at the Japanese wedding banquet celebrating the union between the American groom, Pinkerton, and his Japanese bride, Cio-Cio-San. In the era of Puccini, tea was a gastronomic signifier for the Japanese, since it was already associated with China, as we have seen, but no longer for the Americans, who predominantly drank coffee. The stage directions in the libretto prescribe *jams, sweets, sake, liquors, wines, tea service* (confetture, pasticcietti, saki, liquor, vini e servizi da thè), which Pinkerton describes as "flies, sugar spiders, nests in julep! All the sweets and every delicatessen of Japanese gastronomy" (Mosche, ragni allo zucchero, / Nidi al giuleppe! Tutti I dolci d'uso, / Ogni ghiottoneria / Della nipponeria!).[41] The gastronomic signs in Pinkerton's lines contradict the visual gastronomic signs, since the Japanese viands onstage look entirely unremarkable—showing that Pinkerton's concept of Japan is so biased as to block his perception of reality.

La fanciulla del West also represents the different ethnic and national cultures coexisting in California at the time of the Gold Rush: Anglo-Saxon, Mexican, Native American, African American, Asian American, and even Australian. The group of Californian gold miners gathering at Minnie's barroom "Polka" in 1848, the year Mexican California was annexed to the United States, marginalizes native Californians (Mexicans and Native Americans), creating an opposition between "the Nation and the Other," where the Nation is represented by the newcomers.[42] Different ethnicities are identified immediately through their names and appearance, such as Dick Johnson, "alias Ramirez"; Jack Rance; Billy Jackrabbit, described as "an Indian redskin," and his squaw Wowkle; Jake Wallace, "a traveling camp-minstrel," a role originally interpreted in blackface; and José Castro, described as a "half-breed."[43] Even the group of miners and Minnie (the "Nation") is ethnically diverse.

Gastronomic signifiers help cement this culturally and ethnically heterogeneous group. At the beginning of the opera, they all drink whiskey and eat the only humble food that appears to be available at the Polka: oysters in vinegar (ostriche sott'aceto), while singing the "ritornello americano,"

"Dooda, dooda, day. . . ." Musically and dramatically, as Beth Levy points out in her study of musical representations of the American West, Puccini dramatizes a "collective nostalgia" and "Old World melancholy" even though he represents a "conflation of American types (black, Native, outlaw)" through music quotations and sonic evocations.[44] The gastronomic signifiers are in fact residues of English or Scottish taste transplanted to the American West. Besides the obvious reference to whiskey, the reference to "oysters in vinegar" is a departure from David Belasco's literary source, where Minnie mixes a "prairie oyster," a cocktail made with raw eggs.[45] The common gastronomic culture of "the Nation" is undoubtedly Anglo-Saxon.

The culturally and linguistically marginalized Native Americans are, at the beginning of the second act, tempted to steal Minnie's goodies from the table she sets for her date with Dick Johnson, alias the bandit Ramirez. Minnie's table presents a more varied gastronomic palette: whiskey, cream-filled cookies, a tart, slices of meat, and sugar for the coffee.[46] Unlike Mozart's irreverent servants, they do not dare at first to put their hands on Minnie's food, and Billy only touches the cream filling with his finger to put it back. Later, when they think of their children, Billy Jackrabbit gives his wife Wowkle a little bit of cream (orchestral score's rehearsal number 5, henceforth r.n., with indication *he gives Wowkle a bit of cream on a piece of paper; she licks it avidly*). They then immediately share pipe tobacco, launching the duet, after which he hopes to get some whiskey too after being married. While pipe tobacco still denotes Native American identity as it did in the eighteenth century, whiskey—the drink of the new "Nation" anchored to the British Old World—represents their hope for integration. Julian Budden in his commentary on Puccini's operas labels this scene as comic and points at their "crude appetite for whiskey and jewels."[47] Appetite in fact is what drives the entire community of Californians, a reason this can be considered a "comic opera" as much as *Carmen* is an *opéra-comique*. The Native Americans' appetite is far from "crude," however, since it attaches more to the symbolic reference of the gastronomic signs than to their caloric or alcoholic content.

Minnie's date with Dick Johnson—their act 2 love duet—is also articulated through a deployment of gastronomic signifiers that define and build a common identity as well as the dynamics of the encounter. More than anything, their reactions—the creating and cementing of their relationship—are stimulated by coffee, which is also a neutral drink in terms of identity, allowing the Mexican man and the Anglo-Saxon American woman to meet on common ground. The encounter is at first musically dramatized through nervous syncopations after the increment in pace (allegretto mosso, r.n. 13) and interjection of rapid sixteenth-note scales by flutes playing in parallel seconds. It calms down as they remember their past encounter at the Polka. The crucial shift from the recollection to the acknowledgment of themselves in the present in Minnie's cabin happens as Minnie orders Wowkle to bring the coffee.

Once the coffee is served the meter, key, and tempo change to an indicative "allegretto mosso e giocoso" (r.n. 19), which opens a section where the effect of caffeine is represented musically. It is the most alert episode of the duet, accompanied by an ostinato alternation of the tonic triad D major with the fifth of the chord reiterated in rapid thirty-second-note legato-staccato notes and a pizzicato open fifth on the tonally unrelated B-E bichord. Meanwhile the solo violin plays a legato ascending arpeggio with the harp, followed by chirping replies of the flutes and piccolos in counterpoint with the celesta. This remarkable variety of effects and microgestures happens in just one measure, repeated as an ostinato as Minnie sings with joy, in a light coloratura style that is a rarity in Puccini's work, about her happy life galloping her horse. Minnie's ride leads her to think of the sublime mountains of the Sierra Nevada and from that of her yearning for the sky and heaven through an ecstatic melodic ascent on a stretched-out D-seventh chord.

The following food item is the cream cookie (biscotto alla crema) that sealed the love between the two Native Americans in the previous scene. This dramatic moment was critical enough to be immortalized by a still photograph cataloged as "Del biscotto alla crema?" in the Ricordi Archive: it is an image from the series of photographs from the 1905 Belasco play that Ricordi collected for the production of the opera.[48] Here Minnie offers the cookie to Johnson, who takes it while the orchestra "sings" (cantando) the "love leitmotif"[49] in an andante calmo (r.n. 22), leading to Minnie's reflection that "love is infinite" as the violins open the sound by taking off their mutes. The prelude to their kiss is then Minnie's offering a Havana cigar (r.n. 24). This episode parallels the previous scene with Billy and Wowkle, with the Havana cigar (betraying Ramirez's Latin American identity) replacing the pipe that marked the Native American. Ramirez's repeated passionate request for a kiss (un bacio) in a lyric melody that holds the ground is reminiscent of the African warrior Othello's asking the Venetian lady Desdemona for "un bacio," hoping that love could overcome the difference in race.

After Minnie sends Wowkle away to remain alone, undisturbed, with Johnson, the door opens and a raging snowstorm invades Minnie's room, an allusion to the encounter between Siegmund and Sieglinde in Wagner's *Die Walküre* (1, 1).[50] The love between the Wälsung siblings is also carried out through an exchange of refreshments: "Erquickung schaff' ich" (I'll get some refreshment) she reassures the exhausted Siegmund. She gives him water from a drinking horn, refilling it later with alcoholic "honeyed mead" (Des seimigen Metes / süssen Trank), which they both drink from the same rudimentary cup. The incestuous love between brother and sister is justified by their drive not to corrupt their pure blood. It is relevant that Puccini alludes to this iconic scene of racist ideology in his mixed-race love duet set in California. In doing so Puccini represents a reaction against the myth of racial purity already raging in Europe. While the Wälsungs drink alcohol, the Californian Mexican-American couple drink coffee, carrying on an Enlightenment tradition of taking caffeine to keep at bay the monsters produced by the sleep of reason.

In Bach's Coffee Cantata, Mozart's *Così fan tutte*, Rossini's *Il turco in Italia*, and Puccini's *Fanciulla*, coffee does not retain a consistent denotative function, but the effect of caffeine is consistently dramatized musically, used to stir excitement and emotions. In Rossini and Puccini, sharing food or drink has the effect of establishing or strengthening an intimate bond and excluding those who do not share. This is indeed the main use of gastronomic signs in nineteenth-century opera, as we shall see in the next chapter about Verdi's operas.

CHAPTER NINE

Verdi and the Laws of Gastromusicology

Out of the twenty-eight operas Giuseppe Verdi wrote, two are comic operas: *Oberto* (1839) composed at the beginning of his career, and *Falstaff* (1893) at the end. The remaining works are serious dramas, often tragic.[1] While eighteenth-century opera seria excluded gastronomic signs, Verdi did not discriminate, and his operas offer a summa of the functions and laws of operatic gastromusicology. Bodily realism and the realistic use of gastronomic signs, which were the trademark of comedy, now invaded the world of tragedy, as in *Traviata* or in *La forza del destino*, where Verdi represents the large kitchen of a tavern where patrons are eating a simple supper (2, 1–4), food vendors (3, 6), starving peasants begging for bread (3, 12), and friars serving soup to the poor (4, 1–2).[2]

Verdi's inspiration for injecting bodily realism into tragedy, including the effects of wine or the dramatizing of appetite, even hunger, came from one of his greatest models: Mozart's *Don Giovanni*, an opera that had already evaded the clear-cut separation of serious and comic opera.[3] An early Verdi biographer reports that Verdi's teacher, Vincenzo Lavigna, who had produced Mozart's *Don Giovanni* in Milan in 1814, spent many evenings with his young pupil playing Mozart's opera at the piano and carefully analyzing it. The result, as Verdi's early biographer Arthur Pougin writes, was that "Verdi memorized *Don Giovanni*, admired it, respected it, and it gave him indigestion that lasted for many years."[4]

Verdi uses feasting and fasting gestures primarily to dramatize relationships, following consistent principles that can be summarized in the seven laws of operatic gastromusicology:

No meal can be sad.
No starvation can be happy.
A shared meal or drink is a socially cohesive event.
The presence of food or drink excludes immediate catastrophe (unless the food or the drink is poisoned).
The act of feasting is in itself morally neutral, but a feasting group (or individual) is morally negative when contrasted with a fasting group or individual.
A fasting individual is a hero; a hero is always a sober person.
Music and text may lie, but gastronomic signs never do.

Traviata's Gastronomies

La traviata, premiered in Venice in 1853, uses the familiar religious symbolism of feasting and fasting related to the dichotomy of carnival versus Lent, but it also exemplifies the five functions of food in opera: ritual (including religious meals or fasts), social (establishing or breaking relationships), intimacy (characters exchanging food, often to establish a romantic relationship), denotative (revealing identity), medicinal (affecting the mind or body), and dietary (shaping body size and image).

The libretto's literary source, *La dame aux camélias* by Alexandre Dumas fils, was a realistic novel and play inspired by the life and death of a real *grisette* (courtesan) named Alphonsine Plessis, alias Marie Duplessis, who died of tuberculosis in 1847 at age twenty-three.[5] In Louis Huart's treatise *Psychologie de la grisette* (1841), such women are described as craving "marrons, babas, galettes, vin chaud, bischoff [cookies] et autres refraîchissements analogues." To court a *grisette*, Huart instructs his male audience, one must offer her food. Among the best bait are oranges and chestnuts.[6]

According to the contract between Verdi and the theater of Venice La Fenice, the opera was "to be produced in this theater during the coming 1852/53 season of carnival and Lent."[7] Carnival is explicitly represented in the second-act masked party at Flora's (no. 7, act 2 finale), where a chorus of men dressed as bullfighters sing about the parade of the "fatted ox," a typical French carnival ritual. In the third act, while Violetta is dying, the metaphor of the sacrificial animal recurs in the chorus coming from the street (no. 9, "Baccanale"). Here castanets and tambourines mark every downbeat of the 2/4 measures as if beaten by excited but unrefined players, while the chorus sings, in rhythmic unison, *quinari sdruccioli*, or five-syllable slack lines ending with proparoxytone words accented on the antepenultimate syllable ("Largo al quadrupede"). One year after *Traviata*, another Lenten opera titled *I baccanali di Roma*, by Carlo Romani, used the same meter for a bacchanal chorus, "Al suon festevole, / di tibie e cembali" ("At the festive sound of tibias and cymbals").[8] In *Traviata*, the chorus's rhythmic pattern is doubled by a fanfare of horns, trombones, clarinets, and piccolos that approximate the timbre of ancient folk instruments and eventually play very fast, sliding scales (velocissimo, scivolare) ending on an uncomfortably high A4 in the basses. In the score, Verdi reassures the bass players, "Don't be afraid, basses, of this A: no need to sing it [in tune]; you can slide it as all the other instruments do," encouraging the production of a type of sound associated with a folkish bacchanal.[9]

For a carnival *and* Lent opera Verdi could not have chosen a more fitting, but also more controversial, subject. The librettist Francesco Maria Piave explained to the secretary of La Fenice that Verdi was "in love" with the subject of *La dame aux camélias*, which was then provisionally titled *Amore e morte* (Love and death).[10] The first interpreter of the role of Giorgio Germont, the baritone Felice Varesi, vehemently expressed his consternation over the "very dangerous" representation of a high-class prostitute.[11] Understandably, negotiating with the censors was not easy and contributed to a substantial production delay, causing the opera's premiere to be moved from carnival into Lent (March 6, 1853).

Traditionally, Lenten operas had been based on stories of saints or sacred scriptures.[12] Although Violetta is not exactly a saint, Dumas conceived the story as spiritually edifying: "Christianity is ever-present, with its wonderful parable of the prodigal son, to urge us to counsels of forbearance and forgiveness. Jesus was full of love for souls of women wounded by the passions of men, and He loved to bind their wounds, drawing from those same wounds the balm that would heal them. Thus he said to Mary Magdalene: 'Your sins, which are many, shall be forgiven, because you loved much'—a sublime pardon which was to awaken a sublime faith."[13]

The gastronomic trajectory of *Traviata* reflects the trajectory from the feasting of carnival to the fasting of Lent. At the beginning of the opera, Violetta offers and shares food and wine. In the end, as she dies after sacrificing herself to save the honor of her lover's family, the only objects in her sickroom are laid out on a dressing table to remind us of her past life: an oil lamp, symbol of vanishing life; medicines that are useless; and a crystal glass and carafe of water, symbol of death and purification.[14] Verdi represents the disembodiment of the protagonist through a radical contrast in orchestral texture, which becomes rarefied at the end (no. 11, "finale ultimo"), as Violetta shifts from singing to speaking ("[*parlando*]: cessarono gli spasimi" [the spasms stop]). This textural contrast is so essential to the narrative that Verdi sets it up in the very first measures of the orchestral prelude (no. 1), which begins with the diaphanous sound of solo violins that we will hear again in the death scene. The body of the string section is fibrillated by splitting it into eight plus eight solo, divided violins (soli divisi), whispering, pianississimo, in the very highest register a minor triad that transforms into a major one through a melodic ascent.

The use of gastronomic signs in the opera differs from their use in its literary source. In Dumas's novel, the young lover, Armand (Alfredo), recollects his first encounter with Marguerite (Violetta) at the Opéra Comique, where he offered sugared raisins to the woman, "who ate her raisins without paying any further attention to me." Two years later, he sees an old count offering sweets to Marguerite at the same theater.[15] In both cases the sweets label her as fickle and as a courtesan, who takes food from everyone and pays attention to no one. Later, he and three other friends have dinner at her apartment, where, as Armand recollects, "we laughed, we drank, we ate a great deal at the supper party. Within minutes, the merriment had sunk to the lowest level," and the fun is spoiled by Marguerite's violent fit of coughing.[16] The reader is aware of Marguerite's tragic destiny because the novel starts from its conclusion, the horrifying exhumation of Marguerite's body. The eater is now eaten; the shroud covering her is "completely eaten away at one end," revealing the body, whose "eyes were simply two holes, the lips gone."[17]

Verdi's theatrical representation begins more merrily and ends less lugubriously. The first scene is a dinner party at Violetta's. She is not an avid solitary eater, as in Dumas, but a generous hostess. As the curtain rises, we see "a table richly set for a lavish feast" (tavola riccamente imbandita). All sources are adamant about the immediate presence of food. Verdi, in his autograph sketches, titles the scene "dinner" (cena).[18] The food, china, and silverware, from the moment we first see it, denote a special festive moment, for which Verdi chooses the appropriate tempo indication, "Allegro brillantissimo e molto vivace." The presence of waiters in a private house and the table manners indicate the high class of the hostess and guests.

At Violetta's dinner party, a polka rhythm permeates the soundscape. As Emilio Sala documents, the polka had been introduced in Venice and Paris only a few years before the composition of *Traviata*, and it was associated with the younger generation immersed in the political struggles of the 1848 revolutions.[19] High-class gastronomic signs (high-table manners, china, silverware, and food) clash with the polka as the topos of a new generation trying to disentangle itself from the old logic of class boundaries. The idiosyncratic social environment of Violetta's party, as defined by food and music, echoes the ambivalence of the position of the protagonist and her profession as a *grisette*. Huart indeed maintained that *grisettes* were "defined differently by different classes."[20]

Violetta's house is where people find a safe space to mingle. While Dumas represented this scene as an intimate dinner, Verdi and Piave opted for a banquet where sharing food and wine is a socially cohesive event, typical of communal meals studied by George Armelagos and Peter Farb in their anthropology of eating.[21] The guests appear at first in two divided groups. Some, already in Violetta's salon, are waiting for others who have been gambling at the house of her friend Flora. As soon as the latecomers arrive, Violetta's group playfully reproaches Flora's group with hungry mock anger. Violetta's invitation to drink ("fra le tazze è più viva la festa" [the party is livelier among the cups]) is a gesture of cohesion and a tension reliever. The two groups now become one and the chorus is reconciled, at least temporarily.

But more divisions emerge in the following scene (1, 2) with the entrance of Alfredo and his friend Gastone, marked by a modulation away from the initial A major and by the appearance of a new lyrical theme. As the score prescribes, Violetta "offers her hand to Alfredo, who kisses it," and one measure later, "waiters bring in the food." The scene superimposes the second function of food in opera—the intimate, erotic one—upon the first social, public function. At this point, as Violetta asks if supper is ready and a servant nods, the music stops again to signal another important moment of dramatic articulation, while Violetta invites everyone to sit at the table ("Miei cari sedete").

Violetta refers to the banquet as a place of truth: in a solemn, descending melodic line encompassing an octave, and accompanied only by long notes in the strings, she sings, "È al convito che s'apre ogni cor" (at the table all hearts are opened). The chorus answers as an ever larger and more unified group as the tonality rapidly returns to the tonic, A major. At this point everyone is seated and the dishes start to circulate.[22] From this point on throughout the supper, the relationship between Alfredo and Violetta strengthens, at first by a comparison between the gallantry of Alfredo and the clumsiness of his rival, Violetta's "sugar daddy" Baron Douphol. Douphol refuses to lead the toast—an antisocial if not openly hostile gesture—and he does so without opening his mouth, simply shaking his head and removing himself from the banquet by not drinking or eating. In his study on representations of food in modern fiction, Gian-Paolo Biasin observes that, in the context of narrative, there is a symbolic link between the act of receiving (food or drink) and producing (speech) from the same orifice: "The human mouth is the ambiguous locus of two oralities: one articulates the voice, language; the other satisfies a need, the ingestion of food."[23] Alfredo now replaces Douphol in Violetta's affections, as Violetta pours the wine into Alfredo's glass, after which Alfredo becomes more vocal while the Baron is silenced.

The brindisi "Libiamo" has always been the iconic moment of *Traviata*. An illustration for the toast song ("Ronde") composed for Dumas's play *La dame aux camélias*, as performed at the Théâtre du Vaudeville in 1852 (fig. 9.1) shows the heroine sitting at the dinner table during the toast.[24]

A period illustration published in 1856 in the *Illustrated London News* (fig. 9.2) shows the early interpreter of Violetta, Marietta Piccolomini, in her defining act of celebrating at the table.[25] In this image she is represented

Figure 9.1. Édouard Montaubry, "Ronde" for *La dame aux camélias* (Paris: Leduc, [1852]), frontispiece.

Figure 9.2. "Mdlle. Piccolomini, of Her Majesty's Theatre," *Illustrated London News*, May 31, 1856, 588.

in the first-act dinner and brindisi while raising the goblet next to a full plate of food.

"Libiamo" is a typical specimen of a choral drinking song structured as a ritualized toast.[26] Written with a sweeping waltz rhythm, the piece is a celebration of both communal and intimate joy. It alternates lines sung by Alfredo, Violetta, and a unified chorus. The censors emended Alfredo's invitation to "intoxicate the fleeting hour with voluptuous pleasure" (e la fuggevol ora / s'inebri ~~s'inebbrii a voluttà~~), replacing it with "più lieta scorrerà" (the fleeting hour will pass more pleasantly). They also disliked the invitation to "drink to the sweet shivers that love arouses" (Libiam ne' dolci fremiti / che suscita ~~l'amore~~), replacing "amore" (love) with "licore" (liquor). Likewise, they banned the invitation to drink and enjoy "warmer kisses" while drinking ("~~più caldi caldi baci avrà~~"), replacing this line with "cerchiam felicità" (let us seek happiness). Finally, Alfredo's reference to the cross ("croce e delizia," or "cross and delight") was replaced with "pain" ("duolo e delizia").[27] In a letter to his friend the sculptor Vincenzo Luccardi, Verdi complained that "the censors destroyed the meaning of the drama. They made *Traviata* pure and innocent. Thanks a lot! So they marred every situation and character. A whore must be a whore, always! If the sun would shine in the night there would be no night. In short, they are clueless!"[28]

Verdi managed to retain some of the original Dionysian quality of the drinking song in the music itself. The phrasing of the brindisi theme is slightly irregular, encompassing an unusual number of measures—ten rather than the typical eight.[29] They are grouped as six plus four, with the first group ("libiamo ne' lieti calici" [let's drink from happy goblets]) presenting more extended, lyrical note values than its consequent phrase ("che la bellezza infiora" [as beauty blossoms]). The effect is like an unsteady hastening toward the end, which, when effectively performed, gives the impression that the song is being sung by mildly inebriated partygoers.

This banquet scene exemplifies the first three laws of gastromusicology, as well as the social, intimate, denotative, and medicinal functions of the gastronomic sign in opera. Later in the opera, as we shall see, the dietary or bodily function—the body shape of the singer—emerges as the drama unfolds. Let us move for the time being to other of Verdi's parties, keeping an eye on who accepts or rejects eating or drinking.

Verdi's Parties

In Verdi's operas we find "dry" parties with food but no drinks (*Un giorno di regno*, 1, 1; *Traviata*, 2, 9; *Les vêpres siciliennes*, 2, 7, 3, 5), rowdy parties with drinks but no food (*Alzira*, 2, 1; *I masnadieri*, 3, 3; *Il corsaro*, 1, 1–2; *Les vêpres siciliennes*, 1, 1; *Otello*, 1, 1), parties with food and a toast (*Ernani*, 1, 1; *Attila*, 2, 5–6; *Macbeth*, 2, 5–7; *Traviata*, 1, 1), parties where refreshments are expected but absent (*Un giorno di regno*, 2; *Ernani*, 2, 1 and 4; *Rigoletto*, 1, 1), and offstage banquets (*I masnadieri*, 2, 1). Within this broad array of possibilities, social gatherings present different degrees of social cohesion. The act 1 banquet in *Traviata* offers the highest level of cohesion and yet, as we have seen, even in that case one character excludes himself from the merry, feasting group. The sad truth is that in Verdi's operas there is no good party, no perfect example of Armelagos and Farb's dictum that "eating is the primary way of initiating and maintaining human relationships."[30] The reason Verdi's operas lack a perfect convivial situation is that his dramaturgy often spins toward the tragic climax through a progressive crisis in human relationships and social cohesion.

The opening scene of *Rigoletto* represents a fragmented court, dominated by mistrust, conspiracy, and disrespect. After the short, ominous *preludio*, the curtain rises to reveal a dancing party (festa da ballo) in progress.[31] The Duke of Mantua speaks in a low tone with his courtesan Borsa about his plan to seduce the daughter of his court buffoon Rigoletto. After the libertine cavatina "Questa o quella," in which the Duke explains his indiscriminate taste for women, the guests dance a minuet and the Duke lusts after the Countess of Ceprano, unheard by her husband. Rigoletto now mentions "wine and feasts," listing what the Duke likes in rolling *doppi senari*, set by Verdi as a monotonic patter ending with real laughter (*ridendo*): "gambling, drinking wine, parties and dancing, battles and feasting" (Il giuoco ed il vino, le feste, la danza, / Battaglie, conviti, ben tutto gli sta). Like Don Giovanni, the Duke uses banquets, feasts, and wine not for nourishment, but to amuse himself and as bait to seduce and conquer his prey.

In many parties in Verdi's operas, a cohesive eating group emphasizes and brings to the fore the isolation of an individual. In the banquet scene of the act 2 finale of *Macbeth* (no. 9, "Convito"), a feasting group is contrasted with the troubled Macbeth (2, 5–7).[32] Before the brindisi begins ("Allegro brillante"), the guests gather around a lavish table. The banquet is opened by a toast that, as in *Traviata*, is a *ménage à trois* of the couple and the chorus. However, the brindisi itself (from the allegretto marking) works very differently than in *Traviata*, where the tenor leads the drinking song. Here Lady Macbeth leads the toast, and she does so with a display of coloratura that confers power on her as the unequaled protagonist of the scene. Her cheerful toast is echoed by a faithful chorus, after which a hit man informs the king, in an aside, that he has killed Banquo. The festive party music starts again, but disturbing musical signs appear as soon as the queen notices her husband's suspicious distraction. The ghost of Banquo appears while the joyful party music, marked "morendo" (dying), is engulfed in an explosive minor chord followed by a clashing diminished chord as the king sees the ghost (mm. 204–7). The queen tries to salvage the party after a long, terrifying section in which the music brings us inside a parallel reality populated by Macbeth's nightmares. Lady Macbeth and the chorus repeat the brindisi in a desperate attempt to hide the king's madness, which will irremediably fail after the second appearance of the specter at the end of the second toast. Only Lady Macbeth and the chorus participate in this second toast; Macbeth takes no active part. Macbeth acts as a real party pooper, even worse than Baron Douphol in *Traviata* (who sits alone in a corner). After the second appearance of the specter, his wife is forced to surrender to his antisocial behavior. The party is over as the chorus becomes infected by fear and sings as a troubled, fragmented ensemble, ending the act on an ominous minor sonority.

At the beginning of the second act of *I masnadieri* (2, 1), the isolated, distressed character Amalia appears in the foreground, while the sound of the feasting chorus drifts in, unaccompanied, from offstage as a dissonant happy element intruding on the heroine's anguish. She is alone, kneeling by the grave of her uncle Massimiliano Moor, and we hear a gloomy descending line in the strings, followed by a contemplative melody on a bass pedal ostinato.[33] In the scene, she expresses herself in tragic free-verse lines, "dell'infame banchetto io m'involai" (I flew away from the wretched banquet), contrasting with the convivial rhythms of the unseen a cappella chorus in the allegro vivace: "Let's enjoy ourselves, for fleeting are the hours of laughter; let pleasure lead us from cups to kisses" (Godiam che fugaci / Son l'ore del riso / Dai calici ai baci / Ne godi il piacer). Amalia calls the happy dinner party a "wretched banquet," and the grotesquely cheerful offstage music clashes with the funereal scenery and the heroine's mourning. The gastronomic contrast of the feasting/fasting trope makes the merry and consonant music of the chorus appear dissonant against the heroine's distressed music. From the perspective of the merry chorus, the law "no meal can be sad" stands but, as is often the case in Verdi's operas, somebody's happiness is somebody else's misery.

If no meal can be sad, then no starvation can be happy. In situations where serving food would be appropriate—as, for example, at a wedding banquet—a lack of refreshments is an unpleasant surprise. Although Verdi's characters do not notice the absence of refreshments that would normally be expected, the lack still sends a subliminal message to the audience, signaling that something is wrong.

All Verdi's wedding celebrations are fasting parties. In his operas marriage unions are never happy: either the soprano is condemned to marry a man she does not love, or the wedding ceremony ends in violence. Even Verdi's first comic opera, *Un giorno di regno*, represents a double wrong wedding, and there is no indication in the libretto that food appears onstage. A chorus of waiters and servants praises the beautiful parties and banquets at the house of the Baron, but nobody, including the prospective couples, makes a toast or sits at the dining table.[34] In fact, at the beginning of the second act, the chorus complains that the banquet has not yet started: they are literally starving. Thus, during the act 1 fasting wedding party, the music was stereotypical cheerful banquet music, but the lack of food portended the unhappy mismatch of the two couples. Music lies, but the gastronomic sign speaks the truth.

In *Alzira* (2, 7)—and also at the beginning of the second part of *Ernani*—Verdi again represents unhappy, fasting wedding parties where the gastronomic sign works against the music and the cheerful chorus appears clueless about what is really going on. In *Alzira*, the absence of food suggests that the marriage is wrong, since the Peruvian couple, Zamoro and Alzira, love each other but Alzira is being forced to marry the Spanish conquistador Gusmano. Before the party ends, Zamoro thrusts a dagger into Gusmano's chest, then invites the bride to drink his blood.

Les vêpres siciliennes also presents gastronomic signs that indicate a tragic ending. They also presage rescue, as when the presence of food indicates that a foreseeable catastrophe will be averted at the last minute. The representation of the marriage feast in this opera (2, 6) is particularly grandiose: no fewer than twelve couples are being wed at the same time. Although they are supposedly happy couples, food is absent.[35] The scene starts with a folk-like Sicilian dance, suggesting the flavor of southern Italy with a tarantella. Yet the music is anxiety driven. The E-minor folk dance is both exotic and unnerving: at first its short-breathed syncopations over the stereotypical triplets are characteristic of the dance, but then the music shifts to a pounding single note in the basses on each downbeat, each note reached by a grace note rising anacrusis, giving the impression that the bass players are having trouble finding the note. This folk music effect follows vertigo-inducing slow chromatic descents and other paraphernalia of exotic dance music.[36] The first performance of the opera, premiered in Paris on June 13, 1855, coincided with the first Paris Exposition universelle. Perhaps that was why Verdi does not offer a sympathetic representation of French troops or a positive representation of Italian conspirators.[37] Procida, a Sicilian doctor who is organizing the revolt against the French, plans to play an Iago-like trick: knowing the jealousy of Sicilian men, he hopes to incite a popular revolt by suggesting that the French occupiers will steal their brides. As the French soldiers start dancing the tarantella with the Italian women, tension rises. In the shock ensemble (interdits—accablés), the enraged Sicilian men decide to retaliate in a gradual music-dramatic crescendo. Just as they are ready to attack, a group of French officers and wealthy Sicilian women pass by in a galley eating *sorbetti* and singing merrily, "O bonheur! O délice!" (Oh goodness! Oh delight!) (2, 9), overlapping with the "interdits—accablés" that die down to a single whispered word, "vengeance!" postponing the revenge to the upcoming masked ball. In the following act, the audience expects to see blood. The tyrant Montfort is about to be killed in an instant ("Dans un instant . . . ici!"), but at the peak of the tension, *sorbetto* makes its second appearance (3, 6, *Les sorbes circulent*"), and Montfort is rescued.

The fourth act ends with the Sicilian men and the French soldiers sealing a truce with a toast (4, 5). This could be a moment of general happiness and reconciliation. Alas, the soloists do not join the drinking chorus, signaling that this happy ending is deceptive. In the last-act finale, as Montfort joins the hands of the young couple, the bell sounds. It is the signal for the insurrection that Procida gave to the Sicilian people. The curtain falls as the angry Sicilian crowd, armed with daggers and swords, are about to slaughter the foreign invaders.

The masked ball at the end of *Un ballo in maschera* (3, 7) is another occasion for conspirators to kill a political leader. The target is the governor of Boston. The scene opens with an exhilaratingly loud and fast chorus celebrating love and dance (Fervono amori e danze), in what the libretto describes as a "large and rich ballroom, splendidly lit," populated by a multitude of guests" and attended by black waiters (il servizio è fatto da neri), as would have been the case in colonial Boston.[38] The music is played by an onstage band. Too bad for the governor, no *sorbetti* are served. His former best friend has joined the "terrorists" and stabs him to death. As he dies, the governor pronounces his farewell to his beloved America ("Addio . . . diletta America").

The Drunkards and the Hero

In Verdi's operas, young men who sing and drink together are up to no good. All-male drinking songs belong to a type that David Rosen, in his study of meter and gender in Verdi's operas, describes as the "male-bonding, dangerously high testosterone-level choruses of certain non-sedentary professions, such as pirates, bandits, . . . but not musicologists (which might explain why musicologists rarely star in operas or 'summer block-buster action movies'). . . . This is the kind of music drunken soccer hooligans would howl."[39] These pieces present the duple meter and marchlike rhythms typical of military music and, like gangsta rap, they often celebrate violence and crime. Male drinking choruses are always contrasted to an opposing nondrinking group or a sober individual. In all these cases the drinking (or feasting) group has a negative connotation when contrasted with the fasting characters. This kind of feasting/fasting opposition can convey a political meaning, as in *Les vêpres siciliennes* (1, 1, oppressed Sicilians vs. occupying French soldiers) or in *Alzira* (2, 1, oppressed Inca prisoners vs. Spanish conquistadores) or in *Attila* (2, 5, oppressed Italians vs. barbarian invaders).

Les vêpres siciliennes opens with the French soldiers drinking in a square of Palermo, while Sicilians in the square look angrily at the merry occupants. The two choruses—Italian vs. French—are opposed sonically and visually. As Julian Budden observes, Verdi assigned to each chorus a "distinctive melody, tonality, and rhythmic gait."[40] The original stage manual divides the stage in half: tables with seated soldiers drinking stage right and Sicilians standing stage left without drinking or eating. After more drinking, as the dynamics increase to forte, the soldiers rise from the table holding glasses and bottles, while in the background the Sicilians prepare to attack with daggers in hand.[41]

Spanish soldiers occupying Peru in *Alzira* are much worse than their French counterparts. As in Voltaire's eighteenth-century tragedy, the conquistadores are presented as nationalistic war criminals. At the beginning of the third act of Verdi's opera, they drink and sing with glasses in hand (no. 8, "Mesci mesci"), as they celebrate their "joy after victorious war, carnage, and fury."[42] The score prescribes that the men drink happily ("sbevazzano allegramente") and cling to their glasses when toasting "to Spain." The short staccato phrases of "mesci mesci" are followed by a more lyrically prolonged and legato melody when they sing about the Spanish wine ("vino Ibero") they are savoring, reminding them of the flavor of their fatherland.[43] Within the same number, the tempo shifts from allegro vivace to lamentoso and the brassy sound of the orchestra (which includes a cimbasso, meaning the lowest available brass instrument) gives way to a warm melody of woodwinds in the range of tenors and basses, accompanied by pizzicato strings.[44] This shift corresponds to the entrance of the Zamoro with other "[Native] American prisoners" crossing the stage in chains. The instruments replace their voices, then the lament is interrupted by loud exclamations "Bevi!" (Drink!) from the Spanish soldiers, set as a descending octave leap in the dominant. The contrast between the feasting soldiers and the fasting prisoners is articulated through a radical change in texture, making it sonically striking.

In *Attila*, a chorus of barbarian warriors invading the Italian city of Aquileia is first represented at night among the ruins of the town they have just sacked (no. 2, Introduzione, "Urli, rapine"). The chorus is accompanied by a fanfare of trumpets, trombones, and cimbasso and celebrates "screams, robberies, gasps, blood, rapes, pillage, slaughter, and fire": "the game of Attila," a "rich banquet" of Valhalla. The final scene of the second act (no. 11) again presents Attila's camp at night, lit by fires and torches, where everything is ready for a solemn banquet (solenne convito). The chorus of Huns, Ostrogoths, and Herules ("Del ciel l'immensa volta") announces a new fun day of dismemberment of limbs and heads ("Di membra e teste tronche / godremo al nuovo giorno") over tremolos of the strings and rolls of timpani.[45] The orchestra again features a brassy sound (cimbasso, horns, trumpets, and trombones), but here Verdi foregrounds a comically grotesque melody of short staccato phrases. During the banquet, the Italian woman Odabella appears as the opposing, fasting heroine, sitting next to Attila and dressed as an Amazon warrior. At the end of the banquet, she saves Attila from being poisoned, but only so she can slaughter him with her own sword at the end of the opera.

In the drinking chorus in act 3 of *I masnadieri* (no. 10), the bandits of the collective title celebrate their violent lifestyle, singing at night in a forest by the ruins of an ancient castle. The dark, brassy fanfare of trombones, cimbasso, and bassoons is immediately contrasted with the descending phrase played by the strings in unison.[46] Taking advantage of the absence of their noble, sober leader Carlo Moor, the brigands sing a naughty song ("Le rube, gli stupri"), celebrating "pillage, rape, arson, killing" as their "pastimes and amusements." The juxtaposition of contrasting tempos and rhythms portrays the robbers' erratic, unpredictable lives. The third section of this piece is comically grotesque. The meter shifts from duple to triple, and in an amusing waltz, the robbers whisper in staccato ("sottovoce staccate") over an even quieter orchestra (pppp) about what amuses them most: "the last gasps of murdered fathers, the cries and wails of wives and mothers are music to us, are entertainment for our harsh, stony hearts." In the reprise of the first tempo ("allegro come prima"), they announce that, far from being afraid of being hanged one day, they drink to their own death: "Wetting our gullets with our last wine, la, ra. . . . la la ra . . . we'll leap from this world into the next."

Their leader, Carlo Moor, is a typical Romantic hero, a cultured man who becomes an outlaw out of disgust with humanity. At the beginning of the opera, he appears alone by a tavern, reading a book by Plutarch.[47] The moral and social distance between the hero and his lowlife comrades is emphasized by his physical and sonic distance: the brigands are offstage and their far-off a cappella drinking chorus resounds from the tavern as they sing about wine and daggers ("Col pugnale—e col bicchier!"). Carlo, in a thoughtful *accompagnato* recitative, complains, "Those drunkards are my shameless companions in error!" In the cantabile section, "O mio castel paterno," he evokes the memory of his "father's castle" to distance himself even further from the lowly tavern. In the tempo di mezzo, he reads a letter from his brother warning him not to go back to his father's castle unless he wants to end up eating bread and water in prison. Unsympathetically, the chorus of robbers replies, mockingly, "Bread and water! What a feast!" (Pane ed acqua! Il cibo è grasso!), triggering Carlo's enraged cabaletta.

Ernani starts similarly, except that the bandit chorus is heard in act 1, followed by the hero's entrance. At sunset the outlaw band appears eating, drinking, and gambling, while some clean their weapons. The chorus is introduced by strings with basses doubled by bassoons, playing quiet triplets and lacking the brassy quality of the robbers' chorus, "Hurray! Let's drink!" (Evviva! Beviam!).[48] This drinking song is neither as debauched nor as violent as other male drinking choruses. The hero is introduced in the middle of the chorus (1, 2) and does not join them. In the following number, the sober hero does not despise his fellows as Carlo did.[49] In fact, he begins the recitative by calling them "dearest friends." Nonetheless, the first sonority, modulating away from the previous chorus, tonally distances him from the men drinking. Even in this case the hero asserts his own class and moral difference against and above his carousing, carefree low fellows.

The opening scene of *Il corsaro* (The pirate) takes place in a pirate camp on an island. We hear an a cappella male drinking chorus coming from offstage ("coro interno de' Corsari") in an empty marine landscape in which the "vastness" (ampiezza) of the sea can be admired among the "steep cliffs."[50] The stratagem produces an effect of distance separating the pirates from the stage and contributing through a clever sound effect to create the impression of vastness and void. After the unaccompanied chorus, Corrado enters and starts his accompanied recitative. His loud statement (fortissimo), condemning the wretched wild song of his men ("Fero è il canto"), overpowers the quiet offstage chorus of pirates who continue, undisturbed, their bloodthirsty drinking song: "Let's take pleasure! Who cares if blood drips from our conquering hands? Let the cheer of our cups drown the curses of the dying mariner." The leader and hero in the meantime abstains from drinking, detaching and isolating himself from his bad fellows.

In these three operas about thugs (*I masnadieri*, *Ernani*, and *Il corsaro*), o2the relationship between the hero and the drunkards is one of simultaneous alliance and distance. A character who is unsuccessful in resisting the temptation to join a drinking chorus shows his weakness, and hence his antiheroic nature. This is the case of Dr. Caius at the beginning of *Falstaff* and especially Cassio in the first act of *Otello*. While the hero is merely sober, the antihero is a teetotaler, and when he drinks the consequences are disastrous. Dr. Caius gets robbed and swears that "the next time I get drunk at the tavern it, will be in the company of sober, civil, and devout people."

In *Otello*, Cassio attempts to resist Iago's invitation to drink, but he finally yields and gets hopelessly drunk. The stage manual describes the drinking and the presence of cups and wine, but it omits all mention of food, making the effect of wine that much stronger.[51] Iago's Dionysian drinking song is intoxicating with its rhythmic inequalities and heavy chromaticism. It represents the inebriating effect of alcohol drunk by the festive crowd.[52] The stage manual instructs the actor to avoid any comic representation of drunkenness: "This scene is extremely difficult for Cassio, because the actor must be careful not to exaggerate and fall into an indecent parody of a drunken man: he should not forget that Cassio is an elegant officer."[53] After Iago's third stanza, "Il mondo palpita / quand'io son brillo" (The world throbs when I am drunk), accompanied by syncopated horn figures and disorienting meter shifts, Cassio is still able to reply with a stanza. Following the chorus's refrain, a further disorienting effect is produced by the complex rhythm of timpani palpitating with grace notes on the downbeat, counteracted by the upbeat bass drum and interlocking patterns in the strings and winds. Now Cassio starts to interrupt Iago rather than alternating stanzas, breaking the rules of the drinking game song that until this moment has been played out in a more or less orderly fashion. His singing becomes increasingly fragmented, chaotic, and illogical. He stutters, unable to finish lines, and realistically shifting, as indicated in the score, to "suffocated voice" (con voce soffocata). When alcohol alters the voices of opera characters (their sonic masks), we are at the ultimate stage of embodiment and grotesque bodily realism, a traditionally emblematic characteristic of comedy that now has fully entered the world of tragedy.

Anorexic Women

Female characters' rejection of food reveals distress that results in their rejecting the meanings attached to food, such as earthly life and relations. As Joan Jacobs Brumberg writes in her social history of female anorexia: "Because food functions as a system of signs and symbols with multiple meanings, we must consider the symbolic value of what is rejected."[54] In

Verdi's operas this is even truer than in real life. Anorexic heroines suffer from anxiety caused by the tremendous value placed on virginity (and the fear of losing it), which, as Emanuele Senici points out, became particularly stressful to women in Catholic countries after the 1854 papal proclamation of the dogma of the Immaculate Conception (that the conception of Mary's son Jesus was virginal).[55] Verdi's heroines, affected by what Senici identifies as the "virgin syndrome," conflate anorexia mirabilis and anorexia nervosa in what Rudolph Bell calls "holy anorexia."[56] Bell ascribes two motivations to the anorexic behavior of fasting female saints: the first is self-assertion by means of rejecting food; the second is frustrated erotic desire caused by the disappearance of a beloved person, by the repressed desire for one, or by unrequited love.[57]

As we have seen, Violetta drinks and eats at the beginning of the opera, when she is more sinner than saint, but not at the end, when she turns into a martyr. A spiritual woman, such as Joan of Arc in *Giovanna d'Arco*, never touches earthly food. Luisa Miller, who is more consistently virtuous than Violetta, refuses food from her peasant friends, but not the poison from her lover.

While anorexia nervosa results in lack of appetite, anorexia mirabilis results in sublimated appetite. As Brumberg observes about fasting saints, "Many fasted in order to feast at the 'delicious banquet of God.'"[58] In the case of Luisa Miller, anorexia nervosa and anorexia mirabilis converge in the sublimation of erotic desire. The last act of the opera, subtitled "Poison," begins with Luisa writing a letter, seated at a table that holds an oil lamp, a basket of fruit, and a cup of milk, while the illuminated church can be seen through her window.[59] The opening melody, ominous, windy, and minor in the low register of the strings, gives the food a sour taste. The mournful C-minor chorus of farm girls, sympathizing with Luisa's sadness, ends on a major sonority as one girl encourages her to eat something. Luisa firmly refuses, shifting the harmony back to minor on the word *ripugnanza* (repugnant) as she mentions her aversion to food. Luisa contemplates the delightful heavenly food that will be hers after her final sacrifice, and the harmony shifts back to major, arpeggiated by the flute to evoke the otherworldly sweetness she is imagining ("celesti dolcezze"). The similarity between Luisa's vision and the evocation of celestial food *by the* Commendatore's ghost in *Don Giovanni* is inescapable.[60] Dietary sublimation is rendered through half-note violin tremolo at the point when earthly food is rejected, followed by twisted sixteenth-note figurations in the flute part (scales in Mozart, arpeggios in Verdi). Luisa utters the words of rejection in monotonic, stretched-out, accented syllables, a style reserved for solemn declarations and oaths.[61] In both cases the tremolo has a disembodying effect and is used here, as in other passages involving fasting heroines, to represent transcendental appetite.

Luisa's heavenly banquet is preceded by her final prayer ("Ah l'ultima preghiera") at the sound of the organ coming from the church. While the organ still plays, her lover Rodolfo enters (3, 3). His mention of drink ("bevanda") falls on a loud, dissonant diminished chord representing the lethal content of the drink. Rodolfo drinks and offers some to Luisa ("bevi"), who swallows it in a nauseating chromatic passage. In the tempo di mezzo of the duet (allegro moderato), Rodolfo reveals that now they are both poisoned and will die before the old lamp fades, announcing, "You drank death with me," with the word *morte* sung while pointing to the lethal cup ("additando la tazza") on another diminished chord. After the unhappy couple takes poison, they have enough time and strength left to sing a cabaletta and a trio after the entrance of Luisa's father (3, 4), then Luisa breathes her last as harps prefigure her assumption to the heavenly banquet.

Fat Man Falstaff

Verdi started his training by studying *Don Giovanni* and ended his career with an opera in which the conflation of erotic and gastronomic appetite is essential to the plot. Verdi himself admitted in 1890, "I've wanted to write a comic opera for forty years, and I've known *The Merry Wives of Windsor* for fifty. . . . However, the usual 'buts' which are everywhere always prevented me from satisfying this wish of mine. Now Boito has resolved all the 'buts' and has written me a musical comedy quite unlike any other."[62] Verdi was not the first to shift attention from the women of Shakespeare's play to the corpulent protagonist by making Falstaff the title role. Antonio Salieri had done the same a century earlier. It is significant, though, that Verdi resolved to write an opera about a fat man in 1890 because, as world historian Peter Stearns writes in *Fat History*, "in 1890 success was embodied in corpulence, failure in emaciation."[63] About this time, however, the situation changed and Western societies inverted this equation. Verdi's last opera predates the imminent change of representation and perception of the fat body and the emergence of its sizeist, moralist rejection.

Falstaff is a role that demands a specific body type. To interpret Falstaff, the actor-singer needs to be corpulent and needs to feel good about it. One of the greatest modern interpreters of the role, Ambrogio Maestri, is endowed with the right body shape for the role and is proud of it. Coming from five generations of chefs and butchers and being a respected chef himself, he also boasts a great appreciation for good food.[64] In Maestri we can see a conflation of the singer's persona and his favorite operatic dramatis persona (Falstaff).

It is surprising that in *Falstaff*, where discourse about food is pervasive, nobody eats: there are no banquets, and Falstaff always drinks alone. At the beginning of act 1, Falstaff orders a bottle of sherry (defining his identity as an English gentleman), and the libretto prescribes only one glass on the table, as it does for the next occurrence at the beginning of the second act. At the beginning of the third, Falstaff also drinks, alone, some mulled wine as a remedy to prevent catching a cold after being thrown into the river Thames by the merry wives of Windsor.

In *Falstaff* gastronomic signs, though always realistic, appear in two modalities of representation, the one Biasin calls "cognitive," and the other "tropological." Both belong to the sphere of the figurative (they mean something besides what they denote). In the "cognitive" mode, the drinking or eating character acquires knowledge: in this case, Biasin explains, "food is used to stage the search for meaning that is carried out every time one reflects on the relationship among self, the world, and the others—or among the subject, nature, and history." In the tropological mode, gastronomic signs turn into allegories and symbols.[65] The representation of warm wine in *Falstaff* is used as a realistic remedy against a cold. Yet the symbolic valence of the warm wine clearly emerges in the libretto and score as both cognitive and tropological. Here is the relevant passage (3, 1):

Se non galleggiava per me quest'epa tronfia
Certo affogavo.—Brutta morte.—L'acqua mi gonfia.
Mondo reo.—Non cè più virtù.—Tutto declina.

Va, vecchio John, va, va per la tua via; cammina
Finché tu muoia.—Allor scomparirà la vera
Virilità del mondo . . .
Versiamo un po' di vino nell'acqua del Tamigi.

[If this swollen belly didn't keep me floating, I would have drowned for sure. Ugly death. Water swells me up. Evil world. There is no virtue any more. Everything is in decline. Go, old John, go, go on your way; keep going until you die. Then true virility will disappear from the world. . . . Let's pour some wine into the water of the Thames.]

Arrigo Boito takes remarkable liberties with Shakespeare's text, in which there is no soliloquy corresponding to this section. The librettist retains the essential idea of fertilizing the Thames with fortified Spanish wine (sack): "Let me pour in some sack to the Thames water," says Shakespeare's Sir John (2, 5). Boito adds the concepts of Falstaff's "virility" and the cosmic and moral decline following his death. Cognitively, wine opens a relationship between the self and the cosmos. Tropologically, wine is a metaphor for the insemination of virgin water, a concept metonymically contiguous to virility, which symbolically fertilizes the world.

Verdi introduces Falstaff's monologue with a lugubrious, funereal theme played by low brass and woodwinds with the indication *morendo* (dying).[66] The register expands to four octaves as Falstaff mentions his fat belly (epa tronfia). The address to himself, "Go, old John, go," is singled out by shifting from the recitative mode to a fragment of an aria, incisive as an epitaph in its brevity, with a simple accompaniment on each downbeat to represent his steps, limping after he calls himself old and with chromatic descents on the strings to musically depict the decay of the world after his death. Considering that Verdi was eighty when he wrote this music, this passage appears as one of "Verdi's repeated attempts to personalize *Falstaff*, to assimilate it into his own image," as Roger Parker puts it.[67]

As Falstaff tastes the wine, he "unbuttons his waistcoat" (si sbottona il panciotto), letting his body expand. The orchestral texture thickens in contrapuntal complexity as Falstaff expands and observes the effects of wine. Boito's lines have the ambivalence of a symbolist poem: "The happy globe [both the belly and the head] sets a trilling madness off balance! And the trill invades the world!!!" (Il giocondo globo squilibra una demenza / Trillante! E il trillo invade il mondo!!!). The trill starts with the third flute and engages more and more instruments in a powerful crescendo through to progressive inclusion of the whole orchestra, register expansion, and a shift in the voice from declamation to full-force operatic singing. The passage foreshadows the opera's ending, with its grandiose fugue on the words "Everything in the world is jest" (Tutto nel mondo è burla), celebrating the triumph of Falstaff's Dionysian outlook.

Falstaff's body image expresses his worldview, and both are rejected by the middle-class microcosm of the comedy. One of the characters, Fenton, describes Falstaff's stomach as "hyperbolic-apoplectic bowels" (ventraja / iperbolico-apoplettica), a description that fits Bakhtin's characterization of "the grotesque image of the body" carrying symbols of cosmic fertility, a body that "both swallows and generates, gives and takes." As the Russian critic explains: "Such a body, composed of fertile depths and procreative convexities, is never clearly differentiated from the world but it is transferred, merged, and fused with it. . . . It acquires cosmic dimensions, while the cosmos acquires a bodily nature. Cosmic elements are transformed into the gay form of the body that grows, procreates, and is victorious."[68]

The cavernous emptiness of Falstaff's body is represented sonically at the beginning of the opera in its potentially endless expansion. In the first scene, Falstaff realizes his precarious financial situation on reading a huge bill for the food and wine he has consumed at the Garter Inn: six chickens, thirty jars of sherry, three turkeys, two pheasants, and one anchovy (6 polli: 6 scellini. 30 giarre di Xeres: 2 lire. 3 tacchini . . .). Falstaff's *parlante* is accompanied by an empty fifth played by French horns: a sustained E2 and, above it, a B4, leaving a void of two octaves and a fifth. Time is suspended in this measureless section (senza misura) to depict an unformed void like the primordial chaos. Verdi chooses to score the pedal accompaniment for horns to evoke wide open spaces. The effect of openness is enhanced by scoring an E2, the lowest note on the horn in E—hence the tone that naturally generates the other harmonic sounds, including B4, a naturally perfect fifth. Both are open notes, pure, natural harmonic sounds, free of the muffled tone produced by hand stopping.[69] The sound framed by the horns is left hollow inside, where the voice of Falstaff resonates as if in an empty room, the space of his capacious, empty belly.

His pronouncement, "If Falstaff gets slender, he won't be himself" (Se Falstaff s'assottiglia non è più lui) expresses his concern that for him weight loss would be a loss of identity. The orchestra evokes the image of the slimming body by rarefying the sound texture and leaving emptiness below the piccolo playing in parallel with Falstaff's melody, three octaves above his voice. Falstaff's melody counteracts the textural slimming down by progressively widening its intervals. With the celebration of his "abdomen" (at the line "In quest'addome"), the tempo slows and the agogic indication ("Più lento, maestoso") expresses majestic grandiosity. A powerful crescendo now begins layering broad pentatonic figures in the winds over rapidly pulsating sextuplets in the strings, conveying the idea of thriving biological growth. Boito's text perfectly exemplifies the image of cosmic bodily expansion (I, 1):

FALSTAFF (*alzandosi*):
Se Falstaff s'assottiglia
Non è più lui, nessun più l'ama; in questo addome
C'è un migliaio di lingue che annunciano il mio nome!

BARDOLFO (*acclamando*):
Falstaff immenso!

PISTOLA (*come sopra*):
Enorme Falstaff!

FALSTAFF (*toccandosi e guardandosi l'addome*):
Quest'è il mio regno.
Lo ingrandirò.

[FALSTAFF (*rising*): If Falstaff gets slender, he is no longer himself. Nobody will love him. In this abdomen there are a thousand tongues announcing my name!
BARDOLFO (*hailing*): Immense Falstaff!
PISTOLA (*likewise*): Enormous Falstaff!
FALSTAFF (*touching and admiring his belly*): This is my kingdom. I will expand it.]

With the celebration of Falstaff's majestic body, the orchestral texture expands, gaining gravity and substance, while on the word "kingdom" (*regno*) Falstaff sings his highest pitch on a chord in second inversion, the fifth in the bass further propelling expansion. The register reaches both upward and downward, triumphantly claiming the tonic through a dominant seventh chord with tremolos played by the entire string section, conferring a sense of biological life and organic growth.[70]

Together with the unabashed celebration of the large body, the opera criticizes the societal vilification of fatness, or sizeism. The wives of Windsor, who punish Falstaff for his libertine immorality, see in his body the embodiment of vice, calling him "wineskin," "bathtub," "King of bellies," "cannon," and "voracious whale," pointing out that "oil drips from his greasy fat body" (1, 2). In the last scene (3, 2), they accuse him of being "round as an apple," "big as a ship," and "corrupted and impure," reaching a *stretta* of sizeist insults: "lazy," "glutton," "fatso," "drunk," "rascal," "puffed-up belly," "round face," "bed-smasher," "jersey splitter," "barrel emptier," "chair smasher," "horse destroyer," "triple chin," and most important, "globe of impurity" (globo d'impurità).

Cultural sociologist Abigail Saguy calls sizeism the "immorality frame," conceptualizing it as the cultural regime where "fat is condemned as evidence of sloth and gluttony," hence allowing fatness to be "likened to other sins such as sexual immorality."[71] Fatness and gluttony were never related in medieval theology. Dante does not portray gluttons as fatter than other sinners or saints (*Inferno*, 6), and neither Giotto nor Hieronymus Bosch portrays gluttons in hell as overweight. As Ken Albala writes, in Christian tradition "fat itself was not conceptually linked to gluttony."[72] The medieval theologian Saint Thomas Aquinas, who linked gluttony to libertinism in the Middle Ages, does not attach body types to sinners. Aquinas himself was fat, nicknamed "silent ox" (bovem mutuum), and after his canonization he was portrayed as a fat man.[73] The identification of the fat body type with sin or immorality emerged only in late nineteenth-century Protestant societies when, as Stearns put it, Victorian standards started to conflate pleasure-seeking habits (food and sex) as manifested in the body image. From this time on, "fat became a secular sin" with "moral and emotional overtones," guilt, anxieties, and a division of humankind "between the saved and the lost, the thin and the obese."[74]

The merry wives' remedy for Falstaff's impurity is castration. In the final trio, the women pray to God to make him chaste, to punish him, and to help him repent—"Domine fallo casto!" "Fallo punito Domine," "Fallo pentito Domine!"—and the word *fallo*—"make him"—also has the double meaning of "shortcoming" and "phallus." Falstaff's own response is a prayer asking God to save at least his stomach ("Ma salvagli l'addomine"), a double entendre on the words *ad Domine* (to God) and *addomine* (abdomen). Sir John resists: he never loses his pride in his size and his large stomach. He appears a prophet of the fat pride movements, such as the "I STAND" campaign against "weight bigotry" promoted by San Francisco activist Marilyn Wann.[75]

At the end of the opera, in the magical night scene in Windsor Park (3, 2), Falstaff attempts to seduce two women, Alice and Meg, and to make love to both at the same time. Unlike Don Giovanni, he does not wish to hunt down women and metaphorically eat them. He wishes, instead, to be hunted down, be quartered by the women, and be devoured by them: "Quarter me like a deer for dinner! Devour me!!!" (Quartatemi come un camoscio a mensa!! / Sbranatemi!!!). Falstaff loves to eat and to feed. The concluding chorus, "Tutto nel mondo è burla," which celebrates Falstaff's carnivalesque, comic philosophy, is introduced by the meta-operatic line, "Let's sing a chorus and we'll end the scene," where *scena* rhymes with *cena* (dinner), announcing the banquet to celebrate the union of the young couple: "Then we will go all to dinner with Sir Falstaff" ("Poi con Sir Falstaff, tutti andiam a cena"). As Northrop Fry points out, "In Plautus the audience is sometimes jocosely invited to an imaginary banquet afterwards," which is "an act of communion" and "an invitation to the audience to form part of the comic society."[76] The final imaginary meal in *Falstaff* is shared by everybody. Both the initial and the final meals of the opera (the only meals) happen outside the temporal frame of the represented drama, breaking the time and space boundaries of theater, invading the whole world, celebrating "the gay form of the body that grows, procreates, and is victorious."[77]

CHAPTER TEN

The Callas Diet

It Ain't Over till the Fit Lady Sings

"It's all over for fat lady singers as slimline divas triumph," announced Vanessa Thorpe of the *Observer* in her review of the 2009 Salzburg festival, parading new opera "sylphs" dominating the festival, including Danielle de Niese, Marina Rebeka, Elīna Garanča, Anna Netrebko, and Magdalena Kožená. On the origin of the triumph of slimline divas, John McMurray, responsible for casting at the English National Opera in London, provided a straightforward answer: "The question of weight came up when Maria Callas slimmed down and returned to sing in Visconti's revival of *La Traviata* at La Scala in 1955."[1] This chapter focuses on that critical episode, addressing the epochal shift in opera culture from separation to conflation of the dramatis persona and the singer's persona.

After the Callas diet, singers have generally been expected to fit a particular role or role type, at least where body size defines the role. As we saw in the previous chapter, that is the case with Ambrogio Maestri's interpreting and identifying with the corpulent Falstaff. If "enorme Falstaff" requires a big singer, consumptive heroines like Violetta and Mimì call for slender singers. In Dumas's novel, the literary source of *Traviata*, the protagonist is described as "slender almost to a fault" as a result of tuberculosis, which also affected Mimì.[2]

Body mass became a desideratum, if not a precondition, for certain roles only in the second half of the twentieth century. Before then operagoers did not lose their ancestors' ability to suspend their disbelief when approaching opera, as is apparent with sopranos and altos, mostly castratos, singing the roles of adult male heroes in opera seria and occasionally female roles in opera buffa or semiseria. The same applied to body size, even in the more realistic genre of opera buffa. For example, the singer Gertrude Righetti Giorgi, for whom Rossini created the title role of *Cenerentola* (1817), was far from the slimness of Disney's sylphlike Cinderella (1950). Her portrait (fig. 10.1) emphasizes her plumpness rather than hiding it.

Righetti's feet were probably not the smallest, prompting the librettist to have Cenerentola recognized by a lost bracelet instead of the "little glass slipper," thus eliminating the defining stratagem that gave the title of Perrault's fairytale *Cendrillon, ou La petite pantoufle de verre* (*Cinderella, or The Little Glass Slipper*).[3] The comparison between Rossini's Cinderella and Disney's illustrates the change in body-type aesthetic. As Peter Stearns points out in his *Fat History*, it was precisely with Cinderella that the Walt Disney Company "adopted an impossibly willowy form for heroines," leading to Disney's thinner and thinner princesses imposing what anti-sizeist feminist writer Kim Chernin has defined as the "tyranny of slimness."[4]

In Verdi's *Traviata* the protagonist's body shape is even more relevant to the plot than in *Cenerentola*. In this case change in body perception changed the way reception history was rewritten. The premiere of *Traviata*—so the story goes—was not an immediate success, and modern musicologists blamed the wrong body type of the first interpreter.[5] It is true that Verdi complained about the big fiasco (*fiascone*) of the premiere, possibly exaggerating the extent of the failure, but he did not blame Violetta's interpreter, Fanny Salvini-Donatelli.[6] Indeed, the body shape and size of the first Violetta did not bother the critics either, who were pleased in all respects with her performance and appearance. The local newspaper's review (*Gazzetta di Venezia*) records that at the first night of Verdi's opera at La Fenice (Venice, March 6, 1853), Fanny Salvini-Donatelli was the only singer to be applauded, reporting that "she stole the show, and the audience literally submerged her with an ovation." The following performances of the same production went even better, especially thanks to Salvini-Donatelli's "agility and confidence."[7] The *Gazzetta Musicale di Milano* published a similar, overall positive report that same year.[8] Only in 1914 did the *Encyclopédie de la musique*, by Albert Lavignac, allege for the first time that the protagonist's corpulence caused the fiasco of *Traviata*'s premiere, maintaining that Salvini-Donatelli's "embonpoint" made her interpretation "grotesquely unrealistic."[9] Interestingly, the myth that Salvini's size was the cause of *Traviata*'s failure was generated along with the birth of cinematography and the emergence of a modern obsession for extremely fit female silent-movie stars. For example, the actress and professional swimmer Annette Kellerman practiced and preached

Figure 10.1. Portrait of Gertrude Righetti Giorgi (1793–1862), "so the world may know her and love her (Petrarch)," etching by nineteenth-century anonymous, Bologna, Museo internazionale e biblioteca della musica, "Disegni e stampe" 22053.

slenderness as the highest aesthetic value, campaigning actively to promote weight loss through diet and "daily exercise in the nude before a full-length mirror."[10] Emblematic movies produced from 1909 to 1914 stage her in the roles of swimming characters such as mermaids, sirens, or Neptune's daughter, or indeed as herself, a swimmer, in *The Perfectly Formed Woman* (1910).

In the following decades, cinema became the leading force in shaping visual culture, and slimness became a universal aesthetic value. Beginning with the economic boom of the 1950s, aggressive anti-obesity campaigns were increasingly charged with an array of health, moral, social, and aesthetic values, leading to our current, ideologically biased, medicalization of "overweight."[11] Fashion and movie industries affirmed slimness as a criterion of female beauty during a time when food was extravagantly available, especially in America. This paradox generated enormous pressure on women to practice self-control, while in domestic life they were expected to be in charge of preparing and serving food.[12]

The case of Maria Callas is emblematic. After returning to the United States from Greece in 1945, the twenty-year-old singer indulged in cheeseburgers, pizza, pancakes, and other goodies readily available in the Big Apple. According to Callas's biographer Arianna Stassinopoulos, the singer recorded in her diary that she weighed 218 pounds.[13] In an autobiographical sketch in possession of biographer Renzo Allegri, she wrote, "In America, thanks to a slim diet, my weight went from 218 pounds to 170 pounds."[14] In another autobiographical account signed by Maria Callas and published in the magazine *Oggi* in 1957, she recounts that in New York, at the time of her first audition at the Met (1945), she weighed 80 kg (176 lbs.), which she thought excessive, even considering that she was tall.[15] These slightly contradictory reports suggest that during her early years in New York City the singer was already stressed about her weight, which was likely fluctuating as a result of inconsistent dieting.

In 1947 the twenty-four-year-old Maria Callas moved to Italy. Five years later she adopted a stricter dieting regimen, losing at least thirty more pounds for good and acquiring the ideal body shape for the role of the consumptive Violetta in the 1955 Visconti production of *Traviata*. That Luchino Visconti, a major figure of twentieth-century film history, was responsible for that crucial production of *Traviata* at La Scala is significant because it sheds light on the conflation of operatic and cinematic cultures. Also significant is that during the 1950s the Italian fashion industry abandoned previous ideals of plumpness as a symbol of fertility and motherhood and began to employ slender and even emaciated models. This at first created a disconnect between the wife-and-mother figure established during the Fascist era and the postwar emancipated woman celebrated in fashion magazines and movies.[16]

In this historical context, Maria Callas's transformation from plump to slim appeared as a rejection of the plump housewife and fat soprano in favor of the slender, independent diva. The widely circulated legend that the singer lost her voice as a result of her weight loss has attracted the attention of prominent scholars of vocal music such as Nina Eidsheim, who points out that the controversies surrounding Callas's voice loss use imagery and language that are "saturated with the very body- and gender-related power structures" and that the "narrative fashioned around Callas is one that frequently appears in relation to women."[17] Implicit was not only "look," but gender politics. Because Callas was a sweeping celebrity and tabloids had made her private life more public than her singer's persona, her body became a battlefield on which opposite generational ideologies clashed. Anthropologist Mary Douglas, through a symbolic theory of the body, suggests that there exists a continual exchange of meanings between the social body of shared values and norms and the actual physical body, with the former shaping the latter and the latter mapping the former.[18]

The Callas Diet, or A Body Changed into New Forms

The programmatic opening of Ovid's *Metamorphoses*, one of the most influential books in opera culture, declares that this monumental poem is about "bodies changed into new forms."[19] The third book recounts an extreme case of slimming. The nymph Echo falls madly in love with a handsome boy with a "slender body." Narcissus, being in love with his own image, scorns and rejects the nymph. Heartbroken, Echo "started to waste away" until "the lovely bloom of her flesh lost its moisture and nothing remained of her but voice and bones, then only voice."[20]

Biographical accounts of Maria Callas have focused on her body as the locus of a prodigious transformation. In 1959 *Oggi* published a biographical account of Maria by her first voice teacher, the great Spanish singer Elvira de Hidalgo, who recollects that the first time she met the young Maria in 1939 in Athens, she "had a round face smeared with pimples," she was "tall, big, wearing heavy glasses," was badly dressed (white cap and apron), and "waddled around heavily." As soon as she started singing, however, de Hidalgo "recognized" the voice she had been "secretly awaiting." She closed her eyes so as not to see the body that was producing it, perceiving a disconnect between the voice and the body.[21] The narrative of Callas's diet as the defining moment of her life became canonic after her death in 1977. In 1981, Arianna Stassinopoulos opened her monumental biography of the recently deceased singer by stating, "The life of Maria Callas was both tragedy and fairy tale. As completely as anyone outside mythology, she *transformed* herself from a fat, awkward girl into a woman of magnetic beauty and personality."[22] The same year, Maria Callas's ex-husband, Giovanni Battista Meneghini, published a biography of his wife, recounting her weight loss as a tale of profound transformation not only of her body, but of her entire personality and artistic persona:

> When Maria made her formal debut at La Scala in December 1951 she weighed 210 pounds; three years later, when she opened the 1954–55 season, she had dropped to 144 pounds. Her physique had undergone a drastic change, which in turn influenced her entire way of life. She seemed to be another woman with a different personality. One could say that this change was fundamental for Maria Callas's life and for her artistic activity. Her shedding of all those pounds made opera history. From a kind of clumsy, encumbered whale, Maria was transformed into an elegant woman with the figure of a model.[23]

Meneghini recollects how "in the middle 1950s, especially among women, Maria was more famous for her mysterious weight loss than for her singing."[24] *La divina*—as she was called in the media—acquired the aura of a secular saint, at least in the context to Joseph Roach's understanding of the appellation "divine" in the "theology of pop culture."[25] In 2000, Linda Hutcheon and Michael Hutcheon, in their book about representations of bodies in opera, identify Callas's diet as a major change in the representation and perception of the opera singer's body. They observe that Callas, after her weight loss, acquired the power "to focus public attention on the relation of the body to the voice."[26] In 2013, Callas's intimate friend Giovanna Lomazzi published an interview touching on the singer's "metamorfosi" (a term the interviewer used) by emphasizing how in a matter of months Callas turned from "fat, ugly and badly dressed" to a slender and elegant diva, allowing her to reach "complete maturity, both vocal and physical." By slimming down, Lomazzi continues in her remarkable manifest of the new "tyranny of slimness" in opera, Callas inaugurated a new season in the history of opera, since it happened "at the end of an era of fat and ugly singers. She was the first to understand that there was a need for aesthetic truth."[27]

To understand how a weight-loss diet came to be perceived as a pivotal moment in her life and in opera history, we need to retrace the circumstances surrounding the inception of the Callas diet. Although, as we have seen, Callas started losing weight slowly in the late 1940s, her decisive, radical diet took place in the mid-1950s. As one story goes, after watching *Roman Holiday* (1953), Maria Callas resolved to look like the svelte Audrey Hepburn.[28] The Milanese fashion designer Biki played a pivotal role in the Callas diet. Biki, the granddaughter of Giacomo Puccini, who gave her the nickname, short for *birichina* (naughty girl), reported that when she first met Callas, the soprano appeared "big and clumsy" and "badly dressed." Callas asked the stylist for advice, and Biki agreed to become her personal fashion guru—a sort of fairy godmother—on one condition: she had to lose weight. When Callas did so, Biki renovated her wardrobe: Callas acquired more than 200 dresses, many by Biki, 150 pairs of shoes, 300 hats, and many more items.[29] A photograph taken at Biki Atelier in 1958 shows Maria Callas in a dynamic pose like a fashion model's, between Biki and an unidentified man, probably one of Biki's assistants, in the act of trying on one of Biki's creations.

The Callas diet became legendary through a conflation of opera and real life. In the mythopoeia of Callas's life, two pairs of archetypical food imageries are recurrent: fasting and feasting, the raw and the cooked. According to Lévi-Strauss's theory of mythology, "empirical categories" based on food, such as food intake, fasting, consumption of raw or cooked food, and the offering of food can be "conceptual tools with which to elaborate abstract ideas."[30] In biographical accounts of Maria Callas, gastronomic signs are deployed according to these categories. A case in point is Maria's betrayal of her husband after her infatuation with the tycoon Aristotle Onassis, which on September 21, 1959, *Time* magazine presented as an opera plot, casting Onassis as the tenor, Maria as the soprano, and Giovanni Battista Meneghini, "her aging husband," as the bass. The journalist narrates how Maria's weight loss was the beginning of her emancipation: "Under his [her husband's] loving care, the fat duckling slimmed herself from 213 lbs. into a glamorous creature, and became the most fabulously acclaimed opera singer of her time. . . . Their love, it seemed, thrived on money, and money thrived on love. And yet last week, after ten years of this golden idyll, Callas, 35, and Meneghini, 64, announced that they were 'definitely and irreparably' separated."[31]

Meneghini's account of his wife's betrayal leading to their separation also reads like an operatic scene. His recollection of the night Onassis and Callas paid him a visit at his villa in Sirmione resembles an opera trio. The lovers arrived at 8:00 p.m. on Monday August 17, 1959. "His breath"—Meneghini remembers—"smelled of alcohol." As the driver told Meneghini in an aside, Onassis had already drunk a full bottle of whiskey during the two-hour drive from Milan to Sirmione. Maria was also acting strangely, and her husband suspected she had been drinking as well. Dinner was ready at 9:00, and "Maria behaved like a silly, stupid child. She wanted a fire lit in the dining room fireplace." This observation suggests his exclusion from the repeated toasts that bonded his wife to her lover, similar to the moment when old Baron Duphol is excluded from the brindisi involving Violetta and his rival Alfredo. In Italy, August is the hottest month; the fire was meant to set the stage, but it made the dining room hot as hell, like the end of the dinner scene in *Don Giovanni* when flames rise to devour the libertine. Meneghini recollects, "I was sweating like a donkey and I was unable to eat."[32] In this story the lovers share not only drinks but food, while the old husband is excluded from both.

Meneghini introduces the story of his first encounter with Maria, a girl twenty-seven years younger than he was, by confessing that "ballerinas—so thin and all skin and bones—are not my type. Titianesque, fleshy women appeal to me more." He relates then how the plump Greek American soprano stole his heart at a dinner party during the summer of 1947. As in *Traviata*, their relationship is defined by a shared gastronomic sign:

> The group had almost finished eating, but [Tullio] Serafin said that everyone would stay and keep me company. He asked what I would like to eat. "I am not that hungry. I'll just have a veal cutlet," I said. Sitting across from me at the table was a young girl whom I didn't know, with a plump face and sweet features. She said in perfect Italian, but with a trace of an accent: "Sir, if you don't mind I would like to offer you my cutlet."[33]

From her husband's perspective, the whole love story with Maria begins with feasting and sharing food with her, and it ends with fasting and being excluded from the convivial moment bonding her with her new lover.

In Maria Callas's own account of her first encounter with her future husband, published by the magazine *Oggi* in 1957, location and circumstances are consistent with Meneghini's story. The remarkable difference is that there is no memory of feasting and offering food.[34] Yet the author of the biographical account in *Oggi* gives a lot of attention to food, cooking, and dieting. In the same article there are two large photos of the soprano in her kitchen, which attempt to portray her as a good housewife in the act of preparing food and doing housework (figs. 10.2 and 10.3). The caption of the first photo reads, "Maria Callas's favorite hobby is cooking sweets. Here she is in her kitchen, beating the dough for a ring-shaped cake (*ciambella*)."

The caption of figure 10.3 reads "Milan: Maria Callas in her very modern kitchen, polishing with great care one of her silver dishes. . . . Callas is an excellent housewife; she loves cooking, taking care of furniture, shopping for

Figure 10.2. Maria Callas in the kitchen preparing a cake. *Oggi* 13, no. 3 (January 17, 1957): 15. Courtesy of the Archivi Farabola, Rome.

Figure 10.3. Maria Callas in the kitchen polishing a silver tray. *Oggi* 13, no. 3 (January 17, 1957): 15. Courtesy of the Archivi Farabola, Rome.

trinkets. Usually, while attending to the house chores, she prefers to wear a pair of old pants." Yet it is striking that in the photograph she is wearing not a pair of old pants but a nice dress. The pictures used for the article are carefully staged and rehearsed (some of the originals, showing different takes of the same portraits, are preserved in the Centro Studi Callassiano in the

Academia Maria Callas of Zevio). The silver dish she is supposedly polishing is deliberately used as a mirror, as in the myth of Narcissus, reflecting how Callas wants to appear: not the housewife in the kitchen but herself, the *divina*, seen from below, towering proud, the prima donna at center stage seen from the main floor of the opera house. The effect is repeated in other photos taken in her house with mirrors (figs. 10.4 and 10.5). What we see outside the mirror (the house) stays outside the mirror. What we see in the reflecting dish is a window into the parallel reality of the opera diva.

Evidence from the Callas diet—what she ate—suggests she was not likely to eat the sweets she allegedly loved to cook. Newspapers published widely different accounts of Maria Callas's diet, from her having purposely ingested a tapeworm in a glass of champagne to the fabrication that she had switched from regular pasta to dietetic Pasta Pantanella (Callas successfully sued the company for that falsehood).[35] Callas wrote a document in which she dispels most dietary legends and describes a diet consistent with

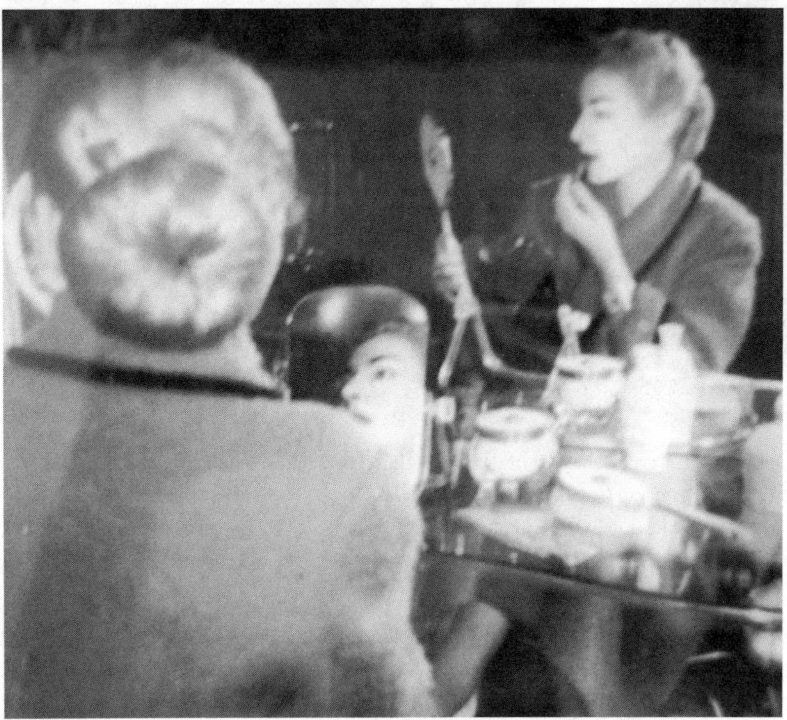

Figure 10.4. Maria Callas applying makeup in her house in Verona, via Leoncino (1954). Centro Studi Callassiano, Accademia Maria Callas in Zevio (Verona), folder 54, 11FG. Courtesy of Centro Studi Callassiano.

Figure 10.5. Maria Callas reading by a painting representing Venus in her house in Verona, via Leoncino (1954). Centro Studi Callassiano, Accademia Maria Callas in Zevio (Verona), collection "Per/für Maria Callas," folder 54, 1FG. Courtesy of Centro Studi Callassiano.

Meneghini's account: "She never ate any kind of pasta, subsisting on grilled meat and raw vegetables, which she ate without seasoning or oil, like a goat. She didn't drink liquor, and only took the smallest amount of wine. She *never* ate desserts."[36] Her war on dessert had already started in 1949, when she wrote a letter to her husband from Buenos Aires in which, after repenting of having "been eating like a wolf," she pledged to go on a diet. "So if you don't want me to look like Caniglia," she wrote, "you should not let me eat much, only grilled meat, raw vegetables, etc. Do not dare to insist. Only three or four weeks and you will see how I will go back to my ideal weight. Promised? And no sweets!!! My dear, I want to look beautiful for you, you know!"[37] It seems implausible that Callas really wanted to look beautiful for her husband by losing weight, considering his predilection for "Titianesque, fleshy women," the reason he found the young Maria attractive before hearing her sing a note or speak a word.

The inconsistency between what Callas was cooking and what she was (not) eating after she started her ascetic diet is striking. She titles one of her autograph recipes *peperata* a version of the gravy sauce used in a Veronese dish called *lesso con pearà* (boiled beef with bone-marrow gravy): "Mix 30 grams of marrow in about a liter of good broth, and when it starts simmering add breadcrumbs until it looks like it's the right texture. Add then a nice handful of [grated] Grana [parmesan cheese], pepper, and a spoonful of butter. Let simmer for two hours. Serve very hot."[38]

This sophisticated and hypercaloric recipe was certainly not part of her typical diet, nor were the other dishes her mother-in-law taught her to cook, such as duck or *baccalà* with polenta.[39] As her husband recollects, "After having spent so much time in the kitchen preparing a particular dish or dessert, Maria would not even taste it if her diet did not permit it."[40] The idea that Callas was so generous that she would suffer hunger while cooking hearty meals for her husband and guests is charming, but not convincing. She in fact rejected the culture of the cooked by pursuing the practice of the raw.

The public image of Callas's domestic life was fully staged, like a theatrical role, making one wonder whether she ever spent any time in the kitchen at all. The picture of Callas as a cook was probably constructed to fulfill the desire of her husband and his mother to project the image of a respectful wife. For example, once Maria's mother-in-law sent her a dishtowel and an apron—two symbolic gifts, likely passed on to the maid.[41] There are personal handwritten notes that the singer wrote to her chef, Elena Pozzan, in which she thanks her for the food but instructs Pozzan to let her sleep.[42] Callas was not doing the cooking in her house, Pozzan was. In a typewritten document titled "Questionario," Maria Callas (who usually wrote with pencils or pens) allegedly wrote, "I adore my kitchen, where I spend many hours cooking succulent dishes," adding, "I do not follow any special diet: different kinds of healthy food, and that's it. Healthy life, simple, far from the confusion and stress of modern society, in the peace of my own home, of my familiar affection and artistic occupation." The document is a bad forgery, a dictated confession. It is written in perfect Italian, in a style very different from Maria Callas's letters and handwritten communications, and it is inconsistent with all the other evidence on her diet and lifestyle.[43] This is one of the many attempts to fabricate a reassuring image of the singer, in line with the traditional family values she was subverting.

Maria Callas, if we can believe her friend Giovanna Lomazzi, was not able or willing to cook at all, "not even an egg."[44] She preferred raw food to cooked, including raw meat. In February 2014, Elena Pozzan revealed that she and Callas had both been repeatedly infected by tapeworm as a consequence of a high-protein diet based on eating uncooked meat.[45] Two years later the great actor Paolo Poli recollected, "I saw her at the Biffi Scala dipping raw liver in a cup of hot broth: she was feeding the beast that was inside her!"[46] The tapeworm was a consequence of her diet, not the cause. The legend of Callas's ingesting the tapeworm in a glass of champagne was only a beautified version of her real "barbarous" diet, which her husband amended in the public image by stating that she ate "grilled meat." In fact, Callas's diet was the rejection of the cooked and the culture it stands for: the traditional image of the woman as "queen of the fireplace," the caretaker of the kitchen fire, the ideal, dutiful housewife.

The first role Callas explored as soon as she started losing weight was Medea, the Greek tragic heroine who kills her children to punish her husband. When asked why she went on such a strict diet, Maria Callas declared that in preparing for her interpretation of Cherubini's *Medea* she realized how important it would be to emphasize and use the angular lines of her face and chin.[47] Her interpretation of *Medea* in the 1953 Maggio Fiorentino, right at the beginning of her slimming diet, was sensational; it revealed Callas as both a great singer and a powerful tragic actress. It is possible that she attended, the same year, Visconti's production of Euripides's *Medea* in Milan, indirectly exchanging ideas on acting.[48] After the loss of her voice in the 1960s, Callas would conclude her career as an actress by playing the nonsinging role of the tragic Greek heroine in the equally sensational 1969 film *Medea* by Pier Paolo Pasolini, who understood, perhaps better than anybody else, the power of her acting as a form of being herself, the complexity of her persona, with her identity struggle and the clash between family values and personal selfhood.[49]

Pasolini, Visconti before him, and later Franco Zeffirelli, who, as we shall see, was equally inspired and fascinated by Callas, were three gay film directors. Reflecting on why so many gay men were and still are fans of Maria Callas, Wayne Koestenbaum offers an array of motivations, among which, on the stage, the style of acting inspired by Greek theater, and behind the scenes "the division, in Callas, between private and public," observing how "the social forces that shaped 'Callas' . . . are the same currents that created the closet and its spectacular opposite, the scene of coming out: Callas and gayness are both symptoms of modern society's pervasive split between silence and speech, secrecy and disclosure."[50] The Callas diet reveals in a different way this very clash and split between her private and public existence, between art and life, the singer's persona and the dramatis persona. Maria Callas changed her body image to become her operatic dramatis personae, first Medea, then Violetta.

Becoming Violetta

Traviata was the first opera Maria Callas attended, in 1938 at age fifteen, at the Pallas Theater in Athens, accompanied by her mother and sister.[51] It seems destiny that her personal story would be superimposed upon Violetta's story. The basic narrative moves from feasting to fasting, from carnival to Lent, but with a twist. While Violetta turns from sinner to saint as consumption liberates her spirit from her flesh, the life of Maria Callas has been recounted as the story of a good daughter and wife turned fallen woman, becoming, in effect, a "traviata." After she acquired the fame of a superdiva and the body of a model, she abandoned her role as a good wife and rejected the traditional role assigned to her gender and marital status. In 1959 she left her husband to pursue her infatuation with Onassis; shortly afterward, her mother published a book presenting her as a selfish, ungrateful daughter.[52] In 1968 the billionaire decided that the singer he had been dating and living with was not going to be a suitable wife, and he instead married Jackie Kennedy, the widow of the recently assassinated US president.[53] In 1977 Callas died virtually alone in her Paris apartment, like Marie Duplessis.

Maria Callas's performance of *Traviata*, opening on May 28, 1955, seemed a real turning point in performance history, the first opera in which she seemed to be impersonating rather than interpreting her role, like a shaman in a ritual of possession. The opera had already been produced twenty-one times at La Scala, and Callas had played Violetta in ten previous productions over the past four years and recorded the opera once.[54] Yet, unlike the tenor Giuseppe Di Stefano (soon replaced), the *divina* never missed a rehearsal, even when Visconti required an unusually high number of them.[55] Her commitment is astonishing considering how busy she was at the time: at La Scala alone, during the season of 1954–55, Callas interpreted the title roles of Donizetti's *Lucia di Lammermoor*, conducted by Herbert von Karajan (January–February), and Gluck's *Alceste*; she played Elisabetta in Verdi's *Don Carlos* (April) and Giulia in Spontini's *La vestale* (this her first collaboration with Visconti, in December); she was Maddalena in Giordano's *Andrea Chénier* (January and February), Amina in Bellini's *La sonnambula* (her second collaboration with Visconti, in March and April), Fiorilla in Rossini's *Il turco in Italia* (April and May), and finally Violetta (May and June), ending the season with another of her favorite parts, the Druid priestess in Bellini's *Norma* (December). During the same short period, Callas also performed outside Milan in an impressive array of operas: *Medea* in Venice (February 1954), *Tosca* in Genoa (March), *La forza del destino* in Genoa (May), Boito's *Mefistofele* in Verona (July), *Lucia di Lammermoor* in Bergamo (October), *Norma* and *Traviata* in Chicago (November), and, in 1955, *Medea* in Rome (January). She also gave a number of concerts and appeared as the star in nine recordings for EMI: *Norma*, *Pagliacci*, *La forza del destino*, *Il turco in Italia*, *Madama Butterfly*, *Aida*, *Rigoletto*, and two anthologies of arias.[56]

One of Callas biographers, Julie Kavanagh, has observed about the Visconti production, "Callas identified with Violetta to the point of obsession."[57] The orchestra conductor, Carlo Maria Giulini, recollected: "For three weeks, Visconti, Callas, and I worked solely on the Violetta character. Only after that did we start rehearsals. Visconti had the great ability to suggest ideas that an *intelligent actress* like Callas assimilated and made her own. In these three weeks the character of Violetta was created: *La Callas became Violetta*."[58] Callas-Violetta was meant to become a model for other Violettas. As Visconti predicted to Maria Callas's husband, "You see, our *Traviata* will last, whatever latecomers and hopeless jerks could possibly say." Visconti concludes, "Thanks to the art of a great actress like Maria future 'Violettas' will be 'Violetta-Marias.'"[59]

Music critic Elvio Giudici offers his vivid impressions of the legendary performance. Like most reviewers of the Visconti production, he was particularly impressed by the realism of the sets and by Callas's new style of acting, which, as he puts it, gave him an "electric shock." He describes the visual aspect of this production as something between film and pictorial naturalism: in other words, between realism and stylized representation of nature. This quality was achieved mostly thanks to sets painted by Lila De Nobili, but also by myriad small details like fresh flowers that Visconti himself picked and put in tall Chinese vases or, in the act 1 dinner scene, silverware that Visconti borrowed from his patrician family. Particularly realistic and "modern" were Callas's movements, which Giudici describes as akin to early cinematic style ("da cinematografo").[60]

The Visconti-Callas production was not universally applauded. Teodoro Celli of *Corriere Lombardo* felt that Visconti's realist approach (he speaks of exaggerated "verismo") clashed with the spirit of Verdi's drama, and that increased influence of the director's persona came to the detriment of the composer's persona.[61] Here, as in films such as *La terra trema* (1948), Visconti was pursuing a neorealistic approach, and critics saw such innovative performance approaches as a break with opera tradition.[62] In truth, the performance tradition of Verdi's operas was being re-created and reimagined during those same years as part of an attempt to pursue "authenticity," a criterion intended as respect for the composer's persona. As Harriet Boyd-Bennett documents in her history of twentieth-century Venetian opera, in 1951 a series of commemorative events and productions to celebrate the fiftieth anniversary of Verdi's death led to the monumentalizing of the composer and the canonizing of his persona and operas, and to considering opera scores "relics."[63] Retrieving his lesser-known operas was being described as "exhumation." Producing Verdi started to become an exercise in "cultural archaeology" that was "out of touch with the postwar generation."[64] Visconti seemed a threat to those who were clinging to Verdian relics, while to those who saw Verdi as "popular culture"—progressive intellectuals in particular—Visconti-Callas were the new heroes for pursuing a "democratization of taste."[65]

The Italian Communist newspaper *L'Unità* praised Visconti's production, saying it "represented the first turning point in the history of staging and set design, showing how opera could be cleansed from conventions and become a modern, live, believable form of performing art."[66] The newspaper critic also pointed out that Verdi's opera itself had been a "great revolution" in staging a real-life prostitute as the heroic protagonist, scandalizing the well-to-do and challenging a false morality. Callas and Visconti, according to the reviewer, rediscovered the real Duplessis in Violetta, while Lila De Nobili's fin-de-siècle setting unmasked luxury as a form of shallow, selfish bourgeois pleasure. In the course of the opera, Violetta turned from "a fallen angel" into "a real woman, as suffering matured her."[67]

The representation of feasting and fasting in Visconti's *Traviata* combines realism with court-rooted convivial values, pursuing a democratization of taste based on sharing aristocratic traditions with a broader sector of society. Visconti was in fact a progressive artist deeply immersed in aristocratic culture. The Visconti family had ruled Milan from the Middle Ages to the early Renaissance and continued to be influential in the twentieth century. Luchino's family attended opera at La Scala regularly. According to the film director, his mother, Carla Erba, gave birth to him on November 2, 1906, one hour before the curtain went up on a La Scala performance of Verdi's *Traviata*, a performance his mother had to miss.[68] Dinner parties at the Viscontis' were highly elaborate, ritualized events. Visconti's awareness of the cultural values of food and its social consumption is apparent in all his movies. The large dinner party scene in *Il gattopardo* (The leopard) gives us a particularly vivid idea of how Visconti understood a formal lavish meal in an aristocratic family palace: elegant but never stiff. The Renaissance intellectual Baldassare Castiglione, in his widespread and foundational manual of good manners, *The Book of the Courtier*, postulated that the basic rule of behavior in high society is the so-called *sprezzatura*, which is the art of appearing natural and at ease, never artificial and rigid, especially at a banquet. The acting style in Visconti's movies, even when actors portray common people, represents an attempt to modernize *sprezzatura* and extend it beyond the aristocratic and wealthy elites to include the middle class as well as the working class.

The lavish table prepared for the dinner party in his productions of *Traviata* shows a resemblance to this later model from *The Leopard*, as one can tell from stage photographs. In the 1955 production of the opera, he used a real dining table with chairs on all sides (fig. 10.6) rather than opting for the traditional solution of leaving the audience side empty as in a tableau of the Last Supper.[69] At each side of the large table, he set two smaller round tables with no chairs on the front. This allowed the actors to move between the tables, but it also re-created a real convivial situation, as if opera had regressed into the convivial rituals that generated it. Visconti kept this solution in his later production of *Traviata* at London's Royal Opera House in 1967 (fig. 10.7). In Visconti's brindisi, different groups that are spatially separated become unified sonically in the choral toast and are *visually* bridged as the protagonists walk between tables.

Visconti's *Traviata* had special influence on Franco Zeffirelli's movie version of the opera (1982). Casting the slim Greek singer Teresa Stratas as Violetta was an attempt to evoke Callas. Zeffirelli, who started his career as Visconti's assistant, became obsessed with both *Traviata* and Callas, pestering the soprano with repeated invitations to make a film version of the opera, an appeal the diva rejected.[70] In his *Traviata*, Zeffirelli takes the representation of food and wine seriously. At Violetta's dinner party in act 1,

Figure 10.6. Erio Piccagliani, stage photograph of Visconti's production of *Traviata*, act 1 (dated May 28, 1955), "brindisi." Rome, Archivio Visconti, ser. 2, U.A. 3/41. Courtesy of the Fondazione Gramsci, Archivio Luchino Visconti.

Figure 10.7. Nato Frascà, sketch for the Visconti's production of *Traviata*, act 1, in London, Royal Opera House, 1967. Rome, Archivio Visconti, ser. 2, U.A. 19, envelope 4: "bozzetto." Courtesy of the Fondazione Gramsci, Archivio Luchino Visconti.

he replicates the idea of the dinner table with guests seating all around, as would be customary in a film set, rather than on three sides as normally done in theater, and shows understanding of important rituals of sharing or rejecting food and drink in real life.[71]

Edward T. Cone, in his influential reflection on authors', characters', and performers' personae, thought that in *Traviata* Verdi failed to create a real presence for Violetta and Alfredo in order to use them to project his own composer's persona.[72] In their production of *Traviata*, Callas and Visconti corrected this by being faithful to the spirit rather than the letter of the text, letting the director's and singers' ideas compete with the composer's. Here and elsewhere, in fact, Callas was pursuing fidelity not to the "truth of the text, but to the truth of her own theatrical instinct," as Luca Aversano points out about her bold interpretations of *Norma*.[73] For example, the 1955 Milanese production of the opera presented the detail, absent in the libretto and the score, of Violetta's self-medicating by drinking alone, as a powerful gesture of bodily realism. It happens after the duet with Alfredo, who suggests to her that there is a higher form of love than sheer pleasure. In the following scene and aria, Violetta begins by reflecting on Alfredo's words, first by repeating, unaccompanied, "È strano . . . !" (How strange . . . !) and, in the slow lyric section, by quoting Alfredo's definition of love as the "heartbeat of the entire Universe, mysterious and stern / . . . cross and delight to the heart" (A quell'amor che è palpito / Dell'Universo intero / Misterïoso, altero / Croce e delizia al cor). As she begins to transform to this true love, in the transitional section (tempo di mezzo), she dismisses her reflections as folly ("Follie, follie"). This resolution launches the last fast climactic movement of her double aria, the cabaletta, in which she declares, "Always free I must fly from joy to joy to experience every pleasure of life" (sempre libera degg'io / Trasvolar di gioia in gioia, / Perché ignoto al viver mio / Nulla passi del piacer). In the middle of her celebration of life's pleasures, Alfredo, from down the street, starts serenading her again about the "mysterious and stern Love." His serenade is accompanied by the harp, evoking the guitar, traditionally used to accompany serenades, as well as heavenly music. His voice makes Violetta waver before reasserting her intention to embrace freedom. At this point Visconti instructed Callas to drink from the wine glasses her guests had left unfinished on the table, desperately attempting to suppress her conversion through intoxication.[74] Elvidio Giudici recollects Maria Callas's powerful interpretation of this scene in Visconti's historical production:

> During the *Andantino* she takes off her jewels, lets her hair down, covers her shoulders with a white shawl, and finally kneels in front of the fire and takes off her gloves. She rises suddenly on "Follie," runs to the table, and balances on the chair while twisting her head backward. Then she stands up. Again she sits, this time on the dining table, balancing herself this time by extending her arms backward and her legs outward. She takes off her shoes and swiftly throws them in the air. Frantically she starts gulping leftover wine from many glasses. She staggers a little, keeps herself steady by holding on to the table. She hears the voice of Alfredo, uncertain if the product of her increasingly clouded mind is a result of her inebriation. She runs to the balcony on the right and stands there without moving, then comes back downstage appearing transfigured.[75]

Paolo Poli, who also attended the Callas-Visconti production, remarked, "The elegance of Callas, her way of inhabiting the role, of being Violetta, was phenomenal." He gives as an example the cabaletta: "The agile passages in 'sempre libera' were vertiginous but precise, charged with excitement and anxiety."[76]

The effects of these stage decisions on the music itself can be heard in a noncommercial live audio recording of Callas and Visconti's production made in 1956 when, owing to the success of the previous year, La Scala programmed *Traviata* again with the same cast, except for replacing Di Stefano with Gianni Raimondi. Compared with the studio recording that Callas made in September 1953 for Cetra, the live recording shows a greater dramatic vibrancy.[77] In the cabaletta "Sempre libera," recorded live, Callas presses against the rhythmic strictures of the pulse with rebellious fluidity but complete confidence. In the cadenza on *gioir*, her portamento is extreme, giving the impression that she is about to skid out of tune. She nonchalantly stretches the syncopated high As and Cs, suggesting that Violetta-Callas does not care whether she slips off tempo. We can better appreciate this recording if we visualize the action of sharing food in the first scene and the effect of drinking too much wine in the last scene. The cabaletta in Verdi's drama represents a character trapped in her role and tragically unable to escape it. In Callas's impersonation it becomes a moment of liberation and therapeutic frenzy that has the cathartic power to grant temporary relief from the androcratic cultural order, to paraphrase anthropologist Ernesto De Martino's theory of female rituals of trance and possession, from Dionysian rituals to Tarantism.[78] From this viewpoint the moment is reminiscent of the drinking frenzy of the bacchants at the end of Politian's *Orfeo* and anticipating the cathartic function of music drama later theorized by the Alterati (chapters 1 and 3 above).

The recording reveals Callas as an interpreter with the courage and ability to possess her characters like a shaman, making them live outside the written score. Roland Barthes writes about the shaman as a narrator without authorial responsibility, in the same essay where he theorizes the death of the author and the life of the reader. We may compare Barthes's reader to a performer taking possession of the text.[79] One can infer from Gilbert Rouget's study of shamanism and trance that when enacting spirits of gods (the equivalent of opera characters) the shaman never presupposes the presence of a script or an author.[80] Because Maria Callas's relationship to the characters she impersonated was akin to shamanic possession, she gained a trance-induced force to push the boundaries of performance into uncharted territory, unburdened by anxiety over fidelity to the composer's voice and authority.

For the scene in which Violetta dies of consumption, Visconti had the option of taking full advantage of his diva's emaciated features. Stassinopoulos wrote that "Maria never looked more bruised or more frail than in the last two acts of this *Traviata*."[81] Compared with Callas's interpretation of the role in Mexico, before her diet (fig. 10.8), the stage pictures of the Visconti production seem taken from a neorealistic movie (fig. 10.9).

In the live recording, Callas whispers over the immaterial texture of the orchestra to convey the idea of bodily consumption. For the second and last time in the opera, before dying Violetta pronounces the words "È strano!" (How strange!). As in holy anorexia, consumption liberates Violetta from the gravity of the flesh. What is strange, she observes, is that she no longer feels any pain. Her very last utterance, "oh gioia" (Oh joy), is an ascending leap of a sixth resolving half a step down. The point of arrival remains harmonically suspended as Violetta dies on a still unresolved major seventh chord, rather than on the closing minor tonic, to convey that her death is not her end, allowing us to imagine her assumption into heaven. Before this final vocal flight, in her 1956 live recording Callas takes Verdi's indication *parlando* ("speaking") less literally. Her half-sung declamatory delivery is an improvised *Sprechgesang*. The hybrid declamation allows Callas to position herself in a liminal zone where she herself is inhabiting the body of her character, letting us believe for a moment that we are hearing Callas-Violetta.[82] Callas, like a shaman, possesses and is possessed by her character, giving

Figure 10.8. Maria Callas as Violetta in the last scene of *Traviata*, Mexico City, Palacio de Bellas Artes, July 1951, Centro Studi Callassiano, Accademia Maria Callas in Zevio (Verona), collection "Per/für Maria Callas," folder 26, 1FG. Courtesy of Centro Studi Callassiano.

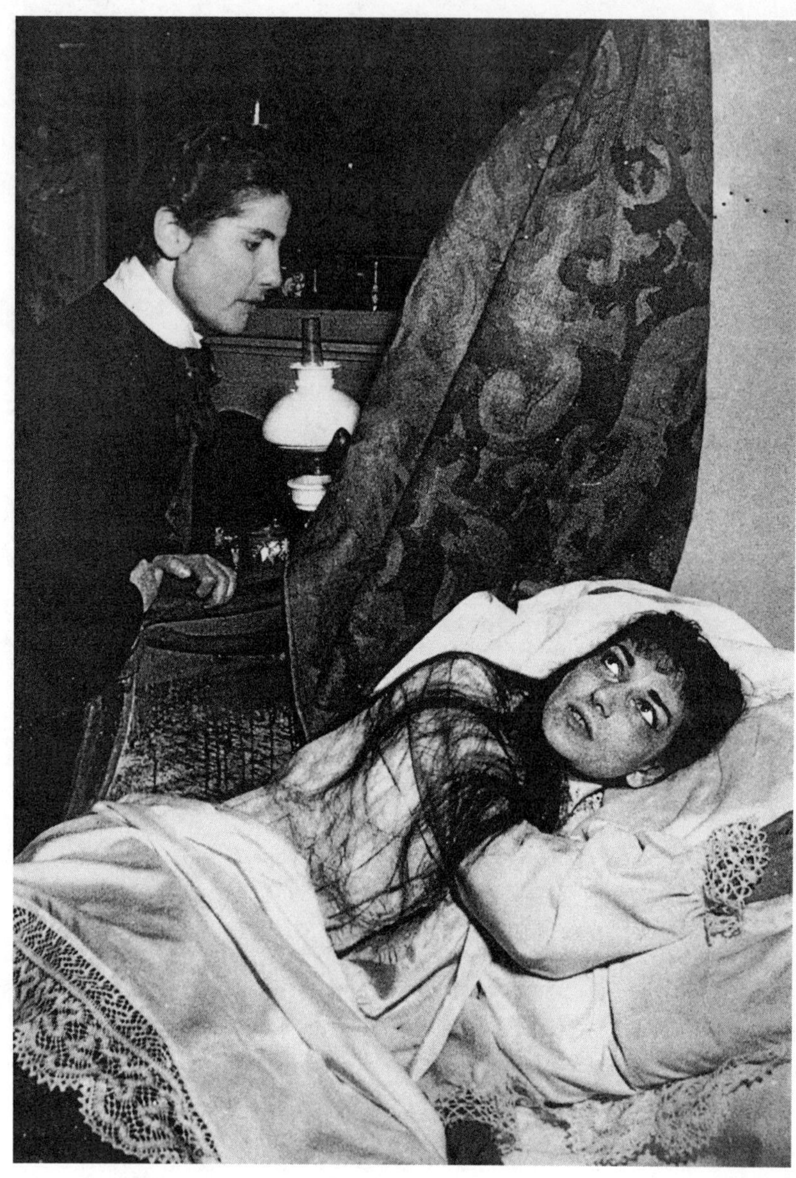

Figure 10.9. Callas posing as Violetta on her deathbed, stage photograph by Erio Piccagliani of Visconti's production of *Traviata*, act 3. Rome, Archivio Visconti, ser. 2, U.A. 3/86. Courtesy of the Fondazione Gramsci, Archivio Luchino Visconti.

birth to a new Violetta, allowing her to step out of the score of a dead author and taking her last breath in freedom.

Conclusion

This book started with a cautionary tale about the risk of conflating the opera stage with real life. It ends with a real-life story of an opera diva whose fame grew as her dramatic life episodes were presented and perceived as operatic scenes, and as her artistic achievements were praised based on her ability to identify with the characters she was impersonating. The story of the Callas diet represents an epochal shift in opera culture from separation to conflation of the dramatis persona and singer's persona, which is in fact a return to the prehistory of opera presented at the beginning of this book. Maria Callas's identification with her characters suggests that her approach to opera was not dissimilar to the trance and possession practiced by the first interpreter of the earliest operatic experiment: Baccio Ugolini in the title role of Politian's 1480 *Orfeo*. The difference is that, by her becoming Violetta outside *Traviata*, Callas's impersonation of the character was not confined by the temporal and architectonic boundaries of a theatrical performance. The public's morbid curiosity about what she ate and how she managed to fast increased the porosity between the world of opera and real life—a life the media presented no more realistically than in an opera.

Flipping through the pages of the "secret" Callas recipe book (*La divina in cucina: Ricettario segreto di Maria Callas*), we encounter delicious dishes that the singer allegedly favored, based on her own handwritten recipes, as well as on what she presumably ordered at restaurants and on recipe books in her personal library. The repertory is heterogeneous in culinary traditions. It includes Venetian classics from simple polenta to liver cooked in butter and onion (fegato alla veneziana), rice and peas with prosciutto, bacon, parmesan, and chicken broth (risi e bisi), bucatini with duck sauce, bruschetta with chicken liver; Milanese ossobuco with porcini; American classics like pumpkin soup, southern fried chicken, Hawaiian lomi lomi salmon, Thanksgiving roast turkey adapted to the Italian food market, cheesecake, and glazed sweet potatoes; French recipes such as escargots à la Provençale (allegedly Maria Callas always ordered this dish at Maxim's in Paris), simple omelets, asparagus soup (potage aux asperges ou crème argenteuil), onion soup (soupe à l'oignon gratinée); Greek recipes like astakós (lobster) with mayonnaise, small meatballs (keftedakia), big meatballs (koftedes), and nut pastries (floyeres).[83] Most of these dishes reflect the culinary traditions of nations Callas identified with, even though her actual strict diet was based on raw meat and vegetables. Both the Callas recipes and the Callas diet are gastronomic signs, carefully chosen, staged, and transmitted to convey meaning and define her character. As such, they work like food in opera: edible props depicting the diva's complex and ambivalent persona in terms of social class through simple and sophisticated recipes reflecting her experience of both poverty and luxury; gender, through homemade food and dishes prepared by professional chefs, reflecting her struggle between the imposed role of traditional wife and her public persona as an independent modern celebrity; nationality and ethnicity, capturing her experience as a resident primarily in the United States, Greece, Italy, and France. Conflating the opera stage with real life can have positive effects after all, once we realize that feasting and fasting have greater value than their nutritional content, that in our own lives, as in opera, we can find beauty and meaning with every sip and morsel we take or renounce, whether alone or in the company of others.

Acknowledgments

In 1995 I received an unusual invitation from Giuliano Bugialli, an opera fan, world-class chef, and cookbook author, who used to entertain opera stars in his Manhattan residence, among them, as he told me at dinner, the insatiable Luciano Pavarotti. One day he decided to write a book on Verdi's favorite recipes and, not having the time to do ground research, he contacted my mentor at the University of Rome, Pierluigi Petrobelli, to whom I will be forever indebted. He told Bugialli he knew a guy. He called me to explain that my mission, should I choose to accept it, was to find evidence to reconstruct Verdi's recipes. Like a farmer, I was supposed to provide the chef with quality produce. At the time I was paying frequent visits to Nino Pirrotta, a Harvard emeritus professor of musicology, to whom I am also indebted, and not only for this book. Our conversations dragged me away from my simple farming job and inspired me to investigate the meaning of food in opera. I became interested in "gastronomic signs." That summer I flew to New York to deliver my findings to the chef, hoping to also get a taste of one of his phenomenal Italian dishes. He took me to a Tex-Mex restaurant in Chinatown. At dinner I unveiled my theory that the representation of fasting and feasting in Verdi's opera is highly meaningful and consistent. He listened attentively while eating, then, after he finished the last morsel, he apologized for changing the subject and for getting down to our business: Verdi's recipes. I gulped the rest of my margarita and told him that to the best of my knowledge Verdi never cooked an egg. But as I could deduce from a letter from Giulio Ricordi to Verdi, dated August 22, 1890, that the composer once sold his publisher a raw pork shoulder from his own farm in Sant'Agata. Ricordi congratulated Verdi for the "exquisite meat" but complained about the "salty bill." Apparently Verdi was selling Ricordi operas he composed while smelling pigs and also selling him the pigs he raised while writing operas. Bugialli fired me, and for good reason. I am grateful to him for introducing me to Tex-Mex cuisine, which has become one of my favorites, and for inspiring me to write this book, which I hope won't get me fired again.

In the following weeks, I shared meals with two Verdi scholars: Harry Powers at Princeton and David Rosen at Cornell. Both encouraged me to pursue the study of gastronomic signs in opera and forget about recipes. Two years later I enrolled in a doctoral program at Cornell, and thanks to David Rosen, I continued my research on food and Verdi's operas, producing my first articles, one published in *Studi Verdiani* (1999) and the other in the proceedings of the conference Verdi 2001. I am grateful to David Rosen, Pierluigi Petrobelli, and Fabrizio Della Seta for their incisive comments and editorial advice. These first essays attracted the attention of a blog called *Improbable Research That Makes You Laugh and Then Think*, but the reactions of some of my peers made me suspect that gastromusicology was making them laugh without making them want to think about it. To be taken seriously, I needed to construct a more solid theoretical frame and study a broader repertory. But considering how time-consuming and risky this enterprise appeared to be, I reluctantly put the project aside.

Then, on May 7, 2012, Daniel J. Wakin published an article in the *New York Times* titled "Don't Sing with Your Mouth Full," in which he addressed the issue of food and opera, and he mentioned my work. I am grateful to him for making me realize that what I wrote many years earlier could still make the news. Slowly I started thawing the project, thanks especially to the warm interest of scholars and editors I would like to thank. The first is Roberta Montemorra Marvin, who commissioned a series of entries from me for *The Cambridge Encyclopedia of Verdi* (2013), including one on "brindisi/toast," and later invited me to present a paper on food in opera at the Opera Studies Forum of the University of Iowa. Independently, Kate van Orden encouraged me to write an essay on Maria Callas's diet for a volume of the *Oxford Handbook Online*, edited by Alexander Rehding (published in 2015). About this time, Marta Tonegutti, acquisitions editor at the University of Chicago Press, expressed vivid interest in the topic and helped me envision a book on it, brainstorming on how to expand my ideas. I am immensely grateful to her for fueling my enthusiasm and also for her harsh but always constructive criticism at every step of a long process. I am also grateful to Dylan Montanari at the Press for keeping me on track, to freelance manuscript editor Alice Bennett, and to the anonymous reviewers who offered different and complementary perspectives on my manuscript, all extremely useful.

Writing the kind of academic books I like requires an enormous amount of time and resources. In 2013 I was fortunate to be granted a large nonresidential grant from the Earhart Foundation, cosponsoring my leave of absence from my faculty position. The University of Notre Dame, where I was a professor at the time, was also extremely supportive, granting me the Founders' and Director's Thirtieth Anniversary Research Award from the Institute of Scholarship in the Liberal Arts (ISLA) and smaller grants and nonmonetary support from the Nanovic Institute, including the help of a fantastic group of scholars reading each other's work in progress, led by Julia Douthwaite. This initial support allowed me, among other things, to conduct research in Italy and to visit libraries and archives in Italy and the United States, some of which were very welcoming. I am grateful to the collector and archivist Stefano Castellani and the director Gianluca Brigo for opening the door of the small museum of the Accademia Maria Callas, at a time when the collection was not available to the public. I am also indebted to the Casa Goldoni and the Fondazione Cini of Venice, to the Archivio Visconti of Rome, to Elena Zomparelli, head librarian of the Conservatory Cherubini of Florence, to Barbara Nepote of the Fondazione Torino Musei, and to John Shepard, head librarian of the Hargrove Music Library of the University of California, Berkeley. In 2017 I joined the faculty of the music department of the University of California, Davis, an institution that immediately supported my research. I am grateful to the provost at the time, Ralph Hexter, an opera enthusiast, for letting me into his very busy office to exchange ideas about opera studies and directing me to the right resources to continue my project in my new institutional home. Among them, the Jan and Beta Popper Endowment in Opera has been crucial for the acquisition of material and resources, allowing me to complete this book. Our music librarians Ruth Gustafson and Nick Carvajal helped make resources available to me even during the difficult time of the coronavirus pandemic when libraries were closed to the public. I also wish to acknowledge publication assistance grants that I received from the Office of Research and from the the College of Arts and Letters of the University of California, Davis, 2020, as well as from the American Musicological Society. The help and support of students and colleagues has been pivotal in developing and testing ideas. At Notre Dame I benefited from a truly interdisciplinary intellectual environment and I was fortunate to get help from my research assistants Mimi Ensley and especially Lesley Sullivan. I want to thank stage designer and architect David Mayernik, classicists Brian Krostenko and Catherine Schlegel, art historian Randy Coleman, English literature professors Ian Newman and Yasmin Solomonescu, German literature scholar Tobias Boes, philosopher Vittorio Hösle, and especially my colleagues in the Program of Liberal Studies, particularly Ficino expert Denis Robichaud and musicologist Chris Chowrimoottoo. Moving to the University of California, Davis, was a difficult choice but good for the progress of this book, thanks to the leading role of the institution and surrounding community in the study, but also in the production and consumption of food and wine. I have been fortunate to benefit from a competent and thorough research assistant, Sarah Miller, and from the advice and support of colleagues who are both academically rigorous and joyfully convivial, including Christian Baldini, Anna Maria Busse Berger, Juan Diego Díaz, Carol Hess, Beth Levy, Sally McKee, Pete Nowlen, Pablo Ortiz, Jessie Ann Owens, Chris Reynolds, and Henry Spiller, while Laurie San Martin has been a very supportive chair during the final stages of production for this book.

I started reading papers related to this book's subject in 1999, including at an eye-opening and mouthwatering conference at Universidad de Las Américas in Puebla, Mexico, devoted entirely to food and culture, then took a long break from presentations about the subject from 2001 to 2013. From 2013, after publication of my "brindisi" article in *The Cambridge Encyclopedia of Verdi*, I frequently presented my gastromusicological work and received much feedback. I am much indebted to Mary Ann Smart, who shortly after I moved to California invited me to present at the colloquium series of the music department of UC Berkeley and discussed with me my work in progress. Similarly, Karol Berger invited me to present my research at the colloquium series of his home institution, Stanford University. I admire him for providing a model of humanism that reconciles tradition and innovation. At Stanford I also had the chance to discuss food in Bertold Brecht's operas with Stephen Hinton, realizing how much more there is to be done than I could do in this book. I am grateful to Lorenzo Bianconi for the opportunity to offer the keynote address at the twenty-first conference of Il Saggiatore Musicale in Bologna, an institution that has been at the forefront of food cultural studies. There I met the great food historian Massimo Montanari, whom I thank for his interest in my work and especially for expanding my understanding of food as culture. I am also indebted to Nicolas Dufetel and other colleagues in France who expressed interest in the study of food in opera within the context of new directions in musicology at the one hundredth anniversary conference of the Société française de musicologie in Paris ("Penser la musicologie aujourd'hui"), giving me hope that today gastromusicology may still make people laugh, but it can also make them think.

Beyond the opportunities offered on an institutional level, I am grateful to many colleagues, students, and friends who helped me locate resources, discuss ideas, read drafts, and share sources in their possession. I thank Luca Aversano, Marco Beghelli, Paola Besutti, Mark Evan Bonds, Rogério Budasz, Michael Burden, Margaret Butler, Mauro Calcagno, Audrey Calefas-Strébelle, Alessandra Campana, Stefano Castelvecchi, Andrea Chagai, Caryl Clark, Paul Corneilson, Francesco Cotticelli, Gabe Dotto, Annagret Fauser, Michael Freyman, Bob Judd, Dorothea Link, Ralph Locke, Paologiovanni Maione, János Malina, Robert L. Marshall, Vittorio Montemaggi, Hilary Poriss, John A. Rice, Ellen Rosand, Aida Shirazi, Elaine Sisman, Michael P. Steinberg, Claire Thompson, David Yearsley, Neal Zaslaw, and Stacy Stout on behalf of the Eataly NYC Flatiron. I am particularly grateful to Anthony R. DelDonna for professional and moral support and Emanuele Senici for his terrific editorial advice on the last chapter. And, speaking of editors, I was very fortunate to work with two exceptional editors, Beverly Wilcox and Paul De Angelis, who helped me at two very different stages of production and offered a treasure of advice on both form and content. Last but far from least, I want to thank Leah Ross, a wonderful editor as well, and also a music and food lover with whom I have the pleasure to share the enjoyment of opera and many happy meals.

Notes

PROLOGUE

1. This quotation, alas, is incomplete. I suspect he did not read the entire sentence as it appears in Mikhail Bakhtin's book: "No meal can be sad. Sadness and food are incompatible (while death and food are perfectly compatible)."

2. Kenneth Bendiner, *Food in Painting: From the Renaissance to the Present* (London: Reaktion, 2005).

3. Gillian Crowther, *Eating Culture: An Anthropological Guide to Food* (Toronto: University of Toronto Press, 2013), 152.

4. Massimo Montanari, *Food Is Culture* (New York: Columbia University Press, 2006).

5. Claude Lévi-Strauss, *The Raw and the Cooked*, trans. John and Doreen Wightman (Chicago: University of Chicago Press, 1983), 164.

6. Mary Douglas, "Deciphering a Meal," *Daedalus* 101, no. 1 (1972): 61; reprinted in *Food and Culture: A Reader*, ed. Carole Counihan and Penny Van Esterik, 3rd ed. (New York: Routledge, 2013), 36.

7. Paraphrasing Daniel J. Wakin, who discusses my essay "Feasting and Fasting in Verdi's Operas" in his article "Don't Sing with Your Mouth Full," *New York Times*, May 7, 2012.

8. Gian-Paolo Biasin, *The Flavors of Modernity: Food and the Novel* (Princeton, NJ: Princeton University Press, 1993).

9. Priscilla Parkhurst Ferguson, *Accounting for Taste: The Triumph of French Cuisine* (Chicago: University of Chicago Press, 2004), 3.

10. Carl Dahlhaus, "What Is a Musical Drama?," trans. Mary Whittall, *Cambridge Opera Journal* 1, no. 2 (1989): 95, expanding on Kerman's philologically incorrect but aesthetically reasonable interpretation of *dramma per musica* as "drama through music," in Joseph Kerman, *Opera as Drama* (New York: Knopf, 1956), 8.

11. Joseph Kerman, "Reading Don Giovanni," in *"Don Giovanni": Myth of Seduction and Betrayal*, ed. Jonathan Miller (Baltimore: Johns Hopkins University Press, 1990), 116: "Mozart, who was a dramatic genius as well as a musical genius, understood the problem

that he was faced with by Da Ponte's cobbled-up libretto. He devised his own radical way of dealing with it, a strictly musical way. In opera, the dramatist is the composer."

12. Pierluigi Petrobelli, "Music in the Theater (apropos of *Aida*, act III), in *Music in the Theater: Essays on Verdi and Other Composers* (Princeton, NJ: Princeton University Press, 1994), 113, first published with the same title in *Drama, Dance, and Music*, ed. James Redmond, 129–42 (Cambridge: Cambridge University Press, 1981); Fabrizio Della Seta, "'O cieli azzurri': Exoticism and Dramatic Discourse in *Aida*," *Cambridge Opera Journal* 3, no. 1 (1991): 49–62.

13. The term multivalence was used by Harold Powers in a paper presented at a conference in Vienna in March 1983 and published in its most complete form as "La Solita Forma and the Uses of Conventions," *Acta Musicologica* 59, no. 1 (1987): 65–90. The term was later adapted to describe the composite nature of operatic expressive parameters and their complex interplay, as in James Webster's "To Understand Verdi and Wagner We Must Understand Mozart," *19th-Century Music* 11 (1987–88): 175–93. James Webster, "Mozart's Operas and the Myth of Musical Unity," *Cambridge Opera Journal* 2, no. 2 (1990): 198, gives a definition of multivalence where parameters may be incongruent. The interest in the incongruence, rather than unity, is prominent in Carolyn Abbate and Roger Parker, "Dismembering Mozart," *Cambridge Opera Journal* 2, no. 2 (1990): 187–95.

14. Sergio Durante, "Analysis and Dramaturgy: Reflections towards a Theory of Opera," in *Opera Buffa in Mozart's Vienna*, ed. Mary Hunter and James Webster (Cambridge: Cambridge University Press, 1997): 315. This concept stems from a well-known provocative essay by Don M. Randel, "The Canon in the Musicological Toolbox," in *Disciplining Music: Musicology and Its Canons*, ed. Katherine Bergeron and Philip V. Bohlman (Chicago: University of Chicago Press, 1992), 10–22.

15. Alessandra Campana, *Opera and Modern Spectatorship in Late Nineteenth-Century Italy* (Cambridge: Cambridge University Press, 2015).

16. Mary Ann Smart, *Mimomania: Music and Gesture in Nineteenth-Century Opera* (Berkeley: University of California Press, 2004).

17. David J. Levin, *Unsettling Opera: Staging Mozart, Verdi, Wagner, and Zemlinsky* (Chicago: University of Chicago Press, 2007), 69–98.

18. Wolfgang Amadeus Mozart, *Don Giovanni*, directed by Peter Sellars, English subtitles by Peter Sellars (London: Decca, 1991), DVD, disc 2, chap. 10.

19. For an overview of patterns of change and continuity in food taste and meaning see Paul Freedman, ed., "Introduction: A New History of Cuisine," in *Food: A History of Taste* (Berkeley: University of California Press, 2007), 7–33.

CHAPTER ONE

1. Gary Tomlinson, *Music in Renaissance Magic: Toward a Historiography of Others* (Chicago: University of Chicago Press, 1993), presents the most thorough contribution to Ficino's philosophical thought relevant to Renaissance music up to Monteverdi's *Orfeo*. On Ficino as music therapist see Angela Voss, "Marsilio Ficino, the Second Orpheus," in *Music as Medicine: The History of Music Therapy since Antiquity*, ed. Peregrine Horden (Brookfield, VT: Ashgate, 2000), 154–72.

2. Giulio Caccini, dedicatory preface "All'Illustrissimo Signore Il Signor Giovanni Bardi de' conti di Vernio" to *L'Euridice composta in musica in stile rappresentativo da Giulio Caccini detto Romano* (Florence: Marescotti, 1600).

3. Nino Pirrotta was among the first music historians to cast doubt on the myth of Bardi's Camerata as the "factory" that created opera. See his "Recitar cantando e aria nei primi decenni della storia dell'opera," in *Li due Orfei: Da Poliziano a Monteverdi* (Turin: ERI, 1969), 307–29. Pirrotta's collection of essays on early opera is available in English translation as Pirrotta, *Music and Theater from Politian to Monteverdi*, trans. Karen Eales (Cambridge: Cambridge University Press, 1982).

4. Claude V. Palisca, "The Alterati of Florence, Pioneers in the Theory of Dramatic Music," in *New Looks at Italian Opera: Essays in Honor of Donald J. Grout*, ed. William W. Austin (Ithaca, NY: Cornell University Press, 1968), 11. Palisca's groundbreaking research, to which I am deeply indebted, is based on the minutes of the academy, the "Diario degli Alterati," Florence, Biblioteca medicea laurenziana, MS Ashburnham 558. The *Diario* has been also examined, with little attention to music, by literary historians, as in the case of Bernard Weinberg, "The Accademia degli Alterati and Literary Taste from 1570 to 1600," *Italica* 31, no. 4 (1954): 207–14. That wine and food were part of their philosophy and not just entertainment has been recognized only recently, in passing, by Paolo Puggelli, "*Del convivio degli Alterati* di Giulio del Bene," *Accademia: Revue de la Société Marsile Ficin* II (2000): 63–88. Puggelli, like other literary historians, disregards the Alterati's role in the creation of opera. I first pointed out the centrality of the theme of wine in the Alterati and Umidi academies in Pierpaolo Polzonetti, "The 'Quantitative Style' in Seventeenth-Century Italian Opera," in *Pensieri per un maestro: Studi in onore di Pierluigi Petrobelli*, ed. Stefano Lavia and Roger Parker (Turin: EDT, 2002), 98.

5. Domenico Maria Manni, *Memorie della fiorentina famosa accademia degli Alterati* (Florence: Stecchi, 1748), 5–6. In the translation I follow the version "designat" (makes possible) chosen by the Alterati, rather than the correct "dissignat" (unlocks).

6. Horace, *Epistles* 2.5.16–19: "Quid non ebrietas dissignat [designat]? Operta recludit, / Spes iubet esse ratas, ad proelia trudit inertem, / Sollicitis animis onus eximit, addocet artis. / Fecundi calices quem non fecere disertum, / contracta quem non in paupertate solutum?" All translations are my own unless otherwise indicated. Original-language citations are included when relevant to explain my choices in the English translation or when the text cannot be easily translated into English.

7. A long list of nicknames and emblems is in Manni, *Memorie della fiorentina*, 5–24.

8. On distillation and natural magic about this time in history I am indebted to papers that John Slater William Eamon and John Rundin presented at the conference "Distillation and Alchemy: Science, Society and Sentiment," University of California Davis, April 27, 2018.

9. Giulio del Bene, "Del convito degli Alterati," Florence, MS Magliabechiano IX, 137, cc. 12r–22r, Bibliotoeca Nazionale Centrale. The speech in the original Italian language is transcribed in Puggelli, "*Del Convivio*," 79–86. The date of the speech was established by Palisca, "Alterati of Florence," 12, based on the *Diario*, i.e., the proceedings of the academy.

10. Del Bene, "Del convito degli Alterati," 12v.

11. Florence biblioteca riccardiana, MS 2471, folio 98, cited in Palisca, "Alterati of Florence," 19–20.

12. Del Bene, "Del convito degli Alterati," 12r–13r.

13. Marsilio Ficino, *Sopra lo amore ovvero Convito di Platone*, ed. Giuseppe Pensi (Milan: ES, 1992), 17. Puggelli highlights the influence of Ficino in del Bene's speech in his introductory essay, "*Del Convivio*," 65–66.

14. Marsilio Ficino, *Three Books on Life*, critical ed. by Carol V. Kaske and John R. Clark (Binghamton, NY: Center for Medieval and Early Renaissance Studies of the State University of New York at Binghamton, 1989), Procemium, 103.

15. Lorenzo Bianconi, "La forma musicale come scuola dei sentimenti," in *Educazione musicale e formazione*, ed. Giuseppina La Face Bianconi and Franco Frabboni (Milan: FrancoAngeli, 2008), 85–120.

16. Del Bene, "Del convito degli Alterati," 13v: "l'alteratione è un mutamento di accidenti, quando il subietto resta il medesimo."

17. Del Bene, "Del convito degli Alterati," 16r.

18. Del Bene, "Del convito degli Alterati," 21r.

19. Del Bene, "Del convito degli Alterati," 18v–19r.

20. Del Bene, "Del convito degli Alterati," 20v.

21. Baldassare Castiglione, *Il cortigiano*, 1.8.1–8.3, following the text established by Amedeo Quondam (Milan: Mondadori, 2002), 83.

22. Lorenzo Giacomini, *Orationi e discorsi di Lorenzo Giacomini Tebalducci Malespini* (Florence: Sermartelli, 1597), 39: "Il cibo e il vino riscaldando e destando gli spiriti, e rinvigorendo il corpo partorisce letizia. Dal altra parte l'aggravamento de la parte sensitiva per li vapori torbidi e impuri, e la diminutione del calore interno preparano a mestizia e a timore, e ci fanno parere pigri, tardi, e inutili." Palisca, "Alterati," 22–29, is well aware of the importance of Giacomini's theories during the critical years leading to the creation of opera, even though in his treatise he does not explore pervasive parallels between food, music drama, and medicine.

23. Giacomini, "De La Purgatione," 36.

24. Giacomini, "De La Purgatione," 39–40.

25. Giacomini, "De La Purgatione," 43–44.

26. Lucretius, *De rerum natura* 1, 931–50. Giacomini, "De La Purgatione," 30, quotes Lucretius a propos of the purgative effects of observing a ship in a tempest from the shore. *De rerum natura* 2, 1–5.

27. Giacomini, "De La Purgatione," 46.

28. Giacomini, "De La Purgatione," 49–50: "Dolore, allegrezza, libidine, ira quando senza offesa de la virtù ricevan sfogamento, per piu agevol maniera si moderano col lasciarli per qualche tempo sino a certa misura sfogare che col costringerli, e violentemente tenerli racchiusi."

29. As in the first lecture of Sigmund Freud, *Five Lectures on Psycho-analysis* [1910], trans. and ed. James Strachey (New York: Norton, 1990), 14.

CHAPTER TWO

1. Eugene J. Johnson, *Inventing the Opera House: Theater Architecture in Renaissance and Baroque Italy* (Cambridge: Cambridge University Press, 2018), 87–93.

2. Anthony M. Cummings, "Music and Feasts in the Fifteenth Century," in *The Cambridge History of Fifteenth-Century Music*, ed. Anna Maria Busse Berger and Jesse Rodin (Cambridge: Cambridge University Press, 2015), 361–73.

3. On the central role of the Church of Rome in the humanist project of retrieving pre-Christian classical culture, see Peter Burkhardt, *The Civilization of the Renaissance in Italy* (New York: Random House, 1954), part 3 ("The Revival of Antiquity"), esp. 135–40. On papal banquets at the time of Leo X, see Cummings, "Leo's Jesters," *Revue belge de musicologie/Belgisch Tijdschrift voor Muziekwetenschap* 63 (2009): 31–65.

4. Bartolomeo Platina, *De la honesta voluptate et valitudine vulgare* (Venice: Ruschoni, 1501), i–ii: "la felicitate è quella voluptate la quale nasce da honesta cagione: cioè è la medicina a lo infermo che produce la sanitate a l'homo." According to Westbury, Platina's was the first gastronomy book ever printed in Italy. Its first edition was published in 1475 in Latin. See Richard Westbury, *Handlist of Italian Cookery Books* (Florence: Olschki, 1963), vi, 176–77; Alberto Capatti and Massimo Montanari, *Italian Cuisine: A Cultural History*, trans. Áine O'Healy (New York: Columbia University Press, 2003), 10, acknowledging Platina's book as a model for the holistic concept of conviviality.

5. Platina, *De la honesta voluptate*, 57, 62, 65, 75.

6. Barbara Ketcham Wheaton, *Savoring the Past: The French Kitchen and Table from 1300 to 1789* (New York: Touchstone, 1983), 36.

7. Plato, *Republic* 614b–617b. On the mystical and aesthetic value of food and wine in Christian, and especially Catholic, liturgy and culture, see Ann W. Astell, *Eating Beauty: The Eucharist and the Spiritual Arts of the Middle Ages* (Ithaca, NY: Cornell University Press, 2006), and Norman Wirzba, *Food and Faith: A Theology of Eating* (Cambridge: Cambridge University Press, 2011).

8. On the representations of "the Table of Christ" as a banquet that "transcends earthly substance" but is no different from iconographies of secular banquets, see Fernand Braudel, *Civilization and Capitalism: 15th–18th Centuries*, vol. 1, *The Structures of Everyday Life*, trans. Siân Reynolds (New York: Harper and Row, 1982), 207–9. Accounts of the cultural issues at play in the representation of food and eating are presented in a special issue of the art-history journal *Predella*: Diane H. Bodart and Valérie Boudier, eds., in *Le banquet de la Renaissance: Images et usages*, special issue, *Predella: Rivista di arti visive/Journal of Visual Arts* 7 (2013).

9. Christina Normore, *A Feast for the Eyes: Art, Performance, and the Late Medieval Banquet* (Chicago: University of Chicago Press, 2015), 1. I am grateful to Marta Tonegutti for calling my attention to this study.

10. Giovanni Battista Rossetti, *Dello scalco del Sig. Gio. Battista Rossetti, Scalco della Serenissima Madama Lucretia da Este Duchessa d'Urbino, nel quale si contengono le qualità di uno scalco perfetto e tutti i carichi suoi, con diversi ufficiali a lui sottoposti* . . . (Ferrara: Mammarello, 1584), 45. Stefano Lorenzetti, commenting on Rossetti's book, suggests comparing the steward to the "conductor of a composite multisensorial orchestra." See Lorenzetti, "'At Every Gesture from the Lord': Music at Banquets, a Cornucopia of the Senses," in *Le banquet de la Renaissance: Images et usages*, ed. Diane H. Bodart and Valérie Boudier, special issue, *Predella: Rivista di arti visive/Journal of Visual Arts* 7 (2013): 22–23. For an equally compelling reading of Renaissance banquets at the Gonzaga court as multimedia

events see Paola Besutti, "Musiche e musicisti alla tavola dei Gonzaga," in *Le tavole di corte tra Cinquecento e Settecento*, ed. Andrea Marlotti (Rome: Bulzoni, 2013), 185–216.

11. Normore, *Feast for the Eyes*, chaps. 1–2.

12. Claudio Monteverdi, *L'Orfeo: Favola in musica di Claudio Monteverdi rappresentata in Mantova l'anno 1607 e nuovamente data in luce. Al Serenissimo Signor D. Francesco Gonzaga, Principe di Mantova, e di Monferato, etc.* (Venice: Amadino, 1609).

13. Norbert Elias, *The Civilizing Process: Sociogenetic and Psychogenetic Investigations*, trans. Edmund Jephcott (Oxford: Blackwell, 2000), 68.

14. Edward Muir, *Ritual in Early Modern Europe* (Cambridge: Cambridge University Press, 1997), 118–26. On a banquet's audience as actors and the expectations for guests' effective performance see also Normore, *Feast for the Eyes*, 47–67, 74–91.

15. Cristoforo di Messisbugo, *Banchetti, compositioni di vivande et apparecchio generale di Christoforo di Messisbugo allo Illustrissimo et Reverendissimo Signor il Signor Don Hippolito da Este, Cardinale di Ferrara* (Ferrara: Giovanni de Buglhat and Antonio Hucher, 1549). Michael Jeanneret, *A Feast of Words: Banquets and Table Talk in the Renaissance* (Chicago: University of Chicago Press, 1991), 51–55, disregards the structural links between music, drama, and food in Messisbugo. The same can be said for the fish feast described below in Mary Hollingsworth, *The Cardinal's Hat: Money, Ambition, and Everyday Life in the Court of a Borgia Prince* (Woodstock, New York: Overlook Press, 2005), 19–23, as well as for Howard Mayer Brown, "A Cook's Tour of Ferrara in 1529," *Rivista Italiana di Musicologia* 10 (1975): 216–41, reprinted as Brown, "A Cook's Tour of Ferrara in 1529," in *Renaissance Music*, ed. Kenneth Kreiner (Burlington VT: Ashgate, 2011): 243–62. More promising is the short but excellent contribution by Nicola Badolato, "Commedie e intermedi musicali ferraresi nei 'Banchetti' del Messisbugo (1549)," in *Le arti e il cibo: Modalità ed esempi di un rapporto*, atti del convegno (Bologna, 15–16 ottobre 2012), ed. Sylvie Davidson and Fabrizio Lollini (Bologna: Bononia University Press, 2014), 177–87, comparing the steward to a stage director (178) and recognizing the presence of deliberate connections between gastronomy and music (184).

16. June di Schino, "Banchetti, vivande e imbandigioni della tavola di Ippolito d'Este," in *Ippoliro II d'Este: Cardinale, principe, mecenate*, atti del convegno (Villa d'Este, Tivoli, 13–15 maggio 2010), ed. Marina Cogotti and Francesco Paolo Fiore (Rome: De Luca, 2013), 455.

17. Hollingsworth, *Cardinal's Hat*, 15–16.

18. On Ippolito as art sponsor see Marina Cagotti and Francesco Paolo Fiore, eds., *Ippolito II d'Este: Cardinale principe mecenate*, atti del convegno, Villa d'Este, Tivoli, 13–15 maggio 2010 (Rome: De Luca, 2013).

19. Mauro Natale, "Lo studiolo di Belfiore," in *Le muse e il principe: Arte di corte nel Rinascimento Padano*, ed. Andrea Di Lorenzo et al. (Modena: Panini, 1991), 404–16.

20. I base this description on the second edition: Cristoforo di Messisbugo, *Libro nuovo nel quale s'insegna il modo d'ordinar banchetti* . . . (Venice: Spineda, 1600), 9r-14v. In his description of this banquet, Brown, "Cook's Tour of Ferrara," 284–86, does not take into account the actual dishes within the courses.

21. The account is in the Archivio di Stato di Mantova (ASMn), Archivio Gonzaga (AG), b2494, c. 274rv, October 14, 1516, cited in Giancarlo Malacarne, *Sulla mensa del*

Principe: Alimentazione e banchetti alla corte dei Gonzaga (Modena: Il Bulino, 2000), 175, and Fanny Kieffer, "La confiserie des Offices: Art, sciences et magnificence à la cour de Médicis," in *Le banquet de la Renaissance: Images et usages*, special issue, *Predella: Rivista di arti visive/Journal of Visual Arts* 7 (2013): 85.

22. Kieffer, "Confiserie," 86, 90–93.

23. Wheaton, *Savoring the Past*, 39.

24. On the banquet as a pedagogical tool in the practice and performance of temperance, see Normore, *Feast for the Eyes*, 105, 129–30.

25. I am grateful to Lesley Sullivan for helping with the translation, which required consulting many period sources. Especially helpful was Bartolomeo Scappi, *The Opera of Bartolomeo Scappi (1570): "L'arte et prudenza d'un maestro cuoco,"* ed. and trans. Terence Scully (Toronto: University of Toronto Press, 2008). The exact number of dishes is not easy to determine since they are not numbered in the original and a few items do not seem to count as a proper dish (as in the case of sugar sculptures).

26. Wheaton, *Savoring the Past*, 6.

27. Tomlinson, *Music in Renaissance Magic*, 4–9. On the practice of semi-improvised music at the banquet see also the articles by Anthony Cummings mentioned in this chapter (see bibliography).

28. L. P. Hartley, *The Go-Between* (London: Hamilton, 1953), 9.

29. The use of the terms diegetic and nondiegetic for these two modes has been convincingly criticized by Stefano Castelvecchi, "On 'Diegesis' and 'Diegetic': Words and Concepts," *Journal of the American Musicological Society* 73, no. 1 (2020): 149–71.

30. On the moresca as an exoticizing dance see Anthony M. Cummings, "Dance and 'the Other': The Moresca" in *Seventeenth-Century Ballet, a Multi-art Spectacle: An International Interdisciplinary Symposium*, ed. Barbara Grammeniati (Bloomington, IN: Xlibris, 2011): 39–60; and especially Ralph P. Locke, *Music and the Exotic from the Renaissance to Mozart* (Cambridge: Cambridge University Press, 2015), 117–25. On performing morescas at the end of the meal, even outside Italy, see Normore, *Feast for the Eyes*, 96.

31. Angela Voss, "Marsilio Ficino, the Second Orpheus," in *Music as Medicine: The History of Music Therapy since Antiquity*, ed. Peregrine Horden (Brookfield, VT: Ashgate, 2000), 161–71; Gary Tomlinson, "Il canto magico dell'Euridice," in "Lo stupor dell'invenzione": Firenze e la nascita dell'opera," atti del convegno internazionale di studi (Firenze, 5–6 ottobre 2000), in *Quaderni della Rivista Italiana di Musicologia* 36, ed. Piero Gargiulo (Florence: Olschki, 2001), 61–72.

32. For representations of the myth of Orpheus at other Renaissance banquets see Cummings, "Music and Feasts in the Fifteenth Century," 366.

33. Monteverdi, *L'Orfeo: Favola in musica*, 100. The moresca was performed as part of the bacchanal staging the killing of Orpheus on at least one occasion during carnival, as maintained by Silke Leopold, *Monteverdi: Music in Transition*, trans. Anne Smith (Oxford: Clarendon Press, 1982), 98. On this issue and the implications of giving the last "word" to the dancing bacchants, see also Karol Berger, *Bach's Cycle, Mozart's Arrow: An Essay on the Origins of Musical Modernity* (Berkeley: University of California Press, 2007), 24. Berger observes that this ending functions as a "corrective to [the] hero's male self-sufficiency" for the all-male audience of the premiere on February 24, 1607.

34. Normore, *Feast for the Eyes*, 42.

35. Rossetti, *Dello scalco*, 1–46. Based on salary records, Hollingsworth, *Cardinal's Hat*, 51, presents a long list of professional figures employed in the kitchen of Ippolito II d'Este.

36. Rossetti, *Dello scalco*, 29–30.

37. Rossetti, *Dello scalco*, 30–32.

38. Rossetti, *Dello scalco*, 1–10, 33–34.

39. Rossetti, *Dello scalco*, 37–38, 127.

40. Rossetti, *Dello scalco*, 50.

41. Rossetti, *Dello scalco*, 53–55, 58, 72–73, 119. Fanfare was also used in banquets in France, Burgundy, Flanders, and other locations, as documented, among others, by Normore, *Feast for the Eyes*, 28, and Wheaton, *Savoring the Past*, 5.

42. Rossetti, *Dello scalco*, 118–27.

43. Rossetti, *Dello scalco*, 137.

44. *Descrizione delle feste fatte nelle reali nozze de' serenissimi principi di Toscana Don Cosimo de' Medici, e Maria Maddalena Arciduchessa d'Austria* (Florence: Giunti, 1608), with an inserted engraving reproduced in Lorenzetti, "'At the Very Gesture from the Lord': Music at Banquets," 31.

45. The role of Emilio de' Cavalieri as organizer of complex banquets has been documented based on a late eighteenth-century historical account and period archival documents at the Archivio di Stato di Firenze by Kieffer, "Confiserie," 87, 91–92. For the leading role of Cavalieri in the creation and early dissemination of opera, see Warren Kirkendale, "The Myth of the 'Birth of Opera' in the Florentine Camerata Deflated with the Roman Gentleman Emilio de' Cavalieri," in Warren Kirkendale and Ursula Kirkendale, *Music and Meaning: Studies in Music History and the Neighbouring Disciplines* (Florence: Olschki, 2007), 205–16.

46. Wheaton, *Savoring the Past*, 43–49. See also Roy Strong, *Splendor at Court: Renaissance Spectacle and the Theater of Power* (Boston: Houghton Mifflin, 1973), 19–56.

47. Venantio Mattei, *Teatro nobilissimo della scalcheria di Venantio Mattei da Camerino per apparecchio di Banchetti a gran Prencipi, secondo il variar delle stagioni . . . dedicato all'Eminentissimo e Reverendissimo Signor Cardinale Giacomo Rospigliosi* (Roma: Dragondelli, 1669).

CHAPTER THREE

1. Mauro Calcagno, *From Madrigal to Opera: Monteverdi's Staging of the Self* (Berkeley: University of California Press, 2012), 18.

2. Angelo Poliziano, *Stanze, Orfeo, Rime*, ed. Davide Puccini (Milan: Garzanti, 1992), 146–17. I translate the word *tumulti* as "carousing" in agreement with Davide Puccini's commentary in the critical apparatus of this edition. I agree with Piccotti, who proposed that the first performance of *Orfeo* took place on February 15, 1480, based on internal evidence (the dedicatory letter) and contextual evidence, such as the festivities in Mantua on that day and the limited presence in Mantua of both Baccio Ugolini (the first Orfeo) and Francesco Gonzaga (the sponsor) during the first months of 1480: Giovan Battista

Piccotti, "Sulla data *dell'Orfeo* e delle *Stanze* di Agnolo Poliziano," *Rendiconti della Reale Accademia dei Lincei, Classe di scienze morali, storiche e filologiche* 23, ser. 5 (1914): 330–34. Further and incontrovertible evidence supporting the idea that the premiere of *Orfeo* was at the end-of-carnival banquet in 1480 is provided by Cynthia Munro Pyle, "Politian's *Orfeo* and the *Favole Mitologiche* in the Context of Late Quattrocento Northern Italy" (PhD diss., Columbia University, 1976), 47–56. In spite of this evidence, in the critical edition of Politian's *Orfeo*, Antonia Tissoni Benvenuti objects to this as the date of composition but does not propose any viable alternative and does not produce convincing evidence against Piccotti's and Pyle's date and place. See her introduction to Angelo Poliziano, *"L'Orfeo" del Poliziano con il testo critico dell'originale e delle successive forme teatrali*, ed. Antonia Tissoni Benvenuti (Padua: Antenore, 1986), 58–70. Pirrotta also finds Piccotti's date and place to be the most plausible but does not exclude other dates, at least for the replicas: *Li due Orfei*, 13, 16, 21. Last but not least, Piccotti's date has been accepted by Donald C. Sanders, *Music at the Gonzaga Court in Mantua* (Lanham, MD: Lexington Books, 2012), 13.

3. Alessandro d'Ancona, *Origini del teatro italiano, libri tre con due appendici sulla rappresentazione drammatica del contado toscano e sul teatro mantoano nel sec. XVI*, 2nd ed., 2 vols. (Turin: Loescher, 1891), 2:365. On Gonzaga's convivial culture and its intimate relation to music and theater see Paola Besutti, "Musiche e musicisti alla tavola dei Gonzaga," in *Le tavole di corte tra Cinquecento e Settecento*, ed. Andrea Marlotti (Rome: Bulzoni, 2013), 185–216.

4. The lavish banquets of Cardinal Riario were praised by Ilarione in a *Dialogus* composed in 1473, as documented in Lucia Gualdo Rosa, Isabella Nuovo, and Domenico Defilippis, eds., *Gli umanisti e la guerra otrentina: Testi dei secoli XV e XVI* (Bari: Dedalo, 1982), 23.

5. A substantial portion of Riario's "De conviviis per dominos cardinales faciendis," is in Camillo Corvisieri, "Il trionfo romano di Eleonora d'Aragona nel giugno 1473," *Archivio della Società Romana di Storia Patria* 1 (1878): 475–91, esp. 479.

6. Giosuè Carducci, introduction to Poliziano, *"Le Stanze," "L'Orfeo," "le Rime" di Messer Angelo Ambrogini Poliziano rivedute su i codici e su le antiche stampe e illustrate con annotazioni di varii e nuove da Giosuè Carducci* (Florence: Barbèra, 1863), ix–ixi. Scholars after Carducci have also ignored the musical aspect, including most recently Paolo Orvieto, *Poliziano* (Rome: Salerno, 2009), 312–23.

7. Nino Pirrotta, "L'Orfeo degli strambotti," in *Li due Orfei*, 13–56. Pirrotta's essay builds on Romain Rolland's intuition that sacred representations with music and Politian's *Orfeo* were the forerunners of opera: Romain Rolland, "L'opéra avant l'opéra," in *Musiciens d'autrefois* (Paris: Rachette, 1908), 19–54.

8. Ireneo Affò, preface to his edition of Politian, *"L'Orfeo": Tragedia di Messer Angelo Poliziano tratta per la prima volta da due vetusti codici ed alla sua integrità e perfezione ridotta e illustrata dal Reverendo Padre Ireneo Affò di Bussetto* (Venice: Luigi Antonio di Ravenna, 1776), 7.

9. Affò's commentary in the 1776 edition of *"L'Orfeo": Tragedia di Messer Angelo Poliziano*, 79–80.

10. Data from OPAC-SBN: Catalogo del servizio bibliotecario nazionale (www.sbn.it).

11. Alfredo Casella, *La favola di Orfeo (1932) di Messer Angelo Ambrogini, detto Poliziano (1472): Musica di Alfredo Casella*, text edited by Corrado Pavolini (Milan: Carish, 1932). Casella's definition of Politian's *Orfeo* as "puro classicismo" is in *I segreti della giara* (Florence: Sansoni, 1941), 97, cited in Antonio Attisani, "Orfeo simplex e Orfeo infelix nell'opera da camera di Casella e Pavolini," *Musica e storia* 7, no. 1 (1999): 77–88.

12. Piccotti, "Sulla data *dell'Orfeo*," 330–34.

13. Berger, *Bach's Cycle*, 38.

14. Arnaldo Della Torre, *Storia dell'Accademia Platonica di Firenze* (Florence: Carnesecchi, 1902), 796–800. On Baccio's improvisatory practice and the circle of improvisers in fifteenth-century Italian humanism, see Blake Wilson, "Canterino and Improvvisatore: Oral Poetry and Performance," in *The Cambridge History of Fifteenth-Century Music*, edited by Anna Maria Busse Berger and Jesse Rodin (Cambridge: Cambridge University Press, 2015), 297–304, referring explicitly to Baccio's improvisations in Politian's *Orfeo*.

15. Pico della Mirandola, *Conclusiones* XXXI no. 2, in *Omnia quae extant opera* (Venice: Scotus, 1557), 159, cited in translation by Voss, "Marsilio Ficino, the Second Orpheus," 163. On Baccio, Pico, and Orphic singing see Voss, "Marsilio Ficino, the Second Orpheus, 169, as well as Tomlinson, *Music in Renaissance Magic*, 185.

16. The most complete account of the textual variants is the critical edition: Angelo Poliziano, *"L'Orfeo" del Poliziano con il testo critico dell'originale e delle successive forme teatrali*, ed. Antonia Tissoni Benvenuti (Padua: Antenore, 1986).

17. Poliziano, *Stanze, Orfeo, Rime*, 145–46.

18. Marsilio Ficino, letter no. 52 to Antonio Pelotti and Baccio Ugolini, dated March 4, 1474, "Poeticus furor a Deo est" ("Poetic frenzy is from God"), in *The Letters of Marsilio Ficino*, trans. from the Latin by members of the Language Department of the School of Economic Science, London, 9 vols. (London: Shepheard-Walwyn, 1975), 1:98–99.

19. *Phaedrus*, 244A–245A, 265B. Quotations from Plato's *Phaedrus* are adapted from *Plato in Twelve Volumes*, trans. Harold North Fowler, vol. 1, Loeb Classical Library (Cambridge, MA: Harvard University Press, 1982), 406–579. On the relevance of *Phaedrus* in the study of music and trance in Greek culture see Gilbert Rouget, *Music and Trance: A Theory of the Relations between Music and Possession*, ed. and trans. Brunhilde Bierbuyck and Gilbert Rouget (Chicago: University of Chicago Press, 1985), 188–201.

20. Ficino, *Commentaries on Plato*, vol. 1, *"Phaedrus" and "Ion,"* ed. and trans. Michael J. B. Allen (Cambridge, MA: Tatti Renaissance Library of Harvard University Press, 2008), 111–13.

21. Ficino, *Commentaries on Plato*, 5 (commentary on *Phaedrus* 245A).

22. Ficino, *Commentaries on Plato*, 53.

23. Normore, *Feast for the Eyes*, 33–35, on the aquamanile representing Phyllis and Aristotle (reproduced in the book), and 46 on the pedagogical function of banquets and entremets and carnival reversals.

24. Piccotti, "Sulla data *dell'Orfeo*," 335–37.

25. William F. Prizer, "Isabella d'Este and Lucrezia Borgia as Patrons of Music: The Frottola at Mantua and Ferrara," *Journal of the American Musicological Society* 38, no. 1 (1985): 1–33, esp. 13–18, documenting that Isabella in Mantua had a much higher budget to sponsor the arts than her sister-in-law Lucrezia Borgia in Ferrara. Her personal musicians

and teachers were Bartolomeo Tromboncino and the lute player Giovanni Angelo Testagrossa, while Marchetto Cara was at the service of her husband.

26. Michele Cordaro, "The Most Beautiful Room in the World," in *Mantegna's Camera degli sposi*, ed. Michele Cordaro (New York: Abbeville, 1993), 11–19.

27. Pirrotta, *Li due orfei*, 17.

28. Berger, *Bach's Cycle*, 24.

29. Calcagno, *From Madrigal to Opera*, 22–23.

30. Politian owned and annotated two incunabula of Ovid's and Virgil's works containing the myth of Orpheus. His marginal notes have been the object of thorough studies, including a chapter of the book-length introduction by Antonia Tissoni Benvenuti to her critical edition of Politian's text, *L'Orfeo*, 104–15.

31. Politian, *Orfeo*, 1–14. Here and henceforth I quote from the critical edition of *Orfeo* presented in Politian, *Stanze, Orfeo, Rime*, 147–82.

32. Politian, *Orfeo*, 20–34.

33. Politian, *Orfeo*, 54–61. Compare with Orpheus's aria "Ecco pur ch'a voi ritorno / care selve e piagge amate" at the beginning of the second act of Monteverdi's *Orfeo*.

34. On the usage of "fistula" as a sexual innuendo, even in early modern English comedy, see Will Stockton, *Playing Dirty: Sexuality and Waste in Early Modern Comedy* (Minneapolis: University of Minnesota Press, 2011), 56, 61, 65, etc. Stockton also alerts readers on the medical use of the term (note 35) explaining its usage in dirty comic jokes.

35. Politian, *Orfeo*, 149.

36. Politian, *Orfeo*, 204–25.

37. On the affinities between Botticelli, Politian, and Ficino see Arnolfo B. Ferrolo, "Botticelli's Mythologies, Ficino's *De amore*, Poliziano's *Stanze per la Giostra*: Their Circle of Love," *Art Bulletin* 37, no. 1 (1955): 17–25. More specifically on Ovid's *Fasti*, disseminated by Politian as a source of Botticelli's *Primavera*, see Lew Andrew, "Botticelli's *Primavera*, Angelo Politian, and Ovid's *Fasti*," *Artibus et Historiae* 32, no. 63 (2011): 73–84.

38. Ovid, *Fasti* 4.90. For literary quotation I adapted translations from Ovid, *Fasti*, trans. James George Frazer, rev. G. P. Goold, Loeb Classical Library (Cambridge. MA: Harvard University Press, 1989).

39. Ovid, *Fasti* 4.603–4. The reference to *Don Giovanni* is from the act 2 banquet scene of the opera: "Non si pasce di cibo mortale / Chi si pasce di cibo celeste" ("Those who feed on Heavenly food do not feed on mortal food").

40. Ovid, *Fasti* 4.606–20.

41. For more on the association of Orpheus with Christ, see Berger, *Bach's Cycle*, 41.

42. Politian, *Orfeo*, indication in italics before line 245: "*Orfeo vien cantando alcuni versi lieti e volgesi.*"

43. Politian, *Orfeo*, 245–47, translating Virgil, *Georg*. 494–95: "Quis et me—inquit—miseram et te perdidit, Orpheu, / quis tantus furor?"

44. Politian, *Orfeo*, 251–52.

45. On homoerotic and homosocial behavior in Ficino and his circle see Jill Kraye, "The Transformation of Platonic Love in the Italian Renaissance," in *Platonism and the English Imagination*, ed. A. Baldwin and S. Hutton (Cambridge: Cambridge University Press, 1994), 76–85; reprinted in *The Renaissance in Europe: A Reader*, ed. K. Whitlock

(New Haven, CT: Yale University Press, 2000), 81–87. See also Wouter J. Hanegraaff, "Under the Mantle of Love: The Mystical Eroticisms of Marsilio Ficino and Giordano Bruno," in *Hidden Intercourse: Eros and Sexuality in the History of Western Esotericism*, ed. W. Hanegraaff and J. Kripal (Leiden: Brill, 2008), 175–208. I am grateful to Ficino scholar Denis Robichaud, who has directed me to this and other relevant literature on Ficino. In his own writings, Robichaud argues that Ficilio's letters suggest his homosexuality should be read in the context of the performance of friendship and his enactment of Plato's persona: see Denis J.-J. Robichaud, *Plato's Persona: Marsilio Ficino, Renaissance Humanism, and Platonic Traditions* (Philadelphia: University of Pennsylvania Press, 2018), 147–48, but also 51–68 about his epistolary friendship with other men and his epistolary persona.

46. Tomlinson, *Music in Renaissance Magic*, 185, based on Rose Theresa, "Engendering Divine Madness," paper presented at the fifty-fifth annual meeting of the American Musicological Society, Austin, TX, October 26–29, 1989.

47. Politian, *Orfeo*, 301–8.

48. Adrian W. B. Randolph, *Engaging Symbols: Gender, Politics, and Public Art in Fifteenth-Century Florence* (New Haven, CT: Yale University Press, 2002), 243, 248, 256–58.

49. Randolph, *Engaging Symbols*, 261–65.

50. Randolph, *Engaging Symbols*, 279.

51. Randolph, *Engaging Symbols*, 266–67, commenting on an influential essay by Natalie Zemon Davis, "Women on Top," in *Society and Culture in Early Modern France: Eight Essays* (Stanford, CA: Stanford University Press, 1975), 124–51.

52. Susan McClary, *Feminine Endings* (Minneapolis: University of Minnesota Press, 1991), 48.

53. Ficino's passages from *De divino furore* are cited, translated, and discussed by Tomlinson, *Music in Renaissance Magic*, 173.

54. Politian, *L'Orfeo*, 309–42.

55. Critical apparatus by Davide Puccini to Politian, *Stanze, Orfeo, Rime*, 175–77.

56. A review of drinking songs in the fifteenth and sixteenth centuries, with special emphasis on the French repertory, is in Annie Coeurdevey, "La célébration du vin dans la chanson polyphonique à la Renaissance," in *"La musique, de tous les passetemps le plus beau": Hommage à Jean-Michel Vaccaro*, ed. François Lesure and Henry Vanhulst (Paris: Klincksieck, 1998), 66–88. This theme has inspired a recording of Renaissance drinking songs by the ensemble La Rossignol, conducted by Domenico Baronio, *In vino: Il vino in musica tra XV e XVI secolo*, CD Tactus TC 400004 (Bologna, 2005).

57. Politian, "Ben venga maggio," *Rime* 122, in Politian, *Stanze, Orfeo, Rime*, 319–22. The anonymous music is published in *Recent Researches in the Music of the Renaissance*, vol. 116, ed. Patrick Paul Macey (Middleton, WI: A-R Editions, 1999). See also Pirrotta, *Li due orfei*, 38–40. Pyle, "Politian's *Orfeo*," 59, defines the final chorus as a "canto carnascialesco."

58. Rouget, *Music and Trance*, 192–201, interpreting and translating Plato, *Phaedrus* 244d–e, identified as Dionysian madness in 265b. Tomlinson, in his account of Platonic furor in the context of Renaissance magic, criticizes Rouget for his "hegemonic

taxonomy" but does not substantially change his interpretation of Dionysian frenzy as therapeutic trance. Rather, Tomlinson enriches it by stressing the well-known connection between Dionysian frenzy and southern Italian tarantism from Apulia by pointing out that Ficino was one of the earliest interpreters of this ritual. Tomlinson, *Music in Renaissance Magic*, 148, 162–64.

59. Tomlinson, *Music in Renaissance Magic*, 164.

60. Ficino, *Commentaries on Plato*, vol. 1, *Phaedrus*, 111, on *Phaedrus* 241d; cf. 117.

61. Luigi Ricci, "Piedigrotta: Commedia in 4 atti di Marco D'Arienzo, musica di Luigi Ricci, rappresentata al Teatro Nuovo l'anno 1852," MS I-Nc 3.3.18–19, 2 vols., vol. 2 (3.3.19), 4r–20v. The indication of representing people eating and drinking during the tarantella comes from the libretto by Marco D'Ariento, *Piedrigrotta: Commedia per musica in quattro atti* (Naples, 1860), 3.1.28. The Neapolitan words of the tarantella are "Viene ccà; non fa cchiù zeza; te remolla Carmenè" ("Come here, do not be shy, give in to me, little Carmen"). The Italian translation of the Neapolitan libretto changes the name of the addressee from Carmen to Rosa to maintain the accent distribution fitting the tarantella rhythm: "Via non esser più ritrosa, / bella Rosa vieni a me": Marco D'Arienzo, *La festa di Piedigrotta: Opera buffa in tre atti*, musica del Maestro Luigi Ricci, traddotta dal dialetto napoletano dall'artista comico Giovanni Gargano (Naples: Cottrau, 1865 [first represented 1852]), 32. The libretto also prescribes tambourines and castanets (tamburelli e nacchere).

62. "Tarantella," in *Folk Music from Italy*, recorded by Walther Hennig for Folkways Records (FW04520_105, 1956), disc 1, track 5. Accessible through the website of the Smithsonian Institution: https://folkways.si.edu/folk-music-from-italy/world/album/smithsonian.

63. Ernesto De Martino, *The Land of Remorse: A Study of Southern Italian Tarantism*, trans. and annotated Dorothy Louise Zinn (London: Free Association Books, 2005), 187–94. On the cry of the *tarantate* see Diego Carpitella's ethnomusicological study, "The Choreutic-Musical Exorcism of Tarantism," published in De Martino's appendix 3, 313.

64. De Martino, *Land of Remorse*, 190–92. The myth of Io is recounted by Ovid in the first book of the *Metamorphoses*.

65. De Martino, *Land of Remorse*, 204.

66. Alexandra Amati-Camperi, "The First Operatic Women: 'Ah fato empio e crudele!,'" *Studi Musicali* 37, no. 1 (2008): 37–57, developing the argument made by McClary, *Feminine Endings*, 39–48.

67. Lorenzo Giacomini, "De La Purgatione de la tragedia: Discorso fatto da Lorenzo Giacomini Te. Malespini Nel Academia de gli Alterati nel Anno 1586," in *Orationi e discorsi di Lorenzo Giacomini Tebalducci Malespini* (Florence: Sermartelli, 1597), 49–50, discussed in chapter 1 above, 8–10.

CHAPTER FOUR

1. David Salazar, "A Comprehensive List of All Opera Companies Offering Free Streaming Services Right Now," Operawire.com (May 25, 2020).

2. Marco Beghelli, "Mangiare all'opera," in *Le arti e il cibo: Modalità ed esempi di un rapporto*, atti del convegno, Bologna, 15–16 ottobre 2012, ed. Sylvie Davidson and Fabrizio

Lollini (Bologna: Bononia University Press, 2014), 245–62, revised in "Dall''Aria del sorbetto' all''Aria della pissa,'" in *Musica di ieri, esperienza d'oggi: Ventidue studi per Paolo Fabbri*, ed. Maria Chiara Bertieri and Alessandro Roccatagliati (Lucca: LIM, 2018), 141–68. The social and economic system formed in the early seasons of Venetian commercial opera were crucial for the formation of a long-lived public opera culture, as explained most clearly by Lorenzo Bianconi, *Il Seicento* (Turin: EDT, [1981]), 163–71, translated as *Music in the Seventeenth Century* (Cambridge: Cambridge University Press, 1989); as well as by Ellen Rosand, *Opera in Seventeenth-Century Venice: The Creation of a Genre* (Berkeley: University of California Press, 1991), 66–109.

3. Roland Barthes, *Elements of Semiology*, trans. Annette Lavers and Colin Smith (New York: Hill and Wang, 1967), 28.

4. Pierre Bourdieu, *Distinction: A Social Critique of the Judgment of Taste*, trans. Richard Nice (New York: Routledge, 2000), 194. Cited from the French edition, Pierre Bourdieu, *La distinction: Critique sociale du jugement* (Paris: Éditions de Minuit, 1979), 218.

5. Colleen Reardon, *A Sociable Moment: Opera and Festive Culture in Baroque Siena* (Oxford: Oxford University Press, 2016), 126.

6. Cristoforo Ivanovich, "Le memorie teatrali di Venezia," in *Minerva al tavolino* (Venice: Niccolò Pezzana, 1686), 410. In the Venetian idiom of the time, *scagno* meant anything you can sit on (*arnese da sedere*)—a chair, a bench, or a stool—as explained in Gasparo Patriarchi, *Vocabolario veneziano e padovano con termini e modi corrispondenti toscani*, 3rd ed. (Padua: Tipografia del seminario, 1821), 172.

7. Beth L. Glixon and Jonathan E. Glixon, *Inventing the Business of Opera: The Impresario and His World in Seventeenth-Century Venice* (Oxford: Oxford University Press, 2006), 16.

8. Glixon, *Inventing the Business of Opera*, 50, 55, 314.

9. Giulio Bistort, *Il magistrato alle Pompe nella Repubblica di Venezia: Studio storico* (Venice: Deputazione veneta di storia patria, 1912; repr. Bologna: Forni, 1969), 233.

10. Giovanni Rossi, "Storia delle leggi e costumi de' veneziani," MS, cited in Nicola Mangini, *I teatri di Venezia* (Milan: Mursia, 1974), 102. Giovanni Rossi was born in 1776 in Venice, where he lived for his entire life. It is possible that he observed what he describes. On Rossi and his monumental and understudied history on Venetian laws and customs, see Claudio Schwarzenberg, "La *storia delle leggi e costume de' veneziani*: Manoscritto inedito di Giovanni Rossi," *Rivista di storia del diritto italiano* 37–38 (1965): 227–33. This testimony is the third and last about the habit of eating dinners at the theater recorded in Bistort, *Il magistrato alle pompe*, 233 (chapter 20, "Le cene nei teatri").

11. Taddeo Wiel, *I teatri musicali veneziani del Settecento: Catalogo delle opere in musica rappresentate nel secolo XVIII a Venezia (1701–1800) con prefazione dell'autore* (Venice: Visentini, 1897), lxix–lxxvi.

12. Wiel, *Teatri musicali veneziani*, xiii–xiv.

13. Wiel, *Teatri musicali veneziani*, xxxiii.

14. Wiel, *Teatri musicali veneziani*, lxviii.

15. Martha Feldman, *Opera and Sovereignty: Transforming Myths in Eighteenth-Century Italy* (Chicago: University of Chicago Press, 2007), 11, 22. For a similar account of the

social rituals of opera, see Daniel Snowman, *The Gilded Stage: A Social History of Opera* (London: Atlantic Books, 2009), in particular chap. 2, "The Opera Business, Italian Style," 29–48; on eating and drinking at the opera, see also 72, 159–60.

16. Margaret Murata, "The Church and the Stage in Seventeenth-Century Rome," in *Sleuthing the Muse: Essays in Honor of William F. Prizer*, ed. Kristine K. Forney and Jeremy L. Smith (Hillsdale, NY: Pendragon Press, 2012), 193. For similar evidence see also Reardon, *Sociable Moment*, 81.

17. Rudolf Wittkower, *Art and Architecture in Italy, 1600–1750*, 3 vols., rev. Joseph Connors and Jennifer Montagu (New Haven, CT: Yale University Press, 1999), 2:71. On the double function of the piazza (or piazzetta) scenes in Torelli's operatic sets and the social functions and theatricality of the piazza in seventeenth-century Venice, see Eugene J. Johnson, "Jacopo Sansovino, Giacomo Torelli, and the Theatricality of the Piazzetta in Venice," *Journal of the Society of Architectural Historians* 59, no. 4 (2000): 436–53. Johnson also stresses that the piazzetta was the locus of frenetic and often theatrical carnival celebrations.

18. Eugene J. Johnson, *Inventing the Opera House: Theater Architecture in Renaissance and Baroque Italy* (Cambridge: Cambridge University Press, 2018), 47–59.

19. Francesco Milizia, *Del teatro* (Venice: Pasquali, 1773), 84–85.

20. Milizia, *Del teatro*, 96–97, and following floor plans.

21. Mladen Dolar, "The Logic of Mercy," in Slavoj Žižek and Mladen Dolar, *Opera's Second Death* (New York: Routledge, 2002), 20. Dolar's observations are indebted to Ivan Nagel, *Autonomy and Mercy: Reflections on Mozart's Operas*, trans. Marion Faber and Ivan Nagel (Cambridge, MA: Harvard University Press, 1991). Daniel Heartz uses the word "clemency" instead of "mercy" but also recognizes it as a pivotal moment in the drama, describing it as a "virtue ardently espoused by the Enlightenment" and maintaining that "clemency" in Mozart's *Idomeneo*, *Die Zauberflöte*, and *La clemenza di Tito* has to be understood as a reference to Masonic enlightened values: Heartz, "La Clemenza di Sarastro: Masonic Benefice in the Last Operas," in *Mozart's Operas* (Berkeley: University of California Press, 1990), 272–75.

22. For a comparison of eighteenth-century opera to the production modes of the movie and television industry, see Reinhard Strohm, *Die italienische Oper im 18. Jahrhundert* (Wilhelmshaven: Heinrichshofen, 1979), 22–23.

23. Margaret R. Butler, "Time Management at Turin's Teatro Regio: Galuppi's *La clemenza di Tito* and Its Alterations, 1759," *Early Music* 11, no. 2 (2012): 285; see also her *Operatic Reform at Turin's Teatro Regio: Aspects of Production and Stylistic Change in the 1760s* (Lucca: LIM, 2001), 9. In "Olivero's Painting of Turin's Teatro Regio: Toward a Reevaluation of an Operatic Emblem," *Music in Art* 14, no. 1–2 (2009): 137–51, Butler offers an impressive list of recent music books that include this image as a representation of a typical eighteenth-century opera night. I am grateful to her for discussing issues related to this image with me and sharing her knowledge on the subject.

24. Milizia, *Del Teatro*, 77.

25. As observed also by Butler, "Olivero's Painting," 139. Butler does not make an explicit claim that the opera theater was analogous to or a mirror of the piazza, but I

believe this is an implicit corollary to her essay. In addition to the painting in figure 4.1, see *Estrazione della lotteria a Piazza delle erbe a Torino*, *mercato in Piazza San Carlo a Torino*, *Piazza di Torino*, and *Piazza del mercato di Porta Palazzo a Torino*.

26. Butler, "Olivero's Painting," 141.

27. Bakhtin, *Rabelais and His World*. The following paragraph is based on chapter 2, "The Language of the Marketplace in Rabelais," 145–95 (quotations are from 153–54).

28. Bakhtin, *Rabelais and His World*, 188.

29. Pierpaolo Polzonetti, "Opera as Process," in *The Cambridge Companion to Eighteenth-Century Opera*, ed. Anthony R. DelDonna and Pierpaolo Polzonetti (Cambridge: Cambridge University Press, 2009), 3–4.

30. Martina Grempler, *Das Teatro Valle in Rom, 1727–1850: Opera buffa in Kontext der Theaterkultur ihrer Zeit* (Kassel: Bärenreiter, 2012), 104–5, cited in Beghelli, "Mangiare all'opera," 255.

31. Cited in Beghelli, "Mangiare all'opera," 250. The habit of spitting from the boxes into the pit is also confirmed by Giuseppe Baretti, *An Account of the Manners and Customs of Italy, with Observations on the Mistakes of Some Travellers with Regard to That Country*, 2 vols. (London: Davis, 1768), 1:58–59.

32. Francesco Cotticelli and Paologiovanni Maione, *Onesto divertimento, ed allegria de' popoli: Materiali per una storia dello spettacolo a Napoli nel primo Settecento* (Milan: Ricordi, 1996), 116. Beghelli, "Mangiare all'opera," 254–55, also discusses archival documents proving how lucrative the *sorbetti* concessions in Roman theaters were.

33. Melissa Calaresu, "Making and Eating Ice Cream in Naples: Rethinking Consumption and Sociability in the Eighteenth Century," *Past and Present* 220 (August 2013): 35, 66–72. See also her essay, "Food Selling and Urban Space in Eighteenth-Century Naples," in *Food Hawkers: Selling on the Streets from Antiquity to the Present*, ed. Melissa Calaresu and Danielle van den Hauvel (Burlington, VT: Ashgate, 2016).

34. Calaresu, "Making and Eating Ice Cream in Naples," 70.

35. [Joseph Addison], *Remarks on Several Parts of Italy, &c., in the Years 1701, 1702, 1703* (London, 1705), 242; Henry Swinburne, *Travels in the Two Sicilies . . . in the Years 1777, 1778, 1779, and 1780* (London 1783), 1:66, both cited in Calaresu, "Making and Eating Ice Cream in Naples," 50–51.

36. Baretti, *Account of the Manners and Customs of Italy*, 2:203–4.

37. John Moore, *A View of Society and Manners in Italy with Anecdotes relating to Some Eminent Characters, written by John Moore M.D. during His Travels through Those Countries in the Years 1777 and 1778*, 2 vols. (London: Bell, 1783), 2: 129.

38. Calaresu, "Making and Eating Ice Cream in Naples," 74.

39. *Brieve e nuovo metodo da farsi ogni sorte di sorbetto con facilità* ([Naples]: Si vendono nella Stamperia del Monaco di rimpetto la Chiesa di S. Liguoro alla strada delli Librari [1690c]). Calaresu, "Making and Eating Ice Cream in Naples," 47, assumes that these recipes were used in aristocratic households. However, the booklet and its contents were in Giambattista Basile, *Archivio di letteratura popolare* 4, no. 8 (August 15, 1886): 63, collecting material from oral tradition and publications, mostly anonymous, for the documentation of lower-class culture.

40. Filippo Badini, *De' sorbetti: Saggio medico fisico* (Naples, 1775), cited in Calaresu,

"Making and Eating Ice Cream in Naples," 61–62, also mentions other contemporary popular cookbooks used for sorbet recipes.

41. Beghelli, "Mangiare all'opera," 251–54; Peter von Lichtensthal, *Dizionario e bibliografia della musica*, 4 vols. (Milan: Fontana, 1826), 3:52; emphasis added.

42. Beghelli, "Dall''Aria del sorbetto' all''Aria della pissa,'" 141–68.

43. The traditional idea that number opera alternates action in recitatives with a sort of "frozen time" for the expression of emotional reactions in lyrical moments (duets, arias, etc.) has been challenged in musicological literature by Luca Zoppelli, *L'opera come racconto: Modi narrativi nel teatro musicale dell'Ottocento* (Venice: Marsilio, 1994), 194, and, more forcefully, by Andrea Chegai, "Muovere l'aria: Jommelli und die innere Handlung (*Il Vologeso*, Ludwigsburg 1766)," in *Musik in Baden-Württemberg*, ed. Ann-Katrin Zimmermann, *Auftrag der Gesellshaft für Musikgeschichte in Baden-Wüttemberg*, Jahrbuch 2014, vol. 21 (Munich: Strube, 2014), 61–110; published in Italian as "Muovere l'aria: Jommelli e l'azione interiore (*Il Vologeso*, Ludwigsburg 1766)," in *Niccolò Jommelli: L'esperienza europea di un musicista 'filosofo,'* atti del convegno internazionale di Studi (Reggio Calabria, 7–8 ottobre 2011), ed. Gaetano Pitarresi (Reggio Calabria: Edizioni del Conservatorio di Musica "F. Cilea," 2014), 298–99.

44. Among the many accounts of this system, readers may want to consult James Webster, "Aria as Drama," in *The Cambridge Companion to Eighteenth-Century Opera*, ed. Anthony R. DelDonna and Pierpaolo Polzonetti, 3–23 (Cambridge: Cambridge University Press, 2009). In the same volume, Gianni Cicali's "Roles and Acting," 66–84, offers a nuanced account of the system of roles in comic opera.

45. Charles de Brosses, *Lettres d'Italie du President de Brosses*, ed. Frédéric d'Agay, vol. 2 (Paris: Mercure de France, 1986), 289–316, excerpts included in translation in Piero Weiss, ed., *Opera: A History in Documents* (Oxford: Oxford University Press, 2002), 83.

46. Giuseppe Tartini, *Trattato di musica secondo la vera scienza dell'armonia* (Padua: Stamperia del Seminario, 1754), 134–35, recounting an episode that occurred in Ancona in 1713 when Tartini was playing violin for the opera theater in this city; cited and discussed in Pierpaolo Polzonetti, "Tartini and the Tongue of Saint Anthony," *Journal of the American Musicological Society* 67, no. 2 (2014): 440. Here I propose Francesco Gasparini's *La fede tradita e vendicata* as the opera with the powerful recitative. However, more convincingly, Sergio Durante proposes Apostolo Zeno's *Ferramondo*, act 1, scene 2, set by Gasparini: Sergio Durante, *Tartini, Padova, e l'Europa* (Livorno: Sillabe, 2017), 20–22.

47. Stefano Castelvecchi, *Sentimental Opera: Questions of Genre in the Age of Bourgeois Drama* (Cambridge: Cambridge University Press, 2013), 201–9. On the eroticism of Barbarina's aria see Christopher Heppner, "'L'ho perduta': Barbarina, Cherubino, and the Economics of Love in *Le nozze di Figaro*," *Opera Quarterly* 15, no. 4 (1999): 644, 647–55.

48. Ursula Mauthe, *Mozarts "Pamina": Anna Gottlieb* (Augsburg: Deutsche Mozart-Gesellschaft, 1986), 9.

49. Dexter Edge, "Mozart's Reception in Vienna, 1787–1791," in *Wolfgang Amadè Mozart: Essays on His Life and His Music*, ed. Stanley Sadie (Oxford: Clarendon Press, 1996), 84; Otto Erich Deutsch, "Mozart in Zinzendorfs Tagebüchern," *Schweizerische Musikzeitung* 102 (1962): 211–18. The Zinzendorf diary entries can be consulted in English

translation in Dorothea Link, *The National Court Theatre in Mozart's Vienna: Sources and Documents, 1783–1792* (New York: Oxford University Press, 1998).

50. Waltraud Heindl, "People, Class Structure, and Society," in *Schubert's Vienna*, ed. Raymond Erickson (New Haven, CT: Yale University Press, 1997), 46–54.

51. Rosand, *Opera in Seventeenth-Century Venice*, 1.

52. Bakhtin, *Rabelais and His World*, 5, 90–92. Bakhtin (5, 74) uses "carnivals" to refer to all feasts that function as a suspension of normal time, such as the "feast of the fools," the "feast of the ass," the "Easter laughter," the feast of St. Stephen, New Year's Day, the feast of the Holy Innocents, the Epiphany, etc.

53. Bakhtin, *Rabelais and His World*, 19.

54. John Evelyn, *The Diary of John Evelyn*, ed. William Bray, 2 vols. (New York: Dunne, 1901), 1:151.

55. Evelyn, *Diary*, 1:213.

56. Benedetto Marcello, *Il teatro alla moda, 1720*, ed. Carmelo Di Gennaro (Milan: Polifilo, 2006), 31, 67.

57. Jean-Jacques Rousseau, *The "Confessions" of Jean-Jacques Rousseau Now First Completely Translated into English* (London: Aldus Society, 1903), book 7, accessed through the Project Gutenberg EBook #3913.

58. Charles Burney, *The Present State of Music in France and Italy, or The Journal of a Tour through Those Countries, Undertaken to Collect Materials for a General History of Music*, 2nd ed. (London: Becket, 1773), 79; emphasis added. On Piccinni's *Il regno della luna* as a revolutionary opera see Pierpaolo Polzonetti, *Italian Opera in the Age of the American Revolution* (Cambridge: Cambridge University Press, 2011), 96–100.

59. Burney, *Present State*, 81–82. For a similar description of an opera seria in a magnificent theater, the San Carlo in Naples, with the royal family present and still a lot of background noise, see Burney, 339.

60. Curtis Price, Judith Milhous, and Robert D. Hume, *Italian Opera in Late Eighteenth Century London*, vol. 1, *The King's Theater, Haymarket, 1778–1791* (Oxford: Clarendon Press, 1995), 9.

61. Cited in Price, *Italian Opera in Late Eighteenth Century London*, 13.

62. Theodore Fenner, *Opera in London: Views of the Press, 1785–1830* (Carbondale: Southern Illinois University Press, 1994), 70.

63. *The Universal Register* (which became the *Times* in 1788), March 15, 1786; both passages reproduced in Fenner, *Opera in London*, 85–87.

64. *Times*, December 29, 1791, in Fenner, *Opera in London*, 365.

65. Judith Milhous, Gabriella Dideriksen, and Robert D. Hume, *Italian Opera in Late Eighteenth-Century London*, vol. 2, *The Pantheon Opera and Its Aftermath, 1789–1795* (Oxford: Clarendon Press, 2001), 285, 288 (on architectural improvement of the coffee room at the end of 1791).

66. Milhous, Dideriksen, and Hume, *Pantheon Opera and Its Aftermath*, 325–29.

67. Burney, *Present State*, 315.

68. Burney, *Present State*, 320.

69. Carlo Goldoni, *Le donne vendicate: Dramma giocoso per musica di Polisseno Fegeio,*

pastor arcade, da rappresentarsi nel teatro Tron di San Cassiano il carnevale dell'anno 1751 (Venice: Fenzo, 1751), 1:1.

70. Burney, *Present State*, 244.

71. Burney, *Present State*, 345.

72. Burney, *Present State*, 347–48.

73. I am grateful to János Malina for this information and for letting me read his essay before its publication: "The Eszterháza Libretti: An Overall Survey," *Haydn-Studien* 11, no. 2 (2017): 223–65. He and his colleagues recently explored new archival sources on the Esterházy theater, including the Esterházy Archives at Forchtenstein (Eszterháza Privatstiftung Archiv, Burg Forchtenstein, EPA, Austria); the National Széchényi Library (H-Bn); the Hungarian National Archives (Magyar Nemzeti Levéltár, MNL) in Budapest; and the library of the Gesellschaft der Musikfreunde (A-gm), Vienna. A published study based on this ongoing research is Ferenc Dávid, Carsten Jung, János Malina, and Edward McCue, "Haydn's Opera House at Eszterháza: New Archival Sources," *Early Music* 43, no. 1 (2015): 111–27.

74. Ulrich Tank, "Die Dokumente der Esterhazy-Archive zur Fürstlichen Hofkapelle, 1761–1770," *Haydn-Studien* 4, nos. 3–4 (1980): 205.

75. Snowman, *Gilded Stage*, 85–86.

76. I am grateful to Dorothea Link for exchanging notes on this matter. See Link, *National Court Theatre in Mozart's Vienna*.

77. Daniel Heartz, "Nicolas Jadot and the Building of the Burgtheater," *Musical Quarterly* 68, no. 1 (1982): 1–31.

78. Dorothea Link generously shared with me her transcription of the account books of the National Court Theater in Vienna, Haus-, Hof- und Staatsarchiv, Generalintendanz der Hoftheater, hereafter cited as HHStA, Hoftheater, SR.

79. HHStA, Hoftheater, SR 11, 6 Apr. 1776–28 Mar. 1777, 16. Similar entries in SR 12, 29 Mar.–26 Sept. 1777, 11; SR 13, 27 Sept. 1777–17 Apr. 1778, 12; SR 15, 2 Oct. 1779–24 Mar. 1780, 11; SR 16, 25 Mar.–29 Sept. 1780, 10; SR 16, 25 Mar.–29 Sept. 1780, 10; SR 17, 30 Sept. 1780–13 Apr. 1781, 10; SR 18, 14 Apr. 1781–29 Mar. 1782, 16; SR 19, 30 Mar. 1882– 18 Apr. 1883, n.p.; SR 20, 1783–84, n.p.; SR 21, 1784–85, n.p.; Link supposes that from here on the account books omit the page devoted to the "Zuckerbackerbestand" because, for accounting purposes, the income was always nil.

80. HHStA, Hoftheater, SR 14, 18 Apr.–2 Oct. 1778, 9.

81. [Louis] de Jaucourt, "Cuisine," in *Encyclopédie ou Dictionnaire raisonné des sciences, des arts et des métiers*, ed. Denis Diderot and Jean Le Rond d'Alembert, vol. 4, *Conjonctif-Discussion* (Paris: Briasson, David, Le Breton, Faulche, 1754), 538. The accuracy of this account is contested by Barbara Ketcham Wheaton, *Savoring the Past: The French Kitchen and Table from 1300 to 1789* (New York: Touchstone, 1983), 43–51.

82. Roy Strong, *Splendor at Court: Renaissance Spectacle and the Theater of Power* (Boston: Houghton Mifflin, 1973), 121–66.

83. John S. Powell, *Music and Theatre in France, 1600–1680* (Oxford: Oxford University Press, 2000), 40, translating a nineteenth-century history of diplomatic exchange between Russia and France.

84. David Charlton, *Opera in the Age of Rousseau: Music, Confrontation, Realism* (Cambridge: Cambridge University Press, 2013), 3–5.

85. Neal Zaslaw, "Observations at the Paris Opéra in 1747," *Early Music* 11, no. 4 (1983): 514–16, reproducing the drawing by Gabriel-Jacques Saint-Aubin, from the Museum of Fine Arts in Boston.

86. In Paris, the standing parterre was often denounced as "barbaric" and "feudal": see Jeffrey S. Ravel, "Seating the Public: Spheres and Loathing in the Paris Theaters, 1777–1788," *French Historical Studies* 18, no. 1 (1993): 173–74.

87. James H. Johnson, *Listening in Paris: A Cultural History* (Berkeley: University of California Press, 1995), 9.

88. Gustave Flaubert, *Madame Bovary*, trans. Mildred Marmur (New York: Penguin, 1964), chap. 15, 210–11.

89. Sally McKee, *The Exile's Song: Edmond Dédé and the Unfinished Revolutions of the Atlantic World* (New Haven, CT: Yale University Press, 2017), 114–27. I am grateful to Sally McKee for exchanging information and ideas on this topic. The image of the Alcazar Theater is also reproduced in her book, page 122.

90. Alexandre Dumas fils, *La dame aux camélias*, trans. David Coward (Oxford: Oxford University Press, 1986), chapter 8, 52.

91. Christopher Small, *Musicking: The Meanings of Performing and Listening* (Hanover, NH: University Press of New England, 1998).

92. Anselm Gerhard, *The Urbanization of Opera: Music Theater in Paris in the Nineteenth Century* (Chicago: University of Chicago Press, 1998), 22; see also Johnson, *Listening in Paris*, 228–36.

93. Snowman, *Gilded Stage*, 159–60.

94. Théo Fleischman, *Napoléon et la musique* (Brussels: Brepols, 1965), 247.

95. Cited in Beghelli, "Mangiare all'opera," 248.

96. Mark Everist, *Music Drama at the Paris Odéon, 1824–1828* (Berkeley: University of California Press, 2002), 22.

97. Honoré de Balzac, "Traité des excitants modernes" [1838], in *Oeuvres complètes de H. de Balzac*, vol. 2, *Oeuvres diverses* (Paris: Société d'éditions littéraires et artistiques, (1908), 73–74.

98. Patrick Barbier, *Opera in Paris, 1800–1850: A Lively History*, trans. Robert Louma (Portland, OR: Amadeus Press, 1987), 33, 167–69; Guy de Maupassant, *Bel-Ami*, ed. Gilbert Sigaux (Quebec: La bibliothèque électronique du Québec, Collection à tous les vents), 510:145–57.

99. My reflections on the similarities between restaurants and concert-hall culture are based on my online publication "Is It Proper to Eat or Drink While Listening to Classical Music?," *Naxos Musicology International* (February 11, 2020). I am grateful to Davinia Caddy, editor of this online platform for music scholarship, for her suggestions and editorial advice.

100. France Rebecca L. Spang, *The Invention of the Restaurant: Paris and Modern Gastronomic Culture* (Cambridge, MA: Harvard University Press, 2000), 180–92 (menu and menu literacy); 152, 236–37 (eating as performance); 152–63 (gastronomic guides and

criticism); and 163 (hiding the kitchen). For a global perspective on the spread of high-class restaurants in the nineteenth century, see Katie Rawson and Elliott Shore, *Eating Out: A Global History of Restaurants* (London: Reaktion, 2019), 51–86. On French *cabarets* and hotel eateries as proto-restaurants in the seventeenth century, see Wheaton, *Savoring the Past*, 73–77.

101. Richard D. Leppert, "The Social Discipline of Listening," in *Le concert et son public: Mutations de la vie musicale en Europe de 1780 à 1914 (France, Allemagne, Angleterre)*, ed. Hans Erich Bödeker, Michael Werner, and Patrice Veit (Paris: Éditions de la Maison des sciences de l'homme, 2002), 459–85.

102. Cormac Newark, "Not Listening in Paris: Critical and Fictional Lapses of Attention at the Opera," in *Words and Notes in the Long Nineteenth Century*, ed. Phyllis Weliver and Katharine Ellis (Woodbridge, UK: Boydell and Brewer, 2013), 35–54. This is also discussed, in the large contest of the cinematic representation and performance of listening, by Giorgio Biancorosso, *Situated Listening: The Sound of Absorbtion in Classical Cinema* (Oxford: Oxford University Press, 2016), 3–4.

103. David J. Levin, "A Picture-Perfect Man? Senta, Absorption and Wagnerian Theatricality," *Opera Quarterly* 21, no. 3 (2006): 491–92.

104. Richard Wagner, "The Art-Work of the Future," in *"The Art-Work of the Future" and Other Works*, trans. W. Ashton Ellis (Lincoln: University of Nebraska Press, 1993), 160.

105. Richard Wagner, "Autobiographic Sketch," in *"The Art-Work of the Future" and Other Works*, trans. W. Ashton Ellis (Lincoln: University of Nebraska Press, 1993), 4.

106. Carl Friedrich Glasenapp, *Das Leben Richard Wagners*, 3 vols. (Leipzig: Breitkopf und Härtel, 1923), 1:288–89, cited and translated by Evan Barker, "Wagner and the Ideal Theatrical Space," in *Opera in Context: Essays on Historical Staging from the Late Renaissance to the Time of Puccini*, ed. Mark A. Radice (Portland, OR: Amadeus Press, 1998), 242–43.

107. Barker, "Wagner and the Ideal Theatrical Space," 263.

108. Wagner, "Art and Revolution," in *"The Art-Work of the Future" and Other Works*, 47.

109. The last performance of the Haymarket Opera Company that I attended was Joseph Haydn's *L'isola disabitata*, which took place in a "regular" theater, the Atheneum Theater in Chicago (September 17 and 18, 2016), where drinks and snacks were not served during the show.

110. David Mayernik, *The Challenge of Emulation in Art and Architecture between Imitation and Invention* (Burlington, VT: Ashgate, 2013).

111. Ethnomusicology never entered in any substantial way the debate on authenticity in music and opera, which focused on the text and its performance. Peter Kivy, who has been at the center of debates on authenticity in opera, does not take into consideration the audience experience in the ritual context of opera culture at different times of history and in different places: see his *Sounding Off: Eleven Essays in the Philosophy of Music* (Oxford: Oxford University Press, 2012), especially chapter 2 on "Authenticities" in music and opera, 33–112, summarizing and expanding his previous contributions on this topic.

112. John Blacking, *How Musical Is Man?* (Seattle: University of Washington Press, 1973), 5.

113. Blacking, *How Musical Is Man?*, 3. See also 25, 31.

114. Mantle Hood, "The Untalkables of Music," *EM: Annuario degli archivi di etnomusicologia dell'Accademia Nazionale di Santa Cecilia* 1 (1993): 142.

115. Robert W. Sneider, *The Voice of the City: Vaudeville and Popular Culture in New York* (New York: Oxford University Press, 1989), 3–25. See also Charles W. Stein, "Introduction," in *American Vaudeville as Seen by Its Contemporaries*, ed. Charles W. Stein (New York: Da Capo, 1984), 3, who draws a neater line between variety and vaudeville based on the presence or absence of alcoholic beverages.

116. Paul F. Berliner, *Thinking in Jazz: The Infinite Art of Improvisation* (Chicago: University of Chicago Press, 1994), 459.

117. Berliner, *Thinking in Jazz*, 452.

118. Scott DeVeaux, *The Birth of Bebop: A Social History* (Berkeley: University of California Press, 1997), 140.

119. Berliner, *Thinking in Jazz*, 467. There is an amateur video recording on YouTube of Ira Sullivan performing at Heidi's Jazz Club of Cocoa Beach (Florida) in 2013 while people eat at the table but also pay attention to the music (https://www.youtube.com/watch?v=1Kz_PhCaWyw, accessed January 10, 2021). The restaurant offers not only snacks but also "serious" meat plates like "Filet Steak Madagascar," "Hausmacher Wurstplatte," "Roasted Duckling," "Dover Sole," Russian "Beef Stroganoff," Wiener Schnitzel, Hungarian Gulyash, and for the unfortunate vegetarians a single item on the menu: "vegetable plate."

120. David Ake, *Jazz Matters: Sound, Place, and Time since Bebop* (Berkeley: University of California Press, 2010), 45.

121. On the norm of playing for eating listeners during the jazz era, even during Prohibition, see William Howland Kenney, "Historical Context and the Definition of Jazz: Putting More of the History in 'Jazz History,'" in *Jazz among the Discourses*, ed. Gabbard Krin (Durham, NC: Duke University Press, 1995), 106.

122. Baldassare Castiglione, *The Book of the Courtier* [1528], trans. Daniel Javitch (New York: Norton, 2002).

CHAPTER FIVE

1. Erich Segal, *The Death of Comedy* (Cambridge, MA: Harvard University Press, 2001), 1–4. For a discussion of the etymology of comedy based on Segal's text I am indebted to Elisabeth Le Guin, *The Tonadilla in Performance: Lyric Comedy in Enlightenment Spain* (Berkeley: University of California Press, 2014), 13.

2. Segal, *Death of Comedy*, 112, commenting on Aristotle, *Poetics* 1449a32.

3. David Kimbell, *Italian Opera* (Cambridge: Cambridge University Press, 1991), 182.

4. Reinhard Strohm, *Dramma per Musica: Italian Opera Seria of the Eighteenth Century* (New Haven, CT: Yale University Press, 1997), 2.

5. Stefano Arteaga, *Le rivoluzioni del teatro musicale italiano dalla sua origine fino al presente*, 2nd ed., 3 vols. (Venice: Carlo Palese, 1785), 2:68.

6. I searched Metastasio's librettos using the website progettometastasio.it, built by the University of Padua. I also consulted and quote librettos from the critical edition Pietro Metastasio, *Drammi per musica*, 3 vols., ed. Anna Laura Bellina (Venice: Marsilio, 2003).

7. Carlo Goldoni, *Drammi comici per musica*, 3 vols., ed. Silvia Urbani (Venice: Marsilio, 2007–16). The University of Padua also maintains an excellent website with most of the Goldoni librettos and many variants (www.carlogoldoni.it), reflecting the printed edition. I resort in a few cases to an earlier edition of Goldoni's complete works: Carlo Goldoni, *Tutte le opere*, 4th ed., 14 vols., ed. Giuseppe Ortolani (Milan: Mondadori, 1935–56), but unless otherwise indicated all the quotations of Goldoni's librettos are from the University of Padua Goldoni website.

8. For a general introduction on Metastasio see Francesco Cotticelli and Paologiovanni Maione, "Metastasio: The Dramaturgy of Eighteenth-Century Heroic Opera," in *The Cambridge Companion to Eighteenth-Century Opera*, ed. Anthony R. Deldonna and Pierpaolo Polzonetti (Cambridge: Cambridge University Press, 2009), 66–84.

9. Letter by Metastasio, in *Tutte le opere*, ed. Bruno Brunelli, 5 vols. (Milan: Mondadori, 1943–54), 4:431–32, cited in Bellina's introduction to the *Drammi per musica*, 1:9.

10. [Ippolito Bentivoglio], *L'Achille in Sciro, favola drammatica da rappresentarsi in musica nel Teatro a S. Stefano in Ferrara* (Venice, 1663), 6. On this see Rosand, *Opera in Seventeenth-Century Venice*, 58. Metastasio's remarks are taken from *Drammi per musica*, vol. 2.

11. Metastasio, *Semiramide*, in *Drammi per musica*, vol. 1, 2, 1.

12. Nicola Porpora, "Semiramide riconosciuta," Dresden, Sächsische Landesbibliothek, MS Mus. 2417-F-2, 3 vols., 2:5–6. This score reflects a production of the opera at the San Carlo Theater in Naples (1739), which was a revamping of a Venetian production of 1729.

13. Gastone Boccherini, *La secchia rapita: Dramma eroicomico* (Vienna: Kurtzboeck, 1772), 2, 12. I am grateful to John Rice for directing my attention to this example. Even though the libretto denotes the genre as "eroicomico," John A. Rice, in *Antonio Salieri and Viennese Opera* (Chicago: University of Chicago Press, 1998), 152, argues that it is a "full-length, three-act comedy, thoroughly Goldonian in form." The minuet appears identical in the manuscript score: Antonio Salieri, "La secchia rapita: Dramma eroicomico," Naples, Biblioteca del Conservatorio di Musica S. Pietro a Majella, MS 30-2-14 (Rari 7.219.202656), 90v–91r.

14. Sam Abel, *Opera in the Flesh: Sexuality in Operatic Performance* (Boulder, CO: Westview Press, 1996), 3–5.

15. Vittorio Montemaggi, *Reading Dante's "Commedia" as Theology: Divinity Realized in Human Encounter* (Oxford: Oxford University Press, 2016), 7–8.

16. Calcagno, *From Madrigal to Opera*, 4, 41–43.

17. I am greatly indebted to Ellen Rosand for exchanging ideas with me on this opera and to her inspiring contribution, *Monteverdi's Last Operas: A Venetian Trilogy* (Berkeley: University of California Press, 2007). On the context of the first performance of *Il ritorno di Ulisse* and its success, see Rosand, *Monteverdi's Last Operas*, 3–8, 52–58. A handy edition of the libretto, with English translation by Derek Yeld and a good piano reduction of the score based on the urtext edition is Monteverdi, *Il ritorno di Ulisse in patria: Tragedia*

di lieto fine in un prologo e tre atti, piano reduction ed. Rinaldo Alessandrini (Kassel: Bärenreiter, 2007). I refer to this edition for both text and music unless otherwise indicated.

18. A reading of political and cultural significance of representations of food in Homer is John Rundin, "A Politics of Eating: Feasting in Early Greek Society," *American Journal of Philology* 117, no. 2 (1996): 181–205. The meanings of food, wine, and the rituals of their consumption follow a complex set of cultural codes in place in ancient Greece. See Paolo Sarpi, *Il senso del cibo* (Palermo: Sellerio, 2005), chaps. 1–3.

19. Also observed by Mitchell Cohen, *The Politics of Opera: A History from Monteverdi to Mozart* (Princeton, NJ: Princeton University Press, 2017), 109.

20. By the time of *Il ritorno di Ulisse*, Lorenzo de' Medici's 1490 poem "Trionfo di Bacco" was already a classic, reprinted in several anthologies and set to music.

21. Homer, *"L'Odissea" d'Omero trasportata dalla greca nella toscana favela*, trans. Federico Malipiero (Venice: Corradicci, 1643), 18.19. Malipiero was a member of the Incogniti academy, like the librettist of Monteverdi's opera: see Rosand, *Monteverdi's Last Operas*, 140.

22. Rosand, *Monteverdi's Last Operas*, 363, 374. For a similar reading see also Cohen, *Politics of Opera*, 112.

23. I agree with Rosand's analysis in *Monteverdi's Last Operas*, 366–69, showing how "Iro's humor derives from his physical being, his speech defect, and his monstrous size and appetites."

24. Rosand, *Opera in Seventeenth-Century Venice*, 250.

25. Iro's lament is not in the *Odyssey*, but the wordplay between *proci* and *porci* appears in Malipiero's translation of the *Odyssey* when Eumaeus, who attends the "Porci d'Ulisse," tells his master in disguise how the pigs are destined for the feasts of the suitors ("per li conviti delli Proci"): Homer, *"L'Odissea" d'Omero*, trans. Malipiero, 14.183.

26. I borrow the terms "sonification" and "rendering," used in film sound studies, from Carolyn Abbate, "Sound Object Lessons," *Journal of the American Musicological Society* 69, no. 3 (2016): 821.

27. The only surviving manuscript score of Claudio Monteverdi, *Il ritorno di Ulisse in patria*, Vienna, Österreichische Nationalbibliothek, Mus. MS 18763, facsimile (Florence: Spes, 2006), does not detail the instruments of the orchestra when presenting obbligato instrumental lines (besides the bass). In this case (page 208 of the facsimile), it presents only the bass and vocal line notated in the tenor clef, which nonetheless does not exclude the possibility of adding instrumental parts, as was customary. The solution of flutes playing in this passage is adopted in the recording of the opera: Monteverdi, *Il ritorno di Ulisse in patria*, Concerto Vocale, conducted by René Jacobs, with Guy de Mey as Iro, Harmonia Mundi France HML 5901427.29, 1992, 2010, three compact discs, CD 3, track 6.

28. Rosand, *Monteverdi's Last Operas*, 373; Rosand, *Opera in Seventeenth-Century Venice*, 37–38. See also Cohen, *Politics of Opera*, 104.

29. Paul Oskar Kristeller, "The Myth of Renaissance Atheism and the French Tradition of Free Thought," *Journal of the History of Philosophy* 6 (1968): 233–43. Kristeller identifies the "fountainhead" of the myth in Ernest Renan's book *Averroès et l'Averroïsme: Essai historique* (Paris: Durand, 1852). Elena Bergonzi presented new evidence supporting

Cremonini's Catholic orthodoxy in her article, "Cremonini scrittore: Gli anni padovani e le opere della maturità," *Aevum* 68, no. 3 (1994): 607–33.

30. Aristotle, "On the Soul," in *The Basic Works of Aristotle*, ed. Richard McKeon (New York: Modern Library, 2001), 535–603.

31. Karol Berger, *Bach's Cycle, Mozart's Arrow: An Essay on the Origins of Musical Modernity* (Berkeley: University of California Press, 2007), 19–20.

32. Malipiero, *"L'Odissea" d'Omero*, book 18, 95; emphasis added.

33. Bakhtin, *Rabelais and His World*. In this book "embodiment" is a pervasive but elusive concept, as Bakhtin does not use this specific term. Gary Saul Morson and Caryl Emerson, *Mikhail Bakhtin: Creation of a Prosaics* (Stanford, CA: Stanford University Press, 1990), 435–36, use "embodiment," explaining that "embodiment as a value is expressed by 'folkloric culture,' in which a hero equals his physicality." Its opposite concept, "potential," produces "symbols of non-coincidence."

34. Bakhtin, *Rabelais and His World*, 19.

35. Bakhtin, *Rabelais and His World*, 22.

36. Bakhtin, *Rabelais and His World*, 23.

37. Bakhtin, *Rabelais and His World*, 407; on this important issue see also 197, 321–22.

38. Bakhtin, *Rabelais and His World*, 370.

39. Bakhtin, *Rabelais and His World*, 435.

40. The "trillo" is a reiterated, accelerating single pitch, and it is finally starting to be performed this way in modern performances. For descriptions of trillo as a repeated pitch, see Giovanni Luca Conforti, *Breve et facile maniera d'esercitarsi ad ogni scolaro* (Rome, 1593), 25, and especially Giulio Caccini, introduction "A i lettori" to *Le nuove musiche* (Florence: Marescotti, 1601), [4]. There is no agreement in the period sources on terminology describing ornamentation. For example, Emilio Cavalieri describes both *groppolo* and *trillo* as modern trills, the former anchoring the upper note, the later the lower note; see his introduction to the *Rappresentazione di Anima e Corpo* [Rome, 1600] cited and translated by Tim Carter, *Composing Opera from Dafne to Ulisse Errante* (Krakow: Musica Iagellonica, 1994), 86–87.

41. Similarly, in act 1, scene 12, Eumaeus confronts Iro by calling him "great eater" (Gran mangiatore) "divoratore" (devourer) and similar appellations. In this scene Iro is also represented as a Polyphemus who mocks the vegetarian shepherd Eumaeus by reminding him, "I eat your companions," meaning the animals Eumaeus takes care of.

42. Malipiero, *"L'Odissea" d'Omero*, book 18, 19–22.

43. Bakhtin, *Rabelais and His World*, 193.

44. All these quotations are from Bakhtin, *Rabelais and His World*, chap. 3, on "Popular-Festive Forms and Images in Rabelais," 196–277.

45. Bakhtin, *Rabelais and His World*, 369–70.

46. Emanuel Schikaneder, *Die Zauberflöte: Eine Große Oper in zwei Aufzugen* (Vienna: Ignaz Alberti, 1791), facsimile reproduction in Wolfgang Amadeus Mozart, *Die Zauberflöte*, K. 620, Facsimile of the autograph score, with introductions by Joachim Kreutzer and Christoph Wolff (Los Altos, CA: Packard Humanities Institute), vol. 6/3, [67–96].

47. Pierpaolo Polzonetti, "Mozart and the American Revolution," in *The Eigh-*

teenth Centuries: An Interdisciplinary Investigation, ed. David T. Gies and Cynthia Wall (Charlottesville: University of Virginia Press, 2018), 202–32. Native Americans were perceived in European culture as similar to American Quakers, who also addressed everybody informally. I agree with Subotnik, who emphasizes the egalitarian worldview projected by Papageno and its opposition to the man of culture and distinction, Prince Tamino: Rose Rosengard Subotnik, "Whose *Magic Flute*? Intimations of Reality at the Gates of the Enlightenment," *19th-Century Music* 15, no. 2 (1991): 138. The essay appears in longer form in her *Deconstructive Variations: Music and Reason in Western Society* (Minneapolis: University of Minnesota Press, 1996).

48. Kerstin Brünenberg, "Sklavenarbeit: Folgenlose Vergangenheit?" in *Von Arbeit und Menschen: Überraschende Einblicke in das Arbeitsleben fremder Kulturen*, ed. Sabine Eylert, Ursula Bertels, and Ursula Tewes, (New York: Waxman, 2000), 53; Jochen Meissner, Ulrich Mücke, and Klaus Weber, *Schwarzes Amerika: Eine Geschichte der Slaverei* (Munich: C. H. Beck, 2008), 102. Louis Nelson gives a chilling account of the systematic whipping, torture, rape, and other crimes committed in sugar plantations in Jamaica and North America during the eighteenth century, based also on period sources published in the mid-eighteenth century, in "The Jamaican Plantation: Industrial, Global, Contested," in *The Eighteenth Centuries: Global Networks of Enlightenment*, ed. David T. Gies and Cynthia Wall (Charlottesville: University of Virginia Press, 2018), 120–43. I am grateful to my colleagues Tobias Boes and Sally McKee for consulting on this issue.

49. [William Fox], *An Address to the People of Great Britain on the Propriety of Abstaining from West India Sugar and Rum*, 10th ed. (London: Gourney, 1791). A large number of witnesses documenting and denouncing slavery of Africans in the Americas are discussed in the contemporary book by Johann Jakob Sell, *Versuch einer Geschichte des Negerschlavenhandels* (Halle: Gebauer, 1791).

50. Jacques Chailley, *The "Magic Flute" Unveiled: Esoteric Symbolism in Mozart's Masonic Opera* (New York: Knopf, 1971), 101 (on Sarastro), 104–5, 188 (on Papageno).

51. Subotnik, "Whose 'Magic Flute'?," 143.

52. Carolyn Abbate, *In Search of Opera* (Princeton, NJ: Princeton University Press, 2001), 78–79.

53. Berger, *Mozart's Arrow*, 282–83.

54. This third stanza does not appear in the Mozart autograph or in the original libretto, but it may reflect the earliest semi-improvised performance tradition of the opera. See Mozart, *Die Zauberflöte*, in the *Neue Mozart-Ausgabe*, II/5/19, ed. Gernot Gruber and Alfred Orel (Kassel: Bärenreiter, 1970), act 1, scene 2, aria no. 2: "Wenn alle Mädchen wären mein, / so tauschte ich brav Zucker ein; / die, welche mir am liebsten wär,' / der gäb' ich gleich den Zucker her. / Und küßte sie mich zärtlich dann, / wär' sie mein Weib und ich ihr Mann. / Sie schlief' an meiner Seite ein, / ich wiegte wie ein Kind sie ein." ("If all the girls belonged to me, I would exchange them for lots of sugar, and then give the sugar to the girl I love. And if she kissed me tenderly, she would be my wife and I her husband. She would sleep with me and I would rock her like a baby"). As Michael Freyman documents in *The Authentic "Magic Flute" Libretto; Mozart's Autograph or the First Full-Score Edition?* (Lanham, MD: Scarecrow Press, 2009), 201, it appears in the printed

score published in Bonn by Simrock in 1814, which "assumes a place of unique importance alongside the autograph" (161). Before then it appears in various manuscripts as well as in the printed piano vocal score (Simrock, 1793), as detailed in the preface to the *Neue Mozart*-Ausgabe, xvii. I am grateful to Neal Zaslaw and Michael Freyman for discussing this issue with me. For early editions with and without the added text, see Werner Wunderlich, Doris Ueberschlag, and Ulrich Müller, eds., *Mozarts "Zauberflöte" und ihre Dichter: Faksimiles und Editionen von Textbuch, Bearbeitungen und Fortsetzungen der Mozart-Oper* (Salzburg: Mueller-Speiser, 2007), 27–29.

55. Chailley, *"Magic Flute" Unveiled*, 101 (on Sarastro), 104–5, 188 (on Papageno).

CHAPTER SIX

1. Marinella Laini, *La raccolta zeniana di drammi per musica veneziani della Biblioteca Nazionale Marciana, 1637–1700* (Lucca: Libreria musicale italiana, 1995).

2. William James Bouwsma, *Venice and the Defense of Republican Liberty: Renaissance Values in the Age of the Counter Reformation* (Berkeley: University of California Press, 1968), esp. 475, showing how important the model of the Roman Republic was for Venetian celebration of republican virtues.

3. Cicero, *On the Commonwealth [De re publica]*, trans. George Holland Sabine and Stanley Barney Smith (London: Macmillan, 1976), 177–78. It is unlikely that the author of the libretto knew Cicero's *De re publica*, but Cicero's narrative and ideology were disseminated in the more popular account by Livy.

4. Richard Miles McKee, "A Critical Edition of Carlo Pallavicino's *Il Vespasiano*," 2 vols. (PhD diss., University of North Carolina, Chapel Hill, 1989), vol. 1, presents a survey of the sources (librettos and manuscript scores) and reception history of this opera. I base my account of its music and drama on his critical edition, as well as on the second edition of the libretto: Giulio Cesare Corradi, *Il Vespasiano, drama per muisca nel nuovo teatro Grimano di S. Gio[vanni] Chrisostomo . . . nella seconda impression con nuove aggiunte, consacrato all'Illustrissimo, e Reverendissimo Monsigno Giovanni Battista Tosio, Abbate e Commendatore perpetuo d'Asola* (Venice: Nicolini, 1680).

5. McKee, "Critical Edition of Carlo Pallavicino's *Il Vespasiano*," 1:13. The cast list was not published in any of the librettos, but it has been reconstructed based on other evidence (range, contracts, published reviews).

6. McKee, "Critical Edition of Carlo Pallavicino's *Il Vespasiano*," 2:119.

7. The bizarre symphony is absent from two of the three surviving manuscript scores of the opera, those corresponding to the Venetian production: Modena, Biblioteca Estense, MS Mus. F.894, dating from 1678, and Venezia, Biblioteca nazionale Marciana MS It. Cl. IV. Cod. 462 (9986), from 1680. The symphony appears in Modena, Biblioteca Estense, MS Mus. F. 898, 65v–67r, prepared for the 1685 productions in Modena and Milan. On the dates of these witnesses see McKee, "Critical Edition of Carlo Pallavicino's *Il Vespasiano*," 1:142 and 2:410–16 for the music. This 3/8 instrumental piece in D major has nothing particularly bizarre about it and is typical courtly, jovial table music. It is possible that different music was improvised for the earlier Venetian productions.

8. McKee, "Critical Edition of Carlo Pallavicino's *Il Vespasiano*," 2:152–53, presenting remarkable similarities with eighteenth-century transcriptions of gondoliers' songs; see Pierpaolo Polzonetti, *Tartini e la musica secondo natura* (Lucca: LIM, 2001), 101–26.

9. Carlo Moderni, *Sardanapalo: Drama per musica da recitarsi nel Teatro di Sant'Angelo l'anno 1679, ristampato con il Prologo e altre aggiunte* (Venice: Francesco Nicolini, 1679), 5–6, where we read that the opera was composed by Domenico Freschi, as confirmed by Cristoforo Ivanovich, "Le memorie teatrali di Venezia," in *Minerva al tavolino* (Venice: Niccolò Pezzana, 1686), 444.

10. Diodoro Siculo, *Delle antique historie fabulose nuovamente fatto volgare e con somma diligentia stampato* (Venice: Gabriel [G]iolito di Ferrarii, 1542), book 3, 42–43.

11. [Jacques Chassebras de Cram], *Mercure galant* (April 1679), 125–26. On the reports on Venetian operas of this time in the *Mercure galant* see Barbara Nestola, "La musica italiana nel *Mercure galant* (1677–1683)," *Recercare* 14 (2002): 99–157. On the attraction of the technology of instrument making at this time see Rebecca Cypess, *Curious and Modern Inventions: Instrumental Music as Discovery in Galileo's Italy* (Chicago: University of Chicago Press, 2016).

12. Moderni, *Sardanapalo*, 1, 1: "*Guardarobba reggio: Sardanapalo, che tra un choro d'Assire donzelle ricama*" (Royal Wardrobe: Sardanapalo in the act of embroidering among a chorus of Assyrian maidens). Domenico Freschi, "Il Sardanapalo," Venice, Biblioteca nazionale Marciana, MS IV, 452 (9976).

13. Roger Freitas, "The Eroticism of Emasculation: Confronting the Baroque Body of the Castrato," *Journal of Musicology* 20, no. 2 (2003): 202–5.

14. Moderni, *Sardanapalo*, 1, 20: "Entro del bagno / Qual ape innamorata, / Nel seno di Nicea / Di sue bellezze al fiore / Vola a raccor il dolce mel d'Amore."

15. I am grateful to Francesco Cotticelli, who clarified for me the use of this invented dialect to represent Moorish slaves in the tradition of semi-improvised Italian comedy (commedia dell'arte) of the time. On the presence of Muslim and African slaves in early-modern Venice, see Alberto Tenenti, "Gli schiavi di Venezia alla fine del Cinquecento," *Rivista storica italiana* 67 (1955): 52–69, and Kate Lowe, "Visible Lives: Black Gondoliers and Other Black Africans in Renaissance Venice," *Renaissance Quarterly* 66 (2013): 412–52. In the commedia dell'arte scenario "Il finto principe," there is a slave named Brunetto (the name suggests his brown skin), who is repeatedly represented in the act of eating or talking about food and cooking "maccheroni." The scenario also prescribes, among the props, a dish of pasta ("piatto di maccheroni") and equipment necessary to cook scrambled eggs onstage ("cose da far frittata"). This scenario has been published in Adolfo Bartoli, *Scenari inediti della Commedia dell'arte: Contributo alla storia del teatro popolare italiano* (Florence: Sansoni, 1880), 181–89.

16. Lorenzo da Ponte, *Il dissoluto punito, o sia Il D[on] Giovanni: Dramma giocoso in due atti da rappresentarsi nel Teatro di Praga* (Prague: Schönfeld, 1787), 2, 12. All subsequent quotations from the libretto are based on this first edition unless otherwise indicated.

17. Nicholas J. Chong, "Music for the Last Supper: The Dramatic Significance of Mozart's Musical Quotations in the *Tafelmusik* of *Don Giovanni*," *Current Musicology* 92 (2011): 17.

18. Frank Lestringant, *Cannibals: The Discovery and Representation of the Cannibal from Columbus to Jules Verne* (Berkeley: University of California Press, 1997).

19. Rogério Budasz, "Of Cannibals and the Recycling of Otherness," *Music and Letters* 87, no. 1 (2005): 1–15.

20. Shirley Lindenbaum, "Thinking about Cannibalism," *Annual Review of Anthropology* 33 (2004): 475–98, offers an overview on cultural constructions of cannibalism in the Western world. See 486–87 for the cited remarks about the eighteenth century.

21. Budasz, "Of Cannibals," 3.

22. Budasz, "Of Cannibals," 6.

23. Budasz, "Of Cannibals," 13.

24. John A. Rice, *Antonio Salieri and Viennese Opera* (Chicago: University of Chicago Press, 1998), 462, 575–85. The libretto shifts attention from the women (as it was in Shakespeare's *The Merry Wives of Windsor*) to the libertine man: Carlo Prospero Defranceschi, *"Falstaff, o sia Le tre burle": Dramma giocoso per musica in due atti (Soggetto inglese) da rappresentarsi negl'Imperiali Regj Teatri di Corte l'anno 1798, musica di Antonio Salieri, primo maestro di cappella della Corte Imperiale* (Vienna: Mattia Andrea Schmidt, 1798).

25. Domenico Poggi, *La locandiera: Dramma giocoso per musica cavato da una commedia dell'avvocato Signor Carlo Goldoni da Domenico Poggi, dedicato al bel sesso . . . da rappresentarsi ne' teatri privilegiati di Vienna la primavera dell'anno 1773* (Vienna: Giuseppe Kurtzböck, 1773). The dining-table seduction scene is set in recitative in act 1, scene 11. Mirandolina's culinary skills inspired a cookbook of period recipes reconstructed based on Goldoni's texts: Flavio Russo, *A cena con la locandiera: Le ricette di Carlo Goldoni* (Turin: Leone Verde, 2004).

26. Poggi, *Locandiera*. The dedication on the frontispiece to the "bel sesso" (beautiful gender) is followed by a quatrain asking women to protect the librettist and to forgive him for his likely imperfect first attempt at writing poetry: "Donne belle proteggete / Questi versi e queste rime; / Se non son come volete / perdonate: son le prime."

27. Maggie Günsberg, *Playing with Gender: The Comedies of Goldoni* (Leeds, UK: Northern Universities Press, 2001), 123.

28. The concept of Don Giovanni as a product of the Counter-Reformation is explored by, among others, Edward J. Dent, *Mozart's Operas: A Critical Study* (1913; repr. Oxford: Oxford University Press, 1991), 120–27, and by Nino Pirrotta, *Don Giovanni's Progress: A Rake Goes to the Opera*, trans. Harris S. Saunders Jr. (New York: Marsilio, 1994), 11–12; Mladen Dolar, on the other hand, states that the Don Juan myth has its roots in medieval morality plays: Dolar, "The Opera in Philosophy: Mozart and Kierkegaard," in Mladen Dolar and Slavoj Žižek, *Opera's Second Death* (New York: Routledge, 2002), 50. For a study of Mozart's *Don Giovanni* as post-Enlightenment, see the collection of essays in Lydia Goehr and Daniel Herwitz, eds., *The "Don Giovanni" Moment: Essays on the Legacy of an Opera* (New York: Columbia University Press, 2006); and on Mozart's operas as bridging Counter-Reformation and "modernity," see Michael Steinberg, *Listening to Reason: Culture, Subjectivity, and Nineteenth-Century Music* (Princeton, NJ: Princeton University Press, 2004), 32. For an analysis of Don Giovanni in terms of religious concern for sin I am indebted to inspiring exchanges of ideas I had with my advisee and former

assistant Lesley Grace Sullivan, whose master's thesis is "Textual Polyphony in Mozart's *Don Giovanni*" (University of Notre Dame, 2016).

29. Tirso de Molina, *El burlador de Sevilla*, ed. Alfredo Rodríguez López-Vásquez, 3rd ed. (Madrid: Cátedra, 1990). The editor discusses the problem of attributing authorship in his introduction and provides information about early performance history (14).

30. The observations on this opera and the literary and operatic tradition of *Don Giovanni* are based on Pirrotta, *Don Giovanni's Progress*, 11–38.

31. Pirrotta, *Don Giovanni's Progress*, chaps. 2 ("The Eighteenth Century") and 3 ("The Immediate Antecedents of Mozart").

32. Anthony R. DelDonna, *Opera, Theatrical Culture and Society in Late Eighteenth-Century Naples* (Burlington, VT: Ashgate, 2012), 61.

33. Lorenzo Da Ponte, *Memorie e libretti mozartiani*, 7th ed. (Milan: Garzanti, 2007); the beginning of part 1 on early encounters with Dante, and part 5 on teaching in New York after 1820. See also 338, 347–48 on Da Ponte's production of Mozart's *Don Giovanni* in New York. The libretto of the New York premiere is Lorenzo Da Ponte, *Don Giovanni: Dramma buffo in due atti, la parte poetica della traduzione da L. D Ponte* (New York: Giovanni Gray, 1826).

34. Thomas Aquinas, *Summa Theologiae* 1–2: q. 84: art. 1.

35. Aquinas, *Summa Theologiae* 1–2: q. 84: art. 2.

36. Aquinas, *Summa Theologiae* 1–2: q. 84: art. 4.

37. Norman Wirzba, *Food and Faith: A Theology of Eating* (Cambridge: Cambridge University Press, 2011), 75–79.

38. Kristi Brown-Montesano, "Holding Don Giovanni Accountable," *Musicology Now*, December 5, 2017, http://www.musicologynow.org/2017/12/holding-don-giovanni-accountable.html, accessed January 12, 2021.

39. Without drawing a direct parallel equating women with food, John Platoff recognizes the similarity between these two arias in his article "Catalogue Arias and the 'Catalogue Aria,'" in *Wolfgang Amadè Mozart: Essays on His Life and His Music*, ed. Stanley Sadie (Oxford: Clarendon Press, 1996), 298.

40. Platoff, "Catalogue Arias," 310–11, observing that this is not the case of Bertati and Gazzaniga's setting of Leporello's catalog aria. A less insightful comparison of the two is in Alfred Einstein, *Mozart: His Character, His Work*, trans. Arthur Mendel and Nathan Broder (New York: Oxford University Press, 1962), 437–38.

41. *Il cuoco piemontese perfezionato a Parigi* (Turin: Giuseppe Ricca, 1766), ed. Silvano Seventi (1766; repr. Bra: Arcigola Slow Food Editore, 1995), chap. 13, 233.

42. In the short, intertwining, minor chromatic string interlude before the repetition of this *a due*, Brown-Montesano recognizes "a fleeting slip of Don Giovanni's ingenious mask, revealing the practiced predator beneath." Kristi Brown-Montesano, *Understanding the Women of Mozart's Operas* (Berkeley: University of California Press, 2007), 69.

43. Kenneth Bendiner, *Food in Painting from the Renaissance to the Present* (London: Reaktion, 2005), 26–27.

44. Dent, *Mozart's Operas*, 161.

45. Among these three styles of late eighteenth-century dance—minuet, folia, and allemande—only the minuet was still in practice as a social dance. This may be an indica-

tion that Da Ponte intended to set the action of the drama at least one hundred years earlier.

46. Hermann Abert, *W. A. Mozart*, trans. Steward Spencer, ed. Cliff Eisen (New Haven, CT: Yale University Press, 2007), 1073.

47. For a different interpretation see Charles Ford, *Music, Sexuality, and the Enlightenmnent in Mozart's "Figaro," "Don Giovanni" and "Così fan tutte"* (New York: Routledge, 2016), 55, who sees in this aria, with its "continuous denial of rhythmic expectations at top speed," an expression of "the destructive negativity of libertine desire through the denial of all musical expectations."

48. *Vocabolario degli accademici della Crusca, edizione seconda veneta accresciuta di molte voci dagli autori della stessa accademia*, 5 vols. (Venice: Francesco Pitteri, 1763), 3:148, para. 31. The meaning "to masturbate" for *menare* is based on the short story in Franco Sacchetti's *Novelle Trecento*, novella 215.

49. John Rosselli, *The Life of Mozart* (Cambridge: Cambridge University Press, 1998), 94; Charles Rosen, *The Classical Style: Haydn, Mozart, Beethoven* (New York: Norton, 1997), 94–95; Robbins H. C. Landon, *Mozart: The Golden Years, 1781–1791* (London: Thames and Hudson, 1989), 170. Nicholas Till, *Mozart and the Enlightenment: Truth, Virtue, and Beauty in Mozart's Operas* (Boston: Faber and Faber, 1992), 212; Abert, *W. A. Mozart*, 212.

50. Abert, *W. A. Mozart*, 1081.

51. On the representation of rape in *Don Giovanni*, with particular attention to the variety of interpretations in videorecorded opera productions, see Richard Will, "*Don Giovanni* and the Resilience of Rape Culture," *Journal of the American Musicological Society* 71, no. 1 (2018): 218–22.

52. Wolfgang Amadeus Mozart, *Il dissoluto punito, ossia Il Don Giovanni*, facsimile of the autograph score included in Wolfgang Amadeus Mozart's *Il dissoluto punito, ossia Il Don Giovanni K. 527, 540a, 540c*, Paris, Bibliothèque nationale de France, Département de la musique, MS 1548 (Los Altos, CA: Packard Humanities Institute, 2009), 447–60.

53. Alessandra Campana, "To Look Again (at *Don Giovanni*)," in *The Cambridge Companion to Eighteenth-Century Opera*, ed. Anthony R. DelDonna and Pierpaolo Polzonetti (Cambridge: Cambridge University Press, 2009), 142.

54. Steffen Lösel, "'May Such Great Effort Not Be in Vain': Mozart on Divine Love, Judgment, and Retribution," *Journal of Religion* 89, no. 3 (July 2009): 388–89.

55. I am grateful to my student Xingyue Zhang for discussing this idea with me and writing a term paper titled "The Ecomedy of Mozart's Operas" (2018). Although aristocrats in opera do not talk about money, in Mozart's time the middle classes found new nobility in making money, as is clear in some comic operas inspired by the American enlightenment: see Polzonetti, *Italian Opera in the Age of the American Revolution*, 247–66, 309–12. On Don Giovanni as a character antithetical to American revolutionary ideals, see Polzonetti, "Mozart and the American Revolution," 217–21. Mary Hunter explored this topic in "Bourgeois Values in Opera Buffa in 1780s Vienna," in *Opera Buffa in Mozart's Vienna*, ed. Mary Hunter and James Webster (Cambridge: Cambridge University Press, 1997), 170–85.

56. Chong, "Music for the Last Supper."

57. Chong, "Music for the Last Supper," 19–21; Wye Jamison [Wendy] Allanbrook, *Rhythmic Gesture in Mozart: "Le nozze di Figaro" and "Don Giovanni"* (Chicago: University of Chicago Press, 1983), 289, relating the reference to the "lamb at slaughterhouse" in Sarti's aria to "Elvira's tempestuous arrival" and her "self-sacrifice." Daniel Heartz, *Mozart's Operas*, ed. Thomas Baumann (Berkeley: University of California Press, 1990), 169–70.

58. Bendiner, *Food in Painting*, 14, 18, 134–35 on representation of the Last Supper, and chapter 4 (205–24) on the interplay between "decorative and symbolic" in food iconography.

59. Lewis L. Robbins, "A Contribution to the Psychological Understanding of the Character of Don Juan," *Bulletin of the Menninger Clinic* 20, no. 4 (July 1956): 166–80.

60. Robbins, "Contribution to the Psychological Understanding of the Character of Don Juan," 176–77.

61. Allanbrook, *Rhythmic Gesture*, 288.

62. Michel Foucault, *The History of Sexuality*, vol. 1, *An Introduction*, trans. Robert Hurley (New York: Vintage Books, 1990), 30–39; literal quotation on 39.

63. Frits Noske, *The Signifier and the Signified: Studies in the Operas of Mozart and Verdi* (The Hague: Nijhoff, 1977), 86.

64. Søren Kirkegaard, *Either/Or*, trans. Alastair Hannay (London: Penguin, 1992), 63–90, esp. 69–70.

65. Dolar, "Opera in Philosophy," 53.

66. Carl Dahlhaus, *The Idea of Absolute Music*, trans. Roger Lustig (Chicago: University of Chicago Press, 1989), 113–14.

67. Brown-Montesano, *Understanding the Women of Mozart's Operas*, xxiii.

68. Bendiner, *Food in Painting*, 43–44.

69. Bendiner, *Food in Painting*, 116.

70. Pierpaolo Polzonetti, "Don Giovanni Goes to Prison: Teaching Opera behind Bars," *Musica Docta* 6 (2016): 99–104, based on the controversial blog with the same title posted on *Musicology Now* on February 16, 2016.

71. As also noted by Allanbrook, *Rhythmic Gesture*, 289, and by Jürgen Maehder, "Essen und Trinken auf der Opernbühne," in *Musikwissenschaft im deutsch-italienischen Dialog: Friedrich Lippmann zum 75. Geburtstag*, ed. Markus Engelhardt and Wolfgang Witzenmann, *Analecta Musicologica* 46 (2010): 322.

72. Lorenzo Da Ponte, *Memorie e libretti mozartiani*, introduction by Giuseppe Armani, 7th ed. (Milan: Garzanti, 2007), 126: "Una bottiglietta di 'tockai'" a destra, il calamaio nel mezzo, e una scatola di tabacco di Siviglia a sinistra. Una bella giovinetta di sedici anni (ch'io avrei voluto non amare che come figlia, ma . . .) stava in casa mia con sua madre, ch'aveva la cura della famiglia, e venìa nella mia camera a suono di campanello, che per verità io suonava assai spesso, e singolarmente quando mi pareva che l'estro cominciasse a raffreddarsi: ella mi portava or un biscottino, or una tazza di caffè, o niente altro che il suo bel viso, sempre gaio, sempre ridente e fatto appunto per inspirare l'estro poetico e le idee spiritose. . . . Mi si assideva talvolta vicino senza muoversi, senza aprir bocca né batter occhio, mi guardava fisso fisso, sorrideva blandissimamente, sospirava e qualche volta parea voler piangere: alle corte questa fanciulla fu la mia Calliope per quelle tre opere e lo fu

poscia per tutti i versi che scrissi per l'intero corso di altri sei anni. Da principio io le permettea molto sovente tali visite; dovei alfine renderle meno spesse, per non perdere troppo tempo in tenerezze amorose, di cui era perfetta maestra. La prima giornata frattanto, tra il 'tockai,'" il tabacco di Siviglia, il caffè, il campanello e la giovine musa, ho scritto le due prime scene del *Don Giovanni*, altre due de *L'Arbore di Diana* e più di metà del primo atto del *Tarar*." For a different translation see Da Ponte, *Memoirs of Lorenzo Da Ponte*, trans. Elisabeth Abbott (New York: Dover, 1959), 174–75. Based on the original spelling of "Tockai" wine with a "K" it is most likely that Da Ponte was drinking the Hungarian Tokaji, easy to find in Vienna. The Tokaji has a high alcoholic content, which explains why it came in a small bottle. The Italian Tocai, from Friuli, is much lighter.

73. Lösel, "'May Such Great Effort Not Be in Vain,'" 389.

74. Abert, *W. A. Mozart*, 1051–52.

75. As I point out elsewhere, Leporello, Don Giovanni, and the Commendatore deliver syllables at three different speeds reflecting their status along the spectrum of comic-seria characters: Pierpaolo Polzonetti, "The 'Quantitative Style' in Seventeenth-Century Italian Opera," in *Pensieri per un maestro: Studi in onore di Pierluigi Petrobelli*, ed. Stefano Lavia and Roger Parker (Turin: EDT, 2002), 114.

76. Scott Burnham, *Mozart's Grace* (Princeton, NJ: Princeton University Press, 2013), 45–47.

77. I am grateful to student Lesley Sullivan for suggesting this idea.

78. Lorenzo Da Ponte, *Il dissoluto punito, o sia Il D. Giovanni. Dramma giocoso in due atti da rappresentarsi nel teatro di Praga per l'arrivo di Sua Altezza Reale Maria Teresa Arciduchessa d'Austria sposa del Ser. Principe Antonio di Sassonia l'anno 1787* (Vienna, 1787), line 1381 bis, cited in the critical edition of the libretto, Lorenzo Da Ponte, *Il Don Giovanni*, ed. Giovanna Gronda (Turin: Einaudi, 1995), 114–15.

79. Bakhtin, *Rabelais and His World*, 407. On this important issue see also 197, 321–22.

80. Bakhtin, *Rabelais and His World*, 369–70.

CHAPTER SEVEN

1. Gillian Crowther, *Eating Culture: An Anthropological Guide to Food* (Toronto: University of Toronto Press, 2013), 138–48.

2. Massimo Montanari, *L'identità italiana in cucina* (Bari: Laterza, 2010). On macaroni as the first recognizably Italian food item see 49–55; on the formation of Italian culinary identity in the late nineteenth century see 53–56. As Montanari acknowledges (94), the first scholar to call attention to Artusi's pioneering role in forming a national culinary identity was Piero Camporesi, in his introduction to Pellegrino Artusi, *La scienza in cucina e l'arte di mangiar bene* (1891; repr. Turin: Einaudi, 1970).

3. National opera traditions are the subjects of different chapters in Anthony R. DelDonna and Pierpaolo Polzonetti, eds., *The Cambridge Companion to Eighteenth-Century Opera* (Cambridge: Cambridge University Press, 2009), part 2.

4. Carl Franz Henisch, *Der Bassa von Tunis: Eine komische Operette in einem Aufzuge*, with music by Franz Andreas Holly (Berlin, 1774), scene 1. On this opera and other singspiels with eating or drinking scenes see Thomas Bauman, *North German Opera in the Age*

of Goethe (Cambridge: Cambridge University Press, 1985), 135 (*Der Bassa*), 169 (*Claudine von Villa Bella*), 276–77 (*Der Spiegelritter*), and 288–90 (*Rinaldo und Alcina*).

5. Braudel, *Civilization and Capitalism*, 1:232–33.

6. Henry Lagrave, *Le théâtre et le public à Paris de 1715 à 1750* (Paris: C. Klincksiek, 1972), 622.

7. [Alain-René Lesage], "Arlequin roy de Serendib," in *Le théâtre de la foire, ou L'opéra-comique, contenant les meilleures pièces qui ont été représentées aux foires de S. Germain et de S. Laurent, enrichies d'estampes en taille-douce, avec une table de tous les vaudevilles et autres airs gravez-notez à la fin de chaque volume*, vol. 1 (Paris: Geneau, 1721), 2.1.19, air no. 10. A possible source of this libretto is a seventeenth-century Italian commedia dell'arte scenario, *Arlecchino creato re per ventura*, as inferred by Francis J. Cormody, "Le repertoire de l'opéra comique en vaudevilles de 1708 à 1764," *University of California Publications in Modern Philology* 16 (1932–33): 409.

8. Priscilla Parkhurst Ferguson, *Accounting for Taste: The Triumph of French Cuisine* (Chicago: University of Chicago Press, 2004), 3.

9. On Harlequin as commedia dell'arte mask, see chap. 12 in Pierre Louis Duchartre, *The Italian Comedy*, trans. Randolph T. Weaver (New York: Dover, 1966), 123–60. Nobel Prize winner Dario Fo immortalized Zanni's insatiable appetite in the monologue "the Zanni Hunger" in his *Mistero Buffo*, imagining this character wishing to eat himself and God with all the angels: Dario Fo, *Mistero Buffo: Comic Mysteries*, trans. Stuart Hood (London: Methuen, 1988). On serenades featuring both Zanni and Arlecchino see Emily Wilbourne, *Seventeenth-Century Opera and the Sound of the Commedia dell'Arte* (Chicago: University of Chicago Press, 2016), 38–42.

10. Daniel Heartz, "*The Beggar's Opera* and *Opéra-comique en Vaudevilles*," *Early Music* 27, no. 1 (1999): 42–53; the idea has been explored much further by Vanessa Rogers, "John Gay, Ballad Opera and the Théâtre de la Foire," *Eighteenth-Century Music* 11, no. 2 (2014): 173–213, adding substantial evidence. I am grateful to Ian Newman for sharing with me early drafts of his monograph *The Romantic Tavern: Literature and Conviviality in the Age of Revolution* (Cambridge: Cambridge University Press, 2019).

11. Elisabeth Le Guin, *The Tonadilla in Performance: Lyric Comedy in Enlightenment Spain* (Berkley: University of California Press, 2014), 8 (literal quotation), 30, 40 (discussion of convivial scenes in opera), 20 (eating at the performance), 78–81 (libretto and score as recipes).

12. Le Guin, *Tonadilla in Performance*, 40, 100.

13. Bakhtin, *Rabelais and His World*, 162.

14. Translated by Le Guin, *Tonadilla in Performance*, 327; on this tonadilla see 39–43.

15. Marvin Harris, "The Abominable Pig," in *Food and Culture: A Reader*, ed. Carole Counihan and Penny Van Esterik (New York: Routledge, 1997), 67–79.

16. The original libretto and a facsimile of the manuscript copy of Galuppi's score from the Biblioteca del palácio nacional de Ajuda and relevant variants are published in Giovanni Bertati and Baldassare Galuppi, *L'inimico delle donne*, with an introduction by Helen Geyer-Kiefl, 3 vols. (Milan: Ricordi, 1986).

17. Adrienne Ward, *Pagodas in Play: China on the Eighteenth-Century Italian Opera Stage* (Lewisburg, PA: Bucknell University Press, 2010).

18. Ralph Locke, *Music and the Exotic from the Renaissance to Mozart* (Cambridge: Cambridge University Press, 2015), 284–86.

19. Ward, *Pagodas in Play*, 166.

20. Bertati and Galuppi, *L'inimico delle donne*, 1:13: "Al suono di Sinfonia entra Zon-Zon cogli altri, che da Sin-Sin vengono condotto ai luoghi loro destinati d'intorno la tavola." The "Sinfonia" appears in the manuscript score, Galuppi, *L'inimico delle donne*, 2:[293–300].

21. Ralph P. Locke, *Musical Exoticism: Images and Reflections* (Cambridge: Cambridge University Press, 2009), 118–21.

22. Jürgen Maehder, "Essen und Trinken auf der Opernbühne," in *Musikwissenschaft im deutsch-italienischen Dialog: Friedrich Lippmann zum 75. Geburtstag*, ed. Markus Engelhardt and Wolfgang Witzenmann, *Analecta musicologica* 46 (2010): 331.

23. Galuppi, *L'inimico delle donne*, vol. 2, act 1 finale, [335–36].

24. Giovanni Bertati, *L'orfanella americana, commedia per musica in quattro atti di Giovanni Bertati da rappresentarsi nel Teatro di S. Moisè per la prima opera dell'autunno 1787* (Venice: Battista Casali, 1787). Pasquale Anfossi, "L'orfanella americana," Genoa, Biblioteca del Conservatorio di musica Niccolò Paganini, MS 13.7.13 (L 8.2).

25. Polzonetti, *Italian Opera in the Age of the American Revolution*, 20.

26. An extensive analysis of this opera is in Polzonetti, *Italian Opera in the Age of the American Revolution*, 202–27, especially 220–23 about the aforementioned episodes.

27. Franco Fido, *Nuova guida a Goldoni: Teatro e società nel Settecento* (Turin: Einaudi, 2000), 48–85.

28. Camporesi, *Exotic Brew*, 36, 46.

29. Camporesi, *Exotic Brew*, 105.

30. As noted in chapter 5 of this book, unless otherwise indicated, all the quotations of Goldoni's librettos are from Carlo Goldoni, *Drammi comici per musica*, 3 vols., ed. Silvia Urbani (Venice: Marsilio, 2007–16), and from at www.carlogoldoni.it.

31. On the abundance of comic representations of hunger in the seventeenth century (the "theater of hunger") see Piero Camporesi, *Il paese della fame* (Milan: Garzanti, 2000), 139–205.

32. Bakhtin, *Rabelais and His World*, chap. 1, 74–90 (Christian carnivals besides the actual carnival before Lent), and chap. 2 (language of the marketplace, including utopian carnival fantasies). I borrow the term "satirical fantasy" applied to *Il paese della cuccagna* from Ted Emery, *Goldoni as Librettist: Theatrical Reform and the "drammi giocosi per musica"* (New York: Peter Lang, 1991), 93–123. On the rituals of *cuccagna* associated with the carnival opera season, especially in Naples, see Martha Feldman, *Opera and Sovereignty: Transforming Myths in Eighteenth-Century Italy* (Chicago: University of Chicago Press, 2007), 196–203. Except for a few numbers, Galuppi's music does not survive.

33. Erich Segal, *The Death of Comedy* (Cambridge, MA: Harvard University Press, 2011), 15.

34. Bendiner, *Food in Painting from the Renaissance to the Present*, 213.

35. E. C. Spary, *Eating the Enlightenment: Food and the Sciences in Paris* (Chicago: University of Chicago Press, 2012), 17.

36. Spary, *Eating the Enlightenment*, 12–15 and chapter 1 ("Intestinal Struggles") on digestive theories.

37. Foucault, *History of Sexuality*, vol. 1, and Michel Foucault, *Madness and Civilization: A History of Insanity in the Age of Reason*, trans. Richard Howard (New York: Vintage Books, 1988). A history of eighteenth-century medicalization conversant with Foucault is offered by Elizabeth A. Williams, *The Physical and the Moral: Anthropology, Physiology, and the Philosophical Medicine in France, 1750–1850* (Cambridge: Cambridge University Press, 1994), and Anne C. Vila, *Enlightenment and Pathology: Sensibility in the Literature and Medicine of Eighteenth-Century France* (Baltimore: Johns Hopkins University Press, 1998).

38. Camporesi documents how, in the Enlightenment, Italian eating habits surrendered to French hegemony in matters of taste, table manners, and healthy diet. Camporesi, *Exotic Brew*, 1, 27–35.

39. Segal, *Death of Comedy*, 15, quoting Virgil, *Georgics* 1.145: "Labor omnia vicit." Ovid, *Metamorphoses*, trans. David Raeburn (London: Penguin, 2004), 1.127–50, describes the Age of "Foul Iron" as a time of fraud and violence; a time of exploitation of foreign countries and their resources, of the disintegration of familial love, and of the end of piety and virtue.

40. Emery, *Goldoni as Librettist*, 109.

41. Umberto Eco, "The Frames of Comic Freedom," in *Carnival!*, ed. Thomas Sebeok (New York: Mouton, 1984), 1–9. Mary Hunter, *The Culture of Opera Buffa in Mozart's Vienna* (Princeton, NJ: Princeton University Press, 1999), 71–73, compares Bakhtin's theory of carnival to Umberto Eco's revisionist theory that casts doubt on the radicalism of carnivalesque uncrownings and subversions of normative order. See also Feldman, *Opera and Sovereignty*, 198.

42. Bakhtin, *Rabelais and His World*, 116–19.

43. Bendiner, *Food in Painting*, 44–50.

44. Braudel, *Civilization and Capitalism*, 1:183–84.

45. I consulted a later version of the libretto: [Giuseppe Palomba], *I zingari in fiera, dramma giocoso per musica da rappresentarsi nel teatro di Cittadella in Bergamo il Carnovale 1791* (Bergamo: Rossi, 1791), 2:3: "Che vagliono i fagiani? / Boccon così bellissimi / Lucrezia sol vi fa." That they are eating goat (*capretto*) can be inferred from the text of the recitative after the cavatina.

46. Giovanni Paisiello, "*Gli zingari in fiera*: Opera buffa in musica originale di Giovanni Paisiello, composta per il Real Teatro del Fondo L'anno 1789," Naples, Biblioteca del Conservatorio di Musica S. Pietro a Majella, MS 16.5.13–14, 2:7v.

47. Camporesi, *Exotic Brew*, 54–56.

48. Pierre Bourdieu, *La distinction: Critique sociale du jugement* (Paris: Éditions de Minuit, 1979). For the English version I consulted Bourdieu, *Distinction: A Social Critique of the Judgment of Taste*, trans. Richard Nice (New York: Routledge, 2000).

49. Bourdieu, *Distinction*, 254, 488–91; Claude Lévi-Strauss, *Le cru et le cuit* (Paris: Plon, 1964), translated into English as *The Raw and the Cooked: Introduction to a Science of Mythology*, trans. John and Doreen Weightman (1969; repr. Chicago: University of Chicago Press, 1983).

50. Bourdieu, *Distinction*, 48.

51. Bourdieu, *Distinction*, respectively 24, 71–73.

52. Bourdieu, *Distinction*, 193–99.

53. Bourdieu, *Distinction*, 247–49.

54. For a discussion of conventional and unconventional aspects of Goldoni's buffa librettos see Franco Fido, "Riforma e 'controriforma' del teatro: I libretti per musica di Goldoni fra il 1748 e il 1753," *Studi Goldoniani* 7 (1985): 60–72. Some of the ideas in this essay have been recapped and expanded by Fido's student Ted Emery in *Goldoni as Librettist*.

55. Bourdieu, *Distinction*, 100–101.

56. Bruno Latour, "On Actor-Network Theory: A Few Clarifications," *Soziale Welt* 47, no. (1996): 369–81; Latour, *Reassembling the Social: An Introduction to Actor-Network-Theory* (Oxford: Oxford University Press, 2005).

57. Latour, Reassembling the Social, 34.

58. Massimo Montanari, *La fame e l'abbondanza: Storia dell'alimentazione in Europa* (Bari: Laterza, 2014), 164–80.

59. Bourdieu, "Postscript," in *Distinction*, 488 (original terms cited from 566–67 of the French edition).

60. Carlo Goldoni, *Gl'innamorati: Commedia rappresentata per la prima volta a Venezia nell'Autunno dell'anno 1759*, in *Tutte le opere*, ed. Giuseppe Ortolani, 4th ed, 14 vols. (Milan: Mondadori, 1959), 7:366.

61. Quoted in Giampiero Rorato, *La cucina al tempo di Carlo Goldoni* (Vicenza: Terra Ferma, 2004), 95, which also presents the recipe for "pasticcio di macaroni" on 115.

62. Adam Geczy and Vicki Karaminas, *Queer Style* (London: Bloomsbury, 2013), 46–56 (quotation on 51).

63. Goldoni refers to Shakespeare multiple times in his works; although he does not mention *Othello* specifically, this tragedy was circulating in Italy, and Venice in particular, at the time: Paul H. D. Kaplan, "The Earliest Images of *Othello*," *Shakespeare Quarterly* 39, no. 2 (1988): 179–80; Giuseppe Ortolani, "Goldoni e Shakespeare, appunti e note," *Rivista italiana del dramma* 4 (1940): 280–301.

64. Braudel, *Civilization and Capitalism*, 1:190–202, documents how eating meat was not a luxury until its decline after 1550. On the association of meat and aristocracy related to the restricted rights to hunt, see Caroline Castiglione, *Patrons and Adversaries: Nobles and Villagers in Italian Politics, 1640–1760* (Oxford: Oxford University Press, 2005).

65. Camporesi, *Exotic Brew*, 36–40.

66. Bendiner, *Food in Painting*, 36–44.

67. Goldoni, *Mémoires*, in *Tutte le opere*, ed. Giuseppe Ortolani, 14 vols. (Milan: Mondadori, 1959), 1:75–77. I am grateful to Claire Thompson for telling me that a modern version of the "glo glo," inspired by Goldoni's description, is now being manufactured by Slovenian designer Oskar Andrej Kogoj.

68. Spary, *Eating the Enlightenment*, 13, 147–50, 197, 282–83.

69. Daniel Heartz, "*Vis comica*: Goldoni, Galuppi, and *L'Arcadia in Brenta*," in *From Garrick to Gluck: Essays on Opera in the Age of the Enlightenment*, ed. John A. Rice (Hillsdale, NY: Pendragon, 2004), 11–39.

70. Cited in translation in Heartz, "*Vis comica*," 17. Cicisbeism was a socially accepted practice of courting well-to-do married women.

71. On cicisbeism in eighteenth-century Italian culture, see Roberto Bizzocchi, "*Cicisbei*: Italian Morality and European Values in the Eighteenth Century," in *Italy's Eighteenth Century: Gender and Culture in the Age of the Grand Tour*, ed. Paula Finden, Wendy Wassyng Roworth, and Catherine M. Sama (Stanford, CA: Stanford University Press, 2009), 35–58, providing a short English version of his book *Cicisbei: Morale privata e identità nazionale in Italia* (Bari: Laterza, 2008). The representation of cicisbeism in opera remains a fertile ground for research. It has been treated by Martha Feldman, *Opera and Sovereignty*, 360–64, among others, but it has not been yet the subject of a thorough study.

72. I consulted the manuscript score, Baldassare Galuppi, "L'Arcadia in Brenta," Modena, Biblioteca Estense, MS Mus. F. 439.

73. *Il cuoco piemontese perfezionato a Parigi* (Turin: Giuseppe Ricca, 1766), ed. Sivano Serventi (repr. Bra: Slow Food, 1995), 250–55, for description of meat and fish pies (*torte*) and *pasta sfoglia*.

74. John Platoff, in his study of catalog arias, discusses this piece in "Catalogue Arias and the 'Catalogue Aria,'" in *Wolfgang Amadè Mozart: Essays on His Life and His Music*, ed. Stanley Sadie (Oxford: Clarendon Press, 1996), 298–89. Platoff concerns himself with the formal aspects of the catalog aria, not with the gastronomic signs or dramatic or political context of this piece.

75. See Claudio Sartori, *I libretti italiani a stampa dalle origini al 1800: Catalogo analitico con 16 indici*, 6 vols. (Cuneo: Bertola e Locatelli, 1990).

76. [Giovanni Bertati], *La vendemmia* (Naples, 1780), where the cast list at the beginning of the libretto spells out the roles as seria, buffa (divided into primi buffi, secondi buffi, and buffo caricato), and *mezzo carattere* roles. Not surprisingly, the seria roles never indulge in food, while the others do. For the analysis of the music I consulted the manuscript score from Dresden, Sächsiche Landesbibliothek, Mus 3491-F-502. The text in the score is the same as the earliest version of the opera [Bertati], *La vendemmia: Intermezzo in musica da rappresentarsi nel teatro dell'Eccellentissima casa Grimani a S. Gio[vanni] Crisostomo* (Venice: Fenzo, 1778), 1:10, 18.

77. Giuseppe Boerio, *Dizionario del dialetto veneziano* (Venice: Santini, 1829), defining *Fòlega* (or *folaga*, *foleghèta*, *folaghetta*) as "sea bird, excellent to eat," and providing its Latin binomial as *Fulica atra*; the *mazzorino* does not appear to have a scientific name, but it has similar but even better "meat" than the *fofano* or *Anas clypeata*. Vincenzo Tanara, *La caccia degli uccelli di Vincenzo Tanara da un manoscritto inedito della Biblioteca comunale di Bologna*, ed. Alberto Bacchi della Lega (Bologna: Romagnoli—Dall'Acqua, 1886), 398–99, explains that the term *mazzorino* was in use in Venice to describe the male of a colorful duck, "the biggest and most beautiful," called *germane* in Tuscany, *malpardo* in Naples, and *capoverde* in Rome. This allows us to identify it as the *Anas platyrhynchos*, or mallard.

78. Anthony R. DelDonna, *Opera, Theatrical Culture and Society in Late Eighteenth-Century Naples* (Burlington, VT: Ashgate, 2012).

79. [Bertati], *La vendemmia: A Comic Opera in Two Acts Performed in the King's Theater at the Hay-Market* (London: Wayland, 1789), corresponding to the manuscript libretto, Bertati, "La Vendemmia: Dramma giocoso per musica da rappresentarsi nel Teatro Reggio di Londra l'anno 1789," 1:10, manuscript at the Huntington Library, CA, John

Larpent Plays, MS coll. 832. This was the official manuscript submitted to Lord Larpent, Examiner of Plays, for licensing in Great Britain.

80. Don Felice Libera, *L'arte in cucina: Ricette di cibi e di dolci. Manoscritto trentino di cucina e pasticceria del XVIII secolo*, ed. Alberto Mazzoni (Bologna: Forni, 2004), recipe no. 577, page 261.

81. Camporesi, *Exotic Brew*, 5–7, 40.

82. Jean-Jacques Rousseau, "Discourse on the Origins of Inequality," in *The Basic Political Writings*, ed. and trans. Donald A. Cress (Indianapolis: Hackett, 1987), 86–87, n. 5.

83. Tristram Stuart, *The Bloodless Revolution: A Cultural History of Vegetarianism from 1600 to Modern Times* (New York: Norton, 2006), 195–99, 295–325.

84. "Lisetta e Caican turco: Intermezzi comici musicali da rappresentarsi nel teatro di San Salvatore l'anno 1733," Venice, Casa Goldoni, MS 59A 96/4, intermezzo primo: "Erba fresca, erba novella. / Ecco qua' l'ortolanella. / Ruccoletta, latughetta, / Fenocchino, salatetta."

85. I consulted Baldassare Galuppi, "Il filosofo di campagna: Opera bernesca in San Samuele l'Anno 1755," Paris, Bibliothèque nationale de France, Départment de la musique, MS X-776.

86. Galuppi, *Il filosofo di campagna*, 1, 2, "Quando son giovine," mm. 1–16.

87. Galuppi, *Il filosofo di campagna*, 1, 1, duet "Candidetto gelsomino," mm. 49–56 ("sol di donna la bellezza").

88. "Se perdo il caro lido" appears in Galuppi, *Il filosofo di campagna*, but not in the piano-vocal score: Galuppi, *Il filosofo di campagna*, ed. Virgilio Mortari (Milan: Carish, 1937), 10–16, features a *mezzo carattere* sentimental aria, "Misera a tante pene," which presents less coloratura than "Se perdo il caro lido" but, like the latter, features a long orchestral introduction and da capo form.

89. Polzonetti, "Mozart and the American Revolution," 214–17.

90. Spary, *Eating the Enlightenment*, 13.

91. Stuart, *Bloodless Revolution*, 227–35. See also Spary, *Eating the Enlightenment*, 254, about the circulation of new ideas on food and health.

92. Spary, *Eating the Enlightenment*, 259–63.

93. Jean-François Marmontel, *Essai sur les révolutions de la musique en France* ([Paris]: Le Noir, 1777). On the ideological implications of Marmontel's Piccinnism and its indirect alignment with revolutionary ideology—including a political reading of *La buona figliuola*, see Polzonetti, *Italian Opera in the Age of the American Revolution*, 9, 142, 172–76.

94. Downing A. Thomas, *Aesthetics of Opera in the Ancien Régime, 1647–1785* (Cambridge: Cambridge University Press, 2002), 227–28.

95. A groundbreaking study of Piccinni's signature opera as a manifesto of the age of sensibility is Mary Hunter's "'Pamela': The Offspring of Richardson's Heroine in Eighteenth-Century Opera," *Mosaic* 18 (1985): 61–76. The ambiguity of class identity in this opera has been carefully analyzed by Franco Piperno in "*La mia Cecchina è baronessa*: Livelli stilistici e assetto drammaturgico ne *La buona figliuola* di Goldoni-Piccinni," *Analecta musicologica* 30, no. 2 (1998): 523–42.

96. Northrop Frye, *Anatomy of Criticism* (Princeton, NJ: Princeton University Press, 1957), 44.

97. Stefano Castelvecchi, *Sentimental Opera: Questions of Genre in the Age of Bourgeois Drama* (Cambridge: Cambridge University Press, 2013), 13–39.

98. Hunter, "'Pamela,'" 65.

99. The score I consulted is Niccolò Piccinni, *La Cecchina, ossia La buona figliuola*, introduction by Eric Weimer (New York: Garland, 1983), facsimile reproduction of the Firenze, Conservatorio di Musica Luigi Cherubini, Biblioteca, MS D I 531, 532, 533. For the libretto I used the edition in Giovanna Gronda and Paolo Fabbri, eds., *Libretti d'opera italiani dal Seicento al Novecento* (Milan: Mondadori, 1997), 619–75, reproducing, with editorial interventions, the edition of *La buona figliuola, drama giocoso per musica* (Rome: [Grossi], 1760). The editors unfortunately omit the cast list present in the original edition of the libretto, which I have consulted. The interesting aspect of the cast is that it included only male singers. The first Cecchina was sung by Tommaso Borghesi, who, as can be inferred by consulting Sartori, *Catalogo*, specialized in female roles. He also played Lesbina in *La fiera di Senigaglia*.

100. Hunter, "'Pamela,'" 62.

101. Piperno, "*La mia Cecchina*," 525–27. On the similarities between *La buona figliuola* and Mozart's *La finta giardiniera* in the context of concealed and finally unveiled social identity, see Jessica Waldoff, *Recognition in Mozart's Operas* (Oxford: Oxford University Press, 2006), chap. 4, esp. 104–5.

102. Goldoni, *La buona figliuola*, 1, 1: "Godo io stessa innestar sul prun selvaggio, / in dolce primavera, or le pesche succose ed or le pera."

CHAPTER EIGHT

1. For eighteenth-century coffeeware design see Hélène Desmet-Grégoire, *Les objets du café dans les sociétés du Proche-Orient de de la Méditerranée* (Paris: Presses du CNRS, 1989).

2. J[ohann] G[ottlob] Krüger, *Traité du caffé, du thé, et du tabac* (Halle: Hemmerde, 1743), 9–10. Giovanni dalla Bona, *Dell'uso e dell'abuso del caffè: Dissertazione storico-fisico-medica*, 2nd ed. (Verona: Berno, 1760), 1–2, maintains that the origin of coffee could be traced to the time of King David and Homer but emphasizes that it was the Arabs who perfected and disseminated coffee.

3. Philippe Sylvestre Dufour, *Traitez nouveaux et curieux du café, du thé et du chocolat: Ouvrage également necessaire aux médecins, et à tous ceux qui aiment leur santé*, 3rd ed. (La Haye: Adrian Moetjens, 1693), cover illustration. The first edition was published in 1685.

4. [Felice Romani], *Il turco in Italia: Dramma buffo per musica in due atti da rappresentarsi nel R. Teatro alla Scala per primo spettacolo* (Milan: Pirola, 1814), 1, 9. The scene with coffee appears in the original source as well, a libretto by Caterino Mazzolà with music by Franz Seydelmann, *Il turco in Italia, dramma buffo in due parti da rappresentarsi al teatro di Corte* (Vienna: Stamperia dei Sordi e Muti, 1789), 1, 6. Consulted score: Gioachino Rossini, *Il turco in Italia: Dramma buffo per musica in due atti di Felice Romani, musica di Gioachino Rossini. Prima rappresentazioni Milano, Teatro alla Scala 14 agosto, 1814*, ed. Margaret Bent, in *Edizione critica delle opere di Gioachino Rossini*, section 1/13 (Pesaro: Fondazione Rossini, 1978), no. 5 "Quartett," 292–354.

5. E. C. Spary, *Eating the Enlightenment: Food and the Sciences in Paris* (Chicago: University of Chicago Press, 2012), 58–68. Markman Ellis, *The Coffee House: A Cultural History* (London: Weidenfeld and Nicolson, 2004), provides an overview of early English coffee culture. Ellis also put together a monumental anthology of sources on the subject: *Eighteenth-Century Coffee-House Culture*, 5 vols. (London: Pickering and Chatto, 2006).

6. Cited in Braudel, *Civilization and Capitalism*, 1:258.

7. Dino Carpanetto and Giuseppe Ricuperati, *Italy in the Age of Reason, 1685–1789*, trans. Caroline Higgitt (New York: Longman, 1987), 264–66; on the reformed cuisine promoted in *Il caffè* see Camporesi, *Exotic Brew*, 46–48.

8. John A. Rice, "Music in the Age of Coffee," *Eighteenth-Century Music* 4, no. 2 (2007): 301–5. Wolfgang's father Leopold apparently preferred alcohol to coffee: see Rudolph Angermüller, "Bier oder Wein für Leopold Mozart," *Mitteilungen der Internationalen Stiftung Mozarteum* 46, no. 1–2 (1998): 1–3.

9. On coffee as a drink for "rich and poor alike," see Spary, *Eating the Enlightenment*, 96, which one needs to take with a grain of salt, considering, as she also notes on 118, the elitist nature of the coffeehouse clientele.

10. Giovanni Battista Felici, *Parere intorno all'uso della cioccolata scritto in una lettera dal conte dottor Giovanni Battista Felici all'Illustrissima Signora Lisabetta Girolami d'Ambra* (Florence: Manni, 1728), 2–4, emphasizes the American origins of chocolate (Jamaica and Mexico), writing that the ancient Americans drank chocolate instead of wine. The Mexican origins and etymology of the word "chocolate" are exposed in Giovanni Battista Anfossi, *Dell'uso ed abuso della cioccolata: Dissertazione storico-medica del dottore Giovanni Battista Anfossi a Sua Eccellenza Pier-Vettore Pisani procurator di S. Marco* (Rovigo: Miazzi, 1775), 15. Count Megalotti describes chocolate as an "elixir from the blessed New World" and an "American julep," as cited by Camporesi, *Exotic Brew*, 73.

11. Gennaro Antonio Federico, *La serva padrona: Intermezzo in due parti*, critical edition of the libretto in *Libretti d'opera italiani dal Seicento al Novecento*, ed. Giovanna Gronda and Paolo Fabbri, 599–617 (Milan: Mondadori, 1997), 603–6.

12. Goldoni, *Il viaggiatore ridicolo*, 1, 1: "Camera in casa di don Fabrizio con varie sedie e tavolino. Don Fabrizio, Donna Emilia, il Conte a seder bevendo la cioccolata, Livietta in piedi, e Giacinto che serve. Tutti: Quanto è buono il cioccolato / Che si beve in compagnia! / La salute e l'allegria / Fa più bella in tutto il dì." Unless otherwise indicated, all the quotations of Goldoni's librettos are from Carlo Goldoni, *Drammi comici per musica*, 3 vols., ed. Silvia Urbani (Venice: Marsilio, 2007–16), available also at www.carlogoldoni.it.

13. Goldoni, *La conversazione* 1, 1; The medical benefits are also praised in Goldoni's comic opera *Il signor dottore* and in many other operas including *L'Arcadia in Brenta*, 3, 1.

14. Lorenz Lütteken, "Negating Opera through Opera: *Così fan tutte* and the Reverse of the Enlightenment," *Eighteenth-Century Music* 6, no. 2 (2009): 229–42, offers an excellent account of coffee culture of the time and on 236 discusses the denunciation of the unhealthy consumption of coffee by dalla Bona's eighteenth-century treatise *Dell'uso e dell'abuso del caffè*, claiming that Da Ponte could have read this treatise in Vienna.

15. Felici, *Parere intorno all'uso della cioccolata*, 41–42.

16. Anfossi, *Dell'uso ed abuso della cioccolata*, 17.

17. Anfossi, *Dell'uso ed abuso della cioccolata*, 27–45, direct quotation from 77–79.

18. Johann Sebastian Bach, *Schweigt stille, plaudert nicht (Kaffee-Kantate)*, BWV 211, ed. Arnold Schering (London: Eulenburg, [1925]), based on the autograph as reflected in the *Ausgabe der Bach-Gesellschaft*. The libretto is mostly by Picander (Christian Friedrich Henrici). This section and the next section of the chapter are based on my paper "Bach and Mozart at the Coffee House," presented at the joint conference of the American Bach Society and the Mozart Society of America, "Bach and Mozart: Connections, Patterns, Pathways," Stanford University, February 13–16, 2020. I am grateful to the colleagues who attended this presentation for the valuable feedback they offered.

19. Buddy Guy, "A Man and the Blues," on *A Man and the Blues*, Vanguard VSD 79272, 1968, LP, side A, track 1: "What can a poor man do / When the blues keep following him around / Get him a half pint of good liquor / And sit there and drink it all down."

20. Werner Neumann, introduction to BWV 211 in *Neue Ausgabe sämtlicher Werke* 1, 40 (Kassel: Bärenreiter, 1969), 193. Bach took a break from the Collegium Musicum from 1737 to 1739. For the dating and location of the first performance see Hans-Joachim Schulze, "Ey! Sweet the Coffee Tastes: Johann Sebastian Bach's Coffee Cantata in Its Time," special issue, *Bach: Journal of the Riemenschneider Bach Institute, Baldwin College* 32, no. 2 (2001): 20. The cantata might have been performed in the private salon of Christine Mariane von Ziegler, as Katherine Goodman maintains, where guests also drank coffee and chatted. Katherine Goodman, "From Salon to *Koffeekranz*: Gender and the *Coffee Cantata* in Bach's Leipzig," in *Bach's Changing World: Voices in the Community*, ed. Carol Baron (Rochester, NY: University of Rochester Press, 2006), 190–218. More likely it was performed in both venues, as Yearsley points out: David Yearsley, *Sex, Death, and Minuets: Anna Magdalena Bach and Her Musical Notebooks* (Chicago: University of Chicago Press, 2019), 154.

21. Hans Ulrich Gumbrecht, *Production of Presence: What Meaning Cannot Convey* (Stanford, CA: Stanford University Press, 2004), 30–31.

22. Jürgen Habermas, *The Structural Transformation of the Public Sphere: An Inquiry into a Category of Bourgeois Society*, trans. Thomas Burger (Cambridge, MA: MIT Press, 1991), 14–43.

23. As documented by Schulze, "Ey! Sweet the Coffee Tastes."

24. "Announcement of the Musical Concerts at Leipzig," in Lorenz Christoph Mizler, *Neu eröffnete musikalische Bibliothek* 1, no. 1 (Leipzig: [September] 1736), included in translation in *The New Bach Reader: A life of Johann Sebastian Bach in Letters and Documents*, ed. Hans T. David and Arthur Mendel, rev. and enl. Christoph Wolff (New York: Norton, 1998), document 187, 185–86.

25. Goodman, "From Salon to *Koffeekranz*," 190.

26. Daniel Duncan, *Von dem Missbrauch heisser und hitziger Speise und Getränke* (Leipzig: Gleditsch, 1707), frontispiece. Cited and reproduced also in Goodman, "From Salon to *Koffeekranz*," 201–2.

27. Yearsley, *Sex, Death, and Minuets*, 181–82. See also Yearsley, "Hoopskirts, Coffee, and the Changing Musical Prospects of the Bach Women," *Women and Music: A Journal of Gender and Culture* 17 (2013): 27–58.

28. Bach, "Ei, wie schmeckt der Coffee süße," on *Coffee Cantata/Peasant Cantata*,

Academy of Ancient Music, conducted by Christopher Hogwood, with Emma Kirby (soprano), Decca 4176212, 1987, compact disc, track 2; compare the same piece in Sumi Jo, *Baroque Journey: Vivaldi, Handel, Bach, Purcell*, Warner Classics 2564 69824-6, 2005, compact disc, track 6. I am grateful to the students in my Bach class at UC Davis, and especially to Jennifer Zhang for discussing the remarkable difference among different interpretations of this piece.

29. "The Well-Caffeinated Clavier," concert by the Philharmonia Baroque Orchestra and Chorale, Friday, February 7, 2020, at the Herbst Theatre, 401 Van Ness Avenue, San Francisco.

30. Lorenzo Da Ponte, *Così fan tutte, o sia La scuola degli amanti: Dramma giocoso in due atti da rappresentarsi nel Teatro di Corte* (Vienna: Società Tipografica, 1790).

31. Wolfgang Amadeus Mozart, *Così fan tutte, ossia La scuola degli amanti*, K. 588, facsimile of the autograph score at the Staatbibliothek zu Berlin–Preußischer Kulturbesitz, Biblioteka Jagiellońska Kraków (Mus. MS autogr. W. A. Mozart 588), Stadt- und Universitätsbibliothek Frankfurt am Main (Mus. Hs 2350), with introductory essays by Norbert Miller and John A. Rice (Los Altos, CA: Packard Humanities Institute, 2007), vol. 1, fol. 13.

32. Spary, *Eating the Enlightenment*, 97–98, 112–19, 143.

33. Camporesi, *Exotic Brew*, 91–95.

34. As one could expect from a Jewish man adopted by a Catholic bishop and ordained abbot: Rodney Bolt, *The Librettist of Venice: The Remarkable Life of Lorenzo da Ponte, Mozart's Poet, Casanova's Friend, and Italian Opera's Impresario in America* (New York: Bloomsbury, 2006), 4–9.

35. Da Ponte, *Così fan tutte* 1, 8: "*Despina*: Che vita maledetta / È il far la cameriera! / Dal mattino alla sera / Si fa, si suda, si lavora, e poi / Di tanto che si fa nulla è per noi. / È mezza ora che sbatto, / Il cioccolatte è fatto, ed a me tocca / Restar ad odorarlo a secca bocca? / Non è forse la mia come la vostra / O garbate signore, / Che a voi dessi l'essenza e a me l'odore? / Per Bacco vo' assaggialo: cospettaccio! / Come è buono! Vien gente (*si forbe la bocca*). / Oh ciel son le padrone: Madame, ecco la vostra colazione."

36. Pierpaolo Polzonetti, "Mesmerizing Adultery: *Così Fan Tutte* and the Kornman Scandal," *Cambridge Opera Journal* 14, no. 3 (2002): 263–96, and Polzonetti, "Mozart and the American Revolution," 220–21. On the political aspects of the Kornman mesmeric group and its role in the French Revolution, see Robert Darnton, *Mesmerism and the End of the Enlightenment in France* (Cambridge, MA: Harvard University Press, 1968), 71–80, 107–25.

37. Letter of Leopold Mozart to his son, in *Mozart Briefe und Aufzeichnungen Gesamtausgabe*, ed. Wilhelm A. Bauer, Otto Erich Deutsch, and Joseph Heinz, 7 vols. (Kassel: Bärenreiter, 1962–78), 2:413, letter no. 467.

38. Nora K. and Vittorio Hösle, *The Dead Philosophers' Café* (Notre Dame: University of Notre Dame Press, 2000).

39. "Benjamin Franklin's milk punch recipe": The photographic reproduction of the handwritten letter to James Bowdoin of Roxbury, dated October 11, 1763, and its transcription, can be read in the digital collection of the Massachusetts Historical Society (accessed June 20, 2020).

40. See chapter 7 on *Le gare generose*. For the contrast between Japan and the United States in *Madama Butterfly*, see Arthur Groos, "Madama Butterfly: The Story," *Cambridge Opera Journal* 3, no. 2 (1991): 125–98, and Ralph P. Locke, *Musical Exoticism: Images and Reflections* (Cambridge: Cambridge University Press, 2009), 202–13.

41. Luigi Illica, *Madama Butterfly*, manuscript draft of the libretto, 330. I am grateful to Arthur Groos for letting me see his own copy of this document, also published in Arthur Groos, "Luigi Illica's libretto for *Madama Butterfly* (1901)," *Studi Pucciniani* 2 (2000): 91–204; sake disappeared in the 1907 Paris revision of the libretto, where the passage was slightly modified, but appeared in the 1904 Brescia and Milan productions: Giuseppe Giacosa and Luigi Illica, *Madama Butterfly da John L. Long and David Belasco: Tragedia giapponese* (Milan: Ricordi, 1904), 21.

42. Annie J. Randall and Rosalind Gray Davis, *Puccini and the Girl: History and Reception of "The Girl of the Golden West"* (Chicago: University of Chicago Press, 2005), 145.

43. The list and description of characters and information about the historical time when the opera is set appear in the original libretto for the premiere: Carlo Zangarini, *La fanciulla del West* (*The Girl of the Golden West*) (Milan: Ricordi; New York: Colombo, 1910), [3–4]. On the blackface role of Wallace and Puccini's interest in hearing African American music to get inspiration for his song, see Randall and Davis, *Puccini and the Girl*, 16–17, 145–46, 173.

44. Beth E. Levy, *Frontier Figures: American Music and the Mythology of the American West* (Berkeley: University of California Press, 2012), 131. For a broader study of the musical characterization of the West through quotations of alleged American styles and songs, see Allan W. Atlas, "Belasco and Puccini: 'Old Dog Tray' and the Zuni Indians," *Musical Quarterly* 75, no. 3 (1991): 362–98. Besides the tunes themselves, Puccini evokes the American sound of the banjo with a special effect by placing paper between the strings of a harp: Giacomo Puccini, *La fanciulla del West* (Mineola, NY: Dover, 1997), act 1, rehearsal number (henceforth r.n.) 20: "Arpa interna: con carta inframezzata alle corde imitando il Banjo."

45. David Belasco, *The Girl of the Golden West: Novelized from the Play* (New York: Dodd, Mead, 1911), 96, 98, 100. The play also refers to "prairie oysters." On the prairie oyster cocktail in nineteenth-century America, see Linda Civitello, *Cuisine and Culture: A History of Food and People*, 2nd ed. (Hoboken, NJ: John Wiley, 2008), 227.

46. Zangarini, *La fanciulla del West*, act 2: stage description, 31–32; on 35 Minnie orders coffee. For a detailed description of the food on Minnie's table see also the original stage manuals: Jules Speck, *La fille du West: Opéra en trois actes (du drame de David Belasco) . . . Mise en scène de Monsieur Jules Speck Régisseur de la scène du Métropolitan Opéra* (Paris: Ricordi, [1910]), 41. Belasco's play presents a slightly different list of comestibles for Minnie's table 350: whiskey, charlotte "susks," "leeming" turnover, biscuit, chipped beef, sugar bowl, coffee.

47. Julian Budden, *Puccini: His Life and Works* (Oxford: Oxford University Press, 2002), 318.

48. Ellen Lockhart, "*Laggiù nel Soledad:* Indexing and Archiving the Operatic West," in *Giacomo Puccini and His World*, ed. Arman Schwartz and Emanuele Senici (Princeton, NJ: Princeton University Press, 2016), 102.

49. For a study of leitmotifs in *La fanciulla* and the labeling of this theme as the one associated with the love between Minnie and Johnson, see Tim Steinke, *Oper nach Wagner: Formale Strategien im europäischen Musiktheater des frühen 20. Jahrhunderts* (Kassel: Bärenreiter, 2011), 80.

50. As noticed also by Budden, *Puccini*, 320, as well as by Michele Girardi, *Puccini: His International Art*, trans. Laura Basini (Chicago: University of Chicago Press, 2000), 310–11.

CHAPTER NINE

1. This chapter is a substantial revision of my articles, "Feasting and Fasting in Verdi's Operas," *Studi Verdiani* 14 (1999): 69–106, and "Anorexia and Gluttony in Verdi's Operas," in *Verdi 2001: Proceedings of the International Conference, Parma, New York, New Haven, 24 January–1 February 2001*, ed. Fabrizio Della Seta, Roberta Montemorra Marvin, and Marco Marica (Florence: Olschki, 2003), 835–47; "Eating and Drinking in Opera: *Traviata* and the Callas Diet," in *Oxford Handbooks Online* [subject: Music, Musicology and Music History, Opera, Ethnomusicology], ed. Alexander Rehding (New York: Oxford University Press, 2015), www.oxfordhandbooks.com.

2. All the references to librettos' act and scene numbers are from *Tutti i libretti di Verdi*, ed. Luigi Baldacci (Milan: Garzanti, 1975), unless otherwise indicated. On the act 2 tavern scene of *La forza del destino*, see Emanuele Senici, "At the Tavern with Manzoni and Verdi: *I promessi sposi* and the Dramaturgy of *La forza del destino*," in *Music as Social and Cultural Practice: Essays in Honour of Reinhard Strohm*, ed. Melania Bucciarelli and Berta Joncus, 336–52 (Woodbridge, UK: Boydell Press, 2007).

3. On Mozart as a model for Verdian opera, see Massimo Mila, *La giovinezza di Verdi* (Turin: ERI, 1974), 26, especially on *La forza del destino*; Pierluigi Petrobelli, "Verdi and *Don Giovanni*: On the Opening Scene of *Rigoletto*," in *Music in the Theater: Essays on Verdi and Other Composers*, with translations by Roger Parker (Princeton, NJ: Princeton University Press, 1994), 34–47; James Webster, "To Understand Verdi and Wagner We Must Understand Mozart," *19th-Century Music* 11, no. 2 (1987): 175–93.

4. Arthur Pougin, *Giuseppe Verdi: Vita aneddotica di Arturo Pougin con note ed aggiunte di Folchetto, illustrazioni di Achille Formis* (Milan: Ricordi, 1881), 102, n. 1. See also Pierpaolo Polzonetti, "Lavigna, Vincenzo," in *The Cambridge Verdi Encyclopedia*, ed. Roberta Montemorra Marvin (Cambridge: Cambridge University Press, 2013), 234–35.

5. Julie Kavanagh, *The Girl Who Loved Camellias: The Life and Legend of Marie Duplessis* (New York: Knopf, 2013); Emilio Sala, *The Sounds of Paris in Verdi's "Traviata,"* trans. Delia Casadei (Cambridge: Cambridge University Press, 2008), 59–61, provides evidence that Verdi became familiar with Dumas's play and its music while in Paris. Dumas's play was also performed in Venice right before the premiere of *Traviata* in the same city.

6. Louis Huart, *Psychologie de la grisette* (Brussels: Aubert and Moens, 1841), 33–34.

7. Marcello Conati, *La bottega della musica: Verdi e La Fenice* (Milan: Saggiatore, 1983), 290–92, presents a transcription of the contract signed by the president of the Gran Teatro La Fenice, Carlo Marzari, in May 1852. On this contract see also the foreword to the critical edition of Giuseppe Verdi, "*La Traviata*: melodramma in tre atti," in *The Works*

of Giuseppe Verdi 1/19, ed. Fabrizio Della Seta (Chicago: University of Chicago Press; Milan: Ricordi, 1997), xii. All subsequent references to the score are from this edition unless otherwise indicated. The circumstances of the commission of *Traviata* are summarized by Julian Budden, *The Operas of Verdi*, rev. ed., 3 vols. (Oxford: Clarendon Press, 1992), 2:115.

8. *"I baccanali di Roma": Dramma lirico in quattro atti, musica del Maestro Carlo Romani da rappresentarsi . . . la Quaresima 1854* (Florence: Galletti, 1854), 1, 4, page 10.

9. Verdi, *La traviata*, no. 9, "Baccanale," 340–41: "Non si spaventino i bassi di questo La: non và cantato ma scivolato come fanno gli stromenti."

10. Francesco Maria Piave to Brenna, S. Agata, October 29, 1852, in Conati, *Bottega*, 302.

11. Varesi to Brenna, Ascoli, November 10, 1852, in Conati, *Bottega*, 303.

12. On Lenten opera see Anthony R. DelDonna, *Opera, Theatrical Culture and Society in Late Eighteenth-Century Naples* (Burlington, VT: Ashgate, 2012), chap. 5, "*Debora and Sisara* and the Rise of Lenten Tragedy," 147–92.

13. Alexandre Dumas fils, *La dame aux camélias*, trans. David Coward (Oxford: Oxford University Press, 1986), chap. 3, 17. In a review of Dumas's play, a journalist called the protagonist a "sainte pécheresse" (saint sinner): Jules Lovoy's review of plays at the Théâtres de Vaudevilles, *Le Ménestrel*, Sunday, May 30, 1852, cited in Sala, *Sounds of Paris*, 59. Linda Hutcheon and Michael Hutcheon describe Violetta as "the disembodied, spiritualized woman [who] manages to be sinner and saint in one" in their book, *Opera: Desire, Disease, Death* (Lincoln: University of Nebraska Press, 1996), 43. A thoughtful study of the Christian message in Dumas's *La dame* and Verdi's *Traviata* is offered by Guido Paduano, "La signora delle camelie, il Moloch e il Vangelo," *Rivista di letterature moderne e comparate* 65, no. 3 (2012): 301–23.

14. Lévi-Strauss, *Raw and the Cooked*, 184–86, 188, 192–91. The analysis of *Traviata* in relation to Violetta's consumptive disease has been the object of important studies by Arthur Groos, "'TB sheets': Love and Disease in *La Traviata*," *Cambridge Opera Journal* 7, no. 3 (1995): 233–60, as well as Hutcheon and Hutcheon, *Opera*, 229–51.

15. Dumas fils, *La dame aux camélias*, chap. 7, 45–46; chap. 8, 52.

16. Dumas fils, *Dame aux camélias*, chap. 9, 64.

17. Dumas fils, *Dame aux camélias*, chap. 6, 37–38.

18. Giuseppe Verdi, *"La Traviata": Autograph Sketches and Drafts*, ed. Fabrizio Della Seta, with facsimile reproductions of the sketches (Parma: Istituto nazionale di studi verdiani, 2000), 105: "cena da Margherita," as Violetta was originally named, after Dumas's Marguerite.

19. Sala, *Sounds of Paris*, 71. On the identification of the opening music as a polka see Fabrizio Della Seta, "Il tempo della festa: Su due scene della *Traviata* e su altri luoghi verdiani," *Studi Verdiani* 2 (1983): 112.

20. Huart, *Psychologie de la grisette*, 6–9.

21. George Armelagos and Peter Farb, *Consuming Passions: The Anthropology of Eating* (Boston: Houghton Mifflin, 1980), 4.

22. Piave, *Traviata*, 1, 2: "They sit down in such a way that Violetta is between Alfredo and Gastone; opposite to her sits Flora, between the Marquis and the Baron; the others sit

as they please. There is a moment of silence while they pass around the plates; Violetta and Gastone speak softly between themselves."

23. Gian-Paolo Biasin, *The Flavors of Modernity: Food and the Novel* (Princeton, NJ: Princeton University Press, 1993), 3.

24. [Jean-Baptiste] Éd[ouard] Montaubry, *La dame aux camélias! Ronde . . . , paroles de M. Alexandre Dumas fils, musique d'Ed. Montaubry* (Paris: Leduc, [1852]), frontispiece. On this printed music sheet see also Sala, *Sounds of Paris*, 113–27.

25. *Illustrated London News*, May 31, 1856, 588–89. The image is based on a print by Colombari representing Piccolomini as Violetta in Siena, 1856: Bibliothèque nationale de France, Département de la musique, Est. Piccolomini M.003.

26. Pierpaolo Polzonetti, "Brindisi," in *The Cambridge Verdi Encyclopedia*, ed. Roberta Montemorra Marvin (Cambridge: Cambridge University Press, 2013), 72; Mila De Santis, "'Triste come une chanson à boire': Ripensando al Brindisi de *La traviata*," *Studi Verdiani* 23 (2012–13): 45–70.

27. Loose manuscript sheets attached to Francesco Maria Piave, *"La traviata": Libretto con note della censura*, Milan, Milano biblioteca nazionale Braidense, Archivio Ricordi, LIBRo 1806.

28. Verdi to Vincenzo Luccardi, Paris, no date but allegedly written after September 8, 1854, in Laura Genesio, ed., *Carteggio Verdi-Luccardi* (Parma: Istituto nazionale di studi verdiani, 2008), no. 42, 91–92.

29. As noted also by Budden, *Operas of Verdi*, 2:131.

30. Armelagos and Farb, *Consuming Passions*, 4.

31. Giuseppe Verdi, "*Rigoletto*: Melodramma in tre atti di Francesco Maria Piave," in *The Works of Giuseppe Verdi* 1/17, ed. Martin Chusid (Chicago: University of Chicago Press; Milan: Ricordi, 1983), no. 2, Introduzione, 8.

32. Here I am referring to the 1865 revision. I consulted the critical edition of the score, Giuseppe Verdi, "*Macbeth*: Melodramma in quattro atti, libretto di Francesco Maria Piave and Andrea Maffei" (Paris 1865 version; Florence 1847 version in appendix), in *The Works of Giuseppe Verdi* 1/10, ed. David Lawton (Chicago: University of Chicago Press, 2005). For a discussion on the 1847 version and its revision of the banquet scene, see the essays by Gary Tomlinson, Ursula Gunther, Francesco Degrada, and John Knowles in *Verdi's "Macbeth": A Sourcebook*, ed. David Rosen and Andrew Porter (New York: Norton, 1984).

33. Giuseppe Verdi, "*I masnadieri*: Melodramma in Quattro atti, libretto di Andrea Maffei," in *The Works of Giuseppe Verdi* 1/11, ed. Roberta Montemorra Marvin (Chicago: University of Chicago Press; Milan: Ricordi, 2000), act 2, no. 6, scena ed aria Amalia.

34. In addition to the libretto in the Baldacci edition cited above, I consulted Giuseppe Verdi, *"Il finto Stanislao" ("Un giorno di regno"), melodramma giocoso in 2 atti di Felice Romani, opera completa per canto e pianoforte* (Milan: Ricordi, 1951), act 1, introduzione.

35. In the wedding scene there is no mention of food in the Italian or the French libretto. For the latter, which I refer to hereafter, I consulted Augustin Eugène Scribe and Charles Duveyrier, *Les vêpres siciliennes: Opera en cinq actes, paroles de MM. E. Scribe et Ch. Duveyrier, musique de M. Verdi, divertissements de M. L. Pétipa. Répresenté pour la première fois à Paris, sur le théâtre de l'Académie impériale de musique, le 13 juin 1855* (Paris: Michel Lévy Frères and Libraires-Éditeurs, 1855), 28. The Italian libretto is included

in Baldacci, *Tutti i libretti di Verdi*. I will refer here to the original French version of the opera.

36. Giuseppe Verdi, *Les vêpres siciliennes: Grand opéra en 5 actes*, vocal score (Paris: Léon Escudier; Milan: Ricordi, [1856]), act 2, no. 6, "Tarantelle et scéne [Robert, Procida, Thibault]: "Voilà, par Saint Denis," 123–26. On the use of exotic style in France and Italy at about this time in history, see Ralph P. Locke, *Musical Exoticism: Images and Reflections* (Cambridge: Cambridge University Press, 2009), chap. 7 on representation of gypsies in Verdi's *Il trovatore* and Bizet's *Carmen*.

37. Vincent Giroud, *French Opera: A Short History* (New Haven, CT: Yale University Press, 2010), 168. Budden, *Operas of Verdi*, 2:169–76. Here Giroud also discusses Scribe's negative description of the Sicilians as "furious, outraged and vindictive" (cited on 174).

38. I follow the scene numbers in the Baldacci edition of Verdi's librettos (cited above). For the score I consulted Giuseppe Verdi, "*Un ballo in maschera" in full score* (Mineola, NY: Dover, 1996), act 3, "The Masked Ball, Chorus [and Canzone]." The opera was set in Boston after four previously considered locations proved unattainable, mostly for problems with censorship, as documented by David Rosen, "A Tale of Five Cities: The Peregrinations of Somma's and Verdi's *Gustavo III* (and *Una vendetta in dominò* and *Un ballo in maschera*) at the hands of the Neapolitan and Roman censorship," *Verdi Forum* 26–27 (1999): 53–66. See also Philip Gossett, *Divas and Scholars: Performing Italian Opera* (Chicago: University of Chicago Press, 2006), 493–513.

39. David Rosen, "Meter and Testosterone: Preliminary Observations about Meter and Gender in Verdi's Operas," in *Una piacente estate di San Martino: Studi e ricerche per Marcello Conati*, ed. Marco Capra, 179–213 (Lucca: LIM, 2000), 190.

40. Budden, *Operas of Verdi*, 2:192.

41. Louis Palianti, *Les vêpres siciliennes: Opéra en cinq actes, paroles de MM. E. Scribe et Ch. Duveyrier, musique de M. Verdi, représenté pour la première fois à Paris sur le Théâtre impérial de l'opéra, le 13 juin 1855.* Collection de mises en scènes rédigées et publiées par M. L. Palianti (Paris: Brière, 1855), 3. The facsimile of this stage manual is available in Robert Cohen, ed., *The Original Staging Manuals for Twelve Parisian Operatic Premières* (Stuyvesant, NY: Pendragon Press, 1991), [263–82].

42. Giuseppe Verdi, "*Alzira*: Tragedia lirica in tre atti di Salvadore Cammarano," in *The Works of Giuseppe Verdi* 1/8, ed. Stefano Castelvecchi (Chicago: University of Chicago Press; Milan: Ricordi, 1994), 2:1: "Mesci, mesci . . .—Vittoria! . . . Vittoria! . . . (*toccando i bicchieri*) / Al Sovrano!—Alla Spagna!—Alla gloria! / Del trionfo la gioria succede / Alle pugne, alle stragi, al furor. / Bevi, bevi . . . È dovuta mercede / Vino ibero ad ibero valor."

43. *Alzira*, no. 8.

44. On the use of the term *cimbasso* in Verdi's operas, see Renato Meucci, "Cimbasso," *Grove Music Online*, 2011, accessed January 16, 2021.

45. Giuseppe Verdi, "*Attila*, dramma lirico in un prologo e tre atti, libretto di Temistocle Solera e Francesco Maria Piave," in *The Works of Giuseppe Verdi* 1/9, ed. Helen Greenwald (Chicago: University of Chicago Press; Milan: Ricordi, 2013), no. 11, "finale secondo."

46. Verdi, *I masnadieri*, no. 10, "Coro di masnadieri."

47. Verdi, *I masnadieri*, no. 2, "Scena ed Aria [di] Carlo."

48. Giuseppe Verdi, "*Ernani:* Dramma lirico in quattro atti di Francesco Maria Piave," in *The Works of Giuseppe Verdi* 1/5, ed. Claudio Gallico (Chicago: University of Chicago Press; Milan: Ricordi, 1985), no. 1, "introduzione."

49. Verdi, *Ernani*, no. 2, "Recitativo e cavatina: Ernani."

50. Giuseppe Verdi, "*Il corsaro*: [melodramma tragico in tre atti] libretto di Francesco Maria Piave," in *The Works of Giuseppe Verdi* 1/13, ed. Elizabeth Hudson (Chicago: University of Chicago Press; Milan: Ricordi, 1998), no. 2, "Coro, scena ed aria Corrado," 15. The indication "coro interno de' corsari senza orchestra" appears in the autograph score; the rest of the stage indications come from the libretto.

51. Giulio Ricordi, ed., *Disposizione scenica per l'opera "Otello," dramma lirico in quattro atti, versi di Arrigo Boito, musica di Giuseppe Verdi, compilata e regolata secondo la messa in scena del Teatro alla scala da Giulio Ricordi* (Milan: Ricordi, [1891]), 10 (list of props for the scene), 21–26 (drinking scene).

52. Verdi, *Otello in Full Score* (New York: Dover, 1986), first act, "Drinking Song: Roderigo beviam!"

53. Ricordi, *Disposizione scenica*, 27: "Tutta questa scena di Cassio è difficilissima, perché l'attore deve studiarsi di non passare una giusta misura, onde non cadere in una indecente parodia dell'uomo ubbriaco: non deve dimenticare che Cassio è un ufficiale elegante."

54. Joan Jacobs Brumberg, *Fasting Girls: The History of Anorexia Nervosa* (New York: Vintage Books, 2000), 7.

55. Emanuele Senici, *Landscape and Gender in Italian Opera: The Alpine Virgin from Bellini to Puccini* (Cambridge: Cambridge University Press, 2005), 107; see also chapter 4 on *Luisa Miller.*

56. Rudolph Bell, *Holy Anorexia* (Chicago: University of Chicago Press, 1985), 1–21, 41–60. Bell's conflation of *anorexia mirabilis* and *anorexia nervosa* has been criticized by Caroline Walker Bynum, *Holy Feast and Holy Fast: The Religious Significance of Food in Medieval Women* (Berkeley: University of California Press, 1987), 4–5, 194–207, and also by Brumberg, *Fasting Girls*, 44–45.

57. Bell, *Holy Anorexia*, 19, 84, 116; on unrequited love as a cause of holy anorexia see 4. Bell uses psychoanalytic theory to interpret the behavior of anorexic female saints such as Saint Margherita da Cortona (92–102), to mention perhaps the most extreme case.

58. Brumberg, *Fasting Girls*, 47.

59. Giuseppe Verdi, "*Luisa Miller*: Melodramma tragico in tre atti di Salvatore Cammarano," in *The Works of Giuseppe Verdi* 1/15, ed. Jeffrey Kallberg (Chicago: University of Chicago Press; Milan: Ricordi, 1992), Atto Terzo (Veleno), no. 12, scena e coro. The score (370) includes the same stage indications as the libretto.

60. As noted also by Budden, *Operas of Verdi*, 1:440.

61. On oaths in Verdi see Pierpaolo Polzonetti, "Giuramento," in *The Cambridge Verdi Encyclopedia*. On the operatic style of setting accented syllables with long notes see Polzonetti, "The 'Quantitative Style' in Seventeenth-Century Italian Opera," in *Pensieri*

per un maestro: Studi in onore di Pierluigi Petrobelli, ed. Stefano Lavia and Roger Parker, 95–114 (Turin: EDT, 2002).

62. Verdi to Monaldi, March 12, 1890, cited in Budden, *Operas of Verdi*, 3:417.

63. Peter N. Stearns, *Fat History: Bodies and Beauty in the Modern West*, with a new preface (1997; repr. New York: New York University Press, 2002), xviii.

64. Michael Cooper, "A Plus-Size Falstaff Grows into His Outsize Part," *New York Times*, December 4, 2013. Maestri shares his thoughts on food and opera in the short documentary, *Opera and Food*, revolving around a dinner he and Lidia Bastianich prepared at Eataly in New York City. This event was held at Eataly Flatiron on March 2, 2016, and was called "An Evening with Lidia Bastianich and Ambrogio Maestri." It was aired on NYC Life (channel 25) and is currently available on You Tube. I am grateful to Stacy Stout, education and events manager of Eataly NYC Flatiron, for the information.

65. Biasin, *Flavors of Modernity*, 16–20.

66. Giuseppe Verdi, *Falstaff: Commedia lirica in tre atti, libretto di Arrigo Boito, prima rappresentazione Milano, Teatro alla Scala, 9 febbraio 1893, partitura*, new and rev. ed. (1983; repr. Milan: Ricordi, 1959); reprinted also as Verdi, *Falstaff in Full Score* (Mineola, NY: Dover, 2014), act 3, pt. 1, rehearsal number 6.

67. Roger Parker, *Leonora's Last Act: Essays in Verdian Discourse* (Princeton, NJ: Princeton University Press, 1997), 106.

68. Bakhtin, *Rabelais and His World*, 24–26 (grotesque body), 339 (quoted passage).

69. Pete Nowlen, *Keys to Transposition: A Method of the Teaching and Learning of Transposition on the Horn* (Ithaca, NY: Ensemble, 2018), 3–4. For the use of the hand-stopping technique in nineteenth-century valve horns, see David R. Sprung, "'Hidden' Stopped Notes in 19th-Century French Opera," *Horn Call* 26, no. 3 (1996): 17–25.

70. On this passage see also the insightful analytical observations by James Hepokoski, *Giuseppe Verdi: "Falstaff"* (Cambridge: Cambridge University Press, 1995), 95.

71. Abigail C. Saguy, *What's Wrong with Fat?* (Oxford: Oxford University Press, 2013), 40.

72. Ken Albala, "Weight Loss in the Age of Reason," in *Cultures of the Abdomen: Diet, Digestion, and Fat in the Modern World*, ed. Christopher E. Forth and Ana Carden-Coyne, 169–264 (New York: Palgrave Macmillan, 2005), 170.

73. William of Tocco, *Hystoria beati Thomae*, cited in James A. Weisheipl, *Friar Thomas D'Aquino: His Life, Thought, and Work* (Garden City, NY: Doubleday, 1974), 44. Aquinas is often represented in iconography as a fat man, as in Carlo Crivelli's fifteenth-century portrait of the saint in the Demidoff Altarpiece, now at the London National Gallery.

74. Stearns, *Fat History*, 63–65.

75. Jackie Wykes, "Introduction: Why Queering Fat Embodiment?," in *Queering Fat Embodiment*, ed. Cat Pausé, Jackie Wykes, and Samantha Murray, 1–12 (Burlington, VT: Ashgate, 2014). Marilyn Wann is the author of an influential book in fat activism, *Fat! So? Because You Don't Have to Apologize for Your Size!* (Berkeley, CA: Ten Speed Press, 1998). See Saguy, *What's Wrong with Fat?*, 164–65.

76. Frye, *Anatomy of Criticism*, 164.

77. Bakhtin, *Rabelais and His World*, 338.

CHAPTER TEN

1. Vanessa Thorpe, "It's All Over for Fat Lady Singers as Slimline Divas Triumph: Opera's New Breed of Slight, Scantily Clad Sopranos Take the Plaudits at the Salzburg Festival," *Observer*, August 15, 2009. For a cultural study of the perception of the fat operatic diva (Deborah Voigt, Maria Callas, and other divas) see Serena Guarracino, "'It's Not Over till the Fat Lady Sings': The Weight of the Opera Diva," in *Historicizing Fat in Anglo-American Culture*, ed. Elena Levy-Navarro (Columbus: Ohio University Press, 2010), 192–212. This chapter is based on my essay "Eating and Drinking in Opera: *Traviata* and the Callas Diet," in *Oxford Handbooks Online* [subject: Music, Musicology and Music History, Opera, Ethnomusicology], ed. Alexander Rehding (New York: Oxford University Press, online publication date August 2015): www.oxfordhandbooks.com.

2. Alexandre Dumas fils, *La dame aux camélias*, trans. David Coward (Oxford: Oxford University Press, 1986), 8. For studies of the consumptive heroines in *Traviata* and Puccini's *Bohème* that consider the medical conditions and symptoms of tuberculosis (TB), see Arthur Groos's three essays: "'TB Sheets': Love and Disease in *La Traviata*," *Cambridge Opera Journal* 7, no. 3 (1995): 233–60; "TB, Mimì, and the Anxiety of Influence," *Studi Pucciniani* 1 (1998): 67–81; and "From *Addio del passato* to *Le patate son fredde*: Representations of Consumption in Leoncavallo's *I Medici* and *La bohème*," in *Letteratura, musica e teatro al tempo di Ruggero Leoncavallo*, ed. Jürgen Maehder and Lorenza Guiot, 57–74 (Milan: Sonzogno, 1995). The theme has also been explored by Linda Hutcheon and Michael Hutcheon, *Opera: Desire, Disease, Death* (Lincoln: University of Nebraska Press, 1996), esp. chap. 2, 29–60.

3. Jacopo Ferretti, "*La Cenerentola, ossia La bontà in trionfo, drama giocoso . . .*" da rappresentarsi al Teatro Valle degl'Illustrissimi Signori Capranica nel Carnevale dell'anno 1817, con musica del Maestro Gioacchino Rossini Pesarese (Rome: Puccinelli, 1817), 2, 8.

4. Peter N. Stearns, *Fat History: Bodies and Beauty in the Modern West* (1997; repr. New York: New York University Press, 2002), 84 (quotation about Disney). See also Kim Chernin, *Womansize: The Tyranny of Slenderness* (London: Women's Press, 1981), 106, in which Chernin claims that a woman suffers in order to adapt her body to cultural expectations. Naomi Wolf's *The Beauty Myth: How Images of Beauty Are Used against Women* (New York: Anchor Books, 1992), and Susan Bordo, *Unbearable Weight: Feminism, Western Culture, and the Body* (Berkeley: University of California Press, 2003), 185–212, conceptualize gender differences in the present cult of slenderness. For a similar take, see Susie Orbach, *Fat Is a Feminist Issue II* (New York: Berkeley, 1982), 27–28.

5. Linda Hutcheon and Michael Hutcheon, *Bodily Charm: Living Opera* (Lincoln: University of Nebraska Press, 2000), 148.

6. Verdi to Luccardi, Venezia, March 9, 1853 (letter no. 30), and Verdi to Luccardi, Busseto, June 7, 1853 (letter no. 32), in *Carteggio Verdi-Luccardi*, ed. Laura Genesio (Parma: Istituto nazionale di Studi Verdiani, 2008), 82–83. Julian Budden, *The Operas of Verdi*, rev. ed., 3 vols. (Oxford: Clarendon Press, 1992), 2:123. Marcello Conati, *La bottega della musica: Verdi e La Fenice* (Milan: Saggiatore, 1983), 325–27.

7. Tommaso Locatelli, "Gran Teatro La Fenice: *La Traviata*," *Gazzetta di Venezia*, March 7, 1853, in Tommaso Locatelli, *Appendice della gazzetta di Venezia: Prose scelte di*

Tommaso Locatelli, vol. 10 (Venezia: Tipografia della gazzetta, 1874), s.v. "Spettacoli," chap. 36, 288–99.

8. *Gazzetta musicale di Milano*, no. 11 (March 13, 1853): 47–48, reproduced in *Carteggio Verdi-Luccardi*, 281–82.

9. Albert Lavignac, *Encyclopédie de la musique et dictionnaire du conservatoire*, dir. Albert Lavignac, première partie: "Histoire de la musique," vol. 2, "Italie–Allemagne" (Paris: Delagrave, 1914), 888.

10. Joan Jacobs Brumberg, *Fasting Girls: The History of Anorexia Nervosa*, rev. ed. (New York: Vintage Books, 2000), 242–43.

11. Esther D. Rothblum and Sondra Solovay, eds., *The Fat Studies Reader* (New York: New York University Press, 2009).

12. Brumberg, *Fasting Girls*, 228–67.

13. Arianna Stassinopoulos, *Maria Callas: The Woman behind the Legend* (New York: Simon and Schuster, 1981), 56. We know of Callas's autobiographical sketch from Giovanni Battista Meneghini, *My Wife Maria Callas*, written in collaboration with Renzo Allegri, trans. Henry Wisneski (New York: Farrar, Straus and Giroux, 1982), 105.

14. Renzo Allegri and Roberto Allegri, *Callas by Callas: Gli scritti segreti dell'artista più grande* (Milan: Mondadori, 1997), 41.

15. Maria Callas et al., "Per la prima volta Maria Callas narra la sua vita," [part I] *Oggi* 13, no. 3, January 17, 1957: 14–17. This corresponds to the memoir published in French translation (without disclosing its source) by Tom Volf, *Maria Callas: Lettres et mémoires* (Paris: Albin Michel, 2019), 35. Maria Callas's height as detailed on her ID card, issued on June 9, 1949, by the City Hall of Zevio, was 1.73 m (5′6″). The ID is preserved in the Centro Studi Callassiano in the Academia Maria Callas of Zevio, folder G51/1.

16. Stephen Gundle, *Bellissima: Feminine Beauty and the Idea of Italy* (New Haven, CT: Yale University Press, 2007); Piero Meldini, *Sposa e madre esemplare: Ideologia e politica della donna e della famiglia durante il fascismo* (Florence: Guaraldi, 1975); Gigliola Gori, *Italian Fascism and the Female Body: Sport, Submissive Women, and Strong Mothers* (New York: Routledge, 2004).

17. Nina Sun Eidsheim, "Maria Callas's Waistline and the Organology of Voice," *Opera Quarterly* 33, nos. 3–4 (2017): 249, 252.

18. Mary Douglas, *Natural Symbols: Explorations in Cosmology* (New York: Routledge, 1996), 69.

19. Ovid, *Metamorphoses* 1.1–4.

20. Ovid, *Metamorphoses* 3.345–98.

21. Elvira de Hidalgo, "La mia allieva Maria Callas, come la ricordo da ragazza," *Oggi* 15, no. 40 (October 1, 1959): 23–24.

22. Stassinopoulos, *Maria Callas*, 10; emphasis added.

23. Meneghini, *My Wife Maria Callas*, 208–9. This book was first published in Italian as *Maria Callas mia moglie* (Milan: Rusconi, 1981).

24. Meneghini, *My Wife Maria Callas*, 208–9.

25. Joseph Roach, *It* (Ann Arbor: University of Michigan Press, 2007), 16–21, 36–40. The secular sacrality of Callas is suggested by the title of the diva's voluminous biography

by Stelios Galatopoulos, *Maria Callas: Sacred Monster* (New York: Simon and Schuster, 1998).

26. Hutcheon and Hutcheon, *Bodily Charm*, 120.

27. Giovanna Lomazzi, interviewed by Marco Cuggiari, "La mia amica Maria Callas," *Corriere di Como*, December 10, 2013.

28. Stassinopoulos, *Maria Callas*, 141–42.

29. Michael Scott, *Maria Meneghini Callas* (Boston: Northeastern University Press, 1991), 106, 128. Items of Callas's wardrobe, including some of Biki's creations, can be seen in the catalog of the 2000 Paris auction of objects from the collections of Laurence Calmels, Frédéric Chambre, and Cyrille Cohen, eds., *Maria Callas: Souvenirs d'une légende; Vente aux enchères publiques des objets personnels de Maria Callas et de ses archives (correspondances, photographies, coupures de presse, rassemblées et conservées par la diva)* (Paris: Calmels, Chambre, Cohen, 2000). In 2012 I visited an impressive collection from Callas's personal wardrobe, including dresses by Biki, which was then preserved at the Centro Studi Callassiano in the Academia Maria Callas of Zevio.

30. Lévi-Strauss, *Raw and the Cooked*, 1.

31. "Love and Money," *Time*, 74, no. 12, September 21, 1959.

32. Meneghini, *My Wife Maria Callas*, 301.

33. Meneghini, *My Wife Maria Callas*, 14–15.

34. Callas, "Per la prima volta Maria Callas narra la sua vita," 14–17. See the comparable biographical sketch published in *Life*, April 20, 1959.

35. Meneghini, *My Wife Maria Callas*, 105. On the story of the dietetic pasta, see 217–19.

36. I am grateful to Renzo Allegri for informing me about Callas's document, in his possession, about her diet, which is allegedly consistent with Meneghini's description. The influence of Biki in Callas's decision to lose weight is confirmed, among other sources, by Giovanna Lomazzi in the interview cited above.

37. The letter is dated Buenos Aires, July 3, 1949, transcribed in Renzo Allegri and Maria Callas, *Maria Callas: Lettere d'amore*, ed. and transcribed by Renzo Allegri (Milan: Mondadori, 2008), 123, 140–41. Maria Caniglia was a heavy soprano twenty years older than Callas. She had been a successful interpreter of Violetta in spite of her size. One can still hear the ovation at the end of her live recording of *Traviata* at Covent Garden in London in 1939: Giuseppe Verdi, *La traviata*, with Beniamino Gigli and Maria Caniglia, Camden Victor 2EA7908-II, June 4, 1939, 78 rpm.

38. Associazione Culturale Maria Callas, *La divina in cucina: Il ricettario segreto di Maria Callas*, ed. Bruno Tosi (Milan: Trenta, 2006), 102. The autograph is reproduced in facsimile.

39. Meneghini, *My Wife Maria Callas*, 106.

40. Meneghini, *My Wife Maria Callas*, 106.

41. Giuseppina Cazzarolli Meneghini to Maria Callas, letter with no date, Zevio, Centro Studi Callassiano in the Academia Maria Callas of Zevio, loose document marked as C/223-1.

42. Uncataloged material in the Centro Studi Callassiano in the Academia Maria Callas of Zevio.

43. "Questionario," uncataloged document in the Centro Studi Callassiano in the Academia Maria Callas of Zevio.

44. Giovanna Lomazzi's personal communication to the Callas archivist and collector Stefano Castellani, whom I thank for the information.

45. I am grateful to Gianluca Brigo for passing me this personal communication on June 11, 2014.

46. Paolo Poli, "Un'artista misteriosa e sconvolta," memoir ed. Jacopo Pellegrini on February 2, 2016, in *Mille e una Callas: Voci e studi*, ed. Luca Aversano and Jacopo Pellegrini (Macerata: Quodlibet, 2016), 368.

47. Interview of Maria Callas by Derek Prouse in the *Sunday Times*, March 19, 1961, cited in Stassinopoulos, *Maria Callas*, 116.

48. Scott, *Maria Meneghini Callas*, 116–17, 124–25; Henry Bacon, *Visconti: Explorations of Beauty and Decay* (Cambridge: Cambridge University Press, 1998), 263.

49. I am indebted to Emanuele Senici for these thoughts on Pasolini's perceptions of Maria Callas. An impressive number of journalistic and critical reports on this controversial film are recorded in Laura Ceccarelli and Marina Cipriani, *Medea di Pasolini: Cronache del tempo e ricordi dei protagonisti* (Rome: Centro Sperimentale di Cinematografia, 2006). Three more essays on Callas's Medea, from Cherubini to Pasolini, are in Aversano and Pellegrini, *Mille e una Callas*.

50. Wayne Koestenbaum, "Callas and Her Fans," *Yale Review* 79, no. 1 (1989): 10–12.

51. Scott, *Maria Meneghini Callas*, 10.

52. Evangelia Callas, *My Daughter Maria Callas*, written in collaboration with Lawrence G. Blochman (New York: Fleet, 1960).

53. The whole affair is recounted in great detail by Nicholas Gage, *Greek Fire: The Story of Maria Callas and Aristotle Onassis* (New York: Knopf, 2000).

54. This information is from the book containing the audio recording of Giuseppe Verdi, *La Traviata*, with Maria Callas (Violetta Valery), Gianni Raimondi (Alfredo Germont), Aldo Protti (Giorgio Germont), conducted by Carlo Maria Giulini, recorded on January 19, 1956, issued in the series La Scala Memories, vol. 3, Skira Classica, 2010.

55. Maria Callas, "Maria Callas narra la sua vita," 34–36. Here Callas accuses Di Stefano of never showing up on time at rehearsals and behaving like a prima donna. See also Scott, *Maria Meneghini Callas*, 153–15, 257–63.

56. Scott, *Maria Meneghini Callas*, 263–66.

57. Kavanagh, *The Girl Who Loved Camelias*, 9.

58. Carlo Maria Giulini's recollection, quoted in Caterina d'Amico de Carvalho, ed., *Viscontiana: Luchino Visconti e il melodramma verdiano* (Milan: Mazzotta, 2001), 58: "Visconti aveva questa grande capacità di suggerire dei pensieri che un'attrice intelligente come la Callas assorbiva e faceva suoi. In queste tre settimane di lavoro si è creato il personaggio di Violetta: La Callas è diventata Violetta"; emphasis added. A list of rehearsal dates is annotated in pencil by Visconti: Rome, Fondazione Gramsci, Archivio Visconti, ser. 2, U.A. 3.3. All cast members were required to attend rehearsals daily from May 16 to May 26, whereas before then rehearsals were sparser. Presumably rehearsals with Callas took place in early May.

59. Visconti to Battista Meneghini, August 13, 1956, in Allegri and Callas, *Maria Callas: Lettere d'amore*, 178.

60. Elvio Giudici, *Il teatro di Verdi in scena e in DVD* (Milan: Saggiatore, 2012), 413–17. Similarly, Fedele d'Amico describes Callas's style of recitation in Visconti's production of *Traviata* as influenced by silent film; see his essay "Luchino Visconti e l'opera," in *Viscontiana*, 17.

61. Teodoro Celli, "Violetta è morta in cappotto e cappello: Più Visconti che Verdi la *Traviata* della Callas," *Corriere Lombardo*, May 31, 1955, cited in Caterina d'Amico Carvalho and Renzo Renzi, eds., *Luchino Visconti: Il mio teatro*, 2 vols. (Bologna: Cappelli, 1979), 1:56–59.

62. Sandro Bernardi, "*La terra trema*: Il mito, il teatro, la storia," in *Il cinema di Luchino Visconti*, ed. Veronica Pravadelli (Venice: Marsilio, 2000), 65–88.

63. Harriet Boyd-Bennett, *Opera in Postwar Venice: Cultural Politics and the Avant-Garde* (Cambridge: Cambridge University Press, 2018), chap. 2, "*A futura memoria:* Verdi's *Attila*, 1951," 64.

64. Boyd-Bennett, *Opera in Postwar Venice*, direct quotations on 65, 69.

65. Boyd-Bennett, *Opera in Postwar Venice*, quotations on 73; see also 83–84 on Verdi in the mass media and as part of the "democratization of taste" framed in the highly polarized political discourse (progressives vs. conservatives).

66. Rubens Tedeschi, "*La traviata* torna giovane con la regia di Luchino Visconti," *L'Unità*, May 28, 1955, 3.

67. Tedeschi, "*La traviata*," 3.

68. Lawrence Schifano, *Luchino Visconti: The Flames of Passion*, trans. William S. Byron (London: Collins, 1990), 1–60; Lino Micciché, *Luchino Visconti: Un profilo critico* (Venice: Marsilio, 1996), 3–6; Pierpaolo Polzonetti, "*Ossessione*: Visconti's Obsession with Verdi," *Italian Journal* 20, no. 10 (2014): 22–25.

69. Erio Piccagliani, stage photograph of Visconti's production of *Traviata*, act 1 (dated May 28, 1955), brindisi. Rome, Archivio Visconti, ser. 2, U.A. 3/41.

70. Meneghini, *My Wife Maria Callas*, 179–82, 205.

71. Giuseppe Verdi, *La traviata*, with Teresa Stratas as Violetta and Placido Domingo as Alfredo, directed by Franco Zeffirelli; film version produced in 1982, Universal 20326, 1999, DVD.

72. On the dialectics between composer's persona and vocal persona I loosely refer to Edward T. Cone, "Some Thoughts on 'Erlkönig,'" in *The Composer's Voice* (Berkeley: University of California Press, 1974), 18. Cone also offers insights on Verdi's failed attempts at creating realistic effects for Violetta's and Alfredo's presence in *La traviata*: see Cone, "The World of Opera and Its Inhabitants," in *Music: A View from Delft; Selected Essays*, ed. Robert P. Morgan (Chicago: University of Chicago Press, 1989), 126–29.

73. Luca Aversano, "Norma sacerdotessa infedele," in *Mille e una Callas*, 152.

74. Zeffirelli staged this scene in a similar way, as did Willy Deker in his 2006 production with Anna Netrebko.

75. Giudici, *Il teatro di Verdi*, 415.

76. Poli, "Un'artista misteriosa," 369.

77. For the recording of the 1956 production of La Scala with Callas and Raimondi, see note 54 above. The studio recording is Giuseppe Verdi, *La traviata*, with Maria Callas (Violetta), Francesco Albanese (Alfredo), Ugo Savarese (Giorgio Germont), Ede Marietti Gandolfo (Flora), Orchestra Sinfonica della RAI conducted by Gabriele Santini, Centra 1246, 1954, LP, 3 audio discs.

78. Ernesto De Martino, *The Land of Remorse: A Study of Southern Italian Tarantism*, trans. and annotated Dorothy Louise Zinn (London: Free Association Books, 2005), 190–92.

79. Roland Barthes, "The Death of the Author," in *Image-Music-Text*, essays selected and trans. Stephen Heath (New York: Hill and Wang, 1977), 142.

80. Gilbert Rouget, *Music and Trance: A Theory of the Relations between Music and Possession*, ed. and trans. Brunhilde Bierbuyck and Gilbert Rouget (Chicago: University of Chicago Press, 1985), esp. 17–29.

81. Stassinopoulos, *Maria Callas*, 142.

82. Similarly, Susan Rutherford experiences the presence of the character Carmen in Callas's 1964 recorded performance of the Habanera: Susan Rutherford, "'Pretending to Be Wicked': Divas, Technology, and the Consumption of Bizet's *Carmen*," in *Technology and the Diva: Sopranos, Opera, and Media from Romanticism to the Digital Age*, ed. Karen Henson (Cambridge: Cambridge University Press, 2016), 88.

83. Associazione Culturale Maria Callas, *La divina in cucina*.

Bibliography

SCORES, LIBRETTOS, AND STAGE MANUALS

Anfossi, Pasquale. "L'orfanella americana." Genoa, Biblioteca del Conservatorio di musica Niccolò Paganini, MS 13.7.13 (L 8.2).

"I baccanali di Roma": Dramma lirico in quattro atti, musica del Maestro Carlo Romani da rappresentarsi . . . la Quaresima 1854. Florence: Galletti, 1854.

Bach, Johann Sebastian. *Sweigt stille, plaudert nicht (Kaffee-Kantate)*, BWV 211. In *Neue Ausgabe sämtlicher Werke* 1/40, edited by Werner Neumann. Kassel: Bärenreiter, 1969.

———. *Sweigt stille, plaudert nicht (Kaffee-Kantate)*, BWV 211. Edited by Arnold Schering. London: Eulenburg, [1925].

Baldacci, Luigi, ed. *Tutti i libretti di Verdi*. Milan: Garzanti, 1975.

[Bentivoglio, Ippolito.] *L'Achille in Sciro, favola drammatica da rappresentarsi in musica nel Teatro a S. Stefano in Ferrara*. Venice, 1663.

Bertati, Giovanni. *L'orfanella americana, commedia per musica in quattro atti di Giovanni Bertati da rappresentarsi nel Teatro di S. Moisè per la prima opera dell'autunno 1787*. Venice: Battista Casali, 1787.

———. *La vendemmia: A Comic Opera in Two Acts Performed in the King's Theater at the Hay-Market*. London: Wayland, 1789.

———. "*La vendemmia*: Dramma giocoso per musica da rappresentarsi nel Teatro Reggio di Londra l'anno 1789," 1:10. Huntington Library, Los Angeles, CA, John Larpent Plays, MS coll. 832.

[Bertati, Giovanni.] *La vendemmia: Intermezzo in musica da rappresentarsi nel teatro dell'Eccellentissima casa Grimani a S. Gio[vanni] Crisostomo*. Venice: Fenzo, 1778.

Bertati, Giovanni, and Baldassare Galuppi. *L'inimico delle donne*. With an introduction by Helen Geyer-Kiefl. 3 vols. Milan: Ricordi, 1986.

Boccherini, Gastone. *La secchia rapita: Dramma eroicomico*. Vienna: Kurtzboeck, 1772.

Caccini, Giulio. *"L'Euridice" composta in musica in stile rappresentativo da Giulio Caccini detto Romano*. Florence: Marescotti, 1600.

———. *Le nuove musiche*. Florence: Marescotti, 1601.

Casella, Alfredo. *"La favola di Orfeo" (1932) di Messer Angelo Ambrogini, detto Poliziano (1472). Musica di Alfredo Casella*. Text edited by Corrado Pavolini. Milan: Carish, 1932.

Cohen, Robert, ed. *The Original Staging Manuals for Twelve Parisian Operatic Premières*. Stuyvesant, NY: Pendragon Press, 1991.

Conforti, Giovanni Luca. *Breve et facile maniera d'esercitarsi ad ogni scolaro*. Rome, 1593.

Corradi, Giulio Cesare. *"Il Vespasiano," drama per muisca nel nuovo teatro Grimano di S. Gio[vanni] Chrisostomo . . . nella seconda impression con nuove aggiunte, consacrato all'Illustrissimo, e Reverendissimo Monsignor Giovanni Battista Tosio, Abbate e Commendatore perpetuo d'Asola*. Venice: Nicolini, 1680.

D'Arienzo, Marco. *La festa di Piedigrotta: Opera buffa in tre atti*. Musica del Maestro Luigi Ricci. Translated from Neapolitan to Italian by Giovanni Gargano. Naples: Cottrau, 1865.

Da Ponte, Lorenzo. *Così fan tutte, o sia La scuola degli amanti: Dramma giocoso in due atti da rappresentarsi nel Teatro di Corte*. Vienna: Società Tipografica, 1790.

———. *Il dissoluto punito, o sia Il D. Giovanni. Dramma giocoso in due atti da rappresentarsi nel Teatro di Praga per l'arrivo di Sua Altezza Reale Maria Teresa Arciduchessa d'Austria sposa del Ser. Principe Antonio di Sassonia l'anno 1787*. Vienna, 1787.

———. *Il dissoluto punito, o sia Il D[on] Giovanni: Dramma giocoso in due atti da rappresentarsi nel Teatro di Praga*. Prague: Schönfeld, 1787.

———. *Il Don Giovanni*. Edited by Giovanna Gronda. Turin: Einaudi, 1995.

———. *Don Giovanni: Dramma buffo in due atti, la parte poetica della traduzione da L. Da Ponte*. New York: Giovanni Gray, 1826.

———. *Memorie e libretti mozartiani*. Introduction by Giuseppe Armani. 7th ed. Milan: Garzanti, 2007.

———. *Piedrigrotta*: Commedia per musica in quattro atti. Naples, 1860.

Defranceschi, Carlo Prospero. *Falstaff, o sia Le tre burle: Dramma giocoso per musica in due atti (Soggetto inglese) da rappresentarsi negl'Imperiali Regj Teatri di Corte l'anno 1798, musica di Antonio Salieri, primo maestro di cappella della Corte Imperiale*. Vienna: Mattia Andrea Schmidt, 1798.

Ferretti, Jacopo. *La Cenerentola, ossia La bontà in trionfo, drama giocoso . . . da rappresentarsi al Teatro Valle degl'Illustrissimi Signori Capranica nel Carnevale dell'anno 1817, con musica del Maestro Gioacchino Rossini Pesarese*. Rome: Puccinelli, 1817.

Freschi, Domenico. "Il Sardanapalo." Venice, Biblioteca nazionale Marciana, MS IV, 452 (9976).

Galuppi, Baldassare. "L'Arcadia in Brenta." Modena, Biblioteca Estense, MS Mus. F. 439.

———. *Il filosofo di campagna*. Edited by Virgilio Mortari. Milan: Carish, 1937.

———. "Il filosofo di campagna: Opera bernesca in San Samuele l'Anno 1755." Paris, Bibliothèque nationale de France, Départment de la musique, MS X-776.

———. *L'inimico delle donne*. With an introduction by Helen Geyer-Kiefl. 3 vols. Milan: Ricordi, 1986.

Giacosa, Giuseppe, and Luigi Illica. *Madama Butterfly da John L. Long and David Belasco: Tragedia giapponese*. Milan: Ricordi, 1904.

Goldoni, Carlo. *Le donne vendicate: Dramma giocoso per musica di Polisseno Fegeio, pastor arcade, da rappresentarsi nel teatro Tron di San Cassiano il carnevale dell'anno 1751*. Venice: Fenzo, 1751.

———. *Drammi comici per musica*. 3 vols. Edited by Silvia Urbani. Venice: Marsilio, 2007–16.

———. *Tutte le opere*. 4th ed. 14 vols. Edited by Giuseppe Ortolani. Milan: Mondadori, 1959.

Gronda, Giovanna, and Paolo Fabbri, eds. *Libretti d'opera italiani dal Seicento al Novecento*. Milan: Mondadori, 1997.

Henisch, Carl Franz. *Der Bassa von Tunis: Eine komische Operette in einem Aufzuge*. Berlin, 1774.

"Lisetta e Caican turco: Intermezzi comici musicali da rappresentarsi nel teatro di San Salvatore l'anno 1733." Venice, Casa Goldoni, MS 59A 96/4.

Mazzolà, Caterino. *Il turco in Italia: Dramma buffo in due parti da rappresentarsi al teatro di Corte*. Vienna: Stamperia dei Sordi e Muti, 1789.

Metastasio, Pietro. *Drammi per musica*. 3 vols. Edited by Anna Laura Bellina. Venice: Marsilio, 2003.

———. *Tutte le opera*. 5 vols. Edited by Bruno Brunelli. Milan: Mondadori, 1943–54.

Moderni, Carlo. *Sardanapalo: Drama per musica da recitarsi nel Teatro di Sant'Angelo l'anno 1679, ristampato con il Prologo e alter aggiunte*. Venice: Francesco Nicolini, 1679.

Montaubry, [Jean-Baptiste] Éd[ouard]. *La dame aux camélias! Ronde . . . , paroles de M. Alexandre Dumas fils, musique d'Ed. Montaubry*. Paris: Leduc, [1852].

Monteverdi, Claudio. *L'Orfeo: Favola in musica di Claudio Monteverdi rappresentata in Mantova l'anno 1607 e nuovamente data in luce*. Al Serenissimo Signor D. Francesco Gonzaga, Principe di Mantova, e di Monferato, etc. Venice: Amadino, 1609.

———. "Il ritorno di Ulisse in patria." Vienna, Österreichische Nationalbibliothek, Mus. MS 18763. Facsimile. Florence: Spes, 2006.

———. *Il ritorno di Ulisse in patria: Tragedia di lieto fine in un prologo e tre atti*. Piano reduction edited by Rinaldo Alessandrini. Kassel: Bärenreiter, 2007.

Mozart, Wolfgang Amadeus. *Così fan tutte, ossia La scuola degli amanti*, K. 588. Facsimile of the autograph score at Frankfurt, Staatbibliothek zu Berlin–Preußischer Kulturbesitz, Biblioteka Jagiellońska Kraków (Mus. MS autogr. W. A. Mozart 588), Stadt- und Universitätsbibliothek Frankfurt am Main (Mus. Hs 2350), with introductory essays by Norbert Miller and John A. Rice. Los Altos, CA: Packard Humanities Institute, 2007.

———. *Il dissoluto punito, ossia Il Don Giovanni K. 527, 540a, 540c*. Facsimile of the autograph score. Paris, Bibliothèque nationale de France, Départment de la musique, MS 1548. Los Altos, CA: Packard Humanities Institute, 2009.

———. *Die Zauberflöte*, K. 620. Facsimile of the autograph score with introductions by Joachim Kreutzer and Christoph Wolff. Los Altos, CA: Packard Humanities Institute; Kassel: Bärenreiter, 2009.

———. *Die Zauberflöte*. In the *Neue Mozart-Ausgabe* II/5/19, edited by Gernot Gruber and Alfred Orel. Kassel: Bärenreiter, 1970.

Paisiello, Giovanni. "Gli zingari in fiera. Opera buffa in musica originale di Giovanni Paisiello, composta per il Real Teatro del Fondo L'anno 1789." Naples, Biblioteca del Conservatorio di Musica S. Pietro a Majella, MS 16.5.13–14.

Palianti, Louis. *Les vêpres siciliennes: Opéra en cinq actes, paroles de MM. E. Scribe et Ch. Duveyrier, musique de M. Verdi, représenté pour la première fois à Paris sur le Théâtre impérial de l'opéra, le 13 juin 1855.* Collection de mises en scénes rédigées et publiées par M. L. Palianti. Paris: Brière, 1855.

[Palomba, Giuseppe]. *I zingari in fiera: Dramma giocoso per musica da rappresentarsi nel teatro di Cittadella in Bergamo il Carnovale 1791.* Bergamo: Rossi, 1791.

Piave, Francesco Maria. *La traviata: Libretto con note della censura.* Milan, Biblioteca nazionale Braidense, Archivio Ricordi, LIBRo 1806.

Piccinni, Niccolò. *La Cecchina, ossia La buona figliuola.* Introduction by Eric Weimer. New York: Garland, 1983. Facsimile reproduction of Florence, Biblioteca del Conservatorio di Musica Luigi Cherubini, MS D I 531, 532, 533.

Poggi, Domenico. *La locandiera: Dramma giocoso per musica cavato da una commedia dell'avvocato Signor Carlo Goldoni da Domenico Poggi, dedicato al bel sesso . . . da rappresentarsi ne' teatri privilegiati di Vienna la primavera dell'anno 1773.* Vienna: Giuseppe Kurtzböck, 1773.

Porpora, Nicola. "Semiramide riconosciuta." 3 vols. Dresden, Sächsische Landesbibliothek, MS Mus. 2417-F-2.

Puccini, Giacomo. *La fanciulla del West.* Mineola, NY: Dover, 1997.

Ricci, Luigi. "Piedigrotta: Commedia in 4 atti di Marco D'Arienzo, musica di Luigi Ricci, rappresentata al Teatro Nuovo l'anno 1852." 2 vols. Naples. Biblioteca del Conservatorio di musica San Pietro a Majella, MS. 3.3.18–19.

Ricordi, Giulio, ed. *Disposizione scenica per l'opera "Otello," dramma lirico in quattro atti, versi di Arrigo Boito, musica di Giuseppe Verdi, compilata e regolata secondo la messa in scena del Teatro alla Scala da Giulio Ricordi.* Milan: Ricordi, [1891].

[Romani, Felice]. *Il turco in Italia: Dramma buffo per musica in due atti da rappresentarsi nel R. Teatro alla Scala per primo spettacolo.* Milan: Pirola, 1814.

Rossini, Gioachino. *Il turco in Italia: Dramma buffo per musica in due atti di Felice Romani, musica di Gioachino Rossini. Prima rappresentazioni Milano, Teatro alla Scala 14 Agosto, 1814.* Edited by Margaret Bent. In *Edizione critica delle opere di Gioachino Rossini.* Section 1/13. Pesaro: Fondazione Rossini, 1978.

Salieri, Antonio. "La secchia rapita: Dramma eroicomico." Naples, Biblioteca del Conservatorio di musica S. Pietro a Majella, MS 30-2-14 (Rari 7.219.202656).

Sartori, Claudio. *I libretti italiani a stampa dalle origini al 1800: Catalogo analitico con 16 indici.* 6 vols. Cuneo: Bertola e Locatelli, 1990.

Schikaneder, Emmanuel. *Die Zauberflöte: Eine Große Oper in zwei Aufzugen.* Vienna: Ignaz Alberti, 1791.

Scribe, Augustin Eugène, and Charles Duveyrier. *Les vêpres siciliennes: Opera en cinq actes, paroles de MM. E. Scribe et Ch. Duveyrier, musique de M. Verdi, divertissements de M. L. Pétipa. Répresenté pour la première fois à Paris, sur le Théâtre de l'Académie impériale de musique, le 13 juin 1855.* Paris: Michel Lévy Frères and Libraires-Éditeurs, 1855.

Speck, Jules. *La fille du West: Opéra en trois actes (du drame de David Belasco). . . . Mise en scène de Monsieur Jules Speck Régisseur de la scène du Métropolitan Opéra*. Paris: Ricordi, [1910].

Le théâtre de la foire, ou L'opéra-comique, contenant les meilleures piéces qui ont été représentées aux foires de S. Germain et de S. Laurent, enrichiés d'estampes en taille-douce, avec une table de tous les vaudevilles et autres airs gravez-notez à la fin de chaque volume. 10 vols. Paris: Geneau, 1724–37.

Verdi, Giuseppe. "*Alzira*: Tragedia lirica in tre atti di Salvadore Cammarano." In *The Works of Giuseppe Verdi* 1/8, edited by Stefano Castelvecchi. Chicago: University of Chicago Press; Milan: Ricordi, 1994.

———. "*Attila*, dramma lirico in un prologo e tre atti, libretto di Temistocle Solera e Francesco Maria Piave." In *The Works of Giuseppe Verdi* 1/9, edited by Helen M. Greenwald. Chicago: University of Chicago Press; Milan: Ricordi, 2013.

———. Verdi, Giuseppe. "*Un ballo in maschera*" *in Full Score*. Mineola, NY: Dover, 1996.

———. "*Il corsaro*: [melodramma tragico in tre atti] libretto di Francesco Maria Piave." In *The Works of Giuseppe Verdi* 1/13, edited by Elizabeth Hudson. Chicago: University of Chicago Press; Milan: Ricordi, 1998.

———. "*Ernani*: Dramma lirico in quattro atti di Francsco Maria Piave." In *The Works of Giuseppe Verdi* 1/5, edited by Claudio Gallico. Chicago: University of Chicago Press; Milan: Ricordi, 1985.

———. *Falstaff: Commedia lirica in tre atti. Libretto di Arrigo Boito, prima rappresentazione Milano, Teatro alla Scala, 9 Febbraio 1893, partiture*. New and rev. ed. 1893. Reprint Milan: Ricordi 1959. Also reprinted as *Falstaff in Full Score*. Minneola, NY: Dover, 2014.

———. *"Il finto Stanislao" ("Un giorno di regno"), melodramma giocoso in 2 atti di Felice Romani, opera completa per canto e pianoforte*. Milan: Ricordi, 1951.

———. "*Luisa Miller*: Melodramma tragico in tre atti di Salvatore Cammarano." In *The Works of Giuseppe Verdi* 1/15, edited by Jeffrey Kallberg. Chicago: University of Chicago Press; Milan: Ricordi, 1992.

———. "*Macbeth*: Melodramma in quattro atti, libretto di Francesco Maria Piave and Andrea Maffei (Paris 1865 version; Florence 1847 version in appendix)." In *The Works of Giuseppe Verdi* 1/10, edited by David Lawton. Chicago: University of Chicago Press, 2005.

———. "*I masnadieri*: Melodramma [in quattro atti] di Andrea Maffei." In *The Works of Giuseppe Verdi* 1/11, edited by Roberta Montemorra Marvin. Chicago: University of Chicago Press; Milan: Ricordi, 2000.

———. *Otello:* Dramma lirico in quattro atti; Partiture. New ed. Milan: Ricordi, 1913. Reprinted as *"Otello" in Full Score*. New York: Dover, 1986.

———. "*Rigoletto*: Melodramma in tre atti di Francesco Maria Piave." In *The Works of Giuseppe Verdi* 1/17, edited by Martin Chusid. Chicago: University of Chicago Press; Milan: Ricordi, 1983.

———. *"La Traviata": Autograph Sketches and Drafts*. Edited by Fabrizio Della Seta, with facsimile reproductions of the sketches. Parma: Istituto nazionale di studi verdiani, 2000.

———. "*La traviata*, melodramma in tre atti." In *The Works of Giuseppe Verdi* 1/19, edited by Fabrizio Della Seta. Chicago: University of Chicago Press; Milan: Ricordi, 1997.

———. *Les vêpres siciliennes: Grand opéra en 5 actes, vocal score*. Paris: Léon Escudier; Milan: Ricordi, [1856].

Zangarini, Carlo. *La fanciulla del West (The Girl of the Golden West)*. Milan: Ricordi; New York: Colombo, 1910.

AUDIO AND VIDEO RECORDINGS

Bach, Johann Sebastian. *Coffee Cantata/Peasant Cantata*. Conducted by Christopher Hogwood, with Emma Kirby (soprano). Decca 4176212, 1987. Compact disc.

Folk Music from Italy. Recorded by Walther Hennig. Folkways Records FW04520_105, 1956. Compact disc.

Guy, Buddy. "A Man and the Blues." On *A Man and the Blues*. Vanguard VSD 79272, 1968. LP.

Jo, Sumi. *Baroque Journey: Vivaldi, Handel, Bach, Purcell*. Warner Classics 2564 69824-6, 2005. Compact disc.

La Rossignol, music ensemble. *In vino: Il vino in musica tra XV e XVI secolo*. Conducted by Domenico Baronio. Tactus TC 400004. Bologna, 2005. Compact disc.

Monteverdi, Claudio. *Il ritorno di Ulisse in patria*, Concerto Vocale. Conducted by René Jacobs, with Guy de Mey as Iro. Harmonia Mundi France HML 5901427.29, 1992, 2010. Three compact discs.

Mozart, Wolfgang Amadeus. *Don Giovanni*. Directed by Peter Sellars. English subtitles by Peter Sellars. London: Decca, 1991. DVD.

Verdi, Giuseppe. *La traviata*. With Beniamino Gigli and Maria Caniglia. Camden Victor 2EA7908-II. June 4, 1939. 78 rpm.

———. *La traviata*. With Maria Callas (Violetta Valery), Gianni Raimondi (Alfredo Germont), Aldo Protti (Giorgio Germont). Conducted by Carlo Maria Giulini. Recorded on January 19, 1956. Issued in the series La Scala Memories, vol. 3. Skira Classica. 2010. CD.

———. *La traviata*. With Maria Callas (Violetta), Francesco Albanese (Alfredo), Ugo Savarese (Giorgio Germont), Ede Marietti Gandolfo (Flora). Orchestra Sinfonica della RAI conducted by Gabriele Santini. Centra 1246, 1954. LP, three audio discs.

———. *La traviata*. With Teresa Stratas (Violetta) and Placido Domingo (Alfredo). Directed by Franco Zeffirelli. Universal 20326, 1999. DVD.

SECONDARY SOURCES

Abbate, Carolyn. *In Search of Opera*. Princeton, NJ: Princeton University Press, 2001.

———. "Sound Object Lessons." *Journal of the American Musicological Society* 69, no. 3 (2016): 793–829.

Abbate, Carolyn, and Roger Parker. "Dismembering Mozart." *Cambridge Opera Journal* 2, no. 2 (1990): 187–95.

Abel, Sam. *Opera in the Flesh: Sexuality in Operatic Performance*. Boulder, CO: Westview Press, 1996.

Abert, Hermann. *W. A. Mozart*. Translated by Steward Spencer. Edited by Cliff Eisen. New Haven, CT: Yale University Press, 2007.

[Addison, Joseph.] *Remarks on Several Parts of Italy, &c., in the Years 1701, 1702, 1703*. London, 1705.

Ake, David. *Jazz Matters: Sound, Place, and Time since Bebop*. Berkeley: University of California Press, 2010.

Albala, Ken. "Weight Loss in the Age of Reason." In *Cultures of the Abdomen: Diet, Digestion, and Fat in the Modern World*, edited by Christopher E. Forth and Ana Carden-Coyne, 169–264. New York: Palgrave Macmillan, 2005.

Allanbrook, Wye Jamison [Wendy]. *Rhythmic Gesture in Mozart: "Le nozze di Figaro" and "Don Giovanni."* Chicago: University of Chicago Press, 1983.

Allegri, Renzo, and Roberto Allegri. *Callas by Callas: Gli scritti segreti dell'artista più grande*. Milan: Mondadori, 1997.

Allegri, Renzo, and Maria Callas. *Maria Callas: Lettere d'amore*. Edited and transcribed by Renzo Allegri. Milan: Mondadori, 2008.

Amati-Camperi, Alexandra. "The First Operatic Women: 'Ah fato empio e crudele!'" *Studi Musicali* 37, no. 1 (2008): 37–57.

Andrew, Lew. "Botticelli's *Primavera*, Angelo Politian, and Ovid's *Fasti*." *Artibus et Historiae* 32, no. 63 (2011): 73–84.

Anfossi, Giovanni Battista. *Dell'uso ed abuso della cioccolata: Dissertazione storico-medica del dottore Giovanni Battista Anfossi a Sua Eccellenza Pier-Vettore Pisani procurator di S. Marco*. Rovigo: Miazzi, 1775.

Angermüller, Rudolph. "Bier oder Wein für Leopold Mozart." *Mitteilungen der Internationalen Stiftung Mozarteum* 46, nos. 1–2 (1998): 1–3.

Aristotle. *The Basic Works of Aristotle*. Edited by Richard McKeon. New York: Modern Library, 2001.

Armelagos, George, and Peter Farb. *Consuming Passions: The Anthropology of Eating*. Boston: Houghton Mifflin, 1980.

Arteaga, Stefano. *Le rivoluzioni del teatro musicale italiano dalla sua origine fino al presente*. 2nd ed. 3 vols. Venice: Carlo Palese, 1785.

Artusi, Pellegrino. *La scienza in cucina e l'arte di mangiar bene*. Edited and with an introduction by Piero Camporesi. 1891. Reprint, Turin: Einaudi, 1970.

Associazione Culturale Maria Callas. *La divina in cucina: Il ricettario segreto di Maria Callas*. Edited by Bruno Tosi. Milan: Trenta, 2006.

Astell, Ann W. *Eating Beauty: The Eucharist and the Spiritual Arts of the Middle Ages*. Ithaca, NY: Cornell University Press, 2006.

Atlas, Allan W. "Belasco and Puccini: 'Old Dog Tray' and the Zuni Indians." *Musical Quarterly* 75, no. 3 (1991): 362–98.

Attisani, Antonio. "Orfeo simplex e Orfeo infelix nell'opera da camera di Casella e Pavolini." *Musica e Storia* 7, no. 1 (1999): 77–88.

Aversano, Luca, and Jacopo Pellegrini, eds. *Mille e una Callas: Voci e studi*. Macerata: Quodlibet, 2016.

Bacon, Henry. *Visconti: Explorations of Beauty and Decay*. Cambridge: Cambridge University Press, 1998.

Badolato, Nicola. "Commedie e intermedi musicali ferraresi nei 'Banchetti' del Messisbugo (1549)." In *Le arti e il cibo: Modalità ed esempi di un rapporto*. Atti del Convegno (Bologna, 15–16 ottobre 2012), edited by Sylvie Davidson and Fabrizio Lollini, 177–87. Bologna: Bononia University Press, 2014.

Bakhtin, Mikhail. *Rabelais and His World*. Translated by Hélène Iswoslky. Bloomington: Indiana University Press, 1984.

Balzac, Honoré de. "Traité des excitants modernes" [1838]. In *Oeuvres complètes de H. de Balzac*, vol. 2, *Oeuvres diverses*. Paris: Société d'éditions littéraires et artistiques, 1908.

Barbier, Patrick. *Opera in Paris, 1800–1850: A Lively History*. Translated by Robert Louma. Portland, OR: Amadeus Press, 1987.

Baretti, Giuseppe. *An Account of the Manners and Customs of Italy, with Observations on the Mistakes of Some Travellers with Regard to That Country*. 2 vols. London: Davis, 1768.

Barker, Evan. "Wagner and the Ideal Theatrical Space." In *Opera in Context: Essays on Historical Staging from the Late Renaissance to the Time of Puccini*, edited by Mark A. Radice, 241–78. Portland, OR: Amadeus Press, 1998.

Barthes, Roland. "The Death of the Author." In *Image-Music-Text*. Essays selected and translated by Stephen Heath, 142–48. New York: Hill and Wang, 1977.

———. *Elements of Semiology*. Translated by Annette Lavers and Colin Smith. New York: Hill and Wang, 1967.

Bartoli, Adolfo. *Scenari inediti della Commedia dell'arte: Contributo alla storia del teatro popolare italiano*. Florence: Sansoni, 1880.

Basile, Giambattista. *Archivio di letteratura popolare*, 4, no. 8 (August 15, 1886).

Bauer, Wilhelm A., Otto Erich Deutsch, and Joseph Heinz, eds. *Mozart Briefe und Aufzeichnungen Gesamtausgabe*. 7 vols. Kassel: Bärenreiter, 1962–78.

Bauman, Thomas. *North German Opera in the Age of Goethe*. Cambridge: Cambridge University Press, 1985.

Beghelli, Marco. "Dall''Aria del sorbetto' all''Aria della pissa.'" In *Musica di ieri, esperienza d'oggi: Ventidue studi per Paolo Fabbri*, edited by Maria Chiara Bertieri and Alessandro Roccatagliati, 141–68. Lucca: LIM, 2018.

———. "Mangiare all'opera." In *Le arti e il cibo: Modalità ed esempi di un rapporto*. Atti del Convegno (Bologna, 15–16 ottobre 2012), edited by Sylvie Davidson and Fabrizio Lollini, 245–62. Bologna: Bononia University Press, 2014.

Belasco, David. *The Girl of the Golden West: Novelized from the Play*. New York: Dodd, Mead, 1911.

Bell, Rudolph. *Holy Anorexia*. Chicago: University of Chicago Press, 1985.

Bendiner, Kenneth. *Food in Painting: From the Renaissance to the Present*. London: Reaktion, 2005.

Berger, Karol. *Bach's Cycle, Mozart's Arrow: An Essay on the Origins of Musical Modernity*. Berkeley: University of California Press, 2007.

Bergonzi, Elena. "Cremonini scrittore: Gli anni padovani e le opere della maturità." *Aevum* 68, no. 3 (1994): 607–33.

Berliner, Paul F. *Thinking in Jazz: The Infinite Art of Improvisation*. Chicago: University of Chicago Press, 1994.

Bernardi, Sandro. "La terra trema: Il mito, il teatro, la storia." In *Il cinema di Luchino Visconti*, edited by Veronica Pravadelli, 65–88. Venice: Marsilio, 2000.

Besutti, Paola. "Musiche e musicisti alla tavola dei Gonzaga." In *Le tavole di corte tra Cinquecento e Settecento*, edited by Andrea Marlotti, 185–216. Rome: Bulzoni, 2013.

Bianconi, Lorenzo. "La forma musicale come scuola dei sentimenti." In *Educazione musicale e formazione*, edited by Giuseppina La Face Bianconi and Franco Frabboni, 85–120. Milan: FrancoAngeli, 2008.

———. *Music in the Seventeenth Century*. Cambridge: Cambridge University Press, 1989.

Biancorosso, Giorgio. *Situated Listening: The Sound of Absorbtion in Classical Cinema*. Oxford: Oxford University Press, 2016.

Biasin, Gian-Paolo. *The Flavors of Modernity: Food and the Novel*. Princeton, NJ: Princeton University Press, 1993.

Bistort, Giulio. *Il magistrato alle Pompe nella Repubblica di Venezia: Studio storico*. Venice: Deputazione veneta di storia patria, 1912. Reprint. Bologna: Forni, 1969.

Bizzocchi, Roberto. "Cicisbei: Italian Morality and European Values in the Eighteenth Century." In *Italy's Eighteenth Century: Gender and Culture in the Age of the Grand Tour*, edited by Paula Finden, Wendy Wassyng Roworth, and Catherine M. Sama. Stanford, CA: Stanford University Press, 2009.

———. *Cicisbei: Morale privata e identità nazionale in Italia*. Bari: Laterza, 2008.

Blacking, John. *How Musical Is Man?* Seattle: University of Washington Press, 1973.

Bodart, Diane H., and Valérie Boudier, eds. "Le banquet de la Renaissance: Images et usages." Special issue, *Predella: Rivista di arti visive/Journal of Visual Arts* 7 (2013).

Boerio, Giuseppe. *Dizionario del dialetto veneziano*. Venice: Santini, 1829.

Bolt, Rodney. *The Librettist of Venice: The Remarkable Life of Lorenzo da Ponte, Mozart's Poet, Casanova's Friend, and Italian Opera's Impresario in America*. New York: Bloomsbury, 2006.

Bordo, Susan. *Unbearable Weight: Feminism, Western Culture, and the Body*. Berkeley: University of California Press, 2003.

Bourdieu, Pierre. *Distinction: A Social Critique of the Judgment of Taste*. Translated by Richard Nice. New York: Routledge, 2000.

———. *La distinction: Critique sociale du jugement*. Paris: Éditions de Minuit, 1979.

Bouwsma, William James. *Venice and the Defense of Republican Liberty: Renaissance Values in the Age of the Counter Reformation*. Berkeley: University of California Press, 1968.

Boyd-Bennett, Harriet. *Opera in Postwar Venice: Cultural Politics and the Avant-Garde*. Cambridge: Cambridge University Press: 2018.

Braudel, Fernand. *Civilization and Capitalism: 15th–18th Centuries*. 3 vols. Translated by Siân Reynolds. New York: Harper and Row, 1982.

Brieve e nuovo metodo da farsi ogni sorte di sorbetto con facilità [Naples]: Si vendono nella Stamperia del Monaco di rimpetto la Chiesa di S. Liguoro alla strada delli Librari, [1690c].

Brosses, Charles de. *Lettres d'Italie du President de Brosses*. Edited by Frédéric d'Agay. 2 vols. Paris: Mercure de France, 1986.

Brown-Montesano, Kristi. "Holding Don Giovanni Accountable." *Musicology Now*, December 5, 2017. http://www.musicologynow.org/2017/12/holding-don-giovanni-accountable.html.

———. *Understanding the Women of Mozart's Operas*. Berkeley: University of California Press, 2007.

Brumberg, Joan Jacobs. *Fasting Girls: The History of Anorexia Nervosa*. Rev. ed. New York: Vintage Books, 2000.

Brünenberg, Kerstin. "Sklavenarbeit: Folgenlose Vergangenheit?" In *Von Arbeit und Menschen: Überraschende Einblicke in das Arbeitsleben fremder Kulturen*, edited by Sabine Eylert, Ursula Bertels, and Ursula Tewes, 51–59. New York: Waxman, 2000.

Budasz, Rogério. "Of Cannibals and the Recycling of Otherness." *Music and Letters* 87, no. 1 (2005): 1–15.

Budden, Julian. *The Operas of Verdi*. Rev. ed. 3 vols. Oxford: Clarendon Press, 1992.

———. *Puccini: His Life and Works*. Oxford: Oxford University Press, 2002.

Burkhardt, Peter. *The Civilization of the Renaissance in Italy*. New York: Random House, 1954.

Burney, Charles. *The Present State of Music in France and Italy, or The Journal of a Tour through Those Countries, Undertaken to Collect Materials for a General History of Music*. 2nd ed. London: Becket, 1773.

Burnham, Scott. *Mozart's Grace*. Princeton, NJ: Princeton University Press, 2013.

Busse Berger, Anna Maria, and Jesse Rodin, eds. *The Cambridge History of Fifteenth-Century Music*. Cambridge: Cambridge University Press, 2015.

Butler, Margaret R. "Olivero's Painting of Turin's Teatro Regio: Toward a Reevaluation of an Operatic Emblem." *Music in Art* 34, no. 1–2 (2009): 137–51.

———. *Operatic Reform at Turin's Teatro Regio: Aspects of Production and Stylistic Change in the 1760s*. Lucca: LIM, 2001.

———. "Time Management at Turin's Teatro Regio: Galuppi's *La clemenza di Tito* and Its Alterations, 1759." *Early Music* 11, no. 2 (2012): 279–89.

Bynum, Caroline Walker. *Holy Feast and Holy Fast: The Religious Significance of Food in Medieval Women*. Berkeley: University of California Press, 1987.

Cagotti, Marina, and Francesco Paolo Fiore, eds. *Ippolito II d'Este: Cardinale principe mecenate*. Atti del convegno (Villa d'Este, Tivoli, 13–15 maggio 2010). Rome: De Luca, 2013.

Calaresu, Melissa. "Making and Eating Ice Cream in Naples: Rethinking Consumption and Sociability in the Eighteenth Century." *Past and Present* 220 (August 2013): 35–78.

Calaresu, Melissa, and Danielle van den Hauvel, eds. *Food Hawkers: Selling on the Streets from Antiquity to the Present*. Burlington, VT: Ashgate, 2016.

Calcagno, Mauro. *From Madrigal to Opera: Monteverdi's Staging of the Self*. Berkeley: University of California Press, 2012.

Callas, Evangelia. *My Daughter Maria Callas*. Written in collaboration with Lawrence G. Blochman. New York: Fleet, 1960.

Callas, Maria, et al. "Per la prima volta Maria Callas narra la sua vita." *Oggi* 13, no. 3 (January 17, 1957): 14–17.

Calmels, Laurence, Frédéric Chambre and Cyrille Cohen, eds. *Maria Callas: Souvenirs d'une legend; Vente aux enchères publiques des objets personnels de Maria Callas et de ses archives (correspondances, photographies, coupures de presse, rassemblées et conservées par la diva)*. Paris: Calmels, Chambre, Cohen, 2000.

Campana, Alessandra. *Opera and Modern Spectatorship in Late Nineteenth-Century Italy*. Cambridge: Cambridge University Press, 2015.

———. "To Look Again (at *Don Giovanni*)." In *The Cambridge Companion to Eighteenth-Century Opera*, edited by Anthony R. DelDonna and Pierpaolo Polzonetti, 140–52. Cambridge: Cambridge University Press, 2009.

Camporesi, Piero. *Exotic Brew: The Art of Living in the Age of Enlightenment*. Translated by Christopher Woodall. Cambridge: Polity Press, 1994.

———. *Il paese della fame*. Milan: Garzanti, 2000.

Capatti, Alberto, and Massimo Montanari. *Italian Cuisine: A Cultural History*. Translated by Áine O'Healy. New York: Columbia University Press, 2003.

Carpanetto, Dino, and Giuseppe Ricuperati. *Italy in the Age of Reason, 1685–1789*. Translated by Caroline Higgitt. New York: Longman, 1987.

Carpitella, Diego. "The Choreutic-Musical Exorcism of Tarantism." In the appendix to Ernesto De Martino, *The Land of Remorse: A Study of Southern Italian Tarantism*, translated and annotated by Dorothy Louise Zinn, 286–315. London: Free Association Books, 2005.

Carter, Tim. *Composing Opera from Dafne to Ulisse Errante*. Krakow: Musica Iagellonica, 1994.

Castelvecchi, Stefano. "On 'Diegesis' and 'Diegetic': Words and Concepts." *Journal of the American Musicological Society* 73, no. 1 (2020): 149–71.

———. *Sentimental Opera: Questions of Genre in the Age of Bourgeois Drama*. Cambridge: Cambridge University Press, 2013.

Castiglione, Baldassare. *The Book of the Courtier* [1528]. Translated by Daniel Javitch. New York: Norton, 2002.

———. *Il cortigiano*. Edited by Amedeo Quondam. Milan: Mondadori, 2002.

Castiglione, Caroline. *Patrons and Adversaries: Nobles and Villagers in Italian Politics, 1640–1760*. Oxford: Oxford University Press, 2005.

Ceccarelli, Laura, and Marina Cipriani. *Medea di Pasolini: Cronache del tempo e ricordi dei protagonisti*. Rome: Centro Sperimentale di Cinematografia, 2006.

Chailley, Jacques. *The "Magic Flute" Unveiled: Esoteric Symbolism in Mozart's Masonic Opera*. New York: Knopf, 1971.

Charlton, David. *Opera in the Age of Rousseau: Music, Confrontation, Realism*. Cambridge: Cambridge University Press, 2013.

Chegai, Andrea. "Muovere l'aria: Jommelli un die innere Handlung (*Il Vologeso*, Ludwigsburg 1766)." In *Musik in Baden-Württemberg*, edited by Ann-Katrin Zimmermann, 61–110. Auftrag der Gesellshaft für Musikgeschichte in Baden-Wüttemberg, Jahrbuch 2014, vol. 21. Munich: Strube, 2014. Published in Italian as "Muovele l'aria: Jommelli e l'azione interiore (*Il Vologeso*, Ludwigsburg 1766)." In *Niccolò Jommelli: L'esperienza europea di un musicista 'filosofo.'* Atti del Convegno internazionale di studi (Reggio Calabria, 7–8 ottobre 2011), edited by Gaetano Pitarresi, 291–354. Reggio Calabria: Edizioni del Conservatorio di Musica "F. Cilea," 2014.

Chernin, Kim. *Womansize: The Tyranny of Slenderness*. London: Women's Press, 1981.

Chong, Nicholas J. "Music for the Last Supper: The Dramatic Significance of Mozart's Musical Quotations in the *Tafelmusik* of *Don Giovanni*." *Current Musicology* 92 (2011): 7–52.

Cicali, Gianni. "Roles and Acting." In *The Cambridge Companion to Eighteenth-Century Opera*, edited by Anthony R. DelDonna and Pierpaolo Polzonetti, 85–98. Cambridge: Cambridge University Press, 2009.

Cicero. *On the Commonwealth* [*De re publica*]. Translated by George Holland Sabine and Stanley Barney Smith. London: Macmillan, 1976.

Civitello, Linda. *Cuisine and Culture: A History of Food and People*. 2nd ed. Hoboken, NJ: John Wiley, 2008.

Coeurdevey, Annie. "La célébration du vin dans la chanson polyphonique à la Renaissance." In *"La musique, de tous les passetemps le plus beau": Hommage à Jean-Michel Vaccaro*, edited by François Lesure and Henry Vanhulst, 66–88. Paris: Klincksieck, 1998.

Cohen, Mitchell. *The Politics of Opera: A History from Monteverdi to Mozart*. Princeton, NJ: Princeton University Press, 2017.

Conati, Marcello. *La bottega della musica: Verdi e la Fenice*. Milan: Saggiatore, 1983.

Cone, Edward T. *The Composer's Voice*. Berkeley: University of California Press, 1974.

———. "The World of Opera and Its Inhabitants." In *Music: A View from Delft*, selected essays edited by Robert P. Morgan, 125–38. Chicago: University of Chicago Press, 1989.

Cooper, Michael. "A Plus-Size Falstaff Grows into His Outsize Part." *New York Times*, December 4, 2013.

Cordaro, Michele. "The Most Beautiful Room in the World." In *Mategna's Camera degli esposi*, edited by Michele Cordaro, 11–19. New York: Abbeville, 1993.

Cormody, Francis J. "Le repertoire de l'opéra comique en vaudevilles de 1708 à 1764." *University of California Publications in Modern Philology* 16 (1932–33): 373–438.

Corvisieri, Camillo. "Il trionfo romano di Eleonora d'Aragona nel giugno 1473." *Archivio della Società Romana di Storia Patria* 1 (1878): 475–91.

Cotticelli, Francesco, and Paologiovanni Maione. "Metastasio: The Dramaturgy of Eighteenth-Century Heroic Opera." In *The Cambridge Companion to Eighteenth-Century Opera*, edited by Anthony R. Deldonna and Pierpaolo Polzonetti, 66–84. Cambridge: Cambridge University Press, 2009.

———. *Onesto divertimento, ed allegria de' popoli: Materiali per una storia dello spettacolo a Napoli nel primo Settecento*. Milan: Ricordi, 1996.

Counihan, Carole, and Penny Van Esterik, eds. *Food and Culture: A Reader*. 3rd ed. New York: Routledge, 2013.

Crowther, Gillian. *Eating Culture: An Anthropological Guide to Food*. Toronto: University of Toronto Press, 2013.

Cummings, Anthony M. "Dance and 'the Other': The Moresca." In *Seventeenth-Century Ballet, a Multi-art Spectacle*: An International Interdisciplinary Symposium, edited by Barbara Grammeniati, 39–60. Bloomington, IN: Xlibris, 2011.

———. "Leo's Jesters." *Revue belge de musicologie/Belgisch Tijdschrift voor Muziekwetenschap* 63 (2009): 31–65.

———. "Music and Feasts in the Fifteenth Century." In *The Cambridge History of Fifteenth-Century Music*, edited by Anna Maria Busse Berger and Jesse Rodin, 361–73. Cambridge: Cambridge University Press, 2015.

Il cuoco piemontese perfezionato a Parigi. Turin: Giuseppe Ricca, 1766. Edited by Silvano Seventi. Reprint, Bra: Arcigola Slow Food, 1995.

Cypess, Rebecca. *Curious and Modern Inventions: Instrumental Music as Discovery in Galileo's Italy*. Chicago: University of Chicago Press, 2016.

d'Amico de Carvalho, Caterina, ed. *Viscontiana: Luchino Visconti e il melodramma verdiano*. Milan: Mazzotta, 2001.

d'Amico de Carvalho, Caterina, and Renzo Renzi, eds. *Luchino Visconti: Il mio teatro*. 2 vols. Bologna: Cappelli, 1979.

d'Ancona, Alessandro. *Origini del teatro italiano, libri tre con due appendici sulla rappresentazione drammatica del contado toscano e sul teatro mantoano nel sec. XVI*. 2nd ed. 2 vols. Turin: Loescher, 1891.

Da Ponte, Lorenzo. *Memoirs of Lorenzo Da Ponte*. Translated by Elisabeth Abbott. New York: Dover, 1959.

———. *Memorie e libretti mozartiani*. 7th ed. Milan: Garzanti, 2007.

Dahlhaus, Carl. *The Idea of Absolute Music*. Translated by Roger Lustig. Chicago: University of Chicago Press, 1989.

———. "What Is a Musical Drama?" Translated by Mary Whittall. *Cambridge Opera Journal* 1, no. 2 (1989): 95–111.

dalla Bona, Giovanni. *Dell'uso e dell'abuso del caffè: Dissertazione storico-fisico-medica*. 2nd ed. Verona: Berno, 1760.

Darnton, Robert. *Mesmerism and the End of the Enlightenment in France*. Cambridge, MA: Harvard University Press, 1968.

Dávid, Ferenc, Carsten Jung, János Malina, and Edward McCue. "Haydn's Opera House at Eszterháza: New Archival Sources." *Early Music* 43, no. 1 (2015): 111–27.

David, Hans T., and Arthur Mendel, eds. *The New Bach Reader: A life of Johann Sebastian Bach in Letters and Documents*. Revised and enlarged by Christoph Wolff. New York: Norton, 1998.

Davidson, Sylvie, and Fabrizio Lollini, eds. *Le arti e il cibo: Modalità ed esempi di un rapporto*. Atti del Convegno (Bologna, 15–16 ottobre 2012). Bologna: Bononia University Press, 2014.

de Hidalgo, Elvira. "La mia allieva Maria Callas, come la ricordo da ragazza." *Oggi* 15, no. 40 (October 1, 1959): 23–24.

De Martino, Ernesto. *The Land of Remorse: A Study of Southern Italian Tarantism*. Translated and annotated by Dorothy Louise Zinn. London: Free Association Books, 2005.

de Molina, Tirso. *El burlador de Sevilla*. Edited by Alfredo Rodríguez López-Vásquez. 3rd ed. Madrid: Cátedra, 1990.

De Santis, Mila. "'Triste comme une chanson à boire': Ripensando al brindisi de *La traviata*." *Studi verdiani* 23 (2012–13): 45–70.

del Bene, Giulio. "Del convito degli Alterati." MS Magliabechiano IX, 137, cc. 12r–22r, Biblioteca nazionale centrale, Florence.

DelDonna, Anthony R. *Opera, Theatrical Culture and Society in Late Eighteenth-Century Naples*. Burlington, VT: Ashgate, 2012.

DelDonna, Anthony R., and Pierpaolo Polzonetti, eds. *The Cambridge Companion to Eighteenth-Century Opera*. Cambridge: Cambridge University Press, 2009.

Della Seta, Fabrizio. "'O cieli azzurri': Exoticism and Dramatic Discourse in '*Aida*.'" *Cambridge Opera Journal* 3, no. 1 (1991): 49–62.

———. "Il tempo della festa: Su due scene della *Traviata* e su altri luoghi verdiani." *Studi verdiani* 2 (1983): 108–46.

Della Torre, Arnaldo. *Storia dell'Accademia Platonica di Firenze*. Florence: Carnesecchi, 1902.

Dent, Edward J. *Mozart's Operas: A Critical Study*. Oxford: Oxford University Press, 1991.

Descrizione delle feste fatte nelle reali nozze de' serenissimi principi di Toscana Don Cosimo de' Medici, e Maria Maddalena Arciduchessa d'Austria. Florence: Giunti, 1608.

Desmet-Grégoire, Hélène. *Les objets du café dans les sociétés du Proche-Orient et de la Méditerranée*. Paris: Presses du CNRS, 1989.

Deutsch, Otto Erich. "Mozart in Zinzendorfs Tagebüchern." *Schweizerische Musikzeitung* 102 (1962): 211–18.

DeVeaux, Scott. *The Birth of Bebop: A Social History*. Berkeley: University of California Press, 1997.

"Diario degli Alterati," Florence, Biblioteca Medicea Laurenzia, MS Ashburnham 558.

Diodoro Siculo. *Delle antique historie fabulose nuovamente fatto volgare e con somma diligentia stampato*. Venice: Gabriel [G]iolito di Ferrarii, 1542.

Di Schino, June. "Banchetti, vivande e imbandigioni della tavola di Ippolito d'Este." In *Ippolito II d'Este: Cardinale, principe, mecenate*. Atti del convegno (Villa d'Este, Tivoli, 13–15 maggio 2010), edited by Marina Cogotti and Francesco Paolo Fiore, 451–70. Rome: De Luca, 2013.

Douglas, Mary. "Deciphering a Meal." *Daedalus* 101, no. 1 (1972): 61–81.

———. *Natural Symbols: Explorations in Cosmology*. New York: Routledge, 1996.

Duchartre, Pierre Louis. *The Italian Comedy*. Translated by Randolph T. Weaver. New York: Dover, 1966.

Dufour, Philippe Sylvestre. *Traitez nouveaux et curieux du café, du thé et du chocolate: Ouvrage également necessaire aux médecins, et à tous ceux qui aiment leur santé*. 3rd ed. La Haye: Adrian Moetjens, 1693.

Dumas fils, Alexandre. *La dame aux camélias*. Translated by David Coward. Oxford: Oxford University Press, 1986.

Durante, Sergio. "Analysis and Dramaturgy: Reflections towards a Theory of Opera." In *Opera Buffa in Mozart's Vienna*, edited by Mary Hunter and James Webster, 311–39. Cambridge: Cambridge University Press, 1997.

———. *Tartini, Padova, e l'Europa*. Livorno: Sillabe, 2017.

Eco, Umberto. "The Frames of Comic Freedom." In *Carnival!*, edited by Thomas Sebeok, 1–9. New York: Mouton, 1984.

Edge, Dexter. "Mozart's Reception in Vienna, 1787–1791." In *Wolfgang Amadè Mozart: Essays on His Life and His Music*, edited by Stanley Sadie, 66–120. Oxford: Clarendon Press, 1996.

Eidsheim, Nina Sun. "Maria Callas's Waistline and the Organology of Voice." *Opera Quarterly* 33, nos. 3–4 (2017): 249–68.

Einstein, Alfred. *Mozart: His Character, His Work*. Translated by Arthur Mendel and Nathan Broder. New York: Oxford University Press, 1962.

Elias, Norbert. *The Civilizing Process: Sociogenetic and Psychogenetic Investigations*. Translated by Edmund Jephcott. Oxford: Blackwell, 2000.

Ellis, Markman. *The Coffee House: A Cultural History*. London: Weidenfeld and Nicolson, 2004.

———, ed. *Eighteenth-Century Coffee-House Culture*. 5 vols. London: Pickering and Chatto, 2006.

Emery, Ted. *Goldoni as Librettist: Theatrical Reform and the "Drammi Giocosi per Musica."* New York: Peter Lang, 1991.

Erdkamp, Paul, Massimo Montanari, Ken Albala, Beat A. Kümin, Martin Bruegel, and Amy Bentley. *A Cultural History of Food*. New York: Berg, 2012.

Evelyn, John. *The Diary of John Evelyn*. Edited by William Bray. 2 vols. New York: Dunne, 1901.

Everist, Mark. *Music Drama at the Paris Odéon, 1824–1828*. Berkeley: University of California Press, 2002.

Feldman, Martha. *Opera and Sovereignty: Transforming Myths in Eighteenth-Century Italy*. Chicago: University of Chicago Press, 2007.

Felici, Giovanni Battista. *Parere intorno all'uso della cioccolata scritto in una lettera dal conte dottor Giovanni Battista Felici all'Illustrissima Signora Lisabetta Girolami d'Ambra*. Florence: Manni, 1728.

Fenner, Theodore. *Opera in London: Views of the Press, 1785–1830*. Carbondale: Southern Illinois University Press, 1994.

Ferguson, Priscilla Parkhurst. *Accounting for Taste: The Triumph of French Cuisine*. Chicago: University of Chicago Press, 2004.

Ferrolo, Arnolfo B. "Botticelli's Mythologies, Ficino's *De amore*, Poliziano's *Stanze per la Giostra*: Their Circle of Love." *Art Bulletin* 37, no. 1 (1955): 17–25.

Ficino, Marsilio. *Commentaries on Plato*. Vol. 1, *Phaedrus and Ion*. Edited and translated by Michael J. B. Allen. Cambridge, MA:Tatti Renaissance Library of Harvard University Press, 2008.

Ficino, Marsilio. *The Letters of Marsilio Ficino*. Translated from the Latin by members of the Language Department of the School of Economic Science, London. 9 vols. London: Shepheard-Walwyn, 1975.

———. *Sopra lo amore ovvero Convito di Platone*. Edited by Giuseppe Pensi. Milan: ES, 1992.

———. *Three Books on Life*. Critical edition by Carol V. Kaske and John R. Clark. Binghamton, NY: Center for Medieval and Early Renaissance Studies of the State University of New York at Binghamton, 1989.

Fido, Franco. *Nuova guida a Goldoni: Teatro e società nel Settecento*. Turin: Einaudi, 2000.

———. "Riforma e 'controriforma' del teatro: I libretti per musica di Goldoni fra il 1748 e il 1753." *Studi Goldoniani* 7 (1985): 60–72.

Flaubert, Gustave. *Madame Bovary*. Translated by Mildred Marmur. New York: Penguin, 1964.

Fleischman, Théo. *Napoléon et la musique*. Brussels: Brepols, 1965.

Fo, Dario. *Mistero buffo: Comic Mysteries*. Translated by Stuart Hood. London: Methuen, 1988.

Ford, Charles. *Music, Sexuality, and the Enlightenment in Mozart's "Figaro," "Don Giovanni" and "Così fan tutte."* New York: Routledge, 2016.

Foucault, Michel. *The History of Sexuality*. Vol. 1, *An Introduction*. Translated by Robert Hurley. New York: Vintage Books, 1990.

———. *Madness and Civilization: A History of Insanity in the Age of Reason*. Translated by Richard Howard. New York: Vintage Books, 1988.

[Fox, William]. *An Address to the People of Great Britain on the Propriety of Abstaining from West India Sugar and Rum*. 10th ed. London: Gourney, 1791.

Freedman, Paul, ed. *Food: A History of Taste*. Berkeley: University of California Press, 2007.

Freitas, Roger. "The Eroticism of Emasculation: Confronting the Baroque Body of the Castrato." *Journal of Musicology* 20, no. 2 (2003): 196–249.

Freud, Sigmund. *Five Lectures on Psycho-analysis*. Translated and edited by James Strachey. New York: Norton, 1990.

Freyman, Michael. *The Authentic "Magic Flute" Libretto; Mozart's Autograph or the First Full-Score Edition?* Lanham, MD: Scarecrow Press, 2009.

Frye, Northrop. *Anatomy of Criticism*. Princeton, NJ: Princeton University Press, 1957.

Gage, Nicholas. *Greek Fire: The Story of Maria Callas and Aristotle Onassis*. New York: Knopf, 2000.

Galatopoulos, Stelios. *Maria Callas: Sacred Monster*. New York: Simon and Schuster, 1998.

Geczy, Adam, and Vicki Karaminas. *Queer Style*. London: Bloomsbury, 2013.

Genesio, Laura, ed. *Carteggio Verdi-Luccardi*. Parma: Istituto nazionale di studi verdiani, 2008.

Gerhard, Anselm. *The Urbanization of Opera: Music Theater in Paris in the Nineteenth Century*. Chicago: University of Chicago Press, 1998.

Giacomini, Lorenzo. *Orationi e discorsi di Lorenzo Giacomini Tebalducci Malespini*. Florence: Sermartelli, 1597.

Girardi, Michele. *Puccini: His International Art*. Translated by Laura Basini. Chicago: University of Chicago Press, 2000.

Giroud, Vincent. *French Opera: A Short History*. New Haven, CT: Yale University Press, 2010.

Giudici, Elvio. *Il teatro di Verdi in scena e in DVD*. Milan: Saggiatore, 2012.

Glasenapp, Carl Friedrich. *Das Leben Richard Wagners*. 3 vols. Leipzig: Breitkopf und Härtel, 1923.

Glixon, Beth L., and Jonathan E. Glixon. *Inventing the Business of Opera: The Impresario and His World in Seventeenth-Century Venice*. Oxford: Oxford University Press, 2006.

Goehr, Lydia, and Daniel Herwitz, eds. *The "Don Giovanni" Moment: Essays on the Legacy of an Opera*. New York: Columbia University Press, 2006.

Goodman, Katherine. "From Salon to Koffeekranz: Gender and the Coffee Cantata in Bach's Leipzig." In *Bach's Changing World: Voices in the Community*, edited by Carol Baron, 190–218. Rochester, NY: University of Rochester Press, 2006.

Gori, Gigliola. *Italian Fascism and the Female Body: Sport, Submissive Women, and Strong Mothers*. New York: Routledge, 2004.

Gossett, Philip. *Divas and Scholars: Performing Italian Opera*. Chicago: University of Chicago Press, 2006.

Groos, Arthur. "From *Addio del passato* to *Le patate son fredde*: Representations of Consumption in Leoncavallo's *I Medici* and *La bohème*." In *Letteratura, musica e teatro al tempo di Ruggero Leoncavallo*, edited by Jürgen Maehder and Lorenza Guiot, 57–74. Milan: Sonzogno, 1995.

———. "Luigi Illica's libretto for *Madama Butterfly* (1901)." *Studi Pucciniani* 2 (2000): 91–204.

———. "Madama Butterfly: The Story." *Cambridge Opera Journal* 3, no. 2 (1991): 125–98.

———. "TB, Mimì, and the Anxiety of Influence." *Studi Pucciniani* 1 (1998): 67–81.

———. "'TB Sheets': Love and Disease in *La Traviata*." *Cambridge Opera Journal* 7, no. 3 (1995): 233–60.

Gualdo Rosa, Lucia, Isabella Nuovo, and Domenico Defilippis, eds. *Gli umanisti e la guerra otrentina: Testi dei secoli XV e XVI*. Bari: Dedalo, 1982.

Guarracino, Serena. "'It's Not Over till the Fat Lady Sings': The Weight of the Opera Diva." In *Historicizing Fat in Anglo-American Culture*, edited by Elena Levy-Navarro, 192–212. Columbus: Ohio University Press, 2010.

Gumbrecht, Hans Ulrich. *Production of Presence: What Meaning Cannot Convey*. Stanford, CA: Stanford University Press, 2004.

Gundle, Stephen. *Bellissima: Feminine Beauty and the Idea of Italy*. New Haven, CT: Yale University Press, 2007.

Günsberg, Maggie. *Playing with Gender: The Comedies of Goldoni*. Leeds, UK: Northern Universities Press, 2001.

Habermas, Jürgen. *The Structural Transformation of the Public Sphere: An Inquiry into a Category of Bourgeois Society*. Translated by Thomas Burger. Cambridge, MA: MIT Press, 1991.

Hanegraaff, Wouter J. "Under the Mantle of Love: The Mystical Eroticisms of Marsilio Ficino and Giordano Bruno." In *Hidden Intercourse: Eros and Sexuality in the History of Western Esotericism*, edited by W. Hanegraaff and J. Kripal, 175–208. Leiden: Brill, 2008.

Harris, Marvin. "The Abominable Pig." In *Food and Culture: A Reader*, edited by Carole Counihan and Penny Van Esterik, 67–79. New York: Routledge, 1997.

Hartley, L. P. *The Go-Between*. London: Hamilton, 1953.

Heartz, Daniel. "*The Beggar's Opera* and *Opéra-comique en Vaudevilles*." *Early Music* 27, no. 1 (1999): 42–53.

———. *From Garrick to Gluck: Essays on Opera in the Age of the Enlightenment*. Edited by John A. Rice. Hillsdale, NY: Pendragon, 2004.

———. *Mozart's Operas*. Edited by Thomas Baumann. Berkeley: University of California Press, 1990.

———. "Nicolas Jadot and the Building of the Burgtheater." *Musical Quarterly* 68, no. 1 (1982): 1–31.

Heindl, Waltraud. "People, Class Structure, and Society." In *Schubert's Vienna*, edited by Raymond Erickson, 36–54. New Haven, CT: Yale University Press, 1997.

Hepokoski, James. *Giuseppe Verdi: "Falstaff."* Cambridge: Cambridge University Press, 1995.

Heppner, Christopher. "'L'ho perduta': Barbarina, Cherubino, and the Economics of Love in *Le nozze di Figaro*." *Opera Quarterly* 15, no. 4 (1999): 636–59.

Hollingsworth, Mary. *The Cardinal's Hat: Money, Ambition, and Everyday Life in the Court of a Borgia Prince*. Woodstock, NY: Overlook Press, 2005.

Homer. *"L'Odissea" d'Omero trasportata dalla greca nella Toscana favela*. Translated by Federico Malipiero. Venice: Corradicci, 1643.

Hood, Mantle. "The Untalkables of Music." *EM: Annuario degli archivi di etnomusicologia dell'Accademia nazionale di Santa Cecilia* 1 (1993): 137–42.

Hösle, Vittorio, and Nora K. *The Dead Philosophers' Café*. Notre Dame, IN: University of Notre Dame Press, 2000.

Huart, Louis. *Psychologie de la grisette*. Brussels: Aubert and Moens, 1841.

Hunter, Mary. "Bourgeois Values in Opera Buffa in 1780s Vienna." In *Opera Buffa in Mozart's Vienna*, edited by Mary Hunter and James Webster, 170–85. Cambridge: Cambridge University Press, 1997.

———. *The Culture of Opera Buffa in Mozart's Vienna*. Princeton, NJ: Princeton University Press, 1999.

———. "'Pamela': The Offspring of Richardson's Heroine in Eighteenth-Century Opera." *Mosaic* 18 (1985): 61–76.

Hutcheon, Linda, and Michael Hutcheon. *Bodily Charm: Living Opera*. Lincoln: University of Nebraska Press, 2000.

———. *Opera: Desire, Disease, Death*. Lincoln: University of Nebraska Press, 1996.

Ivanovich, Cristoforo. *Minerva al tavolino*. Venice: Niccolò Pezzana, 1686.

Jaucourt, [Louis] de. "Cuisine." In *Encyclopédie ou Dictionnaire raisonné des sciences, des arts et des métiers*, edited by Denis Diderot and Jean Le Rond d'Alembert. Vol. 4, *Conjonctif-Discussion*, 537–39. Paris: Briasson, David, Le Breton, Faulche, 1754.

Jeanneret, Michael. *A Feast of Words: Banquets and Table Talk in the Renaissance*. Chicago: University of Chicago Press, 1991.

Johnson, Eugene J. *Inventing the Opera House: Theater Architecture in Renaissance and Baroque Italy*. Cambridge: Cambridge University Press, 2018.

———. "Jacopo Sansovino, Giacomo Torelli, and the Theatricality of the Piazzetta in Venice." *Journal of the Society of Architectural Historians* 59, no. 4 (2000): 436–53.

Johnson, James H. *Listening in Paris: A Cultural History*. Berkeley: University of California Press, 1995.

Kaplan, Paul H. D. "The Earliest Images of Othello." *Shakespeare Quarterly* 39, no. 2 (1988): 171–86.

Kavanagh, Julie. *The Girl Who Loved Camelias: The Life and Legend of Marie Duplessis*. New York: Knopf, 2013.

Kenney, William Howland. “Historical Context and the Definition of Jazz: Putting More of the History in ‘Jazz History.’” In *Jazz among the Discourses*, edited by Gabbard Krin, 100–116. Durham, NC: Duke University Press, 1995.

Kerman, Joseph. *Opera as Drama*. New York: Knopf, 1956.

———. “Reading *Don Giovanni*.” In *“Don Giovanni”: Myth of Seduction and Betrayal*, edited by Jonathan Miller, 108–25. Baltimore: Johns Hopkins University Press, 1990.

Kieffer, Fanny. “La confiserie des offices: Art, sciences et magnificence à la cour de Médicis.” In *Le banquet de la Renaissance: Images et usages*, edited by Diane H. Bodart and Valérie Boudier, special issue, *Predella: Rivista di arti visive/Journal of Visual Arts* 7 (2013): 85–102.

Kimbell, David. *Italian Opera*. Cambridge: Cambridge University Press, 1991.

Kirkegaard, Søren. *Either/Or*. Translated by Alastair Hannay. London: Penguin, 1992.

Kirkendale, Warren, and Ursula Kirkendale. *Music and Meaning: Studies in Music History and the Neighbouring Disciplines*. Florence: Olschki, 2007.

Kivy, Peter. *Sounding Off: Eleven Essays in the Philosophy of Music*. Oxford: Oxford University Press, 2012.

Koestenbaum, Wayne. “Callas and Her Fans.” *Yale Review* 79, no. 1 (1989): 1–20.

Kraye, Jill. “The Transformation of Platonic Love in the Italian Renaissance.” In *The Renaissance in Europe: A Reader*, edited by K. Whitlock, 81–87. New Haven, CT: Yale University Press, 2000.

Kristeller, Paul Oskar. “The Myth of Renaissance Atheism and the French Tradition of Free Thought.” *Journal of the History of Philosophy* 6 (1968): 233–43.

Krüger, J[ohann] G[ottlob]. *Traité du caffé, du thé, et du tabac*. Halle: Hemmerde, 1743.

Lagrave, Henry. *Le théâtre et le public à Paris de 1715 à 1750*. Paris: C. Klincksiek, 1972.

Laini, Marinella. *La raccolta zeniana di drammi per musica veneziani della Biblioteca nazionale Marciana, 1637–1700*. Lucca: Libreria Musicale Italiana, 1995.

Landon, Robbins H. C. *Mozart: The Golden Years, 1781–1791*. London: Thames and Hudson, 1989.

Latour, Bruno. “On Actor-Network Theory: A Few Clarifications,” *Soziale Welt* 47, no. 4 (1996): 369–81.

———. *Reassembling the Social: An Introduction to Actor-Network Theory*. Oxford: Oxford University Press, 2005.

Lavignac, Albert. *Encyclopédie de la musique et dictionnaire du conservatoire*. 11 vols. Paris: Delagrave, 1913–31.

Le Guin, Elisabeth. *The Tonadilla in Performance: Lyric Comedy in Enlightenment Spain*. Berkeley: University of California Press, 2014.

Leopold, Silke. *Monteverdi: Music in Transition*. Translated by Anne Smith. Oxford: Clarendon Press, 1982.

Leppert, Richard D. “The Social Discipline of Listening.” In *Le concert et son public: Mutations de la vie musicale en Europe de 1780 à 1914 (France, Allemagne, Angleterre)*, edited by Hans Erich Bödeker, Michael Werner, and Patrice Veit, 459–85. Paris: Éditions de la Maison des sciences de l'homme, 2002.

Lestringant, Frank. *Cannibals: The Discovery and Representation of the Cannibal from Columbus to Jules Verne*. Berkeley: University of California Press, 1997.

Lévi-Strauss, Claude. *Le cru et le cuit*. Paris: Plon, 1964.

———. *The Raw and the Cooked: Introduction to a Science of Mythology*. Translated by John Wightman and Doreen Wightman. 1969; Reprint Chicago: University of Chicago Press, 1983.

Levin, David J. "A Picture-Perfect Man? Senta, Absorption and Wagnerian Theatricality." *Opera Quarterly* 21, no. 3 (2006): 486–95.

———. *Unsettling Opera: Staging Mozart, Verdi, Wagner, and Zemlinsky*. Chicago: University of Chicago Press, 2007.

Levy, Beth E. *Frontier Figures: American Music and the Mythology of the American West*. Berkeley: University of California Press, 2012.

Libera, Don Felice. *L'arte in cucina: Ricette di cibi e di dolci; Manoscritto trentino di cucina e pasticceria del XVIII secolo*. Edited by Alberto Mazzoni. Bologna: Forni, 2004.

Lindenbaum, Shirley. "Thinking about Cannibalism." *Annual Review of Anthropology* 33 (2004): 475–98.

Link, Dorothea. *The National Court Theatre in Mozart's Vienna: Sources and Documents, 1783–1792*. New York: Oxford University Press, 1998.

Locatelli, Tommaso. *Appendice della gazzetta di Venezia: Prose scelte di Tommaso Locatelli*. 15 vols. Venezia: Tipografia della gazzetta, 1837–79.

Locke, Ralph P. *Music and the Exotic from the Renaissance to Mozart*. Cambridge: Cambridge University Press, 2015.

———. *Musical Exoticism: Images and Reflections*. Cambridge: Cambridge University Press, 2009.

Lomazzi, Giovanni. Interviewed by Marco Cuggieri. "La mia amica Maria Callas." *Corriere di Como*, December 10, 2013.

Lorenzetti, Stefano. "'At Every Gesture from the Lord': Music at Banquets, a Cornucopia of the Senses." In *Le banquet de la Renaissance: Images et usages*, edited by Diane H. Bodart and Valérie Boudier, special issue, *Predella: Rivista di arti visive/Journal of Visual Arts* 7 (2013): 21–40.

Lösel, Steffen. "'May Such Great Effort Not Be in Vain': Mozart on Divine Love, Judgment, and Retribution." *Journal of Religion* 89, no. 3 (July 2009): 361–400.

"Love and Money." *Time* 74, no. 12, September 21, 1959.

Lowe, Kate. "Visible Lives: Black Gondoliers and Other Black Africans in Renaissance Venice." *Renaissance Quarterly* 66 (2013): 412–52.

Lütteken, Lorenz. "Negating Opera through Opera: *Così fan tutte* and the Reverse of the Enlightenment." *Eighteenth-Century Music* 6, no. 2 (2009): 229–42.

Maehder, Jürgen. "Essen und Trinken auf der Opernbühne." In *Musikwissenschaft im deutsch-italienischen Dialog: Friedrich Lippmann zum 75. Geburtstag*, edited by Markus Engelhardt and Wolfgang Witzenmann. *Analecta musicologica* 46 (2010): 319–43.

Malacarne, Giancarlo. *Sulla mensa del Principe: Alimentazione e banchetti alla corte dei Gonzaga*. Modena: Il Bulino, 2000.

Malina, János. "The Eszterháza Libretti: An Overall Survey." *Haydn-Studien* 11, no. 2 (2017): 223–65.

Mangini, Nicola. *I teatri di Venezia*. Milan: Mursia, 1974.

Manni, Domenico Maria. *Memorie della fiorentina famosa accademia degli Alterati*. Florence: Stecchi, 1748.

Marcello, Benedetto. *Il teatro alla moda*, 1720. Edited by Carmelo Di Gennaro. Milan: Polifilo, 2006.

Marmontel, Jean-François. *Essai sur les révolutions de la musique en France*. [Paris]: Le Noir, 1777.

Mattei, Venantio. *Teatro nobilissimo della scalcheria di Venantio Mattei da Camerino per apparecchio di Banchetti a gran Prencipi, secondo il variar delle stagioni . . . dedicato all'Eminentissimo e Reverendissimo Signor Cardinale Giacomo Rospigliosi*. Roma: Dragondelli, 1669.

Maupassant, Guy de. *Bel-Ami*. Edited by Gilbert Sigaux. N.p.: La Bibliothèque électronique du Québec, Collection à tous les vents.

Mauthe, Ursula. *Mozarts "Pamina" Anna Gottlieb*. Augsburg: Deutsche Mozart-Gesellschaft, 1986.

Mayer Brown, Howard. "A Cook's Tour of Ferrara in 1529." In *Renaissance Music*, edited by Kenneth Kreiner, 243–62. Burlington, VT: Ashgate, 2011.

Mayernik, David. *The Challenge of Emulation in Art and Architecture between Imitation and Invention*. Burlington, VT: Ashgate, 2013.

McClary, Susan. *Feminine Endings*. Minneapolis: University of Minnesota Press, 1991.

McKee, Richard Miles. "A Critical Edition of Carlo Pallavicino's *Il Vespasiano*." 2 vols. PhD diss., University of North Carolina, Chapel Hill, 1989.

McKee, Sally. *The Exile's Song: Edmond Dédé and the Unfinished Revolutions of the Atlantic World*. New Haven, CT: Yale University Press, 2017.

Meissner, Jochen, Ulrich Mücke, and Klaus Weber. *Schwarzes Amerika: Eine Geschichte der Slaverei*. Munich: C. H. Beck, 2008.

Meldini, Piero. *Sposa e madre esemplare: Ideologia e politica della donna e della famiglia durante il fascismo*. Florence: Guaraldi, 1975.

Meneghini, Giovanni Battista. *My Wife Maria Callas*. Written with the collaboration of Renzo Allegri. Translated by Henry Wisneski. New York: Farrar, Straus and Giroux, 1982.

Messisbugo, Cristoforo di. *Banchetti, compositioni di vivande et apparecchio generale di Christoforo di Messisbugo allo Illustrissimo et Reverendissimo Signor il Signor Don Hippolito da Este, Cardinale di Ferrara*. Ferrara: Giovanni de Buglhat and Antonio Hucher, 1549.

———. *Libro nuovo nel quale s'insegna il modo d'ordinar banchetti*. . . . Venice: Spineda, 1600.

Meucci, Renato. "Cimbasso." Grove Music Online. 2001.

Micciché, Lino. *Luchino Visconti: Un profilo critico*. Venice: Marsilio, 1996.

Mila, Massimo. *La giovinezza di Verdi*. Turin: ERI, 1974.

Milhous, Judith, Gabriella Dideriksen, and Robert D. Hume. *Italian Opera in Late Eighteenth-Century London*. Vol. 2, *The Pantheon Opera and Its Aftermath, 1789–1795*. Oxford: Clarendon Press, 2001.

Milizia, Francesco. *Del teatro*. Venice: Pasquali, 1773.

Miller, Jonathan, ed. *Don Giovanni: Myth of Seduction and Betrayal*. Baltimore: Johns Hopkins University Press, 1990.

Montanari, Massimo. *La fame e l'abbondanza: Storia dell'alimentazione in Europa*. Bari: Laterza, 2014.

———. *Food Is Culture*. New York: Columbia University Press, 2006.

———. *L'identità italiana in cucina*. Bari: Laterza, 2010.

Montemaggi, Vittorio. *Reading Dante's "Commedia" as Theology: Divinity Realized in Human Encounter*. Oxford: Oxford University Press, 2016.

Morson, Gary Saul, and Caryl Emerson. *Mikhail Bakhtin: Creation of a Prosaics*. Stanford, CA: Stanford University Press, 1990.

Muir, Edward. *Ritual in Early Modern Europe*. Cambridge: Cambridge University Press, 1997.

Murata, Margaret. "The Church and the Stage in Seventeenth-Century Rome." In *Sleuthing the Muse: Essays in Honor of William F. Prizer*, edited by Kristine K. Forney and Jeremy L. Smith, 181–200. Hillsdale, NY: Pendragon Press, 2012.

Nagel, Ivan. *Autonomy and Mercy: Reflections on Mozart's Operas*. Translated by Marion Faber and Ivan Nagel. Cambridge, MA: Harvard University Press, 1991.

Natale, Mauro. "Lo studiolo di Belfiore." In *Le muse e il principe: Arte di corte nel Rinascimento Padano*, edited by Andrea Di Lorenzo et al., 379–444. Modena: Panini, 1991.

Nelson, Louis. "The Jamaican Plantation: Industrial, Global, Contested." In *The Eighteenth Centuries: Global Networks of Enlightenment*, edited by David T. Gies and Cynthia Wall, 120–43. Charlottesville: University of Virginia Press, 2018.

Nestola, Barbara. "La musica italiana nel *Mercure galant* (1677–1683)." *Recercare* 14 (2002): 99–157.

Newark, Cormac. "Not Listening in Paris: Critical and Fictional Lapses of Attention at the Opera." In *Words and Notes in the Long Nineteenth Century*, edited by Phyllis Weliver and Katharine Ellis, 35–54. Woodbridge, UK: Boydell and Brewer, 2013.

Newman, Ian. *The Romantic Tavern: Literature and Conviviality in the Age of Revolution*. Cambridge: Cambridge University Press, 2019.

Normore, Christina. *A Feast for the Eyes: Art, Performance, and the Late Medieval Banquet*. Chicago: University of Chicago Press, 2015.

Noske, Frits. *The Signifier and the Signified: Studies in the Operas of Mozart and Verdi*. The Hague: Nijhoff, 1977.

Nowlen, Pete. *Keys to Transposition: A Method of the Teaching and Learning of Transposition on the Horn*. Ithaca, NY: Ensemble, 2018.

Orbach, Susie. *Fat Is a Feminist Issue II*. New York: Berkeley, 1982.

Ortolani, Giuseppe. "Goldoni e Shakespeare, appunti e note." *Rivista italiana del dramma* 4 (1940): 280–301.

Orvieto, Paolo. *Poliziano*. Rome: Salerno, 2009.

Ovid. *Fasti*. Translated by James George Frazer. Revised by G. P. Goold. Loeb Classical Library. Cambridge, MA: Harvard University Press, 1989.

———. *Metamorphoses*. Translated by David Raeburn. London: Penguin, 2004.

Paduano, Guido. "La signora delle camelie, il Moloch e il Vangelo." *Rivista di letterature moderne e comparate* 65, no. 3 (2012): 301–23.

Palisca, Claude V. "Gli Alterati of Florence, Pioneers in the Theory of Dramatic Music." In *New Looks at Italian Opera: Essays in Honour of Donald J. Grout*, edited by William W. Austin, 9–38. Ithaca, NY: Cornell University Press, 1968.

Parker, Roger. *Leonora's Last Act: Essays in Verdian Discourse*. Princeton, NJ: Princeton University Press, 1997.

Patriarchi, Gasparo. *Vocabolario veneziano e padovano con termini e modi corrispondenti toscani*. 3rd ed. Padua: Tipografia del seminario, 1821.

Petrobelli, Pierluigi. *Music in the Theater: Essays on Verdi and Other Composers*. Princeton, NJ: Princeton University Press, 1994.

Piccotti, Giovan Battista. "Sulla data dell'Orfeo e delle *Stanze* di Agnolo Poliziano." *Rendiconti della Reale Accademia dei Lincei, Classe di scienze morali, storiche e filologiche* 23, ser. 5 (1914): 319–57.

Piperno, Franco. "*La mia Cecchina è baronessa*: Livelli stilistici e assetto drammaturgico ne *La buona figliuola* di Goldoni-Piccinni." *Analecta musicologica* 30, no. 2 (1998): 523–42.

Pirrotta, Nino. *Don Giovanni's Progress: A Rake Goes to the Opera*. Translated by Harris S. Saunders Jr. New York: Marsilio, 1994.

———. *Li due Orfei: Da Poliziano a Monteverdi*. Turin: ERI, 1969.

———. *Music and Theater from Politian to Monteverdi*. Translated by Karen Eales. Cambridge: Cambridge University Press, 1982.

Platina, Bartolomeo. *De la honesta voluptate et valitudine*. Venice: Ruschoni, 1501.

Plato. *Plato in Twelve Volumes*. Translated by Harold North Fowler. Loeb Classical Library. Cambridge, MA: Harvard University Press, 1982.

Platoff, John. "Catalogue Arias and the 'Catalogue Aria.'" In *Wolfgang Amadè Mozart: Essays on His Life and His Music*, edited by Stanley Sadie, 296–311. Oxford: Clarendon Press, 1996.

Poli, Paolo. "Un'artista misteriosa e sconvolta." Memoir edited by Jacopo Pellegrini on February 2, 2016. In *Mille e una Callas: Voci e studi*, edited by Luca Aversano and Jacopo Pellegrini, 367–69. Macerata: Quodlibet, 2016.

Poliziano, Angelo. *"L'Orfeo": Tragedia di Messer Angelo Poliziano tratta per la prima volta da due vetusti codici ed alla sua integrità e perfezione ridotta e illustrata dal Reverendo Padre Ireneo Affò di Bussetto*. Edited by Ireneo Affò. Venice: Luigi Antonio di Ravenna, 1776.

———. *"L'Orfeo" del Poliziano con il testo critico dell'originale e delle successive forme teatrali*. Edited by Antonia Tissoni Benvenuti. Padua: Antenore, 1986.

———. *"Le Stanze," "L'Orfeo," "Le Rime" di Messer Angelo Ambrogini Poliziano rivedute su i codici e su le antiche stampe e illustrate con annotazioni di varii e nuove da Giosuè Carducci*. Edited by Giosuè Carducci. Florence: Barbèra, 1863.

———. *Stanze, Orfeo, Rime*. Edited by Davide Puccini. Milan: Garzanti, 1992.

Polzonetti, Pierpaolo. "Anorexia and Gluttony in Verdi's Operas." In *Verdi 2001: Proceedings of the International Conference, Parma—New York—New Haven, 24 January—1 February 2001*, edited by Fabrizio Della Seta, Roberta Montemorra Marvin, and Marco Marica, 835–47. Florence: Olschki, 2003.

———. "Brindisi." In *The Cambridge Verdi Encyclopedia*, edited by Roberta Montemorra Marvin, 72. Cambridge: Cambridge University Press, 2013.

———. "Don Giovanni Goes to Prison: Teaching Opera behind Bars." *Musica Docta* 6 (2016): 99–104.

———. "Eating and Drinking in Opera: *Traviata* and the Callas Diet." In *Oxford Handbooks Online* [subject: Music, Musicology and Music History, Opera, Ethnomusicology], edited by Alexander Rehding. New York: Oxford University Press, 2015. www.oxfordhandbooks.com.

———. "Feasting and Fasting in Verdi's Operas." *Studi Verdiani* 14 (1999): 69–106.

———. "Giuramento." In *The Cambridge Verdi Encyclopedia*, edited by Roberta Montemorra Marvin, 205. Cambridge: Cambridge University Press, 2013.

———. "Is It Proper to Eat or Drink While Listening to Classical Music?" *Naxos Musicology International* (February 11, 2020), https://www.naxosmusicology.com/essays/is-it-proper-to-eat-or-drink-while-listening-to-classical-music/.

———. *Italian Opera in the Age of the American Revolution*. Cambridge: Cambridge University Press, 2011.

———. "Lavigna, Vincenzo." In *The Cambridge Verdi Encyclopedia*, edited by Roberta Montemorra Marvin, 234–35. Cambridge: Cambridge University Press, 2013.

———. "Mesmerizing Adultery: *Così fan tutte* and the Kornman Scandal." *Cambridge Opera Journal* 14, no. 3 (2002): 263–96.

———. "Mozart and the American Revolution." In *The Eighteenth Centuries: An Interdisciplinary Investigation*, edited by David T. Gies and Cynthia Wall, 202–32. Charlottesville: University of Virginia Press, 2018.

———. "Opera as Process." In *The Cambridge Companion to Eighteenth-Century Opera*, edited by Anthony R. DelDonna and Pierpaolo Polzonetti, 3–23. Cambridge: Cambridge University Press, 2009.

———. "*Ossessione*: Visconti's Obsession with Verdi." *Italian Journal* 20, no. 10 (2014): 22–25.

———. "The 'Quantitative Style' in Seventeenth-Century Italian Opera." In *Pensieri per un maestro: Studi in onore di Pierluigi Petrobelli*, edited by Stefano Lavia and Roger Parker, 95–114. Turin: EDT, 2002.

———. "Tartini and the Tongue of Saint Anthony." *Journal of the American Musicological Society* 67, no. 2 (2014): 429–86.

———. *Tartini e la musica secondo natura*. Lucca: LIM, 2001.

Pougin, Arthur. *Giuseppe Verdi: Vita aneddotica di Arturo Pougin con note ed aggiunte di Folchetto, illustrazioni di Achille Formis*. Milan: Ricordi, 1881.

Powell, John S. *Music and Theatre in France, 1600–1680*. Oxford: Oxford University Press, 2000.

Powers, Harold. "La Solita Forma and the Uses of Conventions." *Acta Musicologica* 59, no. 1 (1987): 65–90.

Price, Curtis, Judith Milhous, and Robert D. Hume. *Italian Opera in Late Eighteenth Century London*. Vol. 1, *The King's Theater, Haymarket, 1778–1791*. Oxford: Clarendon Press, 1995.

Prizer, William F. "Isabella d'Este and Lucrezia Borgia as Patrons of Music: The Frottola at Mantua and Ferrara." *Journal of the American Musicological Society* 38, no. 1 (1985): 1–33.

Puggelli, Paolo. "Del convivio degli Alterati di Giulio del Bene." *Accademia: Revue de la Société Marsile Ficin II* (2000): 63–88.

Pyle, Cynthia Munro "Politian's *Orfeo* and the Favole Mitologiche in the Context of Late Quattrocento Northern Italy." PhD diss., Columbia University, 1976.

Randall, Annie J., and Rosalind Gray Davis. *Puccini and the Girl: History and Reception of "The Girl of the Golden West."* Chicago: University of Chicago Press, 2005.

Randel, Don M. "The Canon in the Musicological Toolbox." In *Disciplining Music: Musicology and Its Canons*, edited by Katherine Bergeron and Philip V. Bohlman, 10–22. Chicago: University of Chicago Press, 1992.

Randolph, Adrian W. B. *Engaging Symbols: Gender, Politics, and Public Art in Fifteenth-Century Florence*. New Haven, CT: Yale University Press, 2002.

Ravel, Jeffrey S. "Seating the Public: Spheres and Loathing in the Paris Theaters, 1777–1788." *French Historical Studies* 18, no. 1 (1993): 173–210.

Rawson, Katie, and Elliott Shore. *Eating Out: A Global History of Restaurants*. London: Reaktion, 2019.

Reardon, Colleen. *A Sociable Moment: Opera and Festive Culture in Baroque Siena*. Oxford: Oxford University Press, 2016.

Renan, Ernest. *Averroès et l'Averroïsme: Essai historique*. Paris: Durand, 1852.

Rice, John A. *Antonio Salieri and Viennese Opera*. Chicago: University of Chicago Press, 1998.

———. "Music in the Age of Coffee." *Eighteenth-Century Music* 4, no. 2 (2007): 301–5.

Roach, Joseph. *It*. Ann Arbor: University of Michigan Press, 2007.

Robbins, Lewis L. "A Contribution to the Psychological Understanding of the Character of Don Juan." *Bulletin of the Menninger Clinic* 20, no. 4 (July 1956): 166–80.

Rogers, Vanessa. "John Gay, Ballad Opera and the Théâtre de la Foire." *Eighteenth-Century Music* 11, no. 2 (2014): 173–213.

Rolland, Romain. *Musiciens d'autrefois*. Paris: Rachette, 1908.

Rorato, Giampiero. *La cucina al tempo di Carlo Goldoni*. Vicenza: Terra Ferma, 2004.

Rosand, Ellen. *Monteverdi's Last Operas: A Venetian Trilogy*. Berkeley: University of California Press, 2007.

———. *Opera in Seventeenth-Century Venice: The Creation of a Genre*. Berkeley: University of California Press, 1991.

Rosen, Charles. *The Classical Style: Haydn, Mozart, Beethoven*. New York: Norton, 1997.

Rosen, David. "Meter and Testosterone: Preliminary Observations about Meter and Gender in Verdi's Operas." In *Una piacente estate di San Martino: Studi e ricerche per Marcello Conati*, edited by Marco Capra, 179–213. Lucca: LIM, 2000.

———. "A Tale of Five Cities: The Peregrinations of Somma's and Verdi's *Gustavo III* (and *Una vendetta in dominò* and *Un ballo in maschera*) at the Hands of the Neapolitan and Roman Censorship." *Verdi Forum* 26–27 (1999): 53–66.

Rosen, David, and Andrew Porter, eds. *Verdi's "Macbeth": A Sourcebook*. New York: Norton, 1984.

Rosselli, John. *The Life of Mozart*. Cambridge: Cambridge University Press, 1998.

Rossetti, Giovanni Battista. *Dello scalco del Sig. Gio. Battista Rossetti, Scalco della Serenissima Madama Lucretia da Este Duchessa d'Urbino, nel quale si contengono le qualità di uno scalco perfetto e tutti i carichi suoi, con diversi ufficiali a lui sottoposti. . . .* Ferrara: Mammarello, 1584.

Rothblum, Esther D., and Sondra Solovay, eds. *The Fat Studies Reader.* New York: New York University Press, 2009.

Rouget, Gilbert. *Music and Trance: A Theory of the Relations between Music and Possession.* Edited and translated by Brunhilde Bierbuyck and Gilbert Rouget. Chicago: University of Chicago Press, 1985.

Rousseau, Jean-Jacques. *The Basic Political Writings.* Edited and translated by Donald A. Cress. Indianapolis: Hackett, 1987.

———. *The "Confessions" of Jean-Jacques Rousseau Now First Completely Translated into English.* London: Aldus Society, 1903.

Rundin, John. "A Politics of Eating: Feasting in Early Greek Society." *American Journal of Philology* 117, no. 2 (1996): 179–215.

Russo, Flavio. *A cena con la locandiera: Le ricette di Carlo Goldoni.* Turin: Leone Verde, 2004.

Rutherford, Susan. "'Pretending to Be Wicked': Divas, Technology, and the Consumption of Bizet's *Carmen.*" In *Technology and the Diva: Sopranos, Opera, and Media from Romanticism to the Digital Age*, edited by Karen Henson, 74–88. Cambridge: Cambridge University Press, 2016.

Saguy, Abigail C. *What's Wrong with Fat?* Oxford: Oxford University Press, 2013.

Sala, Emilio. *The Sounds of Paris in Verdi's "Traviata."* Translated by Delia Casadei. Cambridge: Cambridge University Press, 2008.

Salazar, David. "A Comprehensive List of All Opera Companies Offering Free Streaming Services Right Now." Operawire.com (May 25, 2020).

Sanders, Donald C. *Music at the Gonzaga Court in Mantua.* Lanham, MD: Lexington Books, 2012.

Sarpi, Paolo. *Il senso del cibo.* Palermo: Sellerio, 2005.

Scappi, Bartolomeo. *The Opera of Bartolomeo Scappi (1570): "L'arte et prudenza d'un maestro cuoco."* Edited and translated by Terence Scully. Toronto: University of Toronto Press, 2008.

Schifano, Lawrence. *Luchino Visconti: The Flames of Passion.* Translated by William S. Byron. London: Collins, 1990.

Schulze, Hans-Joachhim. "Ey! Sweet the Coffee Tastes: Johann Sebastian Bach's Coffee Cantata in Its Time." Special issue, *Bach: Journal of the Riemenschneider Bach Institute, Baldwin College* 32, no. 2 (2001).

Schwarzenberg, Claudio. "La storia delle leggi e costume de' *veneziani*: Manoscritto inedito di Giovanni Rossi." *Rivista di storia del diritto italiano* 37–38 (1965): 227–33.

Scott, Michael. *Maria Meneghini Callas.* Boston: Northeastern University Press, 1991.

Segal, Erich. *The Death of Comedy.* Cambridge, MA: Harvard University Press, 2001.

Sell, Johann Jakob. *Versuch einer Geschichte des Negerschlavenhandels.* Halle: Gebauer, 1791.

Senici, Emanuele. "At the Tavern with Manzoni and Verdi: *I promessi sposi* and the

Dramaturgy of *La forza del destino*." In *Music as Social and Cultural Practice: Essays in Honour of Reinhard Strohm*, edited by Melania Bucciarelli and Berta Joncus, 336–52. Woodbridge, UK: Boydell Press, 2007.

———. *Landscape and Gender in Italian Opera: The Alpine Virgin from Bellini to Puccini*. Cambridge: Cambridge University Press, 2005.

Small, Christopher. *Musicking: The Meanings of Performing and Listening*. Hanover, NH: University Press of New England, 1998.

Smart, Mary Ann. *Mimomania: Music and Gesture in Nineteenth-Century Opera*. Berkeley: University of California Press, 2004.

Sneider, Robert W. *The Voice of the City: Vaudeville and Popular Culture in New York*. New York: Oxford University Press, 1989.

Snowman, Daniel. *The Gilded Stage: A Social History of Opera*. London: Atlantic Books, 2009.

Spang, France Rebecca L. *The Invention of the Restaurant: Paris and Modern Gastronomic Culture*. Cambridge, MA: Harvard University Press, 2000.

Spary, E. C. *Eating the Enlightenment: Food and the Sciences in Paris*. Chicago: University of Chicago Press, 2012.

Sprung, David R. "'Hidden' Stopped Notes in 19th-Century French Opera." *Horn Call* 26, no. 3 (1996): 17–25.

Stassinopoulos, Arianna. *Maria Callas: The Woman behind the Legend*. New York: Simon and Schuster, 1981.

Stearns, Peter N. *Fat History: Bodies and Beauty in the Modern West*. With a new preface. 1997. Reprint New York: New York University Press, 2002.

Stein, Charles W. *American Vaudeville as Seen by Its Contemporaries*. Edited by Charles W. Stein. New York: Da Capo, 1984.

Steinberg, Michael. *Listening to Reason: Culture, Subjectivity, and Nineteenth-Century Music*. Princeton, NJ: Princeton University Press, 2004.

Steinke, Tim. *Oper nach Wagner: Formale Strategien im europäischen Musiktheater des frühen 20. Jahrhunderts*. Kassel: Bärenreiter, 2011.

Stockton, Will. *Playing Dirty: Sexuality and Waste in Early Modern Comedy*. Minneapolis: University of Minnesota Press, 2011.

Strohm, Reinhard. *Dramma per Musica: Italian Opera Seria of the Eighteenth Century*. New Haven, CT: Yale University Press, 1997.

———. *Die italienische Oper im 18. Jahrhundert*. Wilhelmshaven: Heinrichshofen, 1979.

Strong, Roy. *Splendor at Court: Renaissance Spectacle and the Theater of Power*. Boston: Houghton Mifflin, 1973.

Stuart, Tristram. *The Bloodless Revolution: A Cultural History of Vegetarianism from 1600 to Modern Times*. New York: Norton, 2006.

Subotnik, Rose Rosengard. *Deconstructive Variations: Music and Reason in Western Society*. Minneapolis: University of Minnesota Press, 1996.

———. "Whose *Magic Flute*? Intimations of Reality at the Gates of the Enlightenment." *19th-Century Music* 15, no. 2 (1991): 132–50.

Sullivan, Lesley Grace. "Textual Polyphony in Mozart's *Don Giovanni*." Master's thesis, University of Notre Dame, 2016.

Tanara, Vincenzo. *La caccia degli uccelli di Vincenzo Tanara da un manoscritto inedito della Biblioteca Comunale di Bologna*. Edited by Alberto Bacchi della Lega. Bologna: Romagnoli–Dall'Acqua, 1886.

Tank, Ulrich. "Die Dokumente der Esterhazy-Archive zur Fürstlichen Hofkapelle, 1761–1770." *Haydn-Studien* 4, nos. 3–4 (1980): 129–333.

Tartini, Giuseppe. *Trattato di musica secondo la vera scienza dell'armonia*. Padua: Stamperia del Seminario, 1754.

Tedeschi, Rubens. "*La traviata* torna giovane con la regia di Luchino Visconti." *L'Unità*, May 28, 1955.

Tenenti, Alberto. "Gli schiavi di Venezia alla fine del Cinquecento." *Rivista storica italiana* 67 (1955): 52–69.

Theresa, Rose. "Engendering Divine Madness." Paper presented at the fifty-fifth annual meeting of the American Musicological Society, Austin, TX, October 26–29, 1989.

Thomas, Downing A. *Aesthetics of Opera in the Ancien Régime, 1647–1785*. Cambridge: Cambridge University Press, 2002.

Thorpe, Vanessa. "It's All Over for Fat Lady Singers as Slimline Divas Triumph: Opera's New Breed of Slight, Scantily Clad Sopranos Take the Plaudits at the Salzburg Festival." *Observer*, August 15, 2009.

Till, Nicholas. *Mozart and the Enlightenment: Truth, Virtue, and Beauty in Mozart's Operas*. Boston: Faber and Faber, 1992.

Tomlinson, Gary. "Il canto magico dell'Euridice." In "Lo stupor dell'invenzione": Firenze e la nascita dell'opera." Atti del Convegno internazionale di studi (Firenze, 5–6 ottobre 2000). In *Quaderni della Rivista Italiana di Musicologia* 36, edited by Piero Gargiulo, 61–72. Florence: Olschki, 2001.

———. *Music in Renaissance Magic: Toward a Historiography of Others*. Chicago: University of Chicago Press, 1993.

Vila, Anne C. *Enlightenment and Pathology: Sensibility in the Literature and Medicine of Eighteenth-Century France*. Baltimore: Johns Hopkins University Press, 1998.

Vocabolario degli accademici della Crusca. Edizione seconda veneta accresciuta di molte voci dagli autori della stessa accademia. 5 vols. Venice: Francesco Pitteri, 1763.

Volf, Tom. *Maria Callas: Lettres et mémoires*. Paris: Albin Michel, 2019.

von Lichtensthal, Peter. *Dizionario e bibliografia della musica*. 4 vols. Milan: Fontana, 1826.

Voss, Angela. "Marsilio Ficino, the Second Orpheus." In *Music as Medicine: The History of Music Therapy since Antiquity*, edited by Peregrine Horden, 154–72. Brookfield, VT: Ashgate, 2000.

Wagner, Richard. *"The Art-Work of the Future" and Other Works*. Translated by W. Ashton Ellis. Lincoln: University of Nebraska Press, 1993.

Wakin, Daniel J. "Don't Sing with Your Mouth Full." *New York Times*, May 7, 2012.

Waldoff, Jessica. *Recognition in Mozart's Operas*. Oxford: Oxford University Press, 2006.

Wann, Marilyn. *Fat! So?: Because You Don't Have to Apologize for Your Size!* Berkeley, CA: Ten Speed Press, 1998.

Ward, Adrienne. *Pagodas in Play: China on the Eighteenth-Century Italian Opera Stage*. Lewisburg, PA: Bucknell University Press, 2010.

Webster, James. "Aria as Drama." In *The Cambridge Companion to Eighteenth-Century*

Opera, edited by Anthony R. DelDonna and Pierpaolo Polzonetti, 3–23. Cambridge: Cambridge University Press, 2009.

———. "Mozart's Operas and the Myth of Musical Unity." *Cambridge Opera Journal* 2, no. 2 (1990): 197–218.

———. "To Understand Verdi and Wagner We Must Understand Mozart." *19th-Century Music* 11, no. 2 (1987): 175–93.

Weinberg, Bernard. "The Accademia degli Alteri and Literary Taste from 1570 to 1600." *Italica* 31, no. 4 (1954): 207–14.

Weisheipl, James A. *Friar Thomas D'Aquino: His Life, Thought, and Work*. Garden City, NY: Doubleday, 1974.

Weiss, Piero, ed. *Opera: A History in Documents*. Oxford: Oxford University Press, 2002.

Westbury, Richard. *Handlist of Italian Cookery Books*. Florence: Olschki, 1963.

Wheaton, Barbara Ketcham. *Savoring the Past: The French Kitchen and Table from 1300 to 1789*. New York: Touchstone, 1983.

Wiel, Taddeo. *I teatri musicali veneziani del Settecento: Catalogo delle opera in musica rappresentate nel secolo XVIII a Venezia (1701–1800) con prefazione dell'autore*. Venice: Visentini, 1897.

Wilbourne, Emily. *Seventeenth-Century Opera and the Sound of the Commedia dell'Arte*. Chicago: University of Chicago Press, 2016.

Will, Richard. "Don Giovanni and the Resilience of Rape Culture." *Journal of the American Musicological Society* 71, no. 1 (2018): 218–22.

Williams, Elizabeth A. *The Physical and the Moral: Anthropology, Physiology, and the Philosophical Medicine in France, 1750–1850*. Cambridge: Cambridge University Press, 1994.

Wilson, Blake. "Canterino and Improvvisatore: Oral Poetry and Performance." In *The Cambridge History of Fifteenth-Century Music*, edited by Anna Maria Busse Berger and Jesse Rodin, 292–310. Cambridge: Cambridge University Press, 2015.

Wirzba, Norman. *Food and Faith: A Theology of Eating*. Cambridge: Cambridge University Press, 2011.

Wittkower, Rudolf. *Art and Architecture in Italy, 1600–1750*. 3 vols. Revised by Joseph Connors and Jennifer Montagu. New Haven, CT: Yale University Press, 1999.

Wolf, Naomi. *The Beauty Myth: How Images of Beauty Are Used against Women*. New York: Anchor Books, 1992.

Wunderlich, Wener, Doris Ueberschlag, and Ulrich Müller, eds. *Mozarts "Zauberflöte" und ihre Dichter: Faksimiles und Editionen von Textbuch, Bearbeitungen und Fortsetzungen der Mozart-Oper*. Salzburg: Mueller-Speiser, 2007.

Wykes, Jackie. "Introduction: Why Queering Fat Embodiment?" In *Queering Fat Embodiment*, edited by Cat Pausé, Jackie Wykes, and Samantha Murray, 1–12. Burlington, VT: Ashgate, 2014.

Yearsley, David. "Hoopskirts, Coffee, and the Changing Musical Prospects of the Bach Women." *Women and Music: A Journal of Gender and Culture* 17 (2013): 27–58.

———. *Sex, Death, and Minuets: Anna Magdalena Bach and Her Musical Notebooks*. Chicago: University of Chicago Press, 2019.

Zaslaw, Neal. "In Vino Veritas." *Early Music* 25, no. 4 (1997): 568–69.

———. "Observations at the Paris Opéra in 1747." *Early Music* 11, no. 4 (1983): 514–16.

Zemon Davis, Natalie. *Society and Culture in Early Modern France: Eight Essays*. Stanford, CA: Stanford University Press, 1975.

Žižek, Slavoj, and Mladen Dolar. *Opera's Second Death*. New York: Routledge, 2002.

Zoppelli, Luca. *L'opera come racconto: Modi narrativi nel teatro musicale dell'Ottocento*. Venice: Marsilio, 1994.

Index

Page numbers in italics refer to figures.